One of *Publishers Weekly*'s Best Books of the Year

"A lyrical, searing memoir. Out of the ashes of . . . misbegotten hopes, Hartley has fashioned a mesmerizing story of pain and loss."
    —*Newsweek*

"[A] pulsating book . . . Hartley, never the hard-bitten war correspondent of stereotype, is seared by the killing fields, by a child rescued from a mass grave, and by the untimely deaths of fellow reporters. But his book is also a tale of furious adrenaline, of not wanting to be far from the action and danger."
    —*The Christian Science Monitor*

"A profoundly moving masterpiece. Whether he's writing about a searing love affair in the middle of a war zone, or describing friendships made and lost in the confusion of the front lines, Hartley's book is heartbreaking, achingly beautiful, and shockingly honest. Rarely has a writer bared his soul to such magnificent effect. This is much, much more than a book about war reporting. It is an extraordinary tapestry of friendships, love affairs, betrayals, and murders that finally come together to give us an intimate and epic portrait of Africa in the twentieth century."
    —Hossein Amini, Academy Award nominated
        screenwriter of *The Wings of the Dove*

"Hieronymous Bosch reincarnated as a frontline correspondent invited to the midnight banquet of Africa's bloody horrors, that's who Aidan Hartley seems to be, an outrageously brave and anguished heart disgorging the never-inert legacies of colonialism."
    —Bob Shacochis, author of *The Immaculate Invasion*

"[Hartley] conjures up with vivid immediacy the frenetic pace of his colleagues, their boozy, buzzing life and gallows humor, and the dangers they faced. What comes across more powerfully still is Hartley's great love for Africa itself, and his great grief at its unhappy modern history."

—*Literary Review*

"Thrillingly charged with an undercurrent of passion."

—Salon.com

"A work of tremendous candor and vigor. Passionately articulated, *The Zanzibar Chest* offers a vision of Africa through the eyes of the war reporter, which is unsettling, compelling, and moving by turns. Reportage, history, family memoir, and personal testimony intertwine in a work of passion and intensity to create a book that is impossible to forget."

—**Aminatta Forna, author of**
The Devil That Danced on the Water

"Mesmerizing . . . engaging . . . This book is a sweeping, poetic homage to Africa, a continent made vivid by Hartley's capable, shining prose."
—*Publishers Weekly* (starred review)

"There is an amazing depth, breadth and grace of fine writing in this book."
—Jim Harrison, author of *Off to the Side*

"Hartley chronicles a decade of encounters with the world's bloodiest conflicts and considers the twisted legacy of colonialism through the microcosm of his own family. Not for the squeamish, these accounts of Ethiopia, Somalia, Bosnia, Rwanda, and other conflicts seethe with shocking and grisly consequences often wrought, in the author's view, by the 'one-size-fits-all solutions' imposed by well-intentioned but clueless Western power structures."
—*Kirkus Reviews*

"A startlingly refreshing perspective on the political, social, and cultural impact of British colonialism in Africa and Arabia . . . an accuracy and veracity seldom seen in Western critiques."
—*Booklist*

The Zanzibar Chest

A STORY OF LIFE, LOVE, AND DEATH
IN FOREIGN LANDS

AIDAN HARTLEY

Riverhead Books
New York

Most Riverhead Books are available at special quantity discounts for bulk purchases for sales promotions, premiums, fund-raising, or educational use. Special books, or book excerpts, can also be created to fit specific needs.

For details, write: Special Markets, The Berkley Publishing Group, 375 Hudson Street, New York, New York 10014.

Riverhead Books
Published by The Berkley Publishing Group
A division of Penguin Group (USA) Inc.
375 Hudson Street
New York, New York 10014

THE ZANZIBAR CHEST

Atlantic Monthly Press hardcover edition: July 2003
First Riverhead trade paperback edition: August 2004
Riverhead trade paperback ISBN: 1-59448-011-7

This book has been catalogued with the Library of Congress.

Printed in the United States of America

10 9 8 7 6 5 4 3 2 1

TO MY WIFE AND MY MOTHER

Contents

From time to time, God causes men to be born—and thou art one of them—who have a lust to go abroad at the risk of their lives and discover news—today it may be of far-off things, tomorrow of some hidden mountain, and the next day of some nearby men who have done a foolishness against the state. These souls are very few; and of these few, not more than ten are of the best.

—*Kim,* by Rudyard Kipling

"That Africa is now but a memory . . ."

BEYOND THE RIVERS OF ETHIOPIA

My father was the closest thing I knew to the immortal. "Our Father, who art in Africa," I prayed as a child of six. He'd always been there. When he died I couldn't believe it. I had moments when I felt haunted by him in ways that were almost physical. They were a comfort to me. At home on the Indian Ocean coast, I swam off the beach and felt he was in the water all around me. On the upcountry plains, I imagined his bones were billowing up in the dust behind the nomads' herds of cattle. I clung on but I felt him slipping away. In my stricken state I longed to pluck something back from oblivion.

The day came for us to go through Dad's belongings. His private territory at home was a coconut-thatched veranda overlooking the beach. He kept his writing desk there and a single bed made of mountain cedar, lashed with thongs of rawhide from an oryx shot many years before. Some of his clothes were still hanging up in there, which described a life of sadhulike simplicity: a few khaki bush shirts and shorts, the *kikoi* wraps we wear in Kenya like sarongs, as well as several pairs of camel-skin sandals.

In the corner of the veranda was a Zanzibar chest, carved with a skill modern Swahili carpenters have forgotten. The old camphor box bore a design of lotus, paisley, and pineapple and it

was studded with rivets tarnished green in the salty air. When I
opened the chest lid, cobwebs tore and something scuttled into a
corner. In the chest was the skin of a lion Dad had tracked down
after it had killed one of his best bulls, a hunting horn, a flute of
apricot wood, and a stack of files. These last contained reports on
missions to southern Sudan, livestock projects for the tribes of
Karamoja, botanical studies, and copious notes about camels.
Always restless himself as a younger man, Dad had spent his last
years devising schemes to help Africa's nomads remain on the
move, beyond the reach of those who wanted to settle them.

Inside one file were my father's handwritten memoirs on
which he had been working for years. I opened a second file and
reached down to grasp the pages. The instant I touched them they
began to crumble in my hands. Time, heat, and the drenching
humidity had ravaged them. Mildew dusted the covers, giving off
that scent of the forgotten. The translucent geckos that roam our
walls had laid their soft, ivory eggs along the spines of the notebooks. White ants and silverfish had eaten into the papers, leaving
a web of brown capillaries. Their tracks threaded through written
words and underlined paragraphs and burrowed into months and
years of recollection. I began to read the papers. I quickly realized I
had stumbled on a secret that had been buried for half a century.
Here were the diaries of the man named Peter Davey, my father's
good friend. Ever since I was a boy, the story of Davey crept in and
out of conversation at home in vague, half-finished sentences. The
tale had always been there, yet my father never properly talked
about it. Davey was a silence, a shadow that moved constantly out
of the corner of one's eye. And now, as if it had been deliberately
dropped into my lap, here was the full and tragic rendition of
Davey's life.

What I found in the Zanzibar chest was a story of lives so
utterly different from my own, so exotic, set in another part of the
world and in another time. I had never believed in any great cause;

I was sent to fight no wars. What I admired most about my father, Davey, and those like them is that they were men of action, whereas I was ever the observer, not the participant, which is the main reason why I'm able to be here to tell this story.

On my flight back to Rwanda I recognised the man who had guided me during the genocide. To be certain of it I looked at his right hand and sure enough, he had no thumb. It had been shot off in the days when he used to wear a red beret and ragged fatigues. Now he appeared in a sharp gray suit carrying a briefcase. As he walked down the aisle past me, our eyes met and his face brightened.

"Frank."

We sat together. Frank, I was reminded from years ago, could talk nonstop. He was one of those men who has suffered immensely, but enjoys the fact that he has lived to tell you all about it. As we flew back to Rwanda, he spoke of battles, massacres and dreams. He recalled the time we marched together on a journey that would haunt us forever. Listening to him speak, I was transported back to those terrible days and felt dizzy to see that here we were, suspended in ether above Africa and toasting each other with little bottles of whiskey served up by air stewardesses.

I descended from the aircraft and felt against my face a blast of hot air carrying familiar smells. I found the faint marks of a mortar bomb impact on the runway tarmac as I walked to the terminal. Inside, the soap statue of the gorilla was back in his glass case. The roads edged by brick red earth and low huts the same. The "Guinness is Good for You" advertisements the same. Guava trees the same. Faces the same. The same, when the truth is that it was changed. Only in our minds, myself, Frank and all the other survivors, did we see a ghost town superimposed on the real city of today. But there were no piles of severed hands by the roadside. No monkey in a bow tie and tuxedo perched in a tree.

I checked into the same room at the Meridien Hotel where we had slept under our flak jackets. I tried to remember. But it was as if nothing had happened. The hotel was back to being what it had been before the fighting. A hotel.

The pool terrace was the place to be these days. This is where the Patriotic Army top dogs and intelligence chiefs drank beer all afternoon. I sat, maintaining a smile, nursing a cold beer, looking over towards the swimming pool. I remembered that the pool had been empty in the war. The UN troops had used it as their water supply when the taps ran dry and they drank every drop. Today, as I watched from the terrace, the Tutsi children of the Patriotic Army leaders, their plump black bodies glistening with wet, were leaping about in a game of water volleyball. For years I had lived in my own museum of horrors in which the Meridien swimming pool had remained empty. Meanwhile in the real world the kids were playing in the chlorinated water as white-gloved waiters carried trays of ice-cold beers to the war veterans and their wives.

From Kigali I drove to Goma, where Lazarus is buried in a mass grave somewhere. I was on the back of a motorbike taxi when two policemen in banana yellow helmets stopped us and shook down the driver for a bribe. Farther up the road that morning Hutu militias had ambushed a truck and killed three traders. The sun was beating down. The volcano on the horizon was smoking, ready to erupt any moment. I stood there watching a passing Congolese girl with hair braided into six-inch spikes and crowds of hustlers striding along in garish pyjama suits. Bicycle taxis with tinsel wound into the spokes. Guerrillas in mirror shades with radios clamped to their ears. And my cell phone rang. I answered and it was my wife Claire, calling from home. "I love you," I said and she replied, "I love you." She told me that at that very moment, when I picked up and she heard my voice on the phone, our baby daughter kicked inside her womb.

At any one time we had six wars, a couple of famines, a coup d'état, and a natural disaster like a flood or an epidemic or a volcanic eruption, all within a radius of three hours' flight from Nairobi. You could take off at sunrise, commute to witness a battle, or hear a starving man breathe his last and be back home by nightfall, in time to file a story, take a shower, then hit the Tamarind restaurant downtown for mangrove crab and Stellanbosch. Or you were dropped off, watching the plane roar away in a cloud of red dust, and you were gone for weeks, out of contact and a thousand miles from help. And each time you returned home after a trip like that for a few days you were as mad as Gulliver talking to his horses.

Those were the years when we hitched rides on dawn flights carrying cargoes of blood plasma, guns, or baby food to bush airstrips. Flights on battered Antonovs, with the word NASDROVJE!—Cheers!—emblazoned on the nose of the fuselage. Flown by Russian crews with the Mongoloid faces of Soyuz cosmonauts from my boyhood stamp collection, their breath sour from drink, on three hundred dollars a month, with girls thrown in, running weapons in the orbit of modern African wars. I recall flights when the passengers sat among boxes of toothpaste and grenades, cement and drums of gasoline. I recall sitting next to a little girl in a frilly pink dress and bonnet and ivory armlets, clutching a yellow-haired Caucasian doll as, below us, broccolilike black forests stretched for a thousand miles, unbroken and empty.

I'd climb aboard the Cessna at first light, in my mind kissing the tarmac good-bye like the pope in reverse. The pilot throttled up, mumbled into his microphone, neck muscles bunching like a bullfrog. On takeoff I used to recite the Lord's Prayer over and over until I got stuck on a line like a mantra—"deliver us from evil, deliver us from evil, deliver us from evil"—as the earth fell away. Ten minutes out from Nairobi and the great gate of clouds opened out, with the pillars of Mount Kenya to the north and Kilimanjaro to the south. Our path led over patchwork peasant lands, sequined with tin hut roofs glinting in the sun; farther out were empty, arid plains, broken up only by smooth brown kopjes and the capillaries of seasonal streams that dissipated into stains of green against the ocher and white desert. Look down and you'd see herds of goats and camels scatter in unison like shoals of fish. Even in this modern day, out here whole grid squares on the tactical pilotage charts were half blank and marked with the words RELIEF DATA INCOMPLETE. They might as well have written "here be monsters." The flights themselves scared the hell out of me before we'd even landed in the eye of another crisis. "I repeat, six souls on board, do you read...?" Often there was no answer. The pilots called Sub-Sahara's airspace "the cone of silence." I couldn't fully appreciate the idea until the day I entered a control tower following a battle at an airport and saw brain, hair, and skull fragments all over the walls. Every time we flew into a cloud I'd hold my breath and think of all the UFO junk we might be on a collision course with: ghost flights, alcoholic Ukrainians shifting cargo, Zimbo arms smugglers, overflying tourist charters, medevacs, drug couriers, patrolling MiGs. There was the tropical weather too, in which minutes after observing clear skies up ahead one saw elevating thousands of feet up out of thin air a black storm with the head of a sledgehammer.

On those flights I'd look down from the sky at takeoffs and landings and see the silhouette of our little aircraft ripple over pulverized cities, refugee camps, the acetylene-white flashes of antiaircraft fire, and countries rich only in lost hopes and broken dreams. What comes to mind when I think of that time in my life are the words of Isaiah 18, which I'd read in Gideons Bibles I'd found in dozens of seedy hotel rooms where I spent so much of my life on the road: "Woe to the land shadowing with wings, which is beyond the rivers of Ethiopia.... Go, ye swift messengers, to a nation scattered and peeled, to a people terrible from their beginning hitherto; a nation meted out and trodden down." That passage makes me think of my circle of friends, the journalists I knew in those years. We were like the swift messengers in Africa.

Sometimes I remember it all again. I am back in that valley at night. I see the silent panic on the livid faces around me with the gunfire roaring in the fog. Or I'm at a field hospital. I put my notebook down to help lift a casualty with his brains spilling personality all over the stretcher, when a mortar bomb slams into the triage room, liquefying patients inside. Or in the famine camp, where at my feet a child crouches like a frog with eyes clouded white as moonstones. And the American nurse is whispering in my ear, "We say the ones like that are circling the drain. You know, like a spider in your bath?"

It all comes back to me. Overnighters, all-nighters, hitching rides on tanks busting down palace gates, sipping dictators' champagne, scoops and whores and house arrests, herograms, smelly socks and Caterpillar boots, the shits, deadlines, dead on arrival, bouts of amoebae and malaria remembered fondly like adventures, beriberi, organ failure, Stalin's organs, brain damage, gas gangrene, coke cut with pig laxative from condoms smuggled in the bowels of living men, oral rehydration salts, satellite feeds, food aid, baby milk, mass burials through a Nikon lens, Huey chopper rides, the pure adrenaline of being in fallen cities decorated with floral mortar bursts and tracers in the sky.

My entire life seems to have been either a prelude or an aftermath to moments such as these. Sometimes for a while I can submerge them and forget. But without warning, the hog-tied corpses of memory bob to the surface once more and then I recognize how much I've loved and missed those days. I suppose this is why people hoard their mementoes. Mine are sundry keepsakes of war and failed states, loot and charms, an odd collection of dictators' portraits, Red Cross press releases, permits from guerrilla armies. Plaintive letters from interpreters left behind after the news went cold. Snaps of friends, gazing over ruined cityscapes, brandishing weapons, smoking joints, posing in mock disguises and states of intoxication, arm in arm. An Ethiopian chopper pilot's visor helmet; river pebbles from Serbia; a concrete fragment of the Berlin Wall. A reject news photo of a Liberian, his skull trepanned by a bullet and daubed over with a Day-Glo smiley face and the caption "Have a nice day!" Buried in a drawer are autopsy reports and black-bordered funeral orders of service. There are voices on tape; if I stand in the next room and listen through an open door, I can ignore their metallic distortion and imagine them to be young and alive once more. All this stuff hangs around like bad luck in my house. I'd throw it all out if it weren't so much a part of me.

Sometimes, the stories themselves can take on their own disturbing vitality. Inside my mind, they play out the what-ifs and maybes, throwing up fresh detail or missing facts I can no longer pin down. Or they spill over into my innocent recollections. Rows of silent infants with swollen kwashiorkor bellies gatecrash the childhood movie of my grandpa tying his runner beans to bamboo stakes in his garden. A gang of executed men in a banana grove falls to the floor as I'm flicking through pictures of my summers at Oxford. All these memories are unfinished business. They seep out of the hidden recesses and coagulate. I confuse the happy ones and the bad ones, where one fuck-up ended and the other began: childhood, or my thirtieth birthday, until I can no longer determine if certain events that still haunt me are either real or imagined, or just excuses for drinking too much, or my yelling rages, or not bothering to get out of bed in the mornings. And sometimes, there are mornings when I get up just so that I can stare at the wall of the room all day.

I recall countless mornings, rooms, and faces. A hut in the suburbs of Nairobi, where the white ants ate the timber walls and the tin roof popped and sighed with the heating and cooling of the days. Back at home on the Indian Ocean beach, like a child again under my mother's care. I have had hours, dawns, waking in strange beds and looking out of windows at deserts, unfamiliar cityscapes, wintry rain, at the airliners coasting in like sharks to land at Heathrow. All that time stuck pacing around in rooms. And when I wasn't there, I was on a road or a flight to some destination that made sense at the time even if it doesn't now. Checking in, checking out. The circular journeys that brought me right back to the point where I had started. It is as if I have slept through an afternoon and waking, found that it is already dark. Time passes. Yet I sometimes sense that no time has passed at all. Sometimes, it occurs to me that if I picked up the phone right now and dialed my old home number the person answering it at the other end would be myself, aged twenty-three.

But it started long before that.

I was going to tell you war stories but I've realized that if I want to make sense of them, there is a wider tale that follows an arc through the generations. You see, it started when I broke down after my father's death. Suddenly I found myself taking stock of everything that had ever happened to me. I remembered the people and the things I had loved, or feared. I recalled my ancestors and my childhood. I lived through my wars again on the journey to recovery, in what the British combat photographer Don McCullin has described as the "peace process." At first I wandered without purpose, but luckily I discovered Peter Davey's diaries in the Zanzibar chest. Sometime later I tucked the papers under my arm and went to Arabia. There I followed the story page by page, mile by mile, and it provided me with a golden thread that guided me out of the labyrinth where I was lost. And for this reason I can't speak of my own story without also telling you about Davey. In these pages I am going to take you to Africa and Arabia and a few other places besides, in different years and over centuries. Forgive me when it proves difficult to keep up, but you'll just have to trust me. For now I want you to keep in mind a day in April 1947. We are in an emerald-green valley beneath the craggy peaks of high Arabia. The land has fallen silent but for the sound of birdsong and the gurgling of water in the cool mountain stream. Youth and innocence are dead. The broad-winged shadow of a vulture circles over three men. One body is that of an African, a sheikh's slave, lying riddled with bullet wounds. Nearby sprawls the figure of Davey. The translucent bone haft of a silver *jambiya* dagger protrudes from his chest and blood soaks his khaki tunic. And standing over the two of them is my father.

My great-great grandfather
Colonel William Temple, VC

Take Me Home to Mama

My father's ancestors were Yorkshire farmers. My great-grandparent Hartleys, remembered chiefly for their habit of sitting up in bed together at home in the seaside town of Bridlington and arguing loudly over the morning newspapers, refused even to set foot outside Yorkshire. I sense the Hartleys' love of home was as important to them as not meddling in the affairs of other peoples overseas. A Hartley was among those who initiated the debate on the abolition of slavery. And David Hartley, a staunch opponent of the American Revolutionary War and a friend of Benjamin Franklin, was Britain's minister plenipotentiary and signed the Treaty of Paris in the autumn of 1783.

All this changed after Britain lost America and spread its empire in the East. My forebears were swept up in a saga that makes an exception of the Bridlington Hartleys. My mother has gathered our family history into a collection of haphazardly arranged scrapbooks. It is a chronicle of tragedy and conquest. Ours is a typical British story spanning generations, in which men, women, and their children sank in ships on faraway oceans, succumbed to fevers in tropical bone yards, and died in small wars, mutinies, and rebellions fought across the crimson atlas of the

British Empire. What survives of each of them in the albums may be only a picture, or an anecdote that fills a few lines. Whole lives are distilled to a single essence, like a well-cut gemstone. Commemorating the life of Great-aunt "Horrible" Hilda, and the love of her husband, is my mother's ring of five Burma rubies. A big champagne diamond and other rings of opal used to set my grandmother off on yet more stories of Antipodean courtships.

As a boy I looked at the faces of my grandfathers and grandmothers, and in those eyes staring back at me through fading paint and sepia I observed a common determination. They were from a tribe absorbed by loyal duty, like my soldier forefather who, starving in the 1688–89 Catholic siege of Londonderry, held off eating his last tallow candle in order to use it to seal his military dispatches. We were indigo planters along the Ganges at the time of the Indian Mutiny. We fled for our lives down the river, but sailed into an ambush on the banks. In a hail of musket fire, the women and children threw themselves into the flood because they preferred to drown than be captured by their "inhuman enemies." Between the Indian Mutiny and the Boer War, Britain fought twenty-nine small colonial wars from Ashanti to the Boxer Rebellion in China. My family fought and perished in a great many of them. One warrior sums up all of them. He was great-great grandfather Colonel William Temple, who fought against the Maoris in New Zealand. In 1863, during the Waikato War on North Island, Temple won a Victoria Cross, the empire's highest military decoration for courage. This was recognition of his bravery while tending his wounded comrades under a hail of intense fire from the ramparts of Rangiriri Pa, a fort of the tattooed Maori rebels. Temple married the magnificent-looking Theodosia, daughter of Major-General T. R. Mould, governor of New Zealand, and she bore him twelve children. Much later, in India, my great-grandfather Gerhardt L'Honneur Sanders, who was to fight in the Boer War siege of Ladysmith, asked Temple's permission to marry my great-grandmother Mabel. The aging colonel, all braid and waxed mustaches, expressed his consent by declaring, "Better for her to be your widow than my unwed daughter!"

Our women certainly led hard lives. At Mabel's wedding, her seventeen-year-old sister Ethel was one of the bridesmaids. Ethel caught the eye of the best man, another army officer named Beames. Beames was a friend of Rudyard Kipling, who based *The Story of the Gadsbys*, his 1899 Indian "tale without a plot," on their courtship. They married and emigrated to Canada, where they became pioneers. Beames turned to drink, abandoning Ethel to raise four children in a remote log cabin. One of her sons grew up to become a sculptor and moved to the United States, where one of his commissions was a monument to the American Indian wars that stands in Washington. My grandfather Colonel Reginald Sanders proposed to my grandmother Eileen after meeting her on home leave at a piano recital before returning to duty in India. By the time her ship arrived in Bombay she had forgotten what he looked like. They met up somehow and married within hours. He took her into the hills to his new married-officer's quarters, carried her across the threshold, and proudly asked her what she thought of it. She burst into tears.

When the colonial peoples had been conquered, we were the rulers, the civil servants, the collectors, the engineers, the planters. We added to the store of scientific knowledge and indulged our national obsession with the classification of nature. Professor James Sanders was a principal of Calcutta University, who died of fever on the ship home in 1871 and is buried in Gibraltar. Douglas Sanders discovered new butterfly species in the hills inland from Chittagong, and his lepidoptera collections can be found in the British Museum. Great-grandfather James Wise worked for the Crown Agents on Cecil Rhodes's unrealized dream of the Cape-to-Cairo railway.

We fed the Great War and the Second World War too.

Great-grandfather Pickard was a shipping magnate who lost his fortune to German U-boats. Great-uncle Bertram was an Indian civil servant, but he died in Flanders. Uncle Alfred Hartley fought at Jutland. Uncle Percy Hartley died in Mesopotamia. Yet another uncle survived the dysentery of that same campaign because, he believed, he had put his trust in a talisman given to him by an Arab friend. In the Second World War one sank in the Hood. Uncle Mike was in Burma. Uncle Norman crashed his Spitfire fighter aircraft and was crippled for life. Noel was a member of the forces that liberated Belsen. Another was a POW of the Japanese and worked on the Burma railway.

In time, the peoples my ancestors ruled won us over to their ways and their nations became more of a home to us than England. Long before the hippies went in search of gurus, my great-uncle Claude acquired a Sikh master in India and founded a society in England to promote his teachings. My grandfather Colonel Sanders devoted forty years of his life to the 48th Dogras, Rajput regiment, and fought alongside his soldiers in the Northwest Frontier, in Aden and Palestine during the Great War, and finally against the Japanese. In photographs he appears in jodhpurs, always with a pipe sticking out of his mouth and a perfectly clipped mustache, painting a watercolor of distant hills, standing, or rifle in hand, with the "mugger" crocodile he has just shot. When Grandpa retired from the Dogras in 1947, at India's independence, he was bereft.

My mother loved India more than anywhere else. She was born in 1925 while my grandparents were on a shopping trip to Lahore. She spent the first week of her life wrapped in cotton wool. Her earliest memories are of waking up at dawn under a tree of blossoms in the garden, in which the family took refuge during an earthquake; of a house on a river, where at night, beyond the garden, jackals howled; eating chapatis in the ayah's quarters; the sight that made her sad of Indians doubled up under the weight of the huge blocks of ice they carried to the European clubs; and of large, cool rooms with fans and cool drinks, regimental displays, and wide, green lawns. Even after half a century in Africa, my mother still said, "Africa is nothing compared to India."

As a boy I asked my mother why our great-grandpas and our great-grannies from families of Yorkshire farmers and Scottish doctors felt the need to leave home and travel all over the world.

"Oh, to get out of the rain, dear," Mother replied.

After several centuries, our British Empire came to an end. Most of my tribe returned to where they had once come from. As a child I used to meet my British relatives on visits in England. We all loved ancient Aunt Connie, who had been married once but recalled little about her husband because it had been so long since he was killed in the First World War. Connie lived with Aunt Vi, a spinster and self-sufficiency enthusiast who kept sheep, a pack of Chihuahuas, and fermented raspberry wine in bottles that exploded in her corridors. But most of the rosy-cheeked cousins I met at weddings and funerals were as strange to me as the country of Britain itself.

My parents were almost the only family members I knew who refused to go back to England. We who had been in India, the Far East, the Antipodes, the Americas, and the South Sea islands stayed on where we had made our last landfall, in East Africa. Once the colonial rulers, our status was now simply that of an appendix to history: powerless, few in number, and, most of all, extremely happy to remain in exile.

Britain was known as "home." Yet for us, it was a distant island, where after all these years it was still raining. It was almost entirely through BBC radio that we kept in touch with an idea of England, which was cleansed by the frequencies of short wave and my parents' vaguely remembered sense of patriotism. England greeted us each dawn with the BBC World Service signature tune, "Lero Lero, Lilli burlero." Wherever we were, Big Ben tolled the hour and Dad, doing his yoga while drinking his early morning tea, gazed out at our adopted landscape, at a rising desert sun, or at the fishermen punting their outrigger canoes into the surf.

At the center of this world was my father. In my eyes, Dad was like an Old Testament patriarch. He was mightily handsome and strong. He had been in the sun so long that his legs, head, and arms were blackish brown, but underneath where he had worn his short-sleeved shirts and shorts his skin was still pale white. He was huge, leather-backed, barrel-chested, larger than mortal, with a large nose, big earlobes, hair of jet, and on the cusp of sixty when my mother gave birth to me. I have a strong mental image of my father as I write this, as a man walking. He walked with big swinging strides. He had walked across entire lands in his day. As an old man he walked too, daily, stopping ever more frequently to survey the view. When he walked a natural euphoria came over him. That is all one can say. It made him happy. It made him remember all the other walks of his life, before cars and aircraft made us rush about and pollute the world. He looked around him and saw the beauty of the land, and saw that he was moving through it at the pace that he wanted, filling his lungs with air, greeting loudly the people he passed on his way.

He was a great storyteller, who came home in his dusty veldskoens with presents that spoke of his travels. He'd produce from his duffel bag a curved Afar dagger in a goatskin sheath, a wooden Somali camel bell, or a gold star brooch for my mother. I remember once he also came home with his Land Rover punctured by three bullet holes. When he slammed the car door and strode off for a cup of tea, I hung back and stuck my fingers into the gashed aluminium. The rare times I ever found Dad sitting down, I'd climb up on his lap and he'd enfold me with one brawny arm, Tusker beer cradled in his other hand. We could be out in the bush but even if we were in a city, the way Dad told a tale in his voice as deep as a drum made it seem as if we were around a campfire out under the stars, in a pool of light cast by flames and encircled by the darkness of a million square miles of imagination.

My paternal grandfather, John Joseph, grew up on the island of Islay, where the Scottish children called him a "Sassenach." He married Daisy, from Queenstown in South Africa's Cape. He worked as a government official and they settled in the Leicestershire village of Kegworth, in a rambling house called Claremont. My father was born at home on July 31, 1907. His earliest memories revolved around ordinary English village family life. Opposite Claremont was the church, where he used to steal pigeon's eggs from the belfry. On Sundays the bells rang out "Nine Tailors Make a Man." In the garden was an ancient mulberry tree, planted during the reign of Charles I, and an old pavement from the ruins of a Roman villa. At the bottom of the garden was the River Soar, where my father and his siblings learned to swim, sail, and fish. England's countryside was still quiet and motor cars were unknown. In summer, one could hear the corncrake and lapwings. Noise arrived only with the outbreak of the Great War, when my father heard the sound of marching boots and horse-drawn equipment echoing through the streets for days on end. He remembered cold winters at his grammar school in Loughborough, and frost-bitten potatoes for lunch. Each week a fresh list of names was added to a scroll of honor in the assembly room to commemorate the old boys killed on the Western Front. He saw zeppelins bombing Nottingham and once the horizon was illuminated by the explosions at Chilwell, a munitions factory where hundreds of women worked. He remembered an elderly spinster aunt's only comment when she heard the detonation: "Oh, what is Cook *doing* in the kitchen?" He was haunted by his memory of the faces of soldiers coming home from the war, still in their trench coats and shouldering their rifles.

Dad recalled later in life that he had not enjoyed school and focused his mind elsewhere, "in the woods and along the river's reedy

banks." His one desire was to roam the countryside. In time he went
to agricultural college, where horses were still used for haymaking,
ploughing, and haulage. He learned to stook sheaves of corn, and he
built turnip clamps, cut and laid hedges, topped and tailed mangles,
hoed root crops, and went turd knocking. A new era in agriculture
was beginning, however, and my father studied soil analysis, artificial
fertilizers, hybrid improvements of crops and livestock, pesticides,
chemicals, and tractors and combine harvesters. In 1927 he was
offered a Colonial Service scholarship to Oxford University.

At Oxford, my father said he learned there was more to the
world than the "bullocks, sheep, and crops" of his childhood and he
"talked of politics and everything under the sun." He began to read
about Africa and in Blackwells he bought Sir Richard Burton's *First
Footsteps in East Africa.* After Oxford he went to study at the Imperial College of Tropical Agriculture in St. Augustine, on the island
of Trinidad. When not studying cotton or coffee, he went out with
his Creole friends shark fishing or iguana hunting. Until then, the
only time he had gone abroad in his life was to France on a cycling
tour. In Trinidad, he was fascinated by the mix of foreign races he
encountered.

My father could have made his life in almost any part of the
empire. Many of his generation went overseas, including his
brother Ronald. I remember Uncle Ronald, a ukulele-playing agricultural college principal in Fiji who had his singing Bulgarian wife
shave him before he turned out of bed each morning. At college in
Trinidad, notices went up offering jobs in everything from rubber
in Malaya and tea planting in Ceylon to ranching in Australia. My
father chose Africa because of his mother, Daisy, who told him stories of life in the Cape in the nineteenth century and remembered
trekking across the veld in an ox wagon when she was still a little
girl. My father was also inspired to live overseas by his paternal
uncle Ernest, whom he loved. Ernest was a businessman in India, a
keen sportsman, and a raffish character with a great sense of humor,

whose daughter grew up to become the actress Vivien Leigh. During the summer of 1928, Ernest and his wife Gertrude leased the house of the Earl of Mayo in Galway and Dad went to join them for a summer's fishing. He fell a little in love with the precocious, adolescent Vivien. "Everybody knew it," a gossipy aunt told me. She gave him a book of poems by Banjo Paterson, signed "To my favorite cousin with love from Viv." My father adored "The Man from Snowy River" for the rest of his life.

On October 10, 1929, he received a letter from the secretary of state for the colonies. It gave news of his appointment as agricultural officer in the Tanganyika Territory and was signed, "I have the honour to be, Sir, your most obedient servant." My father's generation was from a new type of empire builders who were quite different from their predecessors. Before, the British in Africa had pursued an economy of simple extraction and it was as if they believed progress could not involve the mass of black people who lived in their colonies. Thin on the ground, we governed by the system of "indirect rule," via traditional or appointed local chiefs. The surface of East Africa was barely disturbed at first. But in the years after the Great War, the British determined to "develop" the colonies by ensnaring Africa's native peoples in the modern world economy, at the less advantageous end to be sure, as growers of cash crops and payers of tax. This was the mission my father was asked to play a role in and no doubt, at first he believed that it was a noble one, in which the destiny of Africa's remote peoples would for their own benefit at last be joined with that of the outside world.

I have an early memory from home. In the dead of night I am blasted awake by an otherworldly sound. The ocean tide is a distant roar beyond the reef. The house is silent. I call out, and my mother comes into my bedroom. At breakfast next morning, we laugh about the nocturnal disturbance. Dad tells me it was the shout of a honey badger startled by the lights on the veranda. For days and years, I wondered, "Do honey badgers make that noise?" But I have always known that it was my father.

When my mother first met him, my father made his bed point east each night so that he rolled with the world headfirst as he slumbered. He had his ankles tied securely to his bed with strips of bandage, to prevent him from walking in his sleep. Once, in a desert village prone to earth tremors, he slept on the flat roof of a house to get the cool evening breeze. At the dead of night he leapt off the top, landing in the alley below and only woke up when he hit the ground. The villagers, believing Armageddon was upon them, cried out and prayed to Allah. He used to tuck his revolver under the pillow at bedtime during the Mau Mau rebellion in Kenya. And when visiting Nairobi he would stay at my godfather Judge Birkett Rudd's home. One night in the early hours the household was roused by gunfire. Dad was discovered standing, wide awake, peppered in ceiling plaster and staring at the pistol in his hand. In a bad month he had three or four nightmares. During such episodes he gained superhuman strength, enough to hurl himself through high windows. He threw hurricane lamps, tore mosquito nets to shreds, strode about and bellowed the way I had heard that night of the honey badger. He never hurt himself or anybody else. He'd leap clean over my mother as she slept without touching her. When she spoke to him he answered in a voice that was not his own, as if his unconscious body had been possessed. But she grew familiar with this other strange voice and knew that if she kept talking calmly to the sleepwalker, he would after some minutes climb back into the bed they shared. He used to then fall back into a deep sleep, but wake at dawn unaware of all his struggles in the night gone by.

My father began suffering nightmares soon after he came to

Africa. I imagine him setting foot in Dar es Salaam in East Africa for the first time, the aromas of coffee, groundnuts, sesame, coconut oil, and cloves wafting up from the dockside godowns. He had been loaded with piles of items from a Piccadilly tropical outfitters called Griffiths, MacCallister and Crook: solar topee, spine pad, tin bath, lavatory seat, potted shrimps, herring roes, and a double-barreled twelve-bore shotgun thrown in. He was twenty-two.

In Dar es Salaam, he boarded a train that chugged upcountry into the night, the steam locomotive spewing showers of sparks that illuminated the thick bush on either side. After two nights and a day they reached Lake Victoria, where my father's predecessor was at the station to meet him. The official gave him a single sheet of paper of jotted notes describing what the job was all about and boarded the same train, which now returned to the coast. Dad was in charge of a district as large as Ireland and the only way to get around was on foot with porters, or by canoe, or on horseback. My father saw an Africa that was barbaric but at the same time noble, exotic and yet familiar to a young Englishman who had grown up among farmers, self-contained yet also worldly—and that Africa is now but a memory pulverized by history.

The local chief wore a crown of pangolin scales and lived in a palace complex of elaborate grass huts. His wives were adorned with copper bands and beads and their skin was cicatrized with zig-zags, crescents, and paisley whorls. The chieftain was protected by warriors armed with black-powder Tower muskets and spears, carved bows and well-feathered arrows, leather helmets encrusted with cowry shells and zebra manes, ornaments of glass beads and crocodile teeth. But war between neighbors was limited to defense, since it was believed that a leader would die if ever he crossed his own frontiers. True authority rested not in the temporal power of the chief but in the ancestors who resided inside an ornamental elephant's tusk called the "dawa," or medicine. A naked maiden carried the dawa ahead of the chief whenever he walked out and about. The king-makers were the women, since legitimacy in the family line passed from mother to daughter, not father to son. The firstborn princess and heiress made a chief out of her husband when she married him. By these means the misrule of leaders never got out of hand. The younger daughters in the ruling families were considered illegitimate and became the mistresses of outsiders. My father learned all this because soon after he arrived in the country the outcast princess Binti Mwalimu appeared in his bed and stayed with him for seven years. The other whites said he had "gone native," but not only did he not care about that, I think he liked it.

The peasants lived in constant struggle with nature: locusts, armyworm, crop-raiding elephants and baboons, drought, floods, and disease. "I saw a long, dark, ragged cloud appearing," my father wrote of his first sighting of a locust swarm. "It seemed to wave and undulate and to my surprise it was coming closer at a fast pace. The great brown mass darkened the sky above me. I could hear the light, rustling sound of the flight of millions of insects and the sound they made as they collided. ... I remember seeing a whole valley filled with crops reduced to nothing within minutes. I saw an old man sitting in the middle of the remains of his sorghum field, which had been reduced to short stumps. The man had his head bowed and he was weeping. There would be no crop and no store of food for him that season. He was completely ruined."

My father's orders were to make Africans grow cotton. The cash crop was sold, with the prices from Liverpool cabled daily as a guide, and with this money the Africans became part of the wider world and paid their taxes to the government in Dar es Salaam. On the orders of the British the colonial chiefs' overseers flogged Africans who refused to grow cotton. The commodity was so important that my father's local nickname was Bwana Cotton. In time, he negotiated with a local chief to establish a research station breeding new cotton hybrids at a spot called Ukiriguru. This grew up into an institution that is famous in Africa today. The only problem at the time was that the land where the station was to be located was home to two hundred families who would have to be resettled elsewhere.

Dad set off to find a place where the families could be moved farther along the southern lakeshore, intending to look on the shores between the gulf of Emin Pasha and Speke Sound. For this journey the local chief lent my father his war canoe, crewed by sixteen paddlers who shoveled at the oily water and chanted *"Kabule, kabule, keiga, kabule, kwa Majo pshagula, nizere! Tongaka, keiga, kabule, kwa majo: pshagula, nizere!"* "Wind, wind take me home to Mama, I'm coming! Go ahead, wind, and take me home to Mama, I'm coming!" The spear-thin bowsprit, hung with feathery tassels and antelope horns, sliced through the water. The boat left a foaming white wake and skimmed ahead of hippo bulls that charged them under big bow waves. They passed islands ringed by flat rocks that shuddered as dozens of crocodiles that had been basking with their jaws open in the sun bolted and slithered into the depths.

The shores had once been populated, but they were now deserted. Coffee bushes grew as tall as trees and herds of feral goats wandered about. On the island of Zilagora they met a man dressed in motley rags and skins and carrying a black-powder Tower musket with a horn and shot satchel. He said some of his fellow villagers had been devoured by crocodiles waiting in the shallows to swipe at the victims with their tails, who they would then seize and drag back into the water.

The man also talked of an epidemic of sleeping sickness. This had wiped out almost the entire population along the shores of Lake Victoria after the Europeans opened up the heart of Africa and people began to migrate and clear forest land for cultivation. In his time even Dad contracted the sickness and was cured by an Indian vet in Mwanza who injected him with a Bayer drug for cattle.

East African numbers had already been weakened by the

nineteenth-century Arab slave trade. With the Europeans also came sand flies, brought by the Portuguese from Brazil to the port of Luanda, which infected Africa's soils with jigger worms that rotted the feet of the barefoot peasants. Colonial forces invading Sudan and Ethiopia imported cattle infected with rinderpest from the Black Sea and Arabia. The disease spread in a wave from the Horn to Southern Africa, destroying multitudes of cloven-hoofed animals in its path. Smallpox, syphilis, and a battery of plagues from the outside world followed. The Africans who survived, decimated by famine, went to war over what resources remained. East Africa is dotted with monuments to the conflicts and pestilence of that time, such as the Rift Valley town of Eldoret, which means "the place of killing." As the Europeans ventured farther into the interior they discovered swathes of territory where few people survived. My ancestors beheld this scene and assumed that it had always been like this—with the Africans living in a benighted state of perpetual war, pestilence, and famine. They decided the local people were incapable, childlike, vicious, and primitive. Nile explorer Samuel Baker complained there were "no ancient histories to charm the present with memories of the past; all is wild and brutal, hard and unfeeling." Frederick Lugard, among the architects of imperialism in East Africa, claimed that on the cusp of the scramble into the continent, "Europe had failed to realize that throughout the length and breadth of Africa intertribal war was an ever present condition of native life, and that extermination and slavery were practiced by African tribes upon each other." And this view inevitably led to exhortations by men like Captain Ewart Grogan, a father of colonialism in East Africa, that "occupation of Africa with a view to sound colonization, that is, to fit the country as a future home for surplus population, is the obvious duty of the nations which form the vanguard of civilization... to make new markets and open up country for coming generations; to suffer temporary loss for the future benefit of overcrowded humanity."

And so my forebears confiscated this sparsely populated land for themselves and put its original inhabitants to work on it.

My father's party left the man on Zilagora, who refused to leave his island. "I will die here," he said. Some hours later my father's canoe came ashore in the Emin Pasha Gulf, where he engaged a train of porters and trekked inland. The imperial Germans had imposed their rule over this part of Africa by massacring and starving many thousands. The local BaZinza people told my father that the last Caucasian they had seen before him was an officer of the Schutztruppen who had ordered the village chief to be buried alive simply as a warning to others to behave. These people appeared unaware that the British had been their new rulers since Germany's defeat in the Great War. Despite the ravages of disease little had altered the integrity of their culture for centuries. My father passed isolated hamlets of fishermen and stands of millet, tobacco, and plantains. People buried their dead beneath their hut floors and worshiped ancestors who lived in miniature beehive shelters to which they brought gifts of beer and honey. They were also members of a secret cult called the Bachwezi and claimed that their founder, Liangombe, had spoken to the spirits during a spell in the wilderness. His followers entered into trances to commune directly with their ancestors and were able to exorcise spirits from troubled souls.

My father was superstitious. In Tanganyika he knew of a woman who had died of hiccups and because of this, every time he got them he verged on hysteria. He got the shakes when he had to help carry the corpse of a man who had died out in the bush. When I was a child he told me about the terrifying BaFumo witches, who wore black cloaks and carried umbrellas and groaned like zebu bulls. Their job was to sniff out the causes of misfortunes that befell the tribe, like poor harvests or epidemics, and a scapegoat was always found among the hapless peasants. Or the wizards who read the entrails of chickens for omens. There was his story about a witch who transformed her male disciples into hyenas after dark so that when Dad baited zebra meat with poison to kill the scavengers that were harassing local cattle, she declared that he had murdered her sons and cursed him for it. A few days later he was awoken by a loud snuffling and a hyena bolted from under his bed and out of the window.

In those days people along the shores of Lake Victoria practiced cults that had various beasts as their inspiration: members of the porcupine society went into a trance state and danced like their totem animal, trembling under sheaves of spines on their backs. My father became involved in a society that held serpents in great reverence. His English comrades were scandalized when they heard that my father participated in such practices. The cult order trained him to catch snakes by spitting the poisonous juice of a foxglove into their faces. These were kept in pits. Each cult member pared down his snakes' fangs and cut the nail of one of his thumbs at the same time. It was believed that the thumbnail grew at the same pace as the fangs, and when it reached a certain length the thumbnail and the fangs were cut together. Dad used to tell me how snakes sing at night. I never believed him until we were camping in the desert and he said *shush*! Out on the volcanic plain there was a soft moan, like either a frog or a bird. It was a familiar sound, to which I had just never put a name. It was said that snakes also breathed fire like dragons when they sang, and I was sure that out in the desert I could see faint, bluish will-o'-the-wisps. Dad said snakes would not harm him. Once, when he was sitting on a long drop latrine, a cobra shot out from between his legs. He said he stared it down until it slithered off under the door. I have seen Dad pick up a serpent by the tail, nonchalantly swing it around his head, and launch it into the bush. I once saw him shake a snake out of his bedroll in the bush when he got up in the morning.

Continuing on his journey along Lake Victoria's shores, my father and his train of porters arrived at the outskirts of a hamlet.

Ordering the porters to carry on, he went off with a tracker to shoot meat for the pot. They came on two impala rams, standing on an anthill and facing each other. With two clean shots of his rifle, my father killed both stone dead. A clamor erupted in the nearby village. Men, women, and children came running toward the kill. Some elders appeared and became very excited. They announced that my father had carried out an act of great importance. I picture him, a young man trying to comprehend what was being said. Something about totems and prophecies. I have tried to understand what it can be that they said. I imagine the tableau: the white man with his gun, the two horned beasts, almost heraldic, up on their hind legs, antlers pointing at each other, the moment of killing, blood splashing from a hole blasted in each heart onto the earth of the termite hill, the fading light, the peasants chanting *kusinga rugaba, kusinga wombecha.* "I see you, I see the sun."

Singing merrily, men butchered the impala rams and carried the meat back to the village. As my father followed, he heard drumming. Great fires were lit. Darkness fell, the meat was cooked and eaten, and my father was asked to be seated. He watched as a large circle of people gathered to dance. Women beat a rhythm on their rawhide skirts and shook pebble-filled gourds, drummers hammered on lizard-skin tom-toms, while for two hours boys and maidens gyrated violently in a ring. Suddenly a mournful dirge began and two wizards appeared with wildebeest flywhisks. They whisked at the youths who one by one fell to the ground in a trance and began to moan, jerk, and tremble. They began to speak and my father knew enough of the local language to know that they talked in a completely foreign tongue. The youths were using the language of the BaChwezi ancients, having become the oracle between the world of the ancestors and the villagers under that night sky. Questions were asked and translated and the answers came back again. Communing with the dead caused the villagers mirth, but also sorrow and anxiety. The séance over, the dance erupted once more and was still going on when my father went off to sleep. That night he slumbered fitfully. He felt troubled. The next day when he got up, he remembered the purpose of his trip to this hidden corner of Africa, which was to begin opening it up for the resettlement of the two hundred families to make way for the Ukiriguru research station. The elders quickly agreed to make enough land available—there was plenty of space—and allowed my father to survey the site and mark it out with white stones laid in tidy, straight, colonial lines.

Until the day Dad entered the village, the ancestors had held sway over the living. The spirits offered Africans a set of certainties through the endless cycle of the years in a perilous Eden. Rain, harvests, children, disease, drought, and death. In return, the only obligation of the living was to honor the dead. The prophecy was not just that the antelope were to be killed, but that it was my father doing it that day, as a young man of just twenty-three, becoming the agent of irreversible change in that remote corner of Africa. Soon after he walked away from the village the land was cleared. Cotton was planted. Vast deposits of diamonds and gold were discovered. Mines were opened up. Roads, aircraft, politics, wars, and AIDS followed. The rule of the ancestors was buried and forgotten. The new rulers were men who sat in faraway cities. They communicated with the people not via the spirit mediums, but by telegram cables and telephones.

He walked out of BaZinza country and returned to his lake post at Mwanza. From there, he took the train down to Dar es Salaam to attend a friend's wedding as best man. The night of the party, my father had his first nightmare. In his dream there appeared a shadow at his side. A man, but not a man. It threatened my father, who felt he had to attack the apparition before it harmed him. For most of the rest of his life, the dream came back repeatedly to haunt him.

Mother was full of theories to explain the nightmares. They

were mild epileptic fits. Or Dad ate too much cheese at night. Or he had never outgrown his childhood terror of "Mrs. Hicksey," a ghost in Claremont, the English village house where he was raised, that groaned in the attic and was in all probability a faulty water pipe. Nonsense, he said. My father believed he had been bewitched. For half my life I wondered what on earth he meant by that, until I grew to learn that I had fallen under a very similar spell.

My mother used to sit on my bed on Sunday mornings when I was small, telling me about the Burma War. As she spoke she painted her nails and I used to drink in the scent of varnish and picture her in my mind as a young woman on the jungle battlefields. When I urged her to she would go and fetch her box of keepsakes with its photos of her with her comrades in the women's auxiliaries, bullet casings, folded parachute silk, Chindit griffon badges, a captured Japanese rising sun flag, and a little silk wallet containing a Shinto poem praising the emperor, which a British soldier had looted from a dead man.

After spending her early years in India, my mother and her sister, Beryl, were sent to boarding school in Sussex. When the Nazi blitz began Grandpa decided to bring them home to India. They sailed on the troopship *Orion*. As their convoy zigzagged south through the Atlantic, U-boats sank two of the ships. The blackout rules were so strict the cabin portholes were painted black and nobody could even smoke a cigarette on deck after dark. What struck my mother most about her first glimpse of Cape Town was that it was a blaze of lights. In India, refugees were pouring in ahead of the Japanese advances or Malaya and Burma. Mother was sixteen when she volunteered at the Casualty Section of GHQ Simla, where she made bandages and filled out name cards recording the wounded, killed, and missing in action. The next year, in early 1944, she joined the Women's Auxiliary Service (Burma), based at Shillong, in Assam. Among their many tasks, the lady soldiers brewed tea in tin baths for the troops, baked cakes the size of millstones, distributed soap and razors to the troops, typed letters and reports, and sat on the beds of casualties, chatting about home or writing letters for those wounded who were blinded, or had lost their hands.

The Allied forces at last turned back the Japanese advances at Kohima and Imphal. Thereafter they began to drive the enemy back eastward. Mother's unit followed the advance and she was never far behind the front lines. The auxiliaries' CO, known as the General Memsahib, gave her a hand grenade—not to throw but to destroy herself with her honor intact in the event of being captured by the Japs. Even in the hospitals, patients had guns in case the Japs attacked and the medics had so many casualties to work on during a battle that mother knew a young doctor whose hair turned snow white in a single day. During an air raid, she had to jump into a slit trench and she looked up at a dive-bombing Japanese Val that she told me "trembled like a silver leaf in the blue sky."

For all that, what exotic places she saw. She traveled on trucks to Dohazari, in Arakan, Cox's Bazaar, Cachar on the Bishenpur-Silchar track, where "Japs were hiding in the tea bushes"; then Dimapur, Kohima, Milestone 56 on the Manipur Road, and on up to Milestone 82 at Maram, then right into Burma Blue mountains, tracks clinging to vertiginous valleys. "Hot," Mother said it was. "Sandy roads. Tall, tall, tall trees, going on forever. Long grass, green, green. No towns, no people, just camps and rivers ..." In her bathing suit and watched by commandos, she jumped into river pools to gather up fish stunned by cigarette-tin bombs. On the Manipur Road, "tuctoo" lizards sang in the tall trees outside the *basha* huts where she slept. Bandicoots scuttled beneath her bed and in the darkness a gaur, a bison-like creature from the forest, tripped over her tent's guylines.

She saw how battle had stripped the trees bare of branches and leaves. In one of her camps the path between the huts and the long drop latrine was a line of shallow Japanese graves, half exposed by the monsoon rains. Out of one grew a beautiful blue orchid and my mother's commanding officer's only comment was, "They're good for the soil, dear." In an American jungle base, she saw the dried heads of Japanese soldiers rammed onto the gateposts. It was here that she also saw her first movie in color on the big screen: Esther Williams in *Bathing Beauty*, a synchronized-swimming extravaganza. Mother said the Americans were nice, but that the English soldier girls primly refused when the GIs asked them to play Postman's Knock in the jungle in return for cans of pineapple juice and frozen chickens flown in from California.

Troops from all over the British empire made up the Allied army in Burma. Mother encountered soldiers of the West African Division, such as the Nigerians who manned the anti-aircraft batteries. In an air raid once she saw them, illuminated by the muzzle flashes of their guns, dancing a jig after they had scored a hit. One evening the women heard the Africans humming and the sound grew to a crescendo of glorious, homesick singing. They sang, too, in deep voices that made Mother feel sorry for them:

> *Oh, when shall I see my home again?*
> *My Mudda she is da,*
> *My Fadda he is da*
> *When shall I see my native land?*
> *When will I see my home?*

In 1943 she fell in love. She would never tell me much about him, only that his name was Peter and that he was a young British officer in Thirty-six Division. After he was wounded in the leg by a grenade, she was given compassionate leave to visit him. She flew in a troop transport and then drove through the jungles until she arrived at Shillong. Here she waited for days in a house in the forest with two other young women auxiliaries whose husbands had been killed in action. One of them was a friend named Alison, who opened her trousseau, never worn, and offered Mother anything she wanted to borrow. That evening, she went to an old hotel where Peter was convalescing and asked for him. "I sat trembling for a long time by a huge cedar fire. And then at last he came and found me waiting for him."

When Rangoon fell, her unit was assigned to process POWs being liberated from the Japanese prison camps. The CO told the women to talk about only home and happy things to the liberated men. But all they wanted to discuss was what had happened to them. They remembered their ordeals with nonchalance while Mum took down their testimonies in shorthand. She recognized an ex-POW from her father's Indian regiment and invited him and his friends over to the unit's quarters for tea and chocolate cake. Tears in their eyes, all the men could do was stare, unable to eat or drink because they were so used to starving. She saw Peter and was with him when they heard the news of Hiroshima and Nagasaki. After Singapore, she turned down a posting in Japan to return to India. Grandpa was retiring from his regiment. As Mum, Beryl, and Granny sailed for England from Bombay, the Royal Indian Navy was in the process of mutinying. It was the eve of India's independence and my family had been in the subcontinent since the eighteenth century. Mum knew England only from boarding-school days cut short by the Blitz. She hated postwar London, with its whale meat and rationed eggs, but Peter was waiting for her. He was the true reason she went to London, to get married. But some time after the 1946 victory parade, he broke her heart and she cast about for an escape.

In 1938, my father transferred from the Tanganyika colonial service for an appointment as head of agriculture in the Aden Protectorates, Southwestern Arabia. His heart was still in East Africa. During the Great Depression he had bought a small farm called En'nekeraka at Mweiga, on the western slopes of Mount Kenya. En'nekeraka, in the language of the ancestral people who had lived there evoked the sound of pebbles knocking together in the stream below the farmhouse. He aimed to one day retire to the farm, but he was still only thirty-one when he took up his Arabian appointment and the next sixteen years were to be some of the most eventful of his life.

When Dad arrived, Aden was one of the most familiar if unsightly landmarks in the empire. The pocket-sized colony, huddled around the barren mountain of Jebel Shamsan, existed solely for the benefit of the seaport. Then as now, Aden was not so much a single city as a collection of unattractive towns clinging to the volcanic rocks. Imperial officials and shipping agents lived at Steamer Point. On the isthmus of Khormaksar were the military lines and Royal Air Force base and inland from that was the Arab village of Sheikh Othman, where the desert sands blew in from the protectorates. The heart of Aden was Crater, the quarter for Arabs, Jews, Banyans, and international eccentrics. Arthur Rimbaud had pitched up here on his ill-fated scheme to run guns to the Arabs and Ethiopians. The adventurous smuggler Henri de Monfreid passed through here. In the thirties, another Frenchman, the powerful businessman Antonin Besse—who later founded an Oxford college—had built his house on the rocks overlooking Crater and it was here that he entertained the travel writer Freya Stark. In the godowns of the shabby emporium of Crater was a trade in the exotic: Mocha coffee, mother-of-pearl from Abdel Kouri, civet, cinnabar, and ambergris from the island of Socotra; also mass-produced goods, from wall clocks to universal embrocations to underwear from Liverpool. My father walked among crowds of Yemenis, short men from the hills with silver *jambiya* daggers in their belts, or Bedu visiting from the desert, decked out in kilts, snarling in surprise as they scrambled out of the way of passing cars. There were Banyan clerks and Jewish artisans, Bohra tailors, sallow Koranic students from Hadhramaut, Swahili sailors, Somali stevedores, and Chinese exporters of sea slugs and shark fins.

As far as the British were concerned, to protect Aden they had to see what was going on in the wild hinterlands, if not to control them. The inhabitants beyond the borders of Aden were divided into an impossibly complicated mosaic of clan and caste. There were the Gabilis, gun-carrying tribesmen who covered their half-clothed bodies with sesame oil and indigo woad, the Seyyids and Ashraf who believed they were descended from the tribe of the Prophet Mohamed, the nontribal traders and artisans who lived within the walls of tiny hilltop villages, and finally low-caste black serfs and slaves.

In antiquity, the Romans called this land Arabia the Blessed because its inhabitants controlled the trade in frankincense and myrrh, which was harvested in the hills of Oman, the island of Socotra, and in the Horn of Africa. The valuable resins were carried by camel across the desert, via Mecca and Petra, to Gaza and from there to Egypt, Greece, and Rome. In the first century A.D., a Roman legion under Gaius Aelius Gallus had set out to conquer Mareb, capital of the kingdom of Saba, also known as Sheba, and been defeated when the wily Arab guides led the invaders into the waterless deserts. Soon afterward, with the opening of the sea route from India to the Red Sea, the land route fell into decline. The mighty cities built on the back of the trade fell prey to desert raiders and crumbled into the sands.

The British seized the port of Aden in 1837. It was a dirty little village, located on an ancient site and strategically placed. But in the next century, with the completion of the Suez Canal and the invention of coal-fueled steamships, Aden grew as wealthy and as busy as Hong Kong, the key point midway on the passage to India. The interior had been left virtually unexplored, though the British created a buffer zone of treaties of protection with tribes in the hills and deserts surrounding the colony. In the process the British elevated various petty tribal chieftains to the status of sultans, treating them to gun salutes like Indian maharajas when they dropped into Aden to pick up their annual stipends of rifles and silver Maria Theresa dollars from Government House. In return for their pay-offs, the sultans agreed to show allegiance to the British Crown, rather than to the Imam, the sacerdotal ruler of the high Yemen to the north who coveted Aden port and the hinterlands. Otherwise they were left to their own devices, even to the extent that slavery existed under British rule.

On the eve of the Second World War, Britain finally decided on a new "forward policy" to develop the hinterlands. To do that, and to consolidate the protectorate frontiers against incursions from the Imam's Yemen to the north, they enrolled men like Dad to end tribal feuding and establish irrigation farming, police forces, schools, and roads.

One of the first British officials he met in Arabia was Harold Ingrams, the resident adviser to the Hadhramaut, in the Eastern Aden Protectorates. Ingrams was among Britain's most revered Arabists. He told my father he should at all times respect Arab customs, refrain from alcohol, and dress in the local garb. Ingrams himself went in for the authentic look, fluttering about in a Saudi headdress, an Indonesian *lungyi,* a big belt, and silver and ornaments and bracelets. Around his neck he wore a Bedouin leather necklace with a large agate stone. He wore boots and he limped, the result of a wound sustained at the Western Front. Ingrams was famous for negotiating a peace settlement between the warring Hadhramaut clans that was so complicated it involved separate truces to end two thousand long-standing blood feuds. Dad admired Ingrams but thought him somewhat pompous and much later he remembered a ditty about him.

> They call me Headline Harold
> In my home in Hadhramaut,
> Where I toil all day for plenty of pay
> In my simple Saudi suit.

My father adored his job and the fact that he was among just seven Englishmen covering a territory of a hundred thousand square miles. He was in Arabia for sixteen years, which he spent constantly on long journeys, on foot, on horseback, in rickety Vickers Vincent biplanes. He worked with the political officers in the colonial service whose task was to broker peace negotiations to end the perpetual clan conflicts. Refuse to declare a truce and the political officer could call in the Vickers Vincent to bomb a recalcitrant sheikh out of his fortress. Make peace and my father came in as the agriculture officer to reward the tribes and bolster peace by reviving irrigation systems and planting cotton, fruit trees, and food crops. He introduced the husbandry of cotton, but also everything else from cabbages and apricots to large red chickens, to the unsuspecting tribes. He traversed an often hostile country with no more protection than a bodyguard and his skill in talking his way out of tight situations.

In 1949, my mother was offered a job as the governor's confidential secretary in Aden. "How is Aden?" she asked Grandpa, who had fought the Turks there in the Great War. "Bloody awful," he said. She took the job because a first-class ship's passage was part of the deal. At the eleventh hour, they made her fly—because, she later discovered, the woman she succeeded had gone mad and the governor needed a replacement at short notice. When she first arrived in Aden, she stayed with a family in a house overlooking the harbor. The house had a pet ibex, called Jumper, that slept on her bed and trotted about, eating cigarettes. She encountered my father her very first night in Aden during a Scottish dance held at the governor's residence. He was apart from the crowd of Englishmen sitting cross-legged on the floor, cracking walnuts by hurling them against the glass windows.

She did not take much notice of him in the early days, when various other younger suitors pursued her, including a pair of pilots from RAF Eight Squadron, who each had an MG sports car. They turned up in tandem to take her to dances at the Union Club, or picnics and swimming at Gold Mohur beach. There's a black-and-white photo of her, lissome in a black bathing suit, hands on hips, head tilted, a sly smile and laughing eyes, ankle-deep in the surf, flicking water with her dainty foot toward the camera. She looks really quite naughty in the picture, though when I joked with her about this she said primly, "Nonsense—we were quite proper in those days."

My father was a very different sort of man from the dashing young British servicemen. The second time she saw him was during a polo match. He was the team's captain but he turned up late, in dusty clothes, mounted up, yelled a lot, and rode like a Tatar. She liked the look of him. Though he liked his beer and appeared at occasional parties, he was rarely in Aden and spent most of his time in the protectorates among the Arab farmers.

In the Secretariat, a big colonial building of arched windows, latticework, and wide timber verandas, my mother used to have to sort the flow of intelligence reports for the governor. They came in from the senior political officer, Basil "Cloak and Dagger" Seager, a man with a sharp nose, tight lips, pedantic rasping voice, and quick, poor Arabic. He adored intrigue and by telegraph, he sent messages in code or *en clair* in French, Latin, or using obscure literary allusions that took hours to decipher. Or spies in flowing robes arrived at her office with envelopes marked CONFIDENTIAL, inside of which were smaller ones that said SECRET, inside of which were yet smaller ones that said MOST FRIGHTFULLY SECRET.

From these reports and general gossip, Mother began to notice my father's movements. She waited for him. He didn't appear for weeks on end. Then one day after a long time, she heard the heavy step of desert boots ascending the Secretariat's timber stairs. *Clump, clump* they came down the veranda. The next day the boots were gone again. This happened several times. The months passed. She sometimes saw him on her morning rides when she went to the stables at Khormaksar. On the tennis court she found herself opposite him in a game of mixed doubles. At a party to celebrate the King's birthday, she saw him arm in arm with the Sultan Sharif Hussein of Beihan, a magnificent figure she knew from the intelligence files, both of them standing in a flower bed and heaving with laughter at some private joke. And in her office when she heard his boots climb the stairs her heart beat faster. *Clump, clump, clump.* One day, my father's face appeared at her office door.

My mother was beautiful and young, but I've heard it said that Dad fell in love with her when she told him that, as a girl, she had milked a cow called Bumble. He took her horse riding along the beach at Khormaksar, or east along the desert coast to the Abyan Delta where he was growing vast acres of cotton. On overnight trips to the coastal village of Zingibar she stayed with a British married couple to prevent gossip. They went riding in the desert, stopped for picnics, and he fed her polony sausage with mustard and schnapps. Odd combination, she thought. Once they got lost driving across the desert back to Aden, and he wrapped her in his sheepskin cape, waited for the clouds to clear, and navigated his way back by the stars. Mum lived at Steamer Point, Dad on the other side of the colony in the Arab village of Sheikh Othman. One day he said, "Let's get married. We'll save on petrol."

Mum fell in love with Dad because she was a romantic. She was fascinated by stories and wanted to live out an exotic tale herself. She might not have endured as much in the years ahead had she not felt that the adventures he promised to take her on would be worth all the sacrifices she made. She was so slim my father could nearly join his hands around her waist. A Somali woman named Sara stitched her white wedding dress. A handsome RAF padre called them in for a chat and gave them a book entitled *Man, Woman and God.* A riding partner of Dad's named Quill, who had been a POW in Changi, threw a stag party. On January 27, 1951, they married in the garrison church at Steamer Point with a reception to follow. Dad was forty-three, my mother twenty-five. The flowers came from Asmara by plane. The wedding cake was ordered from the Crescent Hotel. The governor laid on his Rolls-Royce to transport the bride. The telegrams were read out.

CANNOT GET OVER NEWS STOP EMPIRE BUILDER LOST
STOP MY CONGRATULATIONS TO YOU AND
COMMISERATIONS FOR THE UNFORTUNATE WOMAN

After the English ceremony my mother changed into an Aertex shirt and slacks. They climbed into a hired car and the Arab driver got angry when he learned the guests had tied tin cans to the rear fender. Later they drove down the beach to Abyan.

Their first night together, they slept in the fort on Khanfar Rock, a promontory overlooking the whole of Abyan. After breakfast next morning, Dad told my mother to change into her riding clothes. They got on their horses; Dad on his stallion al-Qatal, my mother on al-Azraq. They rode their horses to the bottom of the rock, where the mounted Sultan Hussein al-Fadhli and his slave boy on a donkey beside him were waiting. They saw a mass of camel and horseback riders advancing toward them from the village of Zingibar, followed by a great plume of dust. Dad's horse could sense the great crowd and stamped and snorted. The hum of many people became audible. The party rode out in a line and as they approached through clouds of dust a crowd of people on foot and on horses and camels came into view. Turbaned riders, their skin glistening with oil and blue woad, galloped toward them as they fired off salutes with rifles and muskets. "The bullets missed us literally by inches. I felt my hair blow up once from the blast," Mum wrote to her parents. A circle formed and the bride and groom cantered around it as the riders shot in the air, then a cavalcade formed behind them and the whole mass of horses and camels wheeled about in the dust, horses springing and leaping. A bullock was led out into the circle and a swordsman hacked off the beast's head. First my father, then my mother, jumped their horses over the bullock's carcass. They dismounted and were ushered into an enormous tent lit by gas lamps. Inside, they were shown two ornate chairs where they sat, drinking glasses of tea, as a bard sang his blessings for their future together.

"That was a good party," Dad said later, when they had returned to sleep on Khanfar Rock. "I enjoyed that," he said, almost surprised.

My father stopped tying himself to the bed when he grew used to living with my mother. Nor did he make his bedroll head-first with the revolution of the earth. My eldest brother Richard was born twenty months after they married and Dad retired from service in Arabia so that they could settle and raise a family back in his beloved Africa. On the eve of sailing, my mother wrote to Granny and Grandpa: "If ONLY we could be certain of peace, I can see the most *perfect* and *exciting* life ahead ..."

My mother's first glimpse of Africa was a stevedore pushing a wheelbarrow of ivory tusks down the dockside in Mombasa. As he went, he chanted, "Produce of the Congo! Produce of the Congo!" From the coast they drove inland to Mweiga, on the slopes of Mount Kenya, where Dad had bought the farm En'nekeraka during the Great Depression. The farm house was a cedar log cabin and the newlyweds would sit in their dressing gowns, in front of a roaring fire, eating fresh trout from the stream. From the windows in the morning, they saw the legs of a herd of buffalo below the raising blanket of mist as they moved back into the thick surrounding forest.

Soon after my parents settled on En'nekeraka, the Mau Mau rebellion broke out. First my father's cattle were hamstrung by the guerrillas. Then a gang chopped their neighbor into little pieces while he was taking his bath. My parents saw the way things were going and so decided to up sticks and move to Tanganyika. Soon after they left, police burned down the house on En'nekeraka, claiming that it was a late-night meeting house for terrorists.

I clearly remember, at about the age of three, trying to recollect what had happened up to that moment in my life. I looked back to oblivion, all apart from a single conscious moment. In this tiny phrase of time that is with me still, I am sitting up in my cot, crying, in a cool, bluish white room with windows opening out on to a vast, dry landscape. A sublime figure enters the room and, speaking softly, soothes me back to sleep, I suppose, because my memory stops there. My recollection is from my parents' new Tanganyika farm, which they called Langaseni. My mother saved a handful of photographs and scratchy, heat-damaged film from the years there. Otherwise, I have no sense of what Langaseni was like in those days, though I have heard about it all my life from everybody else in the family. From the stories, and they were almost lectures, I formed such a strong mental picture of this African paradise that I feel I could find my way around every single hill and tree of the place. I'd know the horses in the stable, the dogs sunning themselves on the veranda, my elder siblings with their hair flaxen blond, and my father on his horse, riding down the dusty track under thorn trees. As a man I've visited the farm and nothing of my idyll survives.

The ranch was in the dry, rocky plains, between the snowy sugarloaf of Kilimanjaro and the sharp, black mass of Meru. The farm's western boundary was the Red River, colored by fluorine that blackened teeth and bones. Along the east was the Cold River, glacial and blue, flowing among glades of fever trees. To the south was a moonscape of volcanic hillocks like bubbles, covered with sparse, wiry grass, or sands and stunted thorn. On hard red soils to the northwest grew thickets of wait-a-bit thorn and aloes. In the north, on the edge of a plain teeming with game, was Firesticks Hill, Ol'Lekema Jipiparuk. My parents built their first huts here with horse stables made of split euphorbia trees. Later, they built a house of stone with a flat roof like an Arab fort. The walls were of volcanic stone. The roof beams were giant cedar trees Dad had dragged down from Kilimanjaro's forest by ox wagon. The doors and windows were made of camphor and they looked up at the mountains on either side.

At night, lions grunted and roared and the hollow volcanic hill rumbled as rhino cantered by. Coral-colored snakes migrated across the plains en masse in season and in the glade below the home were dark-spotted giraffe, zebra, and impala. In the dry open country were Grant's and Thomson's gazelles, oryx, wildebeest, cheetah, hunting dogs, hyenas, and jackals. In the wait-a-bit thorn were long-necked gerenuk and lesser kudu. Flocks of sandgrouse drank at the salty rainwater pans at dawn and at dusk you could hear the rasping chatter of guinea fowl and partridges preparing to roost.

"We were in a paradise," said my father, "that we can never forget, nor equal."

By the time they arrived, my brother Richard was a baby and my sister Bryony was on the way. "It was good to start a new life on the ranch, with the thought of more children to come, and the great open air," my mother recalled. "I said we were going to be there a hundred years."

They poured what little money they had saved into the farm and borrowed the rest. They started with a small herd of Boran cattle, including a cow that had been slashed on the face by the Mau Mau, a truculent heifer that took exception to anybody wearing a hat, 400 goats, two dogs, Silver the pony, and Jamila, an Arab filly that was my mother's wedding present with three centuries of pedigree, plus a Dodge nicknamed the Red, Red Car. Dad set about building up his herds and bought his stock from the Maasai and European farms in Kenya.

In the bone-dry country, the key to the farm's survival was water. The fluorine in the Red River was slow poison, the Cold River was seasonal according to the rains, and the drums of water they trucked down from pools at Ol Tulali on Mount Meru were thick with baboon shit. When Dad looked across the plains he reasoned there could be water in the ground at the foot of Firesticks Hill, which stood in the way of the line of the Cold River. Flor Visser, an old Boer who had arrived on the banks of Red River in 1904, said, "I tell you, Mister Hartley. You will never find water here."

A plump Swede came to drill at thirty shillings a foot. At first the bit went down through red soil, then clay, then decomposed rock, then volcanic lava to 130 feet. No water. The Swede brought his wife and son down to move in with him in his caravan. The lava got harder and harder. Some days the drilling slowed to as little at eight feet a day. The bit reached 260 feet. No water. The Swede said he was surprised because he had never known a hole that was so completely dry. At 320 feet, no water. The bit went through layer after layer of the glacial mountain Kilimanjaro's roots, the strata of millions of years. At one point, the drill brought up a chunk of timber from a prehistoric forest. Christmas came and went. At 400 feet, Dad announced that the hole was dry. They had failed. "Just one more week," Mum urged. "Please go to 500 feet."

"I told you, British," said Visser. "No water here." There were no wells for miles due to the porous volcanic rock. Everybody knew. And in the remote event of the drill striking water—what then? It would be salty or full of fluorine, you could be sure of that. At 460 feet, no water, and Dad said they were broke. What they would do with no money and no water, they didn't know. It might have come to an end, but that day a car drove up and out got a man my father had known from Arabia. The man announced that the Arab farmers my father had worked with had raised the sum of two thousand pounds for him as a present after he had retired. To my mother's horror, Dad said he could not accept the gift, saying the farmers should use it for their own irrigation works back in Arabia. The visitor said, "That is what they want you to do with it. They say that wherever you have gone, water has followed. And it's time for you to find water with this money yourself."

The next day drilling resumed. The work went on, day after day, until one morning there was an enormous spurt of water. A geyser exploded from the well hole. Clear water spouted in a fountain 160 feet into the air. The water spilled down onto the dry land. It flooded the plain in front of the hill like a flash flood. It gushed at fifteen hundred gallons an hour. There was neither telephone nor radio for miles, but that afternoon Flor Visser drove up in his old Ford truck and parked in front of the fountain of water. He switched off the engine and sat there for hours, staring at the water flooding down and no doubt thinking about the fifty years he had stayed on the arid plains where it had been so hard to make a life. Dad installed a well head that nodded like a huge bird. When the borehole was not pumping, strange humming noises came from the subterranean pipe. It was the thrumming of great Kilimanjaro's volcanic innards. The geyser settled down to a flow of eleven hundred gallons an hour. The water was both fresh and pure.

Our neighbors were the Maasai tribal people and their beloved herds of cattle. Dad knew them well, traded stock at their *bomas*, but also played a cat and mouse game with them when they raided his cattle or poached his scarce grazing. From the top of the hill behind the house, he could see where the Maasai were on the plain, since plumes of dust followed their herds. He would then saddle up his horse and gallop after them like John Wayne with loud "Yehahs!" The Maasai scattered in all directions, their red *shuka* togas flapping. If it was after dusk, Dad stalked them by moonlight and fired his rifle in the air to stampede the cattle off the property. Once a lion killed forty Maasai cattle. It also took Dad's best big gray bull, so he hunted it down, shot it dead and kept the skin forevermore. A crowd of warriors appeared at the house and danced in front of the skin as it hung stretched out and caked with salt. They were in their full regalia of shields, assegai spears, and ocher body paint. In a straight line they danced, stamping their feet, kicking up the dust, toasting "Bwana Harti" and his deed.

Nearby there was a colony of Afrikaner smallholders, who had trekked up from South Africa after the second Boer war to escape the British and settle in German East Africa. They had been led by one of the Malan generals and the families were Pretorius, Van der Venter, Lemmer, Visser, Van Rooyen, and Bekker. In the Great War, they switched sides to help the British when Jan Smuts came up to attack the German East Africa commander Paul von Lettow-Vorbeck in 1916. Pretorius, a scout and hunter, caused havoc for the Germans at Longido when he used lion fat to spook their penned horses. They were picture-book peasants, with blond, barefoot sons, old men with bright red noses, and matrons with huge fat arms. They sat on the *stoeps* of their whitewashed houses, stirring sheep fat with ladles to make soap, as geese and Muscovy ducks waddled about the gardens. Their church doubled as a school and grace was recited over meals at long tables under blue-blossomed jacaranda trees. They ate giraffe-meat sausages and stew made from sheep feet and pig trotters with the hair still on. "You must beat the kaffirs. Else how will you get them to work properly, eh?" one of the mamas told Mother. "Beat them, Mrs. Hartley. You British don't know anything about Africans!" Yet the Boers were themselves Africans, and grew up side-by-side with black children from whom they were inseparable. And everybody knew that old man Pretorius, father of the blue-eyed policeman Jerry, and another boy who drove his truck over the escarpment and was killed in Manyara, lived with his black mistress in a separate house from where his wife stayed in the next-door building, which looked like a railway station. And one of the teenage girls, Katrina, had fallen in love with an African boy and became pregnant by him.

My parents prospered and in time they bought Sarel du Toit's place, Kisimiri, also known as the Top Farm, 7,000 feet up on the slopes of Meru. It was a white mansion with pillars and Dutch gables and a living room that was 99 feet long with big windows overlooking the plains to Kilimanjaro. The steep mountain slopes were carpeted in white pyrethrum flowers and the farm ran a fine herd of Jersey dairy cattle. Mother made butter in a big, hand-driven churn for sale to Europeans in Arusha. She also sold clarified butter, ghee, which was so popular among the Asians that they gave chase when they saw her car coming into town. And the skimmed milk and butter milk were used for the farm workers' rations. Nothing went to waste in those days.

My parents didn't think too much about making money for its own sake, but years later they would muse that while living in this paradise they might also have become rich. Dad went into partnership with a friend, Peter Besse, a son of the great French tycoon Antonin Besse from Aden. Together they built the biggest ranching company in Tanganyika. They were beef barons who ran thou-

sands of head of cattle, leased grazing from the slopes of Kilimanjaro to the coastal plains toward the ocean. With his profits, my
father kept on reinvesting, buying land.

"Your husband doesn't just love Africa," a friend once told my
mother. "He intends to own it."

Ways of life can change gradually, or overnight. The end of British
rule came in 1961. Black rule under the new president, Julius
Nyerere, was intolerable to the Afrikaner settlers. En masse, they
got back in their jalopies and bumped back south from where they
had trekked up nearly six decades before. Visser and his wife
crashed and died on the way, while old man De Wet had a heart
attack two days after leaving the slopes of Meru, where he'd been
raised. Many years later, as apartheid collapsed, some of the survivors joined the ranks of the white supremacist Eugene Terre-
blanche and his AWB brownshirts. They have never stopped
running.

Meanwhile Nyerere flirted with the North Koreans, Chinese,
and Russians. In 1967, the president decreed a program of African
socialism. When it came down to brass tacks, this vague philosophy—
promoted mainly by Nyerere himself in a series of slim volumes—
was less a creed than a way of justifying national theft and
vandalism, which in turn led to destitution across the board. The
socialists began nationalizing white farms without any coherent
plan of what should happen to the properties after they had been
expropriated. Government men arrived and ordered Europeans out.
The Lundgrens were given thirty minutes' notice to leave a farm
where they had lived for three decades. In contrast, the von
Trutschlers were imprisoned in their house for days with no food
but for the eggs the local peasant women smuggled to them. Set-

tlers' bank accounts were frozen and they were allowed to pack only what they could transport on their one-way trip into exile. Some had been on their farms all their lives. They left behind workers, family graves, their possessions—all they had worked for and all they had loved.

Dad saw the way things were going and negotiated to sell his cattle and sheep to the state for cheap. He had done everything he could to avoid politics. At independence, he was not among the vociferous whites who rejected black rule. But neither did he join the Capricorn Society, which aimed to promote good relations between blacks and whites. "I don't need to have little arranged meetings to learn how to get on with Africans," he said. His skill as a rancher was well known, and for this reason the government offered him the job of running all the expropriated ranches grouped in one big block. He stayed on and was allowed to live in his home as part of the deal. Beyond the farm's borders, the transformation of the country was swift. All businesses were nationalized, from big factories to bicycle workshops. Peasants, nomads, and hunter-gatherers alike were herded into collectivized "Ujamaa" villages.

Meanwhile on the farm itself things began to quickly go wrong. A poacher named Hassan Jessa led patrols of policemen onto the land and machine-gunned wildlife, which they loaded onto Bedford trucks and sold to butchers in Arusha. Government officials and their Soviet, Chinese, or Swedish foreign guests became frequent visitors to the farm, which they claimed was a showcase for socialist development. Not a week went by without a plume of dust appearing on the plains, heralding the approach of a convoy of expensive cars. Men with soft hands and collarless safari suits, the fashion inspired by Nyerere's recent visits to North Korea, invited themselves into the home and demanded tours of the ranch, with big luncheons to follow. Dad could do nothing. He amused himself by greeting delegations and taking them off for marathon walks in the hot sun and dust to show them the cattle, the sheep, the spray races, the crushes, and the farm buildings. He earnestly described the agricultural operations in detail, bringing the officials back home for a frugal lunch only when the sun was low in the sky. Once, leading a busload of dumpy Russians, he exclaimed, "Look! Lion spoor. Looks like quite a large male and it's only a couple of hours old." At this the Russians turned tail, puffing and wheezing at a swift pace back to their buses.

Nyerere's disciples in his Revolutionary Party, Chama Cha Mapinduzi, were literally consuming the farm. The president declared that all workers should stand up for their rights, which in many parts of Tanzania resulted in laborers beating up their bosses, then looting their businesses. It all got to be too much when the money needed to run the farm was pilfered from the state ranching corporation. My father decided he had seen enough and so he resigned. The last night we were on the farm, a night I don't remember because I was old enough only to crawl, two lions began roaring at the bottom of the hill. They kept it up until dawn. The Maasai said the animals had come to say good-bye, before the cars were packed up and the family drove away. We camped for one last night between the farm and the border with Kenya. Mum said it was a terrible time. My miserable brothers Richard and Kim and sister Bryony sat with their backs to the fire and against a strong wind blowing dust across the land.

"I cried," my mother always told me. "And Dad cried too, the first time I had seen him cry since his mother died."

"The sequel to all this is so unpleasant to write about that I will try and put it on record and sort it out later," my father wrote as an old man. "It is something disastrous for that beautiful place and the land up on Meru and the house, and our improvements, and everything else. It needs a lot of careful thought." He never did write about it anymore, but he pondered what had happened long and hard. Nyerere's policies collapsed and his books are read no longer. On the farm, what had been a small family business became a Scandinavian-funded aid project, staffed by expatriate experts on salaries paid in Oslo who drove around in gleaming white vehicles. And in time the aid project failed, as schemes of this kind in Africa tend to almost without exception.

Growing up, the loss of my family's paradise was a festering wound, even though I had no personal memory of the thing that hurt me. I grew up feeling that I had been born too late to be part of our greatest adventure. And things were no longer as they had been in the family, down to the smallest detail. Dad never took me riding or deep-sea fishing. Instead I looked at snapshots of my elder brothers proudly holding up their catch. "That white vase," Mum said of an empty receptacle: "I used to fill it with sprays of purple agapanthus every day."

The last I heard, an old caretaker and a gang of bats lived in the house on Firesticks Hill, the place of my first memory, and the roof leaked. The stock is lost, eaten, stolen, or sold. Poachers have wiped out the wildlife. The elephants, the ostriches, and the bullfrogs—the "elphanes," "arse-stretches," and "oggy goggies," as we call them to this day in our intimate family vocabulary of childhood words—are gone. The trees have been hacked down for charcoal to supply the towns. The borehole machinery broke and stopped pumping eleven hundred gallons of clean water a day and the land returned to being a dry desert. My father's beautiful horses, the ones he had imported from Arabia, with their centuries-old Bedu bloodlines, bolted their stables and ran feral across the plains between the mountains. For years afterward, people encountered them, cantering like mustangs. Lions took some, while local peasants captured some of the others, either to eat them or put to them to work pulling carts like donkeys. Up on the slopes of Meru, squatters hamstrung the dairy cows, uprooted the pyrethrum, chopped down the big trees, and replaced it all with fields of marijuana. They occupied the house and made fires on the parquet floors. They tore the tiles off the roof and ripped out the doors and windows, which they carried off to adorn mud huts. They didn't manage to tear down the walls and pillars, and from down below on the plains I myself have seen the ruins gleam brightly like a beacon against the slopes of the mountain.

My father was not the type of man to give up and turn his back on Africa. Nor did he stay in order to retreat into bitterness, as had so many Europeans who found their hopes and dreams dashed but found it was too late for them to start again elsewhere. Instead, he embarked on a dramatic new direction. Having been a colonial officer, then a rancher, he now became a development aid worker himself, ultimately in the same game as the Scandinavian experts who had occupied the ranch on Kilimanjaro. The difference with my father was that he truly was an expert after more than forty years of working in Africa, his adopted home. And so he threw himself into working in the most remote areas of the continent he could find, assisting nomads with the husbandry of livestock and peasants with the growing of crops.

And so in my first coherent memories that run in sequence, in full-color as it seems, I am often in the back of a four-wheel-drive among clanking kettles, piles of rations, and dust, bumping across some drought-blasted plain. I am in camp where wild-haired men squat by the fire and chat with my father about rain and camels. I make my bed out in the open under the stars, or am woken in a village hut by bleating goats or mission hymns, or in a shabby border-town hotel with bare electric bulbs and blue glossy walls.

"We're like a tribe of mechanized nomads," says my mother. To hear this makes me happy. We are like gypsies, living out an adventure in Africa.

The problem was that we couldn't always be on the road with Dad. The roads were dangerous. In Eritrea, Dad lost fifteen of his team to land mine explosions on the roads and it was typical of him that he used this as an excuse to dispense with vehicles in favor of trekking cross-country with pack mules. If only I had been old enough to join him. What walks we might have had together.

Instead, our new way of life was filled with good-byes and absences and flights with my mother to see him wherever he was. These were long journeys with endless waits in airports. Our fellow passengers were often the new Soviet or Chinese officials who had appeared with Africa's liberation from its European masters. I remember asking a group of men —my mother tells me they were Soviets—to read a story from my Disney comic book. They peered at the pages, looked worried, and shook their heads.

We'd arrive in hot and sticky capitals and have to wait for Dad while he was traced out in his wilderness with his livestock and nomads. In Mogadishu, Somalia, we were invariably confined to whichever hotel compound we were checked in to due to the upheavals outside. We stayed at the Croce del Sud, known as the Sweaty Crotch. Nearby was the Shebelle, a.k.a. the Scratchy Belly. The city erupted in anti-Western riots when Apollo 11 landed Neil Armstrong and Buzz Aldrin on the moon and the mosque preachers declared that it was either American lies or blasphemy.

Soon after the moon landings, the Somali president was assassinated and the army took over. Each afternoon I'd watch from the Sweaty Crotch as soldiers goose-stepped down the street. Many years later I worked out that this was when the dictator president Mohamed Siad Barre had seized power in a coup d'état. During one parade, while my mother and sister were out shopping at the bazaar, I filled a soda bottle from the tap, went back to the room's balcony, and emptied the contents onto the heads of the spectators below. The consequences were dire, for within a few minutes there were loud voices and a hammering at the door. I hid in the bathtub until Mother returned, when she had to promise a group of irate men that I had not pissed on them.

Finally we'd be summoned to desert reunions with my father. These trips survive in my mind only as a jumble of images like one of our heat- and dust-damaged family films. We flew for hours and so slowly that we could see the shadow of the Dakota propeller aircraft on the scrub below. On landing at a Somali airfield I broke loose from my mother and burrowed between the sandal-shod brown legs of men in turbans and women in flowing robes. I knew I would recognize him because he would be the only white man in the crowd. But how was I to behave when I met my father? How warmly would Dad kiss Mum and did they still love each other? And what was this strange life my father lived, among such fierce people?

On Sundays in Somalia, the cooks used to hack the chickens' heads off with loud *bismillahs*, then allowed the headless bodies to dance about behind the kitchen. I have a sequence of other disjointed memories: of mosquito larvae in our table water, flexing like red commas magnified in the distorted bowl of the jug; playing Ping-Pong with pasty-faced Chinese commissars in the local hotel; the bleeding toes I got from barefoot soccer with the tough Somali boys; my brother Kim and I on Lido Beach, where camels were slaughtered so that guts lay in bluish puddles on the coral sand; the northern Somali highlands, on a mountain called Ga'an Libah, the Lion's Fist, where Kim and I tried and failed to rescue a goat from our lunch table; a cave of prehistoric paintings of red handprints and herds of eland stalked by cats and men with alien heads. Once I stood on the banks of a dry riverbed, feeling wind on my face, hearing a rumble, then seeing a wall of brown water explode from around the corner as the flash flood approached.

Another time we visited Dad in a big white Arab fort on the Indian Ocean. His housemates were American hippies, young men and women my mother now tells me were from the Peace Corps.

Dad wore a bandana, grew his hair down to his shoulders, and listened to Led Zeppelin. He was learning yoga and at dusk he practiced his *asanas* on the flat roof while looking out over the sea. It was the end of the 1960s, Timothy Leary was urging the world to "turn on, tune in, and drop out," and Dad was sixty-two years old.

After Somalia came Ethiopia. In the summer that I was first taken to see my father there, rumors had been circulating of starvation among the peasants outside the capital, Addis Ababa. My teenage sister Bryony was with him, and together they filled the car with loaves of bread and Arabian dates packed in baskets. On the road to Bati, they found thousands of Oromo peasants whose crops had withered in drought and highland frost. When my sister stood at the back of the truck tossing out the bread and dates, the hungry mob rioted. After Bati, they drove down into the Rift Valley and Denkalia. The local Afar nomads, normally tough enough to inhabit the hottest and most inhospitable place on earth, were dying too, since their livestock was gone. A tragedy was unfolding due to all the usual causes: civil war, overpopulation, and misuse of the land and rivers in the name of modern development.

On the edge of the Danakil Depression, the dead and dying all around him, Dad sat down and wrote a message, which he handed to a runner, who took it to the nearest post office for cabling to Addis Ababa. This was before the days when African famines were the news stories they are today. There were no rock concerts, T-shirts, or advertisements in the paper. But with that message, news of what was happening soon reached Europe. A BBC team flew to Bati and their TV film exposed the truth. When the pictures were shown in Addis Ababa, it helped the tide of revolution that toppled the medieval dictatorship of Emperor Haile Selassie. Back on the plains of Bati Dad sat down by himself. "The camps lie broken down on hill and plain, / Skulls, bones and horns remain," he wrote. "No shouts, no songs of fighting, or of love, / But from the bare thorn tree above, / So sadly calls the mourning dove....

Was this your ravaged land, / The work of God, or was it Man's own hand?" For me this just about sums up what happened all over Africa in the twentieth century.

The Addis Ababa I remember was, as usual, a place of waiting for days in a dark, smelly hotel. The TV broadcast almost back-to-back episodes of *Sesame Street*. In short slots between the programs, the revolutionaries who had taken over the TV station showed footage of the emperor feeding his lap dogs filet steak interspersed with images of stick figures, crying babies with distended bellies, flies cramming into their eyes and mouths. After a few minutes of this, the programming would return to *Sesame Street*.

In the square outside the hotel was a black stone statue of the Lion of Judah, the symbol of Abyssinia's emperors. At the foot of it I found a boy, my age, with his hands out begging.

"I am hungry," the boy whimpered. I tried not to look at him. "I have not eaten for three days."

Even today I can picture the boy's grimace and his outstretched hand. As we moved away a shout went up from the seething pedestrians at street level below the black lion's statue. People were looking up. At the summit of a high building was a young man and I saw that he had a flag wrapped around his shoulders. He jumped. The flag flapped like a parachute that refused to open as he fell to the pavement. I heard a big sigh and a crowd formed where the man had landed, as figures in uniform appeared at the top of the building. These images fed my dreams of monsters: the starving boy, the man with the flag, the emperor's dogs eating minced steak, and the horrid Big Bird and the Muppets of *Sesame Street*.

When I look back now I also see us as the disaster family. I had only just learned to write when I sent my father this letter: "Dear Dad we had a good holidays. Come home now love from aidan xx." But family holidays were really only trips to accompany my father on an assignment to where the latest human catastrophes were being staged. I recall we went on a fishing trip to the Bale Mountains in southern Ethiopia. Dad vanished, while we caught amazing trout in a highland landscape of giant lobelias and fragrant African heathers. My father would join us some days and at night he told me not to wander too far from the tents in camp. The local hyenas had gained a taste for human flesh because there had been so many bodies scattered in the district and live infants were being carried off.

It was hard to know exactly where, or what, we could call home. Almost wherever we went, the newly free Africans warned my parents that for people of our sort the writing was on the wall. They associated us with an imperialist past they wanted to put behind them. Instead, they found we stubbornly refused to leave. Kenya was the one exception in all of East Africa. We had much to be thankful for as Europeans in Kenya. The founding president Jomo Kenyatta could have kicked us out or robbed us like Nyerere. He might have been inclined to do so, since we had imprisoned him during the Mau Mau rebellion prior to independence. Instead he waved an olive branch. At a rally of whites in the Rift Valley town of Nakuru in 1964, he had said: "We are going to forget the past and look to the future. I have suffered imprisonment and detention; but that is gone, and I am not going to remember it. Let us join hands and work for the benefit of Kenya . . ." I was born a year after he made that announcement, and as I grew up all races lived alongside one another.

My parents at last found a family base on Kenya's coast, south of the Swahili village of Malindi, on the white sandy beach near Leopard Point, so named because a column of dead black coral like a cat's head stood out on the reef at the southern end. My mother oversaw the building of a small house, with walls of coral and a roof of *makuti* thatch made of coconut-palm fronds knotted on open mangrove pole rafters. Inside were Zanzibar chests, BaZinza

tribal stools, David Shepherd prints of Aden, Bukhara carpets my
father had haggled from dhow *nakhoda* captains at Mombasa's
Kilindini harbor, and cedar beds slung with rawhide thongs of oryx
and zebra skins. The bathrooms and verandas were scattered with
shells, fragments of coral, and Indian Ocean flotsam and jetsam.
The cement floor was black and cool underfoot. Charo, our house
servant, polished them each day with two halves of a fibrous
coconut, then wrapped rags around his feet and buffed the surfaces
until they shone like obsidian. At night we sat outside and gazed up
at the blanket of stars. On the rare occasions he was home, Dad
pointed up to the constellations that guided ships' captains and
Arab caravans, or the stars of the Africans, who used the constellations to tell them when to plant or harvest their crops.

Before I was old enough to read the books in my father's
library, kept off on a side veranda that served as his office, I knew
each by their pictures, weight, and smell. I remember the portrait
of Burton's scarred face, which so attracted me in the signed copy
of *First Footsteps in East Africa*. Livingstone reminded me of my
father, but I recoiled at the odor of Stanley's *In Darkest Africa* and
the man himself resembled a cruel schoolmaster in a silly hat.
There was Joseph Thomson's *Through Masai Land* with the engrav-
ing of the author, his black-powder gun and helmet being tossed by
a giant buffalo; Frederick Courteney Selous's *A Hunter's Wanderings
in Africa*, the spine repaired with a heavy needle and thread, with a
kudu head embossed in gold on the red cover; Captain Stigand's
The Land of Zinj, eaten into a honeycomb by white ants; the spewing volcanoes of Duke Adolphus Frederick of Mecklenburg's *In the
Heart of Africa*; the bugs in G. D. Hale Carpenter's *A Naturalist on
Lake Victoria*; the slaughtered lions laid out in J. H. Patterson's
Man-Eaters of Tsavo; and the pygmies, tattooed warriors, and men
with filed teeth in Sir Harry Johnston's *The Uganda Protectorate*.

Mum gave us each something to plant in the garden. My eldest brother Richard's tree was a bombax, with a knobbly trunk

that grew ever so slowly. Kim planted a Norfolk pine with crazy branches in the circle of hibiscus next to the house. Bryony's was a frangipani, fragrant and delicate. Dad scattered the seedpods of a Red Sea saltbush that grew into blue-gray fleshy clumps along the high-water mark. Mum loved her Adenium desert roses. This plant had a few plump branches that produced pinkish or dark red blooms aboveground. But like a vegetable iceberg, underground was a massive, tuberous bulb. Much later I, too, was given a tree. I can't recall what it was except that it was dubbed the "whacker" plant because Dad ripped it up to give me a thrashing with it on the only occasion he ever beat me.

At the north end of the beach was the sandy pool, where I learned to swim at eighteen months with my armbands on, bum in the air and my eyes open underwater. When I was older I joined my brother Kim and went out with the fishermen, who taught us the names for all the fish, shells, and corals. Fragments of blue ceramic and celadon washed in with every tide, reminders of Chinese traders from six centuries before. On the southern end of the village bay stood a pillar dedicated to the Holy Ghost, erected by Vasco da Gama, who had sailed from here to India in 1498. Below the beachfront mosque, surrounded by tall phallus-shaped tombs of forgotten notables, townspeople haggled over the day's catch. In the labyrinth of houses of coral and mud and wattle lived a rich mix of cultures from all over the Indian Ocean. Bajuni fishermen, Giriamas in grass skirts balancing pots and banana branches on their heads. The ironmonger was a Hadhramauti who served ginger tea and did not let my mother pay for bags of nails. Our tailoring was done by a bearded Bohra, who had a row of men working on foot-pedaled Singers outside his shop. The news agent was a Pakistani we called Frankenstein, because his teeth were brown from chewing betel nut. There was Archie Ritchie, an old game warden who wore a lilac-breasted roller bird on his shoulder, and his wife, Queenie, whom the village Arabs called "the Queen"; Terence

Adamson, who had had half his jaw torn off by one of his brother George's lions, and who taught me how to divine for water with a forked stick; Laly, who took us snorkeling; Max, a German-Irish baron, who was captured on the Eastern Front and survived years in Siberia as a POW, when snow blew in through his cell window; Max's wife, Anna, a Seychellois beauty whose first husband had been killed by a charging elephant; Gigi, a singer at the Dhow Nightclub, famous for her rendition of "Malaika," the most famous Swahili pop song, about a man too poor to marry his girl; Gigi's boyfriend Knut, a Dane who had been a circus clown and could walk a straight line on his hands but not his legs when he was drunk. And there was Marujin, a Catalonian marquesa whom I held in awe. She wore heavy silver bracelets up each arm that click-clacked as she glided barefoot through her dark, cool house. On the walls were tantric designs and she had a huge copper tray piled with the ivory, smooth fragments of cowry shells. For hours I listened to her speak as she sat cross-legged on her veranda.

"One thing we know is that we're not Europeans. We know that, but we're also not Africans. What we are, I don't know, but we're not Europeans . . ." Marujin said the mind was the "lunatic in the house," the cricket in the cage relentlessly chirping "tchya-ko, tchya-ko, tchya-ko." She said anything we learned came to us spontaneously, when the mind was still and serene.

As a small boy I had a string of fevers, but my parents were offhand about medical treatment. My mother had seen the inside of hospitals only to give birth and I grew up, barefoot and in shorts, to believe Dad's superstitions that visiting a doctor might make an illness more critical rather than cure it. At home our first-aid box had been stocked with Mercurochrome, antiseptic powder, universal Chinese eye ointment, a few stuck-together bandages, and a blue bottle of milk of magnesia. Aspirins were rare, while antibiotics were banned. Home cures and local remedies were warmly approved of: hot cooking oil for earache, hot brine for a stomachache, and a poultice of pawpaw and honey for jigger worm boils, cuts, thorns, or sea urchin spines in our feet. If we had fever Mum plucked leaves from the neem trees in our garden for hot infusions. When Charo suffered a stroke that paralyzed one side of his body, Dad took him to a witch doctor who buried him alive for half an hour, with very positive effects. For me, only malaria had led to a visit to the dreaded Dr. Zoltan Rossinger, a Viennese Jew who had escaped Hitler. The doctor charged Africans nothing and all others the normal price—except for Germans, from whom he demanded double.

My brother Kim and I spent a lot of our time with an old man named Mohamed. Polio had stunted one of Mohamed's legs, which dangled useless and childlike, and he eked out a pittance hawking shells to the growing number of white tourists. He sat all day long on his coconut mat in town, resplendent among the mother-of-pearl of nautiluses, triton conches, and the pink, pouting lips of spider shells. We sat cross-legged listening to him, as he told us stories about storms on the ocean, dugongs, and the Glory of the Seas, rarest among all shells. As he spoke he paused to expertly spit quids of red betel nut juice for dramatic emphasis, or roll a fresh nut into a leaf and tuck it into his cheek to chew.

Some days, he would take us down to the beach where fishermen caulked their careened boats while buyers haggled over beached shark carcasses. The sand glittered with mica. It was the same beach from which Mohamed's slave ancestors had been herded aboard dhows bound for Arabia. On land, he lurched about on crutches but out on the ocean from his outrigger canoe he flipped into the sea and swam like a merman. We used to hand-line in the waters beyond Vasco da Gama's pillar, staring into the water, yanking the line, hoping for brilliant reef fish to bite. Mohamed tied his line to a horny big toe and dozed off, springing alert at the slightest nibble.

Once my brother pulled out a fish with a domed forehead and

a sailfin. Mohamed gave it his Swahili name, *filusi*, fine to eat and very special. In English it is the coryphene. In Spanish it is more beautifully known as the dorado, meaning "gilded," because of its iridescent gold flanks. Mohamed seized hold of the fish and told us to watch closely. As the dorado suffocated its pigment, sheathed with a patina of stippled green, was transfigured for a brief instant like a beam of sunshine on a church mosaic. Mohamed held the fish as its strength drained away. With it, the light in the dorado's brilliance faded. When the process was complete, Mohamed picked up his knife and sliced open her belly, removed the guts, and tossed the body to the bottom of the canoe, where it turned the color of tarnished lead.

My mother decided it was time for us to be educated outside Africa with its revolutions and wars. My siblings were taken out of their Kenya schools. I remember the time they first left by plane to go to boarding school in England. They had to swap their African uniforms of gingham shirts and khaki shorts for thick socks and gray felt blazers that made them look cold even before they were out of the equatorial sunshine. They went on ahead to Europe and my mother followed with me. We settled on a small hill farm in Devon. It was a rugged, pagan spot: a thatched longhouse of whitewashed cob, a great barn with timbers like a ship, views over Dartmoor, oak and elm woods, blackthorn hedges, clover pastures, a millpond and a stream, granite troughs and rookeries. This was modern England, but our neighbor on one side still ploughed with horses, stooked his hay with a pitchfork, and was unable to write apart from sign his name on a bank check. On the other side of us was the poet Ted Hughes. After we met him one day in the fields, Mum said he "looked like a man who has been struck by lightning."

We had sheep, cattle, horses, and a black dog called Bruce. My eldest brother Richard attempted rearing pigs but he grew to know each porker by name so he couldn't face sending them to the butcher. I kept ducks and chickens, goats, rabbits, and guinea pigs. Lambing started when it was still cold and muddy in spring as the first crocuses poked through the snow. May carpeted the wood floor with bluebells. In summer wildflowers dusted the meadows and we fished for trout in the little streams and the pond. Richard helped Mum run the farm. He ploughed and harvested and made hay, helped by a laborer who had a hook where his hand should have been. Richard was so strong he could pitchfork a bale of hay high onto a trailer. In autumn we had fights throwing apples and harvested bags of them for delivery to Mr. Inch, the cider maker who said he threw in a rat to improve the flavor of his brew. In winter, it rained a great deal but some mornings you'd wake up, and it was sparkling sunshine, with the entire landscape covered with hoarfrost or snow.

Richard was dispatched to a school in Scotland, where it was felt that he might grow up tough doing Outward Bound courses, mountain rescue, and skiing. My sister Bryony went to where Mum and Granny had both been educated. Kim attended a school in Berkshire where boys wore First World War navy uniforms, complete with brass buttons, whitened belts, and spit-and-polished boots. So began our long separation from both Dad and Africa, the years of being knocked into shape on a rainy little island. It is impossible to exaggerate the effect that British schools had on my siblings. They had been raised in wild liberty and happiness. They were now rootless and appeared exotic to the local children. They were confronted by petty, brutal school discipline and the unfamiliar British class system. Already from an unorthodox background, the counterculture of the sixties and seventies swept them off their feet and they were always climbing over walls to abscond for parties in London.

I remember Richard with shoulder-length hair and sideburns,

a sheepskin coat, and flares. He came home with languid, older girlfriends and freaks in clapped-out cars. I recall fighting over the gramophone when I wanted to play my record of "Elephants on Parade" from *The Jungle Book* instead of Led Zeppelin's "Stairway to Heaven." Bryony had big eyelashes and puppy fat and she wore lime-green and bright yellow miniskirts and knee-length boots. For a time she lived in a bedsit above a coin-operated laundrette off Elgin Crescent in London. Later, Kim got into disco and grew an Afro.

I remember my first day at school, aged six, when I held my mother's hand and walked up the gravel driveway, past the big stone pillars topped by griffons at the school gates. In front of us was the Victorian Gothic edifice of Ravenswood, on the edge of Exmoor. I looked up at Mum and said, "I'm not going to cry . . ."

The headmaster invited us into his study and asked us to sit down.

"You are most welcome to Ravenswood. Do you have any questions?"

"Yes," I said. "I am told that the planet Pluto has vanished. Could you please explain why?"

Mum went back to Africa to see my father and sent me postcards of elephants and landscapes with colorful stamps. I used to stare into those pictures for hours at a time and long for home in Kenya. School was a hard place to which I became completely adapted. The terms unfolded into years and I recall friends and times that were happy. Still, the memories of Ravenswood and its cold dormitories, with names like Drake and Ivanhoe, still get me like the chilblains.

When Mum was overseas, I'd visit my grandparents and Grandpa sympathized with me about school because he'd hated it too. He joked that if I survived Ravenswood, I'd be able to easily deal with being a POW, if there was ever another war, or as a convict if I ever did anything wrong. It's true I never felt I had to put on such a tough act as I did there. In the playground we played chicken, seeing how close a knife could be thrown at our feet without flinching. The masters beat us regularly but we didn't much care. We'd stuff sheets of blotting paper down our Y-fronts—to absorb the impact—and after a thrashing show off our welt-reddened bare bums to our classmates. The food was inedible but one couldn't "get down" until finishing one's plate. When I went home for the first time, Mum asked me what we were given to eat. "Munched-up meat and hardened potatoes," I told her. We had grayish fish that floated in scum; mashed orange swede; pickled purplish beetroot; toad-in-the-hole and semolina and tapioca pudding.

We were the first generation after the end of the British Empire, but in geography class our aging school atlases still showed large parts of the world colored red. The masters were mostly ex-military or police types like our geography teacher, an Indian army major who reminisced about "when I was in the Punjab." To our delight, he ran our class like his old regiment and barked out parade-ground commands in Hindi. He could throw a piece of chalk with deadly accuracy across the classroom at a daydreaming boy. And if you got an answer wrong he'd yell "Balderdash!"

I quickly learned about Britain by watching television when my mother took me home to the farm in Devon. We had no TV in Kenya, but so much of what the boys talked about at school came from kids' shows and sports on the box. I watched it to find common ground with my peers, among whom one needed to be able to speak and act like Scooby-Doo and Mutley the Dog. The program I genuinely liked most was the *Magic Roundabout*. After that came the news. My mother insisted on watching this and so I would stick around because once in front of the box it was hard to unglue my eyes.

I remember one news night very clearly. The pictures were of troops on the move, refugees, rice paddies, and palm trees. A young American soldier was crying. "I want to go home. I want to go home." My mother looked cross and said, "They're always so emotional. The British never behaved like that."

"Maybe they're scared," I remember saying.

"Of course they're scared," Mum said. "But you should never show it."

A reporter did a piece to camera, speaking into a big handheld microphone. A roar suddenly grew audible. The camera lurched away from the correspondent and zoomed in across the paddies to get a shot of a fighter jet plunging into the earth a mile away. The shot held for a few seconds, the sound of the impact explosion distorted above the muffled shouts off camera. The reporter came back in frame and resumed his story as a column of black smoke rose from the crash site behind him. From that moment on, I think my bags were packed and I was ready for a life in news.

My father took little active interest in my schooling, and he seldom read my end-of-term reports. But once he visited me at Ravenswood to deliver a lecture about the Danakil Depression, which became amazingly detailed about the Afar and their livestock in the deserts along the Red Sea coast. On that occasion, I suppose my African background was so exotic to my peers that a child said to me after Dad had driven away, "That wasn't your father!"

I promised the boy that he was.

"How can that be?" the boy jeered. "He's very old. And anyway, I thought your father came from Africa." I replied that he did.

"Well then, why isn't he a black man?"

At the end of term, I longed to break out like any other boy, anxious to leave that dungeon for a spell. In summer or sometimes at Christmas, I'd fly home to Kenya on a special BOAC flight called the Lollipop Special packed with schoolchildren. Down at the beach house, I'd kick off my squeaky black shoes and socks and feel the sand between my toes again.

At thirteen I went up to Sherborne School, in Dorset. The town was Saxon, built on a *scire burne,* a clear stream; the school had been founded by the boy king Edward VI, and for generations it had fed the ranks of England's soldiers and administrators. In my memory, I seem to have spent a large amount of time in church. During the sermons in the abbey, I'd gaze up at the old flags that hung in lines above our pews, Union Jacks and regimental colors torn by cannonballs and stained by battles in the four corners of Britain's Empire. I filed out of chapel a thousand times with the organ striking up Bach's Toccata and Fugue in D Minor. As I descended the steps I'd look up at the walls of names memorializing all the school's old boys who had been killed in the succession of wars, always bringing my eyes to rest on one, Cowan, whom my mother had known in Burma.

As a teenager, I spiked my hair and bleached it with peroxide, and learned to smoke, drink snakebite, and take poppers and speed. I quickly found the Africans again at Sherborne and together with two Nigerian brothers I formed a rock band. Our keyboardist was from the Cayman Islands. The Nigerians played drums and lead guitar. At first we called ourselves Vic Virus and the Exploding Parasites. Our lyrics were cascades of punk nihilism fused with a Commonwealth beat. We wanted our music to have a message, so we changed our band name to The Starving Millions. At our only concert, I came on stage wrapped head to foot in red ink–soaked hospital bandages and sang about world poverty.

Out in Africa, I think my father grew lonely and perhaps felt burdened by the responsibility of a family from which he was separated for so much of the time. On the rare occasions I saw him in

England or Africa, he never took me in hand. He wasn't one to dispense fatherly advice, or to listen to fears or dreams. He could have had authority over me, if only he had wanted to. He was a stranger to me, though I was in awe of his greatness. It was my mother who laid down the rules and did all the bringing up. Dad paid the bills and came home once in a blue moon. When he was with me he wasn't much good at football, cards, or games. I never went with him to a museum and rarely to the cinema, which in Malindi had films projected onto a big white wall under the stars.

The year my puberty kicked in, I was a bomb primed to go off. I had grown to be happy in England. That summer, I spent my days playing in the fields and along the streams with boys from the neighboring farms. My skin was as brown as an impala's. At home I had persuaded a girl named Alice to take her breasts out and let me kiss them while we played in the hay barn. In school dormitory that summer term, we had run about the sloped rooftops naked, and cut lead from the guttering.

"How wonderful it must be to have such a close family," I would hear older people saying when I was small. It made me feel secure and comfortable. I knew about broken homes but knew instinctively that this would never happen to us. My confidence that all was well was shattered one day when I found my mother by herself in the kitchen weeping. At first she would not tell me what was wrong. She stopped crying, but over the coming days, she sank into a state of depression, sitting alone in her darkened room for hours at a time. She stopped taking care of the house or cooking meals. I recall foraging in the larder myself. My mother's moods took on a frightening pattern. She was fine in the morning. By eleven o'clock she had become listless. If I spoke to her, she didn't answer. If she bothered to reply at all, she spoke slowly and her voice had a disembodied, metallic tone. Instead of disciplining me if I misbehaved, she became sarcastic. Her face sagged. On her rare shopping trips, she would buy several bottles of Martini.

For nearly a year I had not seen my father, who was in Ethiopia. By now I was used to his absence. Our Father who art in Africa. But now Mum told me Dad had taken an Ethiopian mistress.

Mother said that before they were married, she knew the wife of another man who used to look at Dad "like a snake." There had been others, some situations embarrassing, most of them absurd. In most cases my mother had handled the problem with style.

"He's been doing it for years," she shrugged.

It reminded me of the story of my aunt Gertrude, wife of my father's favorite uncle Ernest Hartley. When they lived in Calcutta, Gertie learned about Ernest's constant philandering with other women. Being a Catholic, divorce was not an option and perhaps she loved him enough not to leave him, but she did not let his behavior go unpunished. One evening she held a lavish dinner party and when Ernest entered the room he realized all the female guests were the married women with whom he had had his affairs.

In my father's case, though, what was much worse on this occasion was that he had fathered a child with his Ethiopian girlfriend.

I panicked. Would this mean that my father would leave us, that we'd lose our home in Devon? Would I have to leave school? I imagined my mother having to struggle to care for us with no money. Worst of all, I worried that we would never return to Africa. We would be condemned to a life with no exits in cold, gray England. I knew I had to protect my mother, but I didn't know how. I felt guilty that I could not do something to help her. I began hating both of my parents for ending my childhood in this way. I had expected an adolescence as carefree and irresponsible as those of my elder siblings. But suddenly the limelight was snatched away from me. I remember thinking the family had become a TV soap opera. My mother would fly into a terrible rage if ever even the word "Ethiopia" was mentioned. For months I did not want to see my father ever again. At the same time I was terrified that this might come to be true. I pictured the Ethiopian as more beautiful than I could imagine in the real world. How else could my father have left my beautiful mother? There were times when I could not believe that he had been disloyal. But my mother showed me proof, in the form of letters written to lawyers in Addis Ababa.

The next time I did see him, it was back at the Kenya coast. I can't express how awkward it was. I remember we were walking together down the beach. Those evening walks to Leopard Point in the monsoon breeze almost always succeeded in blowing away anxiety. Our minds were distracted by the fish in the coral pools, the flotsam and jetsam along the high-tide mark, or the plovers and ghost crabs lurking about their holes on the wide, white arc of rippled sand. But this evening was different and the heated quarrels of the day did not vanish but instead formed a heavy silence between us all. My father strode out in the way he normally did: shoulders back, chest out, arms swinging. He was no longer a young man, but he was still much stronger than I was.

Along the way we met a neighbor out strolling with her dogs. We stopped to talk, and the woman spoke proudly about how her children were doing in their studies, travels, marriage plans. At this, Dad grabbed my brother and me each by the shoulder and declared, "These are my useless sons." I wanted to fight him. Right there on the beach, I sized him up and considered my chances. We were both shirtless and we stood facing each other when I spoke to him. "One day, I'll be stronger than you."

For that, he dragged me halfway up the path from the beach to the house, pulled a planted sapling out of the ground, and thrashed me with it. For a time I hated my father, and I jeered at

him for being "a dirty old man." But instead of ending our relationship, his failings became the first reason we'd ever had for intimacy.
At the age of fifteen, I saw that he was full of faults and in many
ways a failure. He became a great deal more human thanks to the
absurdity of his position, and as a result of this we had our first real
conversations. My mother remained the head of the house and our
figure of authority, while I became friends with my father.

Our first family reunion for about a decade took place on
Dad's birthday in 1980. We camped at Lake Naivasha, in Kenya's
Rift Valley, and the whole family fought all weekend. Mum called it
the Third World War Weekend. Dad must have suffered confusion
about what best to do about his two families, but he capitulated
completely to my mother. They were reunited. I remember Mum
going around the house, inscribing every book with both his and
her names. The farm in Devon was sold and Mum moved back to
Kenya. In time the entire crisis blew over; my parents returned to
being a double act as they had always been, on the road, like mechanized gypsies.

On my mother's insistence, Dad took us along on some of his
long road trips, so that many of my school holidays were spent on
magical safaris along dusty red roads into deserts and forests. Along
the way my father's fascination with the people and places of Africa
rubbed off on me. He frequently pointed out of the car window at
trees or hills and after hours of driving he would break into singing
Slim Dusty's "The Pub with No Beer," weaving the car from side to
side on the corrugated dusty track. Around the campfire at night he
continually spoke of the future, of his ambitions and hopes and
schemes with the energy of a young, idealistic man.

"Come, my friends!" he'd boom, with a raised glass of red
wine in one hand, a raw onion or hunk of cheese in the other, commanding silence while he recited his favorite lines of Tennyson.

"'Tis not too late to seek a newer world!"

He missed what Africa had once been. When we drove

through sprawling towns he would describe how a few decades before this had been a savannah of swaying grass teeming with game. But the environmental destruction was still taking place, before our very eyes. At age sixteen I remember visiting the Cherangani Hills in western Kenya, where the forest was so thick the sunlight barely pierced the canopy of mighty trees to the track along which we drove. A few months later we passed down the same road and for miles around the trees had been felled and burned and the view was bruised, eroding earth to the distant horizon.

After sixty years in the continent, my father had come to believe that the Europeans had committed an unforgivable error by sweeping away the traditional culture and economy that Africans had evolved over centuries. The nomad who valued nothing more than his cattle stayed on the move because he knew that to settle would mean death. And yet wherever we went, we saw the new independent African governments, backed by white "development experts," repeating the mistakes of the long past colonial rulers, forcing the nomads into sedentary lives, to put up fences, live in tin huts, to swap their magnificent beads and togas for the castoffs and ragged clothes of the "civilized" West. The missionaries did their damage too and one Sunday I recall arriving in a northern Kenyan hamlet where nomads were gathering in the hope of food handouts from the foreigners, having lost most of their livestock to drought. As they trekked in the American Baptists' overseers were handing out polyester trousers and T-shirts with slogans that were meaningless to their wearers. Some of the proud warriors were stalking around in flowery blue plastic bath caps. The missionaries had surrounded the village with loudspeakers rigged up onto tall poles and when it came time for a church service the sermon was broadcast at full volume, so that no matter where the nomads were, they would be harangued and cajoled to convert to Christianity and turn their back on their past lives in return for the food and clothes they were receiving.

For all my father's enthusiasm his attempts to assist people by enhancing, rather than destroying, their traditions were almost certainly in vain. What he showed me on those road trips had more of an effect on me than anything I learned at school. I had witnessed real injustices, poverty, the arrogance of power, the ignorance of the foreigners, the obliteration of proud cultures and beautiful landscapes.

After three happy years at Oxford, I went to London's School of Oriental and African Studies (SOAS), formerly a famous training ground for those who wanted to make their lives elsewhere, and now a hotbed of dissidents from the Third World. I set off for Africa almost on the day I had graduated with my master's. I hitched down through Europe and met a friend in Cairo. We did Egypt the whole summer: ruins, bazaars, and beaches, all fueled by arak, across-the-counter diazepam, and hashish from vendors down in the souk who sold bitten-off measures spat out onto balanced scales. Before I headed south we took a taxi out to Giza, where we dodged the tourist police and gully-gully men and clambered up the great limestone blocks of the Mycerinus pyramid. We reached the summit and there among the graffiti of generations I scratched my name next to another one etched in copperplate. Pickard. Perhaps he had been one of Napoleon's soldiers, but Pickard had also been my grandmother's maiden name. Had we been here before? From the top of that monument, 4,500 years old, we watched the sun sink into the desert. A hot wind whipped over the pyramid's stones with the roar of myriad voices. Darkness fell. The tungsten lights of the *son et lumieré* show flipped on, illuminating us like prisoners in a gaol break for the audience of package-tour holidaymakers. We descended the dark side of the tomb, sliding from one block to the next, scared of slipping and dashing our brains out on the fall down.

I took a train to Aswan, where I embarked on a ferry across the lake to Wadi Halfa and from there on up the Nile by steamer. Lashed alongside the boat, port and starboard, were barges, so that we became a sailing village of backpackers, Sudanese, livestock, market goods, and kiosks serving *foul* beans and tea. The crew were constantly drunk on arak. When they weren't under the influence, they assembled to pray on the flat roof of the boat five times daily, leaving the vessel to churn on unguided. It was the dry season upriver in East Africa and we ran aground for hours at a time on sandbanks. I sat on the deck enclosed in mosquito mesh, day-dreaming. We continued southward past little sailboats and fellahin and desert hills dotted with acacias and the Nubian ruins at Meroë. At Dongola I disembarked and took a market truck to Khartoum across a desert called the Belly of Rocks and out there the Milky Way was clearer than I remembered seeing it since I was a child.

On the journey I sat next to a very black man in a brilliant white turban. He touched me on the arm and said, "From here on my friend, this is Africa ..."

He asked me where I came from. Without pausing I proudly said, "Here. Africa is where I was born." He smiled.

One evening I lay on my bed in some fleapit village hotel on the Nile riverbanks, woozy from the last of my Cairo supply of diazepam. A song was playing on the radio downstairs in the hotel café. It wafted up the dirty concrete stairs and under the door to where I lay. The hubbub of men's voices fogged the Arabic lyrics, but as I sweated on my bed and listened I distinctly heard the words:

> *Hopeless journey, hopeless journey,*
> *Nothing but a*
> *Hopeless, hopeless, hopeless journey ...*

When I was growing up, my father gave me only a few pieces of advice. I asked him, Where I should live? What should I do?

"Make your life somewhere else other than Africa, a place where there's lots of space," he wrote in a letter to me. I asked where he had in mind.

"Canada," he replied. My father was a colonial settler, who had been searching for new frontiers his whole life.

I was looking for a home, not a Canada. And the only home I had ever really had was as a boy in Africa. The memory of that time still had a compelling power over me. As an adult it came back to me in sounds, colors, and smells: a mango's diesel taste, the smell of dust after rain, and the sounds of a picking guitar on the radio. A lost time when the sun shone, before life grew complicated.

My father's second piece of advice was that he thought I should "never work for anybody except yourself." This contradicted everything he had done himself and indeed whatever my ancestors had done, which involved selfless service to monarch and country. In previous generations I might have served in the empire's army and fought a string of rebellious potentates, or enrolled as a colonial officer to be posted to a remote station, or struck out as a pioneer. But however much I might dream of my opportunities in Africa, this was the 1980s—not the 1880s—and if I wanted to have the same adventures in East Africa as a European, I had few choices about what I might do. I could run safaris for tourists into the ever smaller areas of bush to show them dwindling herds of wildlife. I could be a pilot, flying anything from contraband to oil prospectors into unmarked dirt airstrips. I might become a missionary or a humanitarian aid worker, which was often the best-paid option. Or I might be able to run a small business manufacturing something like car parts in the industrial areas of Nairobi, Dar, or Kampala. I could pursue any of these activities just as long as I didn't make so much money that I would attract the envy of a politician. I should also keep my mouth shut about the steady decline of the nation going on around me. Since I would live under a brutal dictatorship just about wherever I lived in Africa—and on account of my white skin, which disqualified me from participating in the politics of my own homeland—I must be blind to the corruption, killings, and general misrule. Alternatively, I might become a journalist and confront these things head on, which is what I decided to do.

As the descendants of soldiers and farmers I never heard my parents express an opinion, either good or bad, about journalists. The only relative of mine who became a foreign correspondent was Donald Wise, my raffish first cousin, once removed. South African–born Don was captured by the Japanese in Singapore during World War II. He was a POW in Changi jail and worked on the Burma railway, where seven thousand men died. After the war he tracked communists in Malaya, then settled in Nairobi, where he wrote for the *Daily Express* and, later, the *Daily Mirror*. Don was my stuff of legend. He had done it all, from covering the big stories—Mau Mau, Biafra, Katanga, Idi Amin's Uganda, Aden, Cyprus, Vietnam—to hanging out with Hemingway, whom he tracked down after the author had survived a plane crash on a hunting safari. Don had a sense of humor and energy that was so well loved that colleagues said the effect of his arrival on a story, sporting a splendid mustache and impeccably dressed however grim the dateline, was like that of a champagne cork being popped. In the days when news dispatches carried a proper dateline, identifying both the place and the day from which the report was filed, Don traversed the Congo to the Atlantic port of Banana and carefully timed his story so that it would read "Banana, Sunday."

On graduating from the School of Oriental and African Studies in 1988, I had watched some of my friends enter careers in which their sole aim was to make lots of money. Others vanished on adventures. I had renewed my love of Africa's history and began to plot my return to my homeland. I telephoned Michael Holman, the Africa editor of London's *Financial Times*. He called me into his office overlooking Blackfriars Bridge on the Thames and I came away feeling I had met my mentor. Michael was a white Zimbabwean and a respected elder in the world of African journalism. He had stood trial for refusing to serve in Ian Smith's white military during the Rhodesian civil war and afterward had fled to Zambia, where he began to work for the FT. From there he moved to London, but he had never lost his dedication to Africa.

"You have a one in ten chance of making a living out of it," Michael told me that day. "If you do, you won't have to prove yourself in any other way."

"What happens then?" I asked.

"One day, you get to be me," he replied, gesturing at his cubicle office with its window looking out at the diagonal rain of England.

He gave me a short briefing and within half an hour I had been appointed a stringer for the FT. In the jargon of the news world, being a stringer meant I had a loose loyalty to the newspaper as their "man on the ground," though the organization would pay me only for what was published, per thousand words. I had wanted a job that would get me home to Kenya, which was also the hub for the East Africa press corps. But Michael told me there was already a correspondent in Nairobi, so he offered me a spot in neighboring Tanzania.

Advice for young foreign correspondents

JOURNALIST PLUS PLUS

After Egypt and Sudan I overlanded southward until I got to the Indian Ocean port of Dar es Salaam, where in 1929 my father had landed at the same age as I was then. I had mixed feelings about Tanzania, associating it not only with all my father's early adventures but also with the unhappiness caused by the expropriation of my family's ranch land in West Kilimanjaro. But at the same time I had grown to admire Julius Nyerere, together with the other great black nationalists such as Fanon, Cabral, Nkrumah, and Lumumba. I was transformed during my year at SOAS, when I buried myself in the library reading books by and about these men. I grew ashamed of my British colonial past and believed that the only way I might atone for my presence in Africa would be to openly confess the wrongdoings of my people and to rail against the continuing exploitation of the continent by the "rich world."

It swiftly dawned on me that I had fetched up in a place that was off the map in terms of news. Dar es Salaam means "haven of peace." Translated another way, it could also be "backwater." I was too wet behind the ears to appreciate the color copy just begging to be written here: tales of man-eating lions from Songea; insurrections on the spice islands of Zanzibar; the vanishing glacial snows of Mount Kilimanjaro. No news meant no money. I was reduced to sleeping on the roof of a derelict house near the beach. An unvaried diet of maize or rice takes its toll on a man who's not used to it, but what the poorer citizens thrived on in roadside kiosks was all I could afford. And since I rarely got near a tap to bathe, my crazed appearance at interviews with diplomats or bureaucrats caused them sufficient alarm not to invite me back. At any other time, I would have written home with news of Lillian's health. Lillian was from among the ranks of our deceased spinster aunts, known in the family as the Grenadiers because they were straight-backed and haughty. My mother had miraculously resurrected Lillian to become the family code for "please send money." In the paranoia of postcolonial Africa, Mum had coined a glossary of such code words to maintain privacy in telegrams. Waycott was "the police." Toad was the "immigration department." Never was a letter written to say Aunt Lillian was in rude health. Once Dad was tramping about the Danakil desert when a runner appeared, having traveled far from Addis Ababa. By his grave face, the runner clearly knew about the tragedy described in the telegram from my mother that he handed over. How scandalized he must have been to see my father erupt into laughter when he read: LILLIAN DYING STOP SCHOOL FEES UNPAID STOP

I could have written home now, but I didn't because I was out to prove myself. I often think I should have just stayed on that roof and my life would have taken a different path. Instead, I met a man named Buchizya Mseteka. Buchizya, Buchi to his friends, was a big Zambian with a wooden fetish face, professorial glasses, luminous white teeth, and a tufted goatee. Born his father's first son after seven daughters, he claimed his name translated into English meant "the Unexpected One." To me, this is exactly what he was. He dressed in snakeskin moccasins and flashy suits roomy enough for his generous buttocks and a belly that, he said, proved he was a man of prestige. A Big Man. I on the other hand, as he pointed out almost as soon as I had met him, resembled a hippie with my copy of *Africa on a Shoestring,* sandals made from old car tires, tatty jeans, tousled hair, and heat-fried pink skin.

Buchi was the Dar es Salaam stringer for the wire agency Reuters. Two young men, our ways were bound to cross, since there were so few members of the local press corps. Most local African journalists worked for the *Daily News* and Shihata, the state news agency. Some of them were good writers and had a nose for stories. But as employees of the great, flabby system of Chama Cha Mapinduzi, the Revolutionary Party, they were required to toe the line. There was a TASS correspondent, who ignored the news and threw himself into attempting to rehabilitate two Russian ladies who had defected from the Soviet Union to become whores. There was an Indian stringer, who owed his modest wealth not to journalism but to selling secondhand clothes out of his office on Samora Machel Avenue. Then there was Jim, a radioman who smoked a pipe and wore glasses with thick black frames, a porkpie hat, and a bow tie.

When Buchi invited me over to eat at his place, I gratefully accepted. The Zambian's huge frame suggested that he ate well. Indeed he did. Come lunchtime of the following day, Buchi and I were seated in easy chairs. His Zambian girlfriends laid out on doily-covered side tables bottles of beer and plates of delicate maize meal, fried cabbage, and kapenta fish. After they had served us, they withdrew to the kitchen, eyes down, gently clapping their hands.

A series of drinking bouts in open-air bars followed, with us shouting above the blurred racket of Lingala music. Tanzania's breweries, on the rare occasions that they produced anything, they served up lager that tasted of stale piss. Our drink of choice was Tusker, imported from Kenya. It is the oldest beer brewed in East Africa and is named after the elephant that in 1912 killed one of the company's founders. No drink in the world slakes one's thirst so perfectly after a day in the heat than a well-chilled Tusker. Buchizya and I used to drink until we could barely stand. At the end of an evening we staggered away down pungent-smelling, pot-holed streets, Buchi warbling in his melodic Bantu voice the tune that was on every pair of lips at that time in Africa about how "we will sing our own song."

One day, in an offhand manner, Buchi invited me to share his apartment on Cotton Road, rent free. After that I slept on his sofa beneath the churning overhead fan, or on the balcony under the clothesline. Below the apartment was a bar. From morning until night, one could hear happy voices, flip-flopped feet shuffling to music, the squawks of chickens and goats being slaughtered, and the aroma of roasting fat wafting up the stairs. In the middle of Buchi's living room sat a big deep freezer, more of a status symbol than a place to cool our beer since it had the capacity to store more than we could drink in a fortnight. The heat of the days in Dar es Salaam was so moist that the air was viscous. It was as if time itself slowed. Some days it got so hot we gave up hunting stories and fled back to the apartment, where we took turns climbing into Buchi's deep freezer to cool down with the door closed. It smoked as one emerged refreshed, but the torpor returned within seconds.

Buchi also had a video cassette recorder, but only three tapes: *One Flew Over the Cuckoo's Nest*, a hard-core porn flick, and poorly recorded coverage of a socialist nations athletic event that had taken place in Yugoslavia sometime in the early 1980s. We watched each of those videos more times than I can count. When guests dropped by I had to move from the sofa and this happened at all times of the day and night. Buchi would spread out onto the couch and ostentatiously put a tape on. We'd all have to sit there and watch. It didn't seem to matter who the guest was or which video played, just so long as people knew Buchi's TV was top of the line.

* * *

I soon fell in among Buchi's friends. Most of them were South African guerrillas, who had fled apartheid. Tanzania was a Frontline State, although not much fighting was in progress. Pretoria was thousands of miles away. The guerrillas were township kids, not peasants, yet they were housed in camps deep in the bush, where they were expected to grow vegetables and attend ideology classes. They preferred town, where they came drinking with us. During these sessions they happily taught me, a white son of colonialism, a chant whose refrain went: "One settler! One bullet! SETTLER, SETTLER! BULLET, BULLET!"

The guerrillas and I had one common struggle, which was chasing women. In this we were in awe of Buchi, who led a life more sexually complicated than I considered possible. Females came and left Cotton Road at all times of the day and night. To the guerrillas, he'd boast about his conquests as if he were winning wars.

"First, intelligence: find the target. Next, send in the flowers to soften her up. Then I say, Okay boys, it's time to go in with the infantry and air force and pound, *Boom boom*, until she begs for a cease-fire!"

Buchi would stand up to do an obscene jig, snapping his fingers to a rhythm, imitating a female's howls of pleasure.

"Tchwa! *Ooooh*! Tchwa! Mercy!"

He'd also crow about his victories with white women, which he described as redressing the wrongs of European colonialism.

"They get to experience the mysteries of the African man, whereas me, I'm on a one-man crusade to punish as many white women in bed as possible. Tchwa! Mercy!"

The men sitting with us would splutter into their beers at this. I'd struggle to put up a defense, but Buchi was relentless.

"I think we'll all agree you white boys are sexually the weaker race, licking toes and reading stories and then it's all over? I get the job done properly!"

Dar was as licentious as Byron's Venice. Everybody, whether married or single, seemed to be caught up in a web of sexual intrigue. Foremost among the voluptuaries were the Zambians who worked at the local railway corporation. They threw bacchanalian parties, where they drank brandy and danced the rumba. The floor would be packed with bodies—lissome typists with senior controllers, the young clerks with fat managers' wives in explosively hued, shimmering cocktail dresses. The bands were large ensembles of singers, toasters, brass sections, ranks of guitarists, and percussionists, together with girls who'd grind their hips and flash their plump, brown buttocks. The lead vocalist might be in a loud Congolese shirt, dabbing his brow with a hanky, eyes rolling, lips pouting, crooning in his soft bass lyrics of poor men falling in love.

> *Malaika, nakupenda malaika!*
> *Angel, I love you my angel!*

On these nights I'd try to dance like my African friends and end up sweating and leaping about happily whooping. I'd look across the floor and see how Buchi was barely moving. He displayed an intense rhythmic energy with a wonderful economy of movement, mesmerizing his partner with half-closed cobra eyes, a slight rocking of the pelvis, and a positioning of the hands and elbows.

The working day lasted from dawn until two in Dar. It was a hangover from the colonial era. Siesta time was given over to fornicating. Nobody asked questions. The answers were both too obvious and therefore too dangerous. As a result the entire scene was shrouded in secrecy. To commit adultery was expected. To be caught, I sensed, would lead to extravagant violence.

I remained a bemused spectator in all of this, until one day I found myself seduced by a railwayman's wife from the golf club.

Buchi was out at the airport, so we sneaked into his room and flipped on the air-conditioning system. Her braided hair revealed itself to be a wig, which to my consternation she removed. Naked, she was like shiny rubber to touch. I produced a condom.

"Don't worry about that," she said.

"We must," I stammered.

"You will like it better without," she said.

"Always use socks," Buchi warned me later. A "sock" was a condom. We all knew what AIDS was, although these were the days when the prostitutes of Dar es Salaam still hung their socks out to dry before reusing them.

"Never *nyama kwa nyama*, flesh on flesh," Buchi lectured. He made a piston movement of one forefinger sticking into the hole of his left fist. I took his advice, but even after using the condoms I'd stay awake at night for weeks, staring at the overhead fan and praying that I was sorry and I'd never do it again. Until the next time I did it.

One day the janitor knocked on our door and Buchi answered it. The man complained loudly that our condoms had blocked the apartment building's drains. Buchi drew himself up to his full height.

"And what would you have us do, my brother? Endanger lives by not wearing socks?" He waggled his belly in a characteristic display of indignation.

"It poses a threat to the public health!"

I'd rise at seven and wash in a bucket of cold water with a bar of red Lifebuoy soap. Over a breakfast of samosas, a filterless Rooster, and bubblegum, I cracked open the *Daily News*. In time, the door to Buchi's bedroom swung open. Buchi emerged with a bath towel wrapped around his great middle, gave out a thunderous sneeze, and complained of his thumping hangover. "Oooh my bratha! I'm hanging," Buchi would say. "I'm hanging all over!"

Me the *mzungu*, the white man, in my tire sandals. Buchi waddling along in his pinstripe suit, mopping his thick neck with a handkerchief. We must have seemed an odd pair in the streets of Dar, thronging with men in crisp white shirts, ladies in glittering ball gowns or *kanga* wraps, all tiptoeing among broken pavements, puddles, sucked mango pips, and goat bones.

But Buchi and I made a splendid double act. My white skin got us in to see the Brits or Yanks. Except that they let on nothing because, I sense, they knew little about the local situation. Buchi's black skin opened the doors of government ministers or the chiefs of state utilities. Except that they were never in. We'd rouse secretaries who lay slumped over typewriters of monstrous size. "He's not around. Try tomorrow," said the secretaries with heavy-lidded eyes.

Rarely, the official was "around" and we were shown in. He'd be sitting in his Mao suit beneath a portrait of Nyerere, commonly known as *Mwalimu*, or "the Teacher." After thirty years he was still the undisputed leader of the Revolutionary Party.

"*Shikamu, Ndugu*," we'd say. "I hold your feet, Comrade." This combined the traditional greeting for elders that dated back to the days of slavery with the modern socialist form of address.

"*Marahaba*," he'd reply. "You're too kind."

Further pleasantries were exchanged for some minutes. It was considered ill form in Tanzania to get straight to the point. Finally we all fell silent. Only then would Buchi ask for information. This roused the official to open and close his desk drawers, stare at the ceiling, or look at us and politely demur. Even the simplest of subjects, such as the figures for coffee exports, appeared to be matters of national security. In fact, we suspected it was for a more mundane reason. He didn't know and, more to the point, the figures didn't exist.

Things had once been different for Tanzania, as the Cuban ambassador told us at open air lunches over roasted meat. He had been here since Che Guevara had traveled to Congo in '65. He said those days and the later, heroic wars of the seventies were now just memories.

"What hope had existed at independence from colonial rule! What ambitions we had," said the Cuban.

Nyerere had imposed his personal philosophy of African socialism in the 1967 Arusha declaration.

"In our country work should be something to be proud of," Nyerere had said in the sixties. By the eighties, many white expatriates in Dar still reverently called him the Teacher. So did the Africans, but sunk in a poverty brought about by Nyerere's dreams, they were being bitterly ironic. The joke was now that Tanzanians pretended to work, while the state pretended to pay them.

The Cuban ambassador said the presidents of Africa like the Teacher, once liberators, had grown into a group of old crocodiles. Africa was their wallow. It was a still, hot pool into which nothing fresh had run for years.

"Now when the Teacher saw a herd of giraffe grazing in a coffee estate, even he had to admit his revolution had failed," said the ambassador.

"But some of us still believe in the ideas of socialism and self-reliance."

"Oh yes," said Buchi in his baggy suit and moccasins. "*La lutta continua*. The struggle goes on, my brothers."

I wandered off to hike along the Lake Victoria Nyanza shore. I tramped from one mission station hospital to another, dossing on the dirt floors of peasant huts in villages with the banana groves sewn with freshly dug AIDS graves. I crossed by dhow to Zanzibar, where I interviewed dissidents while sipping glasses of tamarind juice and slept on the beach in coconut palm leaf huts. I languished in bars with Buchi.

At a roundabout in downtown Dar, a monument stands to the *askari* African soldiers and porters who died in terrible numbers in East Africa during the Great War. One day while Buchi and I were walking in the street, he pointed up at this and said, "We've been screwed ever since you whites came into this continent. You came with a Bible in one hand and a shovel in the other, to dig our minerals and fuck our women. Then you made us fight your wars."

I became lazy, forgetting that, despite my relaxed Dar es Salaam timetable, my London newspaper had deadlines to maintain, pages to fill. I filed so little, so late that eventually my editor Michael Holman kindly said he had to let me go. An achievement, I thought, since I didn't even have a proper job to lose.

Life in Dar es Salaam was a financial struggle, but had I not left I would have been able to survive on odd stringer jobs probably for the rest of my life. There would have been no end to the beers, the rumba dancing, and the sensuality. But it all came to an abrupt end one day. I remember my last evening in Dar. We were at the radioman Jim's place. Fela Kuti was playing on an old gramophone. I sat on the window ledge, gazing across rusty tin rooftops, pied crows and swallows wheeling through the sky, antique Morris Minors clattering down the street, lines of laundry, and palm trees waving in the evening breeze.

"Hey, punk," said Jim. He stared at me as he puffed on his pipe. "Have you heard the news from Khartoum?"

Jim told me that the military had overthrown the democratically elected prime minister. There was nothing special in this and Jim was simply making conversation. The Sudan was always having coups. Yet I immediately saw that this was an opportunity I could not squander. I went back to the flat in Cotton Road, found a number for *The Times* in London, called, and asked for the foreign editor. To my astonishment he came on the line and said yes, by all means he would take copy from me. The paper's Cairo correspondent had not been able to get to Khartoum. I could file until he made it, if he ever did. I thought it was worth the chance. Next morning, I raised cash up to the maximum limit on my American Express card and bought a flight to Sudan.

My Khartoum flight connected via Nairobi, where a gang of foreign correspondents came on board. They stuck together in a group, chain-smoked cigarettes, and continually ordered drinks from the stewardesses, with whom they flirted. The flight left Nairobi but in midair the captain announced that the military junta that had seized power in Khartoum had closed Sudan's airspace. We were diverted to Addis Ababa, where the Ethiopians kept us in the departure lounge. We sat among large numbers of West African pilgrims bound for Mecca. I sat in my plastic chair nursing a stale sandwich. I had grown used to the friendly company of Buchizya and the African press corps in Dar es Salaam, but I was too shy to introduce myself to these foreign correspondents. It was like arriving in a new school.

The hours turned into evening. The pilgrims crowded into the bathrooms to wash, spraying water through their noses, sticking their feet and bottoms in the basins. They came out and lined up for evening prayers. I watched them and envied their sense of faith and community. I was confused about which was the correct way to live my life and I saw no greater purpose in it than to live it to the full. After praying they settled into circles, telling their beads and chatting over ginger coffee poured from thermoses. I pictured them at home in villages and tents under Saharan night skies. At last they wrapped their turbans around their heads to cut out the fluorescent glare and slept on the dirty linoleum floors. Picking their way through this sea of supine *hajjis* I saw a young English correspondent with the features of Dennis the Menace chatting with a handsome American. Both were my age. They held out their hands.

"Julian Ozanne of the *Financial Times*," said the Englishman. I recognized the name. He was my Nairobi counterpart working for Michael.

"Eric. *U.S. News and World Report*," said the American. "You?" I introduced myself and confessed I didn't work for anybody, but that I might file to *The Times* if the Cairo correspondent didn't make it first.

"Why wouldn't he make it?" asked Eric. He gave me a friendly pat on the arm. "Look, tell me if I can help with anything."

We waited in that airport lounge for three entire days. By the time Khartoum's airspace opened up and the flight departed Addis I was disheveled, unshaven, and in need of a bath. The lounge café had charged high prices in dollars and a big dent had already been made in my funds. We landed in Sudan's capital and exited the aircraft to a blast of hot desert air. In the arrivals building a gigantic officer with blue-black skin checked my passport and said, "No visa. You cannot enter Sudan. You must get back on the aircraft." The flight was headed for Cairo. I remonstrated with the officer, but he shook his head. He didn't look like a man who'd accept a bribe. The only payment he needed was the power his uniform gave him. He nodded to two soldiers who herded me to one side. Julian was next in line. The officer checked his passport, found a valid visa, and waved him through.

"And what about my colleague?" Julian said, fixing the man with a determined stare. "The general has personally called for the international press to come to Sudan. I have an appointment to see him tomorrow morning with my colleague here. The general's not going to be happy if you deport any of us." The officer looked doubtful. "Where is your letter of invitation?" he asked. "At the foreign minister's office," Julian replied. "Telephone if you like." The lines were clearly down. Julian's bluff worked. The officer called me back to his desk and stamped my passport.

Most of the journalists were staying at the Hilton. I couldn't afford that and so I checked into the Acropole, a shabby Greek-run place with a friendly atmosphere, despite the damage from a recent bombing by Islamic militants. Already the shooting was over in Khartoum and the story had, after several days, gone completely cold. It was downpage news, but I reminded myself that at least I had a string. But what to write about? I felt out of my depth and so I decided to pay my colleagues a visit. On the banks of the Nile, the Hilton had its own cool microclimate, food supply, piped music, and soaps in the lavatories. It was an American spaceship that had landed on the dusty planet of Sudan. Walking into the lobby, I encountered a man in a white suit and a jet-black toupee dictating copy down the lobby phone.

"*Stop!* New par! Tanks rumbled through streets, as civilians dived for cover like stray cats ... No! T for Tommy ... *Tanks!* ... No! N is for *nuts* ..."

He had lots of quotes, from Western diplomats and "sources close to the military ..." Not for the last time, I felt like I was a step behind the action, because I hadn't seen any such military displays or panicked civilians. To my eyes, a pall of inertia hung over the city. In fact I could barely even see Khartoum. Sandstorms locally known as the *haboob* whipped the streets in the daytime, producing an ominous twilight. *Haboobs* were famous for the confusion they produced. A Boeing pilot had once ditched on the Nile, mistaking it for the airport runway. "Taxi?" I'd ask at reception, to which the concierge would shake his head. "*Haboob!*" By evening, the *haboob* would settle into sand drifts at every street corner, ready to go airborne again in the heat of the next day. Before dusk, I observed everybody scampering home. A bobbing mass of them swathed in white turbans and leopard-skin slippers, they looked like workers toiling in some gigantic laundry. "Taxi?" I asked in the street. They shook their heads. "Curfew!"

Eric was in the Hilton lobby, smoking. I went over to him and asked who the man in the white suit and toupee was.

"The Cairo *Times* correspondent," he said. "Listen, you can still try writing for the specialist magazines like *Africa Confidential.*"

I told him I knew little about Sudan, certainly not enough to write for the kind of publications read by diplomats and spies. Eric advised me to bluff it. I realized I'd have to. The cash from my credit card was now half gone and I had no prospect of making any more. I spent more precious dollars telephoning *Africa Confidential* from the Hilton foyer, despite the fact that I knew the lines were tapped, and to my astonishment the editor commissioned me.

Shrouded by the curfew and the *haboob,* the junta's new generalissimo, Bashir, had yet to reveal himself. Nobody knew anything about him, since until now he had been isolated in a jungle garrison several weeks' boat journey up the Nile. In a transcript of his only statement so far, I thought I detected a motive for his coup d'état, cryptic though it was. "We will no longer eat bitter aloes on the frontiers," he had said. On state TV, the junta repeatedly broadcast pictures of the ousted prime minister's garage. It was stacked with tins of tomato puree. Puree certainly seemed to be a vital ingredient in much of the local food. Apparently the prime minister had purchased his mountain of tins with diverted state funds. They looked rusty and past their sell-by date to me. I saw that this hardly made a news story. What was I to say? That the Islamic fundamentalists were up in arms over a variation on Lord Acton's dictum? "Puree tends to corrupt and absolute puree corrupts absolutely."

One respected correspondent, meanwhile, did not appear to budge from the Hilton foyer, but seemed to be always parked on a sofa next to a trolley piled with cakes. To remain here and still have so much to file made me think he must be a true expert. "How long have you covered *the* Sudan?" He winked at me. "This is my first time here!" He jerked his head toward the dining hall. "What a dump, eh?"

My mounting panic was partly due to the fact that I knew that if I didn't file, I would have no way of retrieving the costs of the telex, hotel, or flights. I told Eric and Julian that all was going well. At hotel mealtimes, I claimed to have a bad stomach and refused ordering from the menu, but waited until I could secretively nip along to a roadside-shack café to order an aluminium plateful of *foul* beans and coriander with a wheat chapati.

It was my first opportunity to observe up close the other foreign press corps on a story. I noticed that as soon as they began socializing they forgot their rivalries. I sat straining to overhear something useful about the Sudanese coup, but the correspondents made no mention of it. Instead they swapped scurrilous anecdotes about great former colleagues. ("Said he could get laid anywhere, right? So then the desk sends him to Red China during the Cultural Revolution. Nobody thinks he can do it. Six weeks later a postcard arrives with nothing on it but the words 'Gobbled in the Gobi!'") I learned that correspondents were strangely sentimental about the past. Today's stories seemed to be small beer compared to the momentous events of even a few years ago, when titans had walked the earth. The trade of journalism also appeared to have gone into some kind of terminal decline.

A Reuters correspondent covering fascist Italy's invasion of Abyssinia in 1935 sent a cable to Fleet Street headquarters to complain about the quality of the water in Addis Ababa. The solution, he proposed, was to send him crates of champagne. Even today, correspondents conformed to long-held customs. Fiddling expenses or making outrageous claims was a matter of professional pride to the foreign correspondent.

A good stringer, particularly, had to be clever at massaging claims, since he or she was paid far too little in "wordage" fees to keep body and soul alive. One had to resort to a mass of tricks to which editors, who had been in the field themselves, were honor bound to turn a blind eye. Bogus receipt books, forged signatures, black-market cash transactions all came in handy. As long as you wrote down a claim on a receipt and had it stamped all over in purple you'd be all right. Years later I made an expense for a thousand dollars, itemizing it as payment for the services of two prostitutes for a banker I wanted to interview and management never questioned it.

At the end of the meals, I saw them tip the waiter to give them extra blank receipts. One explained to me how it worked.

"Every trip, I try to make enough to buy myself a nice piece of electronics, see? A video, or some speakers . . ."

I was astonished to see one of them rummaging through a wastepaper bin full of discarded receipts at the restaurant entrance.

I became desperate. I knocked on doors, pleading with the other correspondents to tell me where I was going wrong.

"Please tell me what's happening?"

"No, I'm not going to help you just like that," said the BBC correspondent Lindsey Hilsum.

"Pleeeaaase."

"No."

Finally, I went to Julian and Eric and they tried to calm me down. Short of writing my copy, however, they could do little. Up in my room, as my filing deadline loomed, I scribbled a first paragraph. Crossed it out. Screwed the paper into a ball. Wrote another. Screwed it into a ball. And so on, until I had no pages left in my notepad and began work on the hotel stationery. What could I write, when I saw nothing *The Times* man did? Nobody had agreed to speak to me, so I had no quotes, facts, or figures. My taxi driver was the only Sudanese who gave me any comment on the political situation. He said: "Army bad! Army bad!"

I was close to despair, when there was a knock on my door. It was Eric, with a camera slung over his shoulder. "Come with me," he said. "All right," I said gratefully. The foyer doors parted with an electric sigh and we emerged into the *haboob* and clambered into a battered taxi.

I never saw Eric hot, ruffled, unkempt, or miss a story, no matter which jungle, slum, or refugee camp he fetched up in. He made covering Africa look easy. And when a day's journalism was done he'd tell you unprintable tales full of laconic humor, between heavy exhalations of cigarette smoke and always a crazy laugh at the end. Eric had been raised in St. Joseph, Missouri, and I think he'd grown up wanting adventure thanks to the example of his father, William Ransdell, who had joined up with the U.S.A.F. at eighteen. As a navigator in the nose of a B-17 bomber his old man had flown thirty-five daylight missions over Germany, through ribbons of flak and Nazi fighters, with engine shutouts, two crash landings and raids so perilous that on one sortie two-thirds of the bomber group got shot down. By the time Eric was at journalism school he had traveled all over Asia and Australia but he found his cause when he learned what was happening in apartheid South Africa. "The more I read, the more I came to feel that what was happening in South Africa was one of those pure evils, utterly black and white, just like the one my father had fought in Germany," he told me. He touched down in Johannesburg in 1985, soon after the townships exploded. The sudden rush of being in this place— comrades toyitoyi-ing around burning tire barricades,

Casspirs filled with soldiers in riot gear, witnessing Desmond Tutu's church sermons—changed his entire life. Back at home he wrote an article about what he'd seen that won a William Randolph Hearst award. But when he attempted to return to South Africa Pretoria rejected his visa, so he had no choice but to head for "liberated" black Africa, and now here we were.

Minutes later our taxi stopped at the gates of army headquarters. We got out next to a large Soviet tank and Eric moved off a few steps to speak with a sentry. To my astonishment, the guard nodded and called an officer, who marched us into the heavily fortified military complex until we entered a dark office, where a man sat behind a huge desk. By the spade-sized epaulets on his shoulders, I knew him to be an officer. By his shy and deferential manner, I took him for a lowly fellow in the chain of command. We engaged in a little small talk. The officer had a habit of blinking very fast so that his eyelids fluttered.

"You are English?" he asked me with a smile. I said I was, but that I had been raised in Africa.

"Ah, I love England very much," the officer said, disregarding my claim to an African identity. "Manchester United is my team. What is your team?" I have no opinion about football but I wanted to put him at his ease. "Chelsea," I ventured.

"You are a Christian?" I said I was, deciding to go along with this quietly.

"You must know that I myself attended the Oxford University," the officer said complacently. Blink blink.

"Oh? Which college?"

"Ah, Oxford Street," he replied, blinking faster as he smiled so widely that he exposed his gums.

After some minutes of this I saw it was time for me, the eyes and ears of the world, to seize control of the situation. It was time for me to begin my career in earnest. I was being nudged forward by the ghost of my great predecessor, the twenty-three-year-old war correspondent Winston Churchill, who had been in this place when he covered Kitchener's defeat of the Mahdist forces at the Battle of Omdurman in 1898.

With just the right tone of firmness I thought appropriate, I asked, "And when do we get to interview His Excellency the President?"

There was an embarrassed silence. Eric stared at me agape. The Sudanese with the giant gold epaulets had stopped blinking. Somewhat apologetically, the Sudanese replied, "I *am* the President."

It's July 11, 1989, and we are belted in as the Kenya Airways flight taxis for the runway. We're homeward bound for Nairobi after the military coup in the Sudan. We're tired and dirty after an eighteen-hour delay out of Khartoum due to sandstorms followed by a technical-hitch stopover at Addis Ababa's Bole airport. The aircraft is half empty. Eric is next to me and across the aisle is Julian, pulling on a fag after the no-smoking lights have come on. The three of us barely know one another, but what's about to happen will bind us together forever. This moment is when it all really begins. This is why years later I like to fancy that the people who make up my story, even the ones who are not on the plane that day, fill all the vacant seats. And so I look down the aisle and see, half turning to look at me, the faces of Jonathan, Buchi, Hos, Dan, Afrah, Carlos, Bald Sam, Shafi, Lizzie. And among them are dozens of other ghosts and fellow travelers we met along the way.

Our Boeing 707 accelerates and lifts off. Within seconds it becomes clear that we are failing to gain altitude. Julian rests his head against the seat in front of him and exclaims dolefully, "We're not going to make it!" The aircraft banks in a tight circle. Through my porthole the wing is vertical, skimming peasant huts and fields.

We hit the ground halfway down the runway. The jets scream in reverse thrust. Overhead compartments crash open, spilling bags and tubes and yellow masks. We spin, tilt, the wheels give way, as the fuselage torpedoes down a mountainside. The port wing buckles and rips away. Din of turbines, tearing metal, electronics, and then silence.

My panic is over before it even had a chance to begin. In the hush that follows we crouch in the brace position, like churchgoers. Eric cackles, "Are we home already?"

Across the way, a passenger with zigzag tribal scars across his forehead points out of his porthole and yells, "It is burning! We are burning!"

Orange flames billow from the smashed portside wing. The passenger cabin fills with fumes and black smoke. I begin to choke as I struggle to rip off the safety belt. We are all suffocating.

Julian heads downhill toward the aircraft's nose. Instinct tells me to vault up the steep incline to the starboard rear emergency exit. I can see through the smoke that Eric has the same idea as he moves up ahead of me. At the exit, a flight attendant blocks our path. His skin has gone a tinge of green. "Take your seats!" he yells. He is rooted to the spot, as if paralyzed.

Eric punches the flight attendant in the face and pushes past. He turns the emergency handle and wrenches open the door, causing the inflatable chute to billow out to the hillside below. Both of us grab the steward and push him out of the plane headfirst, then follow ourselves. The whole scene's in slow motion as I slide down. I see black smoke, red flames, a fountain of white foam lathering up over the prone aircraft. Walking up the gashed muddy slope I see, in among the debris of orange life jackets and clothes and paper cups, an old man moaning, clutching at his bloody leg out of which sticks a jagged bone. Stretcher crews are skidding down the hill. Off to one side, the Ethiopian soldiers are using the butts of their AK-47s to keep back a crowd of peasants in rags intent on looting the crash site.

We regroup back on the tarmac apron, where an airport bus is waiting for us. "Bloodyfuckinghell," we all agree and light up our fags. Once out of the airport, we rush to file our stories. Only when we talk to our desks do we realize that our harrowing experience in the heart of Africa is not news. It means nothing to anybody but us, yet the crash brings us together as comrades, in a way that no pleasant experience could do.

The flight to Nairobi next day feels like the safest I've ever taken. I'm buoyed up and borne along by the laws of probability on my side that I couldn't be in a plane crash two days in a row. Ever after, Julian's way of coping with air travel is to start talking very loudly just before takeoff about the time he crashed in Africa, until the stewardesses come to ask him to desist because he's frightening the other passengers. Eric claims he has no fear of flying. "Doesn't bother me in the least," he says. "In fact, I feel blessed by the great airline gods, which is why I think I'm always getting bumped up to business or first class." I walk away and forget for years how afraid I am. But on a takeoff hundreds of flights later, every second of the crash comes back to haunt me. I am transformed into one of those unsettling passengers next to you: palms sweating, bare-toothed with fear, and possessed of a high-altitude belief in God. And so it is with many of my memories.

At the end of the nineteenth century the British constructed a railway from Mombasa on the Indian Ocean to Lake Victoria. The project acquired the name the Lunatic Express, being hugely expensive and built for no ultimate reason other than for the vague objective of securing the headwaters of the Nile. The most challenging section of this incredible feat of engineering was to cross the Great Rift Valley. On the last staging post before the precipitous rift escarpment, the British ordered their workforce of Indian coolies and soldiers to pitch their lines of white tents in neat rows on the black cotton soils. Here the flat plains, which teemed with wildlife, suddenly rose up like a wave to break over the Rift near the Ngongs, a ripple of volcanic hills that looked like a giant fist. The staging post quickly became Nairobi, named for Ngare Nairobi, or the Cold River, which snaked across the plains. Having built a railway, the British had to justify its cost. The bureaucrats arrived in Nairobi. A stone magistrate's court was constructed and the trading houses and banks that followed went up along muddy streets wide enough to allow a wagon and eight span of oxen to turn a full circle. The Africans were ordered to pay poll taxes to the bureaucrats. To do this, the Africans came to work and live in shanties. The white settlers arrived to establish plantations and ranches so that the railway would have something to transport. And so the foundations of modern Kenya were laid, created by white men, then worshiped by the mission-raised blacks after they took power following their independence.

I was born within sight of Nairobi's railway terminus, at the Mater Misericordia hospital in the industrial area. The midwife Sister Assunta delivered me and cooed over me for my name, Aidan, was that of the saint who had converted the heathens of the Western Isles of Scotland. My mother gave the hospital a jacaranda tree that grows in the garden to this day. My birth came just after Kenya's independence from Britain in 1963, when postcards showed a city with lush gardens and wide, tree–lined avenues with only the occasional car traveling on them. "Jambo from the Green City in the Sun," said the postcards and the tourist brochures. Even in the Technicolor memory of my childhood, I remember Nairobi was still small enough for people to say hello as one strolled the pavement.

If you live in a place you hardly notice the changes. You have to return after a long absence, as I did in 1989. In the gap since my boyhood, Nairobi had been transformed into a dirty, crime-ridden place, surrounded by slums. I heard that when it rained in the shanties, the poor people's shacks slid down the muddy hillsides. Coldwater City. Nobody knew what the population was except that it was rising. The hacks nicknamed it "Nairobbery" (derelict Dar es Salaam was "Dar-Is-the-Slum" and Uganda's war-devastated capital Kampala was known as "Kampothole"). But with the crowding and danger came a vibrant urban atmosphere as fizzy as a chilled Tusker with its cap popped off.

I remember walking into the Chester House press center on Koinange Street for the first time. Downtown was still defined by the little grid of streets from the colonial era. Concrete structures rose around me, nosing up through the slum smog: ministries, multinationals, agencies of the United Nations. From a street corner, I watched the teeming scene: office workers in their frayed shirt collars and cheap suits stepping over beggars, shoeshine boys, vendors selling spreads of newspapers. *Drum* magazine splashing the headline "Luo Girls are Best in Bed." The white plutocrats in their short sleeves, the youngish European females we called leatherettes because the tropical sun had ravaged their white skin, the hippies, the Kenya cowboys, the Somali café crowd, Asians in their banks and trading houses, the young black middle-class kids in their baggy trousers and wet-look coifs, the Big Shiny Men in their air-conditioned BMWs, or the processions of tourists in khaki safari hats, window-shopping for *taka taka* souvenirs from Eden. Rising above the chaos of downtown's Uhuru Highway was a string of giant advertising billboards. "Tusker," they read. "My Country, My Beer."

Julian and Eric both worked at the Chester House foreign press center and they were the ones who showed me around. It was in a shabby block, up a dark staircase, past a florist that offered special bouquets for funerals and a drink shop that gave a discount on production of a press card. Delegations of rebels, dissidents, and sundry sinister creatures turned up daily to address press conferences. They spoke about distant wars, stuffed ballots, ethnic cleansings, and cattle raids from places far off the map. Others were on missions more personal. Shaka Zulu Assegai, a black American, gave frequent pressers, declaiming in jive how the government should recognize his claim to be an African. A variety of men declared that they had a cure for AIDS, one a date for Armageddon. Or they needed help. Torture victims came in off the street to show their scars from prison. An aging Tutsi king announced to the world that he was looking for a wife.

Julian walked me down a passage that was stuffy and dark because the lights were broken. Grimy yellow doors bore the plaques of famous names, from the BBC to Japan's *Asahi Shimbun*. Julian was a figure like the Artful Dodger: he knew everybody and he seemed to be involved in every scam going. The way he explained it to me, the Nairobi press corps had a subculture all its own, like a school or prison with arcane rules, slang, and legends. I thought of my great cousin Donald Wise, who had long since moved on, though little seemed to have altered since his day. Reporters still punched out their reports on telex tape and photos were sent on analogue barrel transmitters. Julian took me to meet the new doyen of the Chester House pack, Mohamed Amin.

"So you're an Africa boy," Mo said when we met. He was among the few journalists I ever knew who acknowledged how important my adopted home was to what I did, because I believe we shared the same complex emotions about the place. What we had in common was rooted in two entirely different family histories in the British Empire. Mo had been born in poverty, the son of a Muslim stonemason who was among the indentured laborers shipped in from India to construct the Lunatic Express. Mo had bought his first box camera as a boy in Dar es Salaam and a few years later he started Camerapix. At first it was a little photo studio of the type one sees all over Africa, but Mo saw his opportunity in the political upheavals of the day and went into news. His first scoop was to cover Zanzibar's 1964 revolution that overthrew the sultan. Camerapix had since then grown to be one of the largest TV and photo agencies in Africa. Mo had covered every big story on the continent in the past three decades, often working a still camera and film camera at the same time: the heady days of independence from colonial rule; Africa's "winds of change"; the clowning of Idi Amin, who had expelled seventy thousand Asians and led Uganda into darkness; Central Africa's coronation of Emperor Bokassa, modeled on Napoleon Bonaparte's. His greatest triumph was his TV footage, voiced over by the BBC's Michael Buerk, of the first pictures to break the 1984 Ethiopian famine, which would eventually kill a million people. Mo's pictures whipped up publicity, rock songs, and concerts that raised funds for food that probably saved a further two million from hungry deaths. He may have seemed diffident but he was as conceited as hell and never let you forget about his fame.

Mo proudly showed me his office. Covering the walls were framed snaps of Mo with Bob Geldof, Queen Elizabeth giving Mo his MBE medal, Mo with Sidney Poitier, Mo with sundry Third World despots, honorary degrees, TV awards, and a platinum disk of the song "We Are the World."

"If you don't publicize yourself, nobody else ever will," he told me.

Mo's right-hand man was Brian Tetley, a white Kenyan who had grown up in England's north. Brian was a tabloid man out of central casting: crumpled, boozy, a chain smoker, a bankrupt with chronic woman problems. Brian had been crafting snappy leads in Africa since colonial times. He was always kind to the likes of me, young correspondents just starting out. "Lovely story! You should be proud of yourself!" he'd say when one did something right. "Let's go and have a steak and drink some Tuskers!" Tetley drank so much that Mo was rumored to often pay his bar bill instead of a salary. But he was a survivor. His scalawag charm got him out of endless scrapes.

Once Tetley was staggering home in the early hours and a mugger materialized with a knife and demanded money. "Do you honestly think a white man walks through Nairobi at three in the morning if he has any money?" asked Brian. The thief lowered his knife and walked Brian home, saying that he would protect him from other muggers. Brian invited his new friend in for a drink. They parted three days later after a marathon drinking binge, the best of friends.

Then there were the war heroes, men who were believed to be so full of lead that they triggered airport metal detectors. Reid Miller of the Associated Press kept a sliver of shrapnel encased in Perspex on his desk as a paperweight. The metal was flecked with dried blood, Reid's blood, and had been extracted from a wound he had suffered in a Nicaragua bomb outrage. The UPI stringer Miles Bredin had once dealt antique lace in England, where he had bought and sold an evening dress once made for Napoleon III's wife, the Empress Eugénie. TV man Nick Hughes wore collarless shirts of an identical design every day of his life, and when the factory was going out of business he went out and bought four hundred of them. There was a long-haired, dope-smoking cameraman from Southern Africa I called the Rock Spider, who had served as a conscript in the apartheid army and fought in Angola. There were white linen–suited eccentrics still stuck in the colonial era, angry campaigners we called the Laptop Bombardiers and sundry burned-out cases, sunk by drink or running from divorces. And then there were the guys like Duke, a boyishly handsome German kid, blond with a tan and freckles, like a model in a Ralph Lauren Safari perfume advert. He made sure he looked good on a battlefield, loved guns, read *Soldier of Fortune,* and kept up with the latest gadgets: a flak jacket with a specially designed personal logo, a GPS navigator, multiblade knives, night-sight goggles.

As it turned out there was work for me in Nairobi with *The Times.* The paper's regular correspondent was losing interest in his string but was passionately interested in marlin fishing in the Indian Ocean. I encouraged him to go with his tackle and sun lotion, leaving me to cover an inquest into the death of Julie Ward, a young British woman. The victim was an attractive blond white female who had been kidnapped out on safari, held for days by her African captors, in all likelihood gang-raped, then hacked to pieces with a machete and burned on a petrol-soaked bonfire. Despite overwhelming evidence for this, Kenya's police claimed she had committed suicide. The authorities suggested she had climbed an acacia thorn tree, hacked off her own head and limbs, and thrown her dismembered self into a campfire below. They were taken aback when the woman's father, John Ward, questioned their version of events. It was a perfect British newspaper story, especially given the regime's incompetence at managing a cover-up. In court, Chief Justice Mango rolled us in the aisles with his banter. "Who the hell are you?" he demanded of the Wards' family lawyer, Byron Georgiadis, well into the inquest. "Oh," said Mango when Byron reminded him. "All whites look alike to me." When we weren't in court, I joined the tabloid hacks on their death knocks, when we pestered poor John Ward for quotes. My salacious reports went down well in London and my hopes soared that I'd get *The Times* string when the correspondent got sacked for taking too many angling trips. In time, this happened and the correspondent retired to write a book he called *Fishing in Africa.*

But my hopes to become the new *Times* man in Nairobi were quickly dashed. I heard that the paper had appointed an old friend of mine named Sam Kiley. Sam had also been born at Nairobi's Mater Misericordia hospital. We had met at Oxford, where he'd run the university's dramatic society. He had toured Africa with his student actors, performing Shakespeare in village squares and slum bus parks. I recalled that as an undergraduate he had dyed his hair green. But in the period between Oxford and Kenya, during which Sam had attended Sandhurst and done a spell in the Gurkhas before taking up journalism, he had lost most of his hair. He shaved off the rest and wore a black turban against the sun, so that he resembled a handsome pirate. I think that all his life he'd wanted to be a movie actor, but although one of his nicknames was "Yul," as in Brynner, he never made it into that world. Being a foreign correspondent was probably the next best thing. He had a whiplike wit and spoke in machine-gun bursts. To me, Sam was Bald Sam. In return he called me Aidey Boy Baby. Or, more unfortunately, "AIDS."

After *The Times* I managed to get a string for the *Time-Life* bureau chief, a white-haired Vietnam veteran. This man kept his head down and filed a story so seldom that I wondered if the magazine's correspondents were advised to think very carefully about telling the editors in New York about Africa's dramas because it might only irritate them. A decade of *Time*'s covers hung in frames on the bureau chief's office walls. The continent of Africa had graced the cover about three times in ten years and I seem to recall one of the stories was about mountain gorillas. I greatly admired the Vietnam vet, whom I recall sitting in a rocking chair smoking marijuana—he'd had to give up the booze after some embarrassing behavior—as he lectured me about my work ethic. When I told him I was going out on a date with a girl he yelled, "A girl? Go out and get some stories, for chrissakes! When I was your age I was chasing stories, not *pussy!*"

In time the Vietnam vet was posted to Istanbul. His replacement was a woman who had previously been a Roman Catholic nun. She kept me on but asked me to work together with a stringer named Cemlyn-Jones. He was a silver-bearded ex-Reuters correspondent, whom we nicknamed "Grumbling Bones." Grumbling Bones never spoke of his past. There was also a photographer who sometimes worked for *Time*. Jo Louw was a South African from Kimberley. He had started out in the sixties photographing the jazz scene in Soweto, then escaped apartheid to arrive in America at the time of the civil rights movement. Years later he had washed up in Nairobi. Jo didn't make a lot of money and I asked him how he lived. "My wife has a chicken farm," he said with a twinkle in his sad eyes. One day over beers we were talking about our favorite news pictures of history and I brought up the photo of Martin Luther King Jr.'s assassination. In the picture, an aide kneels over the dying man on a motel balcony while others point to from where the shot was fired. It's no masterpiece, but I said whoever took it was in the right place at the right time. "That's my picture," Jo said. "You're bullshitting me," I said. No, he went on, he was standing next to King that day in Memphis, Tennessee, April 4, 1968. And here we were, I thought in awe, having a beer in Kenya two decades later.

I used to get roaring drunk with Grumbling Bones, who was an aficionado of Spanish culture and also an Irish republican. When well oiled he held forth about *rizo negro*, went on to bull-fighting, and finished the evening by singing Irish freedom songs. Late one night he said to me, "What the fuck are you wasting time for on a magazine like this? Go and do something that's fun, full of passion, don't piss your life away on a weekly fucking magazine."

The Bunker was in a ghastly concrete tower that rose above the exhaust and slum-fire smog of downtown Nairobi. The lift didn't have a thirteenth floor so the one I exited claimed to be the four-teenth. Up on the wall next to the door hung a plaque of the agency's ticker-tape logo and a portrait of the founder, the Baron

Julius Reuter. The Bunker became my base for the better part of my twenties. Entering for the first time I observed a scene of bedlam. Two women sat in front of big typewriters, humming hymns, reciting the Gospels with loud amens.

Passing deeper into the room, I found reporters with their feet up on desks, swearing and groaning over the din of chattering machines. Curtains of green text on screens shimmered in the gloom. A stench of chemicals and greasy food hung in the air. A large black-and-white photo of a policeman whipping a crowd of children hung on the wall. A man sat in the corner twiddling the knob on a big radio, monitoring broadcasts in African vernaculars.

A photographer shambled out of his darkroom. His name was Hos Maina and he had a fearful bruise on his forehead, slurred his speech, and fumbled as he handled his camera or tried to roll a print onto the barrel transmitter. He looked like a drunkard. "Car crash," I was later told. "Brain damage." I advanced on through to the far corner of the office to a glass cubicle. Inside, a big map of the region hung on the wall. It was an expanse of green and sandy yellow, most of it quite empty. The pink lines of frontiers were arbitrarily straight, drawn by men from all over Europe who had met a century before to carve up the continent with pencils and rulers. On the desk was a photo of a woman and two girls and also a cartoon of the type sold in kiosks in the city's slums. In grotesque detail, the drawing depicted what was described in the caption:

IF A DOG BITES A MAN THAT'S NOT NEWS
BUT IF A MAN BITES A DOG THAT'S NEWS

Behind the desk, with his feet up on it, was a man shouting into a telephone. He was handsome and swarthy, with a shaggy black haircut in the style of a seventies footballer, large sensuous lips, and great arms and shoulders that he kept shrugging in crablike gestures. His name was Jonathan.

He was the Welsh son of a wartime Spitfire hero and economics professor, George Clayton. After the London School of Economics he had started out on a local paper writing about cats stuck up trees and when he finally scored his post at Reuters nothing had ever made him so happy.

Jonathan was an excellent journalist and my mentor in the trade. I first met him at a Nairobi nightclub called Lips. Three sheets to the wind, he had his arms out wide and seemed to be buying the entire bar a beer. I asked for his card. A few days later we met at the Delamere Terrace. It was at the end of the dry season, when jacarandas scatter their purple blossoms along University Way. "Drinking in excess doesn't make you sexier," said a notice above the bar. "Or richer," I read, "or more sophisticated." Friday-night drinkers milled around: Kenya Cowboys, businessmen, hacks, whores, and tourists in pith helmets. "Just drunk," the notice concluded.

"But look laddie, the story in this place ..." Jonathan said to me, squinting cross-eyed over a bottle of Tusker. He shrugged and made curious circular gestures with his hands. "... Africa!" he roared. "It's wide open for a beach bum like you. You're young! You're hungry!"

He stopped, looked around in surprise. Almost as if he was pinning a medal to my chest, then and there, he awarded me a string.

"Dream job, my lad. What you want to do is get out there, to where there's nothing but warm beer and smelly pussy, and bring us back some *real* stories."

He painted my destiny for me. What he wanted was to have me cover the huge zones on the African map that were under rebel control. There was no way of doing it except to be there for long periods. Remote and pulverized by war, these areas were almost entirely cut off from the outside world, and lacked twentieth-century gizmos like phones or telexes. To travel into those places was to enter a topsy-turvy universe, where the warriors, who could be Maoists by day or naked aboriginals who followed witch doctors and prophets by night, were armed to the teeth with Cold War weaponry.

"See, I can't lose a staffer on full pay for more than a few days. Out of the question, unreasonable. I need all the help I've got in the office ... All hands on deck ... No, no. no," Jonathan tutted. He pointed at me like Lord Kitchener.

"But you, I need a beach bum, backpacker like you, lad. You're young and hungry, won't bleat about working too hard. You're a man who actually likes the shit holes of Africa. Nobody would miss you—except perhaps your Mama ... ?"

Jonathan came to his rhetorical climax. His arms helicopter-ing, he painted before me the flashing lights and billboard of my future. My eyes watered at the prospect. I sensed Jonathan's motives from the start. He knew he could pay me chicken feed. If I got my legs blown off, he and Reuters could legally wash their hands of me. But in return I'd get to cover areas few reporters ever had the privilege to report on.

"You have fun, but make me look good," he said. We shook on it then and there.

Jonathan adored a good story. "Make it sing, lad," he'd say, shrug-ging his arms pincerlike, his hands brushing an imaginary key-board. "Make it sexy ... but always pass it by a second pair of eyes," he'd say, "before you push the titty that transmits your finely crafted copy to the World Desk." And news loved Jonathan. "Never a bor-ing story," he said. "Only a boring correspondent." It was uncanny, but wherever he went, war, famine, pestilence, and death never straggled far behind. He was like a lightning conductor for the hor-rors that were to shortly chug out of the telex day and night.

In those later ordeals, I'll never know how Jonathan stayed

sane, or where he got the strength to go on. Perhaps he genuinely blew off steam by drinking rivers of booze in seedy African bars. I saw him cry when he sang the great Welsh song "Why is there such sadness in those dark eyes, Oh my Myfanwy?" When I picture Jonathan it is with a huge smile and tears gushing down ruddy cheeks.

At Reuters headquarters the great veterans of news admired Jonathan because he was a foreign correspondent of the old school, while some gray new corporate types whispered that he was a bit of a cowboy when it came to management. From my point of view it was among his best qualities. He was clever at screwing cash out of the company accountants so that his stringers got paid better and went on more news trips to the field. His team adored him. I grew to know him as a rare creature on this earth, a truly good man.

Baron Reuter was a German who, in 1840s Britain, launched a daily dispatch of homing pigeons with bourse reports tied to their feet in little silk purses. He invented the modern idea of news, that the winner is he who delivers information widely, accurately, and first. After pigeons came the railway, then undersea telegraph cables, telephones, and finally satellite communications and the Internet.

Africa has been a dateline since Pliny the Elder made his much quoted observation *Ex Africa Semper Aliquid Novi:* Out of Africa always comes something new. Strange tales, great wealth, endless conflict. Among the first wars Reuters ever covered occurred in Africa. In 1867, a correspondent journeyed with General Napier on the expedition into the mountains of Abyssinia to defeat the Emperor Theodore and sack his fort with its priceless library at Magdala. The expeditionary force was composed of a column of men, mules, elephants, even a railway constructed across the Red Sea plains on to the site of the fabled city of Adulis. Among the biggest Reuters scoops of all time came out of Africa too, with the relief of Mafeking during the Boer War. Queen Victoria herself famously demanded to see the telegram that conveyed the news, which the correspondent had smuggled out to the nearest cable office in a train driver's sandwich. Africa was the perfect Reuters dateline. "War correspondents must be up and doing on the clash of arms," wrote Angus Hamilton, who returned to London, sick, to see his doctor after the Boxer crisis when he heard of a bloody setback for British troops in Somaliland in 1901. "So, with the possibility of an immediate departure before me, I preferred an interview with Baron H. de Reuter to that with my medical man. The Managing Director of that wonderful news service received me without delay, and before many minutes passed arrangements were completed for my journey to the scene of the hostilities."

Africa had been big news in the past. In the nineteenth century, together with correspondents' reports there were explorers' accounts of "discovering" the great mountains, lakes, and rivers of darkest Africa's interior. What preoccupied the minds of Victorian audiences when they read about eastern Africa was the abolition of the Arab slave trade, not a thirst for imperial conquest. For this reason, the Christian explorer David Livingstone was a hugely popular figure. When he went missing, the foreign correspondent H. M. Stanley—who had also covered Napier's expedition against Abyssinia's emperor—was paid to go and look for him. Their meeting on Lake Tanganyika is among the most celebrated news scoops of all time.

A century later, Africa was rarely considered worthy of much attention. Editorial interest in foreign news had been declining for years across the board. The wags used to say that as far as a Western editor was concerned, the death of a single white American equaled five Israelis, fifty Bosnian Muslims, or fifty thousand Africans.

Coverage did not even begin to do justice to the myriad stories in the vastness of Africa. It takes longer to fly from Cairo to Cape Town than it does to fly from Cairo to London. But Jonathan asked me to imagine an editor on a newspaper in the West. He regarded Africa almost as a single country, not as a continent of nearly sixty states with hundreds of languages.

"Most *mzungus* don't even know Angola or Gabon are countries," Buchi had complained in Dar es Salaam. "They probably think they're wild animals, you know, with horns and spots that you photograph in game parks."

When Liberian strongman Samuel Doe met Ronald Reagan at the White House, the American president asked the Washington press corps to welcome "Chairman Mo."

Important stories could be ignored simply because they were too complicated. The ones that made the headlines were often the ones that were easier to understand: blacks against whites in apartheid South Africa; tall Tutsis against short Hutus in Rwanda— although even then some hacks called them Hutsis and Tutus. News in sub-Sahara was like a tree that fell in the forest. It might pass unheard. Or it might take weeks to reach our ears. And when we wrote the story, some town taken by rebels, or an epidemic, or a gold mine collapse, our reports were often lost on the wire, which chugged out all the news from the rest of the world. Jonathan told me that there was only one sure way of selling a story from Africa to an editor. It was what is called in the trade "color": a quirky opening vignette, a twist of pathos, the exotic or the bizarre.

Yet Africa was made for news photography. I tried my hand at this and got coaching from a Reuters man sent out from London. "You asked me what makes a picture," he said to me. "It's the three K's, mate. That's Kids, Kittens, and Kunts." Another time he held my negatives up to the light critically. "Remember this, mate," he said. "The way a good news picture is framed is like the best kind of sex: upright—and tight."

Reuters transmitted word of President Abraham Lincoln's assassination to London in a breathtaking twelve days in the era before the laying of the first transatlantic telegraph cable. By the

1990s the world desk in Fleet Street measured our timings against our rivals in seconds.

You broke a big story with a flash, when six bells pinged out on the telex:

******Lincoln dead—official.

Details were amplified at breakneck pace in the following seconds and minutes with bulletins, then urgents and expanded leads, weaving in quotes and facts and analysis. You came in at every possible phase and angle on the news, ending with an overnight look at the day ahead.

"Then?"

"Then we nip out for a pint," said Jonathan.

Next day, or when a story finally died away, the news desk would broadcast how well we had done, showing our beats and losses depending on the time we got the news out:

Lincoln shot at theatre ... Reuters 0858 GMT, Associated Press 0920, Agence France Presse 0909.

They also told us how a report had "played," or how many times newspapers used a Reuters story in preference to those by the competition.

Our performance was scrutinized at "morning prayers," a daily conference of top editors in Fleet Street. When we scored well, a congratulatory message from the bosses known as a herogram tinkled over the service wire. If we lagged on a story the teleprinter spat out a nasty message, known as a "Bollockogram" in the journalist's language of cablese:

pronairobi exnewsdesk. why uu unfile? agencies have king of lesotho abdicating. what yr plans? rgds jmc

Reuters covered absolutely everything that might take place in our regional beat of thirteen African countries. The agency made its profits from financial news. It traditionally lost money covering wars and disasters, though it had been these stories that had won the agency its prestige: the Franco-Prussian War, the May 1900 relief of Mafeking in the Boer War, the two world wars, the end of empire and the collapse of the Berlin Wall. For all of us, the bang-bang assignments were considered a reward after spells of shining our bottoms on office chairs while grafting over dull business copy. And the bureau file, which on any given day might include updates on local stock exchange reports, football results, money exchange rates, tea auctions, the safari rally, a conference of travel agents, engineering tenders, rows between the IMF and finance ministries, arrivals and departures of the pope, and dignitaries on state visits.

On duty, we rotated the task of being "copy taster," or sitting in the "slot." This meant you kept a watch on the flow of copy in and out of the bureau. Sloppily written stories were telexed or dictated via the stringers based in all corners of our patch. This all had to be rewritten, complete with snappy lead and well-crafted body, before sending off to the news desk.

"If you want to be good, it's not all about hogging the glory, but about giving it away," Jonathan lectured.

"You may as well learn right away that it's turning sows' ears into silk purses, and giving some wanker in the field the byline even if he doesn't deserve it."

I liked being copy taster, because I could farm out the crap I didn't want to deal with myself to some other mug who wasn't skiving off duty in the newsroom. Since whoever got fifteen hundred words of turgid French from Madagascar was bound to be nursing a hangover, chatting to a lover on the phone, or downing a plate of burgers and chips, known as "buggers and chimps," they'd inevitably put up some resistance. But as copy taster you were the boss. In the slot seat, perched on my revolving ergonomic chair in front of the blinking curtain of on-screen text, I felt like Luke Skywalker taking on the Empire's Death Star.

Reuters aspired to be fast, accurate, and objective, but the really admirable fact about working for the company in those days was also that it was the agency of record: it put out a story because it had happened, not simply due to its effect on the share price. As a result, we had the integrity and power to put on the wire a tragedy in Africa that nobody else had taken any notice of. You heard it from us first, full stop.

When there was a big story, we had to keep filing and filing, nourishing the wire's bottomless appetite. Jonathan referred to this as "feeding the beast." Soon I learned we were on call twenty-four hours, like doctors tending to a sick world. After the lazy days in Dar es Salaam, this came as a rude shock to the system. Reporters from other bureaus would come down to reinforce us when there was a big story and I'd observe them. They were always moving, always awake, like cartilaginous fish. One jiggled his knees furiously under the table and his body shivered as he typed at the keyboard. Another chain-smoking woman used to become very worked up as she rushed to beat a deadline, and once I saw how she, apparently unable to suck enough nicotine into her system, stuffed a whole cigarette into her mouth and chewed up the raw tobacco.

I had to be alert. Every waking hour I was haunted by the fear that I was missing a story. In my sleep I tossed and turned, dreaming of ringing phones and of ticker tape. I felt hunted by time.

Every third weekend I had to be on call in the office, if I wasn't away on assignment. I used to come in after an all-nighter on Ecstasy and Tuskers with my head feeling as if it had been grilled in a microwave. I'd work right through Saturday alone, pass out overnight on the floor of the photographic darkroom, wake up stiff-limbed, and carry on until Sunday night.

From the Reuters windows you could watch regular riots, armed robberies, and necklacings. Once a stray bullet smashed one of our windows. Between the office block and the roundabout on Kenyatta Avenue and Uhuru Avenue was a piece of muddy dead ground where touts washed cars, hustled pedestrians, and sold strings of tribal beads. At lunchtime street evangelists set up an amplifier and yelled sermons. The secretaries at reception, Margaret and Rose, listened to these intently with amens and hallelujahs, but the rest of us ignored the warnings of impending apocalypse.

Some of my family lived in Nairobi when I first arrived back in the city. I put up a tent in my brother Richard's garden and lived in it for several months. I then shared a house with a bohemian Irish artist and a Francophone pilot who regularly brought home different girls scantily dressed in lycra hot pants, micro-minis, or glittering sequinned boob tubes. One day, Julian invited me to move in with him. I had no car and commuted to and from town on stuffed, stereo-blaring *matatu* communal taxis. But now that I had a decent string with Reuters, I could at last afford to pay my own rent. The house on offer with Julian was spectacular. It was also dirt cheap, as it belonged to another correspondent who had been deported, so we went ahead.

Set in a big garden, the house resembled an alpine *schloss*. For this reason, we christened it the Ski Chalet. From the balcony, on a clear day, you could look out across the plains all the way to Mount Kilimanjaro. A man named Celestine scythed the grass by hand. Celestine was a son of one of Kenya's proud farming tribes, but when he first appeared he was so poor he didn't even own a pair of shoes. He told me that a missionary had selected his name when he was baptized. I pictured an Italian father, set down in the eye of Africa and surrounded by vistas of maize, referring to his book of saints' days. In idle moments I wondered what a man with a name derived from the word "heavenly" was doing in the mud, blood, and beer of my world, and if this was mysteriously significant. A string of canonized popes were Celestines. In the fifth century, Saint Celestine I attacked the Pelagian heresy, which held that we are innately good and capable of exercising our free will to avoid sin, rather than being dependent on the grace of God for our redemption. The thirteenth-century ascetic, Celestine V, is the only pope ever to have resigned and he appears at the gates of Hell in Dante's *Inferno*. Over the years, I came to appreciate Celestine as among the most decent and gentle of people and I don't mean to be patronizing when I remember my Kipling and say, "you're a better man than I am."

In case of armed robberies we had a night guard, a Maasai with lop ears, armed with an assegai, who held loud, schizoid arguments with himself all night long. With the house came two mongrels, Cassandra and Ditch, and Figaro, a spayed female cat. At long last I was able to purchase my first car, a battered red machine that I took to be the height of luxury. Friends drifted in and out of the house, staying a night or a few months. Eric was one of them, and he'd pitch in an old jeep with a Klaxon that played sixteen distinct African folk tunes.

I cannot convey adequately how much trouble Julian and I got into. The lies we told women, the drink, the narcotics, the money we squandered on harebrained schemes, the time we wasted enjoying ourselves. We filled the house with trophies from stories, from empty artillery casings to portraits of deposed dictators that stared down from the walls. Stuck up on the kitchen fridge was a photo of Farzad Bazoft, a British stringer executed in Iraq for spying on Saddam's chemical weapons dumps in March 1990. Press IDs, phone cables, cameras, and dirty clothes clogged up the hall. The bookshelves were stacked with Amnesty International reports, dry academic tomes, and well-thumbed war classics.

I discovered Julian was, like Bald Sam, yet another Kenya-born boy from the Mater Misericordia. I sometimes had the existential thought that Julian, Sam, and I had been swapped at birth and that Julian was me, I was Julian, and Sam was somebody else. All of us as the sons of empire had the capacity to live in a state of perpetual nostalgia of the kind I have now, as I write this, thinking back to those days. Julian's whole life in Africa seemed to be about trying to rediscover some idyll of childhood. "Africa is the place of our lost hopes and our broken dreams," he told me. "But I wouldn't want to live anywhere else." His family had moved to South Africa soon after his birth. His parents had separated and his mother became deeply intimate with King Moshoeshoe of Lesotho. This gave Julian an upbringing in the splendor of an African monarch's palace.

We had both rebelled against our backgrounds by flirting with the left. Julian had handed out copies of *Socialist Worker* at Underground train stations as an undergraduate at the London School of Economics. I had once taken the words of Julius Nyerere to heart. But six months back on the ground in Africa had transformed us into skeptics. We were among foreign journalists who knew even less than we did about Africa and so we reckoned we were already old hands in the long grass of the continent. We were both competitive over who knew the most. Half the time I felt that he wanted to have me nearby so that he could keep an eye on me. He had an urge to win everything. He cajoled and bullied his way into your head until he knew you better than you did yourself. Had he not been a correspondent, he would have made a good cult leader. Instead he had a passport supplied with extra pages to make room for the accumulation of colorful visa stamps, from Angola to Zimbabwe. He had a natural nose for the news, or what he called "nooze." He loved the adrenaline, the rush. "And at my back, I always hear," Julian would yell after me as I rushed into work, "Time's winged chariot hurrying near . . ."

Julian's talent was immense. But when he got a scoop he swanned about with his herograms and held forth at dinner, speaking louder than anybody else. Whereas I enjoyed sleeping rough and being on the road, hardship for Julian was a hotel room without a mini-bar or CNN. I was more accomplished at bush craft. I could hot-wire a car. My knowledge of the alphabet soup of obscure guerrilla factions, their ethnic bailiwicks and ideologies, traditional lore and anecdotes handed down from my father and the old colonials—these I reckoned were unmatched among the hack pack. To this Julian responded sententiously, for he was much given to such Wildean comments as "Your mind is like a junk shop stuffed full of curiosities: some of them priceless, others of no value whatsoever."

Soon after I got to Nairobi, TV showed the footage of the solitary figure standing in the path of a tank trying to enter China's Tiananmen Square on June 3, 1989. A few months later, a friend of mine who was present the day East German border guards sledgehammered the first hole through the Berlin Wall at Potsdamerplatz on November 12 brought me back a fragment of crumbly concrete, which from then on I carried with me like a talisman.

We never thought that such distant rebellions could disturb the doldrums that men like our own Kenyan leader, President Daniel arap Moi, had brought to Africa. But in 1989 people began to talk of Africa's "second winds of change"—the first having been the independence from colonialism some three decades before. Overnight, much of what I had learned about African politics at the School of Oriental and African Studies had become as redundant as the Kremlinology of those who wanted to know what was going on in Moscow after the Soviet Union's disintegration. It was time to throw the books away. The lessons were on the streets, where events unfolded at breakneck speed. At the time, we felt greater hope than at any time before. It is hard now to properly evoke the euphoria of that brief season. It was like a huge weight lifting from people's shoulders.

Fear and hopelessness lay like a blanket of poisonous smog on Nairobi. Everybody blamed Moi, but then Moi was omnipresent. Moi's face with its goatlike eyes stared down from every office wall.

He created the annual holiday of Moi Day. There was a Moi international airport, a Moi South Lake Road, a Moi Bridge, a Moi Stadium, a Moi University, and dozens of Moi Schools. Banknotes and coins bore a youthful version of his face. Youths wore Moi T-shirts and women wore *kanga* cloth wraps with his portrait positioned over their bottoms. Moi was the most merchandized brand in Kenya. Moi's supporters behaved as if Moi *was* Kenya. Police cleared traffic off the roads and lined the avenues of Nairobi a half hour before Moi swept past in a motorcade. Several of the vehicles, which numbered thirty or so, were identical Mercedes with smoked glass so that would-be assassins would not know which one Moi was riding in. Moi employed the biggest Washington and London PR firms to promote his image, which was of a man with whom the West could do business. He carried an ivory knobkerrie with a silver tip, but somehow this was less crude than the fly whisks, leopard-skin hats, combat fatigues, or white handkerchiefs of his fellow African leaders. He turned out in expensive suits, always with a buttonhole rose from one his farms. In fact, Moi was the quintessential African dictator. On Monday, the back pages of the newspapers often ran a photo of Moi singing hymns. He gave sermons exhorting Kenyans to avoid greed, but his own wealth was rumored to be fabulous. In the 1980s he was yet another African leader greatly inspired by men like Nicolae Ceaus,escu of Romania and Kim Il Sung of North Korea and after visiting Pyongyang he ordered plans to be drawn up to build an eight-story statue of himself in Nairobi's Uhuru Park. The project was shelved when it was realized that the nation's coffers were empty. He couldn't have cared less for Kenya. Academics compared Moi's regime to nineteenth-century Bonapartism and penned journal articles with titles like "Après Moi, le deluge."

Dictatorship smothered Kenya's vitality. The radio played little great African music and certainly nothing new. A year in, year out favorite of the state broadcasting corporation was Dolly Parton.

The news had no real news, just endless presidential openings or soapbox speeches. There was plenty of opposition to Moi's regime but the dissidents either operated underground or they were locked up and knee-deep in the water dungeons of Nyayo House.

Moi was too clever to start jailing correspondents, but he set his red-shirted party goons on black journalists and used deportation as a threat against the Europeans. It was incredibly effective in shutting up the press corp members who enjoyed living in Nairobi. To me, the danger of expulsion hung over me like the sword of Damocles when I wrote about Kenya. I found the prospect of being exiled from my home and family almost too unbearable to contemplate and at first I had no courage to deal with it. The mood at the end of the 1980s made the decision for me.

In early 1990 Kenya's much-liked foreign minister Robert Ouko was murdered. It sparked a campaign to end Moi's one-party rule, which degenerated into a season of riots in Nairobi. They used to erupt in the slums between home and the Reuters office at the Bunker downtown. We could pop out for a cruise to watch the fighting, get a mouthful of tear gas, file, and then go off to eat crab served with a crisp white wine at the Tamarind restaurant. In the slums we got attacked by all sides. I was with Mo Amin and his cameraman "Mo" Shafi once, driving at speed, when a concrete block thrown by protesters came through the windscreen. A mile down the road the police arrested us at gunpoint. They set about me with an ax handle and opened a gash on my head. I came to in the back of a truck lying next to a rioter who had wet his trousers with fear. At the police cells, Mo Amin told the cops who he was. "The famous Mohamed Amin!" they said, suddenly turning nice and giving us back our shoes. "A very famous man. Let me shake your hand."

All of us at the time felt that the new revolutions would elevate Africa. For the past three decades, the continent had become a nasty, primitive joke in the papers. Just before the Berlin Wall came down the world had been treated to the atavistic rebellion of Alice Lakwena's Holy Spirit Movement in Uganda, which aimed to seize power and rule by the Ten Commandments. The Lakwenas, as they were dubbed, advanced into battle covered in a nut oil they believed would turn bullets to water. They chanted hymns and the James Bond theme—*bo–bo–bo–bom–ti–pom–pom*—threw Coca-Cola bottles, believing them to explode like grenades, and executed anybody found riding bicycles on Sundays. It didn't seem that things could get much worse. But they did. In late 1990 President Samuel Doe of Liberia was captured by the forces of rebel militia chieftain Prince Johnson. One evening, Johnson and his wife held a soireé for friends and journalists to watch a screening of a home snuff movie. This ran highlights of Doe's torture and execution. Johnson was the star of the show, in which he lopped off the deposed president's ears followed by his penis and testicles.

Change was never going to much resemble the Velvet Revolution of Prague or the other events of 1989 across eastern Europe, except perhaps the gun battles that overthrew Romania's Ceauşescu. More often that not, Africans chose war rather than the ballot box to sweep away the old dictatorships.

"What do you need to start a guerrilla war?" my friend Buchizya once asked the Marxist Congolese rebel leader Laurent-Desire Kabila.

"Ten thousand dollars and a satellite phone," replied Kabila. "You use the dollars to recruit enough fighters to raid the local police stations for their guns. The phone you use to call the world's press after the attack."

Men like Kabila underscored how in Africa it was hard to determine the dividing line between the political and the criminal. "With that box of matches, with our necklace, we shall liberate this country," Winnie Mandela had declared in 1986, unleashing the ANC's campaign to murder rivals in public. A woman guerrilla, of my age, told me how when you necklaced a man—poured gas into a tire, slung it around his neck, and set fire to it—the heat was so great the skull popped like an egg in a microwave oven. We saw such things not only in Soweto but across all of sub-Saharan Africa.

The point was that everybody hoped that the violence would come in a brief spasm, for a greater good. And so, for me, it was both a thrill and a privilege to see Africans whipping up the second winds of change. The first wind had blown awry and now they had another chance. Every day, I looked for reasons to be optimistic for Africa. Peace might break out; a good rain fall; bumper harvests roll in; world coffee prices revive; the IMF disburse a loan; elections be scheduled; an economy record a GDP growth of 7 percent. Any journalist who cared about Africa wanted to believe in a brighter future. One's creative challenge was not only to dwell on the despair but to find a way forward with hopeful stories. In the summer of 1990, I was given an assignment to write about the popular reaction of Africans to the World Cup. When striker Roger Milla pushed Cameroon's Indomitable Lions into the World Cup quarterfinals with a 2–0 win against Colombia, I wrote about how people were dancing all over Africa that day. Africa had climbed up another level in the eyes of its own sons and daughters. Africans wanted more. It didn't matter that Cameroon was knocked out in the next game. As the 1990s dawned, people felt that at last, in so many ways and after so many false starts, Africa had a bright future ahead. "The appetite grows as you eat," Milla said after the Colombia match.

I remember the holiday atmosphere of the early nineties: the Nairobi democracy riots, the season of protests across the continent, the cities that fell like dominoes as the superpowers' proxy wars climaxed. Julian came back from the riots in Kinshasa and told me the looters had hot-wired a Mercedes in a car showroom and driven it out through the display windows only to crash into a wall directly opposite. They had left behind a graffito, MERCI POUR LA

FETE, on the dealership wall. "Thanks for the party." None of us knew where Africa was heading, but it was incredibly exciting to witness Africans fighting for everything, starting with the right to fill their bellies.

It was also a thrilling place to be a correspondent. Africans thirsted after news of any kind. In Africa, the so-called bush telegraph transmitted news of an event across great distances as if by magic, so that people in the street seemed to know of an event before we did with our satellite communications. They greeted you with a request for what you'd heard in the place you'd just come from. They begged you for your three-day-old newspaper, for a photocopy of a banned magazine, for batteries for their radios, for your pen so that they could take notes as you spoke to them about what was going on in the world. Some apparatchik with power over life and death might say imperiously, "And you are from?" And I'd reply Reuters. He would suddenly look anxious and he'd say, "Ah, writers!" As if we had a monopoly on the profession. "Eh! I know you," said a Kenyan politician. "No, no, no. You are not a journalist?" "I am indeed, sir." "No, no, no. You are a journalist *plus plus!*" By that he meant spy, a tool of the Western world, the CIA, MI6, Mossad, or South Africa's BOSS. Senior dissidents courted you. Waiters and taxi drivers, a constant source of information for any foreign correspondent, did you big favors. One felt far more important than in fact one was in reality. In the first couple of years I went along with it, happy to be on the road.

Moroni, Grande Comore, August 1989 After picking up my open-top Mini Moke at the airport on the island of Grande Comore, I had to stop on the road to bang my head against the steering wheel. Was I really being paid to do this? Flown to a story on an Indian

Ocean archipelago, where Bob Denard, veteran freebooter of all Africa, and his gang of mercenaries had seized power. Told not to worry about the money, just to toss off reams of color on Denard, who had invaded Katanga (on a bicycle); who was condemned to death in absentia for an attempted coup in Benin; who had been a hired gun in Angola, Chad, and Côte d'Ivoire. The copy virtually wrote itself—even Denard knew that: he had sold the rights to his life story to Hollywood. In the Comoros, Denard had invaded, installed a new president, and stayed on with his white mates, "*les affreux,* the terrible ones," to head a praetorian guard. On this archipelago, where they cultivated plantations of ylang-ylang perfume, he had found contentment, converted to Islam, and married a local girl. "I hate the traffic of Paris," he said once, "but I adore the scent of ylang-ylang." In 1989, his French and apartheid South African paymasters refused to renew his contract to protect president Ahmed Abdallah. Soon afterward, the president was shot dead. Denard was in the room at the time of the murder, but when he stood trial later in France, he was acquited, claiming he did not pull the trigger. The rumor I heard at the time was that the president had also been gutted from throat to groin like a goat. "Just keep it coming," exclaimed my editors on the news desk. Denard's men, *les soldats perdus,* raced about in jeeps bearing the insignia of a yellow shield and bat with outstretched wings. "Do you know any mercenaries?" I asked the woman at the car hire desk when I picked up my keys. "Yes, I'm married to one," she said. "Don't let him see us talking." I felt like I had walked onto a James Bond movie set and that I should be in a white tuxedo, holding a dry martini. Each morning one of Denard's men, tanned and leathery, would walk his little white poodle along the beach past my hotel room window. Gleefully, I dictated to the copy desk.

Croupiers in the local casino complain that the mercenaries become ferociously drunk STOP I myself saw one slap his revolver on the roulette table when his number failed to come up STOP NEW PARAGRAPH

Three weeks after the coup d'état, the Foreign Legion swooped in on Puma helicopters and expelled Denard. His men demanded "an honorable departure," not to be "slaughtered in the waves like lambs." They left in a South African C-130 loaded with crates of lager. Denard flew home to retirement in France, where the perfume of ylang-ylang would have to come out of a bottle. Before going home I climbed the slopes of the high volcano on Grande Comore with a couple of villagers. As we walked in the cool high altitude, we came upon a carpet of wild strawberries. It could have been a spring day in Europe, except that far below was a tropical scene of palm trees strung along a white beach, and beyond, the turquoise ocean. The beauty made me catch my breath.

Rwanda, October 1990 Is this the front line? It should be a school. The soldiers all appear to be twelve years old. I have no sense of where we are, or who's winning, or why I am here.

I can hear awful, terrifying noises rumbling through the mist of rain from up ahead. It sounds for all the world like an African god who wails and groans with despair at what his people have come to. Is this the front line?

We advance down the road, toward the whooshing sounds. Incoming, outgoing. From up ahead comes a cloud of smoke. It approaches us along the road. The whole column takes cover in a ditch.

"We're not near the front line, but beyond it," I think to myself. "And now we're going to get fucking killed."

A flapping noise grows audible. I see it is an armored car

being driven on its rims, the smoke rising from the burning rubber of shot-out tires. Perched on the turret is a guerrilla with a large pink swimming-pool parasol raised above his head, clutching a bottle of champagne.

At Gabiro, the president's shooting lodge, casualties are all over the place. Retreating government forces have polished off most of the food, including the pet chimpanzees. Rebel boys are pursuing a white rabbit around the swimming pool. The president left behind all his crystal and a very fine cellar. I select a bottle and I drink from it as I trampoline on the leader's bed.

Outside, a female radio correspondent, my friend Catherine Bond, is interviewing a rebel commander. The booze mixed with fear makes me feel deliciously numb. The hillside below us is on fire and a battle is still in progress. The grass is covered with boots, left behind by fleeing peasant boys in the government army who could run faster in bare feet. A *kidogo*, or child soldier, sways after them, swigging from a bottle of claret in one hand and dangling a white rabbit by the ears in the other.

This has to be the biggest story in the world. I say to Catherine:

"This is it. We've arrived. The front line."

Ethiopia, March 1991 An incident famous among journalists occurred in 1991, during the early months of Croatia's desperate war for independence from Belgrade. In the town of Osijiek, Eduardo Flores, a correspondent for the Spanish paper *La Vanguardia* and a follower of the Catholic sect Opus Dei, called his colleagues to his own press conference. At the event, he announced that he could no longer be merely a spectator in the war that pitted Catholic Croatians against the Serb Orthodox-dominated Yugoslav

National Army. From that day onward he, Eduardo Flores, would throw away the pen in order to take up the gun. An International Brigade of some one hundred foreign volunteers was formed. Being a mercenary went to Flores's head and when he migrated from covering the story to becoming the story himself, he didn't like it. In Croatia he was suspected of being behind the murder of a Swiss correspondent. Flores got sucked into the Balkans conflict and who knows what else. Some time later, he was found dead in mysterious circumstances, not on the battlefield but in an apartment on some nameless street.

Flores was a man who crossed the line and became more involved than any of us would ever hope. I often fantasized about crossing the line from being a journalist to being a participant. Yet I always thought that to become an activist would be "unprofessional." All foreigners who have become the groupies of one side or another in Africa come out looking bad when their convictions prove to be naive in the extreme. But after covering a story day in, day out for a time, no correspondent can possibly remain detached— although in order to maintain the ruse that we are impartial we pretend to being as dispassionate as lawyers or doctors—so ours is an imperfect position. And in a war one's sympathies inevitably attach themselves to whichever side one is traveling with. The climax of the Ethiopian civil war was like that for me.

"Remember, lad," Jonathan had nudged me just before dawn at a Nairobi bar we used to hang out in called Buffalo Bill's. "No story is worth dying for." We finished our beers and tottered out of the bar. Jonathan swerved off home and I took a battered taxi out to the airport. In departures I felt suddenly lonely and wanted to call somebody, but it was too early even for Dad's morning cup of tea, and anyway I was drunk, so I just boarded my flight to Khartoum.

At the Acropole I contacted the guerrillas, who smuggled me down the long road south across the Ethiopian frontier. We passed through desert, then mountains. A brown river, the Tekeze, was swollen in angry spate. A guerrilla plunged in with a cable tied around his waist, disappearing into the water. Struggling against the current, he emerged on the far side and tied the cable to a tank, which towed us across as the river roared above the bonnet. On the other side we all danced a jig. I gazed back across the water. I was the only European journalist in rebel-held Ethiopia, and as the waters rose with the first rains of the season I understood that nobody else would be able to follow me. At the same time, my dispatches could be made only by the unreliable means of the guerrillas' own HF radio.

Now that we were across the river my companions, thin little men and women with fuzzy Afro hairstyles and plastic sandals, hailed old comrades in cracked, desert voices. They bumped right shoulders and made soft kissing noises in greeting.

It had taken months of work persuading the rebels to agree to take me into Ethiopia's arid, mountainous north. All the while, I had monitored the rebels' radio, with its burst of AK-47 fire for a signature tune. There were reports of set-piece battles, with fantastic claims of casualties in the tens of thousands, and now Mengistu Haile Mariam's regime, four months after the disintegration of the Soviet Union, was imploding.

A convoy formed, and from then on we moved mainly at night. By dawn, we halted and we rested, with the vehicles camouflaged under the spreading flat branches of a grove of acacia trees or among the rocks of a kopje. At such times I'd read, or talk, or just study the faces of my sleeping fellows.

I already believed that the rebels' cause was worthy, and their story romantic. They were fighting to overthrow a tyrant, Mengistu Haile Mariam. A gang of ten students from Addis Ababa University had taken to the bush sixteen years before. They were inspired by Marx, the Black Panthers, and Orde Wingate, the British guerrilla-warfare expert who had led the World War II invasion against the Italian fascists in Abyssinia and restored the emperor to his throne. Yet they were unable to survive alone in the arid bush and relied on the local shepherds to take them in. In the early days they robbed banks and hit police stations. With the spoils, they were able to equip their peasant recruits. Over time, the gang had swelled into a combined army of a hundred thousand, complete with commando and tank units.

In the meantime, Mengistu had destroyed his nation. He exterminated the aristocracy. The emperor himself had been asphyxiated and stuffed down a pit latrine in his own palace grounds. Mengistu followed this up with the Red Terror, a pogrom in which thousands of students were massacred. He prosecuted war against the Eritrean and Tigrayan separatists with Soviet backing, conscripting hordes of youths, indebting the nation, and feeding the popularity of his enemies. A million perished in the 1984 famine, while Mengistu celebrated the revolution's tenth anniversary with planeloads of whiskey and six-hour speeches. The dictator took a famous Mao Tse-tung quotation on popular support for rural rebels to explain a policy of peasant "resettlement" that won the help of the United Nations. "The people are like the sea and the guerrillas are like the fish swimming in that sea. Without the sea there will be no fish. We have to drain the sea." In all, seven hundred thousand peasants were forcibly transported to the western jungles around Gambella, where many died of fever and hunger.

Meanwhile the rebels, holed up in mountain trenches for years on end, had engaged in bitter, protracted quibbles over Marxist doctrine. A thirteen-page Maoist document sparked bloody factional fighting between the military groups, mainly highland Christians from Tigray and neighboring Eritrea, while the guerilla leadership was beset by internal purges. Finally, in Eritrea Issayas Afeworki, "he of the Golden Tongue," succeeded in poisoning and shooting his way to supremacy, while the ideologue Meles Zenawi came out on top in neighboring Tigray. In his wisdom, Meles decreed that henceforth he would follow the model of Albania, the last nation on earth that annually reprinted the works of Joseph Stalin.

Meles now slept across from me under a thorn tree. He resembled a young, chubby-faced, butterscotch Lenin, down to the goatee. When I told him so he looked mighty pleased. But in his interviews, Meles had diplomatically dropped his Marxism in favor of his idea of "ethnic democracy," which I enthusiastically attempted to understand.

"We can sleep when we die," Girmay, my guerrilla escort, said every morning when he shook me awake. He was a kid, trying to grow his own Lenin goatee and in constant fear of his superiors. His stock responses to my requests were "it is forbidden," or "it is not your program."

Each time I was allowed to press on down the road, we were ordered to halt in the next village while my guides awaited further orders and kept me under guard. I languished in Axum, where avenues of stone obelisks erected in worship of the sun by pre-Christian kings reminded me once again how ancient are the civilizations of Africa; Adua, where Emperor Menelik inflicted the worst defeat ever suffered by an Italian army; Mekele, where I was imprisoned in a damp house while Marxist-Leninist parades carried on outside. Girmay refused to transmit my dispatches by radio. "It is forbidden," he said worriedly. I behaved well until one day I could tolerate it no longer. I exploded with rage. I would return to Khartoum. The river is still in flood, Girmay told me. "I don't care," I said. I aimed to go via Eritrea, I declared, pointing at a long route across the map. "It is forbidden," said my hosts, who then confined me back in my hut.

Being under house arrest changed little. Every day we ate lentils or *wat,* a hot chile sauce with pancakes of sour *injera* bread. *Injera* is made out of the local *teff* grain and to the uninitiated it tastes like an old spongy kitchen mop, but this improves over time. Starting with the fingers of my right hand, the smell of hot chile sauce spread over my body. When I shat I got used to the ring of fire and even my turds looked like hot chile *wat.*

Girmay forbade me to move out of the compound, even to take walks. I sat about writing my notes, compiling as detailed a history of the guerrilla army as possible. I read my *Don Juan.* We wore ourselves out playing with my pack of cards that had naked ladies on them. I childishly took the piss out of those I saw as my captors by peppering my talk with insults wedged quickly inside normal sentences, thus: "Erm, Girmay, *youbloodyfuckingcunt,* pass the salt, please." Girmay, whose English was not so good, would do as I asked and then look confused as I collapsed giggling. Gradually, I withdrew to my bed, losing the wish even to behave childishly.

Poor Girmay, it wasn't his fault. To cheer me up, he organized sightseeing trips—the Challenge Road, which the rebels had constructed by hand, grain distributions, political meetings. It was a magical land of sheer-sided inselbergs known as *ambas,* of hanging valleys, oxen, holy men, golden, beehive-shaped stooks of straw, and attractive peasants with braided biblical hairstyles and crucifixes tattooed on their foreheads.

Edward Gibbon, in his *Decline and Fall of the Roman Empire,* wrote that the Ethiopians had "slept a thousand years, forgetful of the world by whom they were forgotten." To me it seemed that if indeed they had ever woken up, they had stayed awake long enough only to pick up a copy of *Das Kapital,* which had promptly helped them doze off again. Rebel territory was a land held in a time warp, where revolutionary utopia and medievalism coexisted. A peasant, swathed in white cotton robes, might chant slogans before murals of Marx, Lenin, and Engels, then go off to kiss the cross of a monk. Isolated by war, the beauty of the place had been left intact because it was a free-fire zone. In unique ways, conflict had stunted what our era calls progress, which goes hand in hand with the obliteration of both indigenous culture and the environment.

At Axum, Girmay took me to see the town's obelisks, erected

by kings who had worshiped the sun and moon. I met hermits who dwelled in caves and visited a monastery, reached by being winched up a cliff in a basket, where priests read illuminated parchment Bibles. In this part of Ethiopia, there are said to be more churches and monasteries per square mile than anywhere else in the world.

We talked often about visiting Lalibela, the cluster of churches hewn out of solid rock, which was still in a contested area. Legend says the churches were built on God's orders, to create a pilgrimage site closer to home than the Holy Land. The Lord allowed King Lalibela an allotted span to finish the task. The masons failed to meet the divine deadline, however, so at the eleventh hour angels descended from heaven to complete the job.

Farther down the road I visited a monastery in a hidden valley enclosed on three sides by cliffs, which could be reached only by climbing down a precipice, using hand- and footholds worn away over centuries. At first one heard only the wind blowing through the canyons, but as we descended a chorus of voices became audible. Groups of young initiate monks came into view, perched on ledges and under trees, chanting the scriptures. Beneath overhanging rocks dripping with moisture, there was a shrine to Saints Peter and Paul, guarded by a hermit in a yellow cloak who insisted on washing my feet. The monastery itself was perched on a shelf halfway down a sheer rockface so that it seemed to hang suspended in midair, swathed in mist above a knot of trees strung with lianas and lichens.

The monks never left the valley. On death, they were entombed in holes carved into the solid cliff face. They grew all their own food in tidy fields where herds grazed and collected water from a trickle that dripped from the rocks. They welcomed us with *injera* bread and *sewa* beer, which they blessed, and they chattered away like rescued castaways. Their madness came as no surprise to me, since they sat out in the burning days and the cold nights, mortifying the flesh and carving the word "God" into the rock thousands of times. One told me a story about a monk from this place who had flown on a magic carpet to convert the Armenians. The holy men were but dimly aware that a war had been going on for thirty years. Sometimes they heard the rumble of distant artillery, saw the horizons light up, or heard an aircraft, but the killing had passed them by. For me, it was as close to utopia as one could get.

It reminded me of Samuel Johnson's *Rasselas,* the story of the Abyssinian prince exiled to the Happy Valley from which it was impossible to escape. "The sages who instructed them, told them of nothing but the miseries of publick life, and described all beyond the mountains as regions of calamity, where discord was always raging, and where man preyed upon man." Rasselas and his restless friends who want to see the world escape the valley for Egypt, where they attempt to pursue their own free will. After reaching no conclusions on how to find personal happiness, they return to their prison. Many times have I felt that, had I been able to, I would willingly have done the same, had I such a place to go back to.

Each day, the BBC news spoke of the coming showdown in Addis Ababa, and speculated on the situation in northern Ethiopia. "Hello!" I yelled at the radio. "I'm here!"

At last, one night we left in a rush, heading south again, until we neared the front line. We slept in trenches where bombardments and infantry charges were being stepped up. We heard bombs down the line and later saw a casualty, his head cracked open like an egg and his lungs sucked out by the shock of a vacuum bomb.

I petulantly demanded to see some proper fighting. "To prove that it's truly taking place." So Girmay and his fellows yomped me out to a mountain pass near Dessie where from behind a rock I watched an ambush on a retreating government column. Our machine guns and rocket-propelled grenades opened up on the lead truck and then the convoy behind that came to a halt. The government conscripts had no fight left in them and they were sitting ducks. The skirmish died down and the fighters hurried Girmay and me down the valley while they got down to looting the bodies and smashed vehicles for booty.

I was curious rather than shocked to see my first dead body on a battlefield. I saw it as a rite of passage on the road to some kind of truth. As a boy I had seen crows pecking out the eyes of dead lambs. I had seen a cow's bloated body in a ditch slithering with eels. At that time for me, the human skeletons scattering the field of an infantry charge were no more shocking than these things. It was only much later that the sunken, scarecrow forms scattered on the cold plains of Ethiopia returned in my mind and by then the memories made me weep with guilt.

As we marched down the valley, we passed a wounded conscript lying on his back alone among some eucalyptus trees. He waved at me. I can still see his liquid eyes. Can we go back, I said. Go back and help him. I had that same feeling that one has passing a tramp on a winter's day on a city street. Nothing more. Our escort refused to stop, and I looked back to see the man's eyes trailing me as we marched off, leaving him behind.

The miserable survivors were pushed in with the other POWs captured as Dessie fell. Twenty thousand of them, all marching in a line. I thought the Tigrayans would be jubilant at seeing the humiliation of their enemies. A band of guerrillas in heavy metal T-shirts—"Disciples of Destruction"—had vanquished on a grand Soviet-trained army with its tanks, ranks, and tinned food. But nobody rejoices at the sight of defeated men, a horde of hungry tramps, without boots or belts to hold their trousers up.

On the road, I found myself thinking of the boy who was, at least in terms of the blood that flowed in his veins, my Ethiopian half brother. I'd rarely considered his existence, having deliberately put him out of my mind when I was the age that he would be now. I'd always believed that thinking of him would be a disloyalty to my

mother. I had only a vague notion of where he lived, and because it
was a complicated story I hadn't told Girmay about the boy. As the
war swept southward toward the gates of Addis Ababa, I grew anxious for his safety. Knowing that I had flesh and blood possibly in
the line of fire in Ethiopia made the war a curiously personal experience. Had I known where to find him I confess that at that time I
would not have had the courage to track him down and meet him
face to face.

In Kombolcha we picked up three bodyguards and scrounged
a 4 x 4 off the local quartermaster. Within five minutes I'd crashed
it into the back of a T-54 tank, punctured the radiator, and limped
back to the depot, where I was allowed to hot-wire a second vehicle.
My bodyguards were hardened brutes. But I remember them cooing over a poster in a bar, which reminded me that they were youths
who had been robbed of their own childhoods. The picture was one
of those paintings of a waif in ragged clothes, with outsized eyes
and a tears trickling down its cheeks. "Miss You," the caption
declared.

At Debre Berhan, I saw a group of guerrillas lead away a man
in government uniform. I was close enough to see the expression on
his face and hear him talking quietly with his captors. Then Girmay
grabbed my elbow and urged me to come away. As we walked off I
looked back to see the guerrillas form a semicircle around the man.
A muffled burst of shots. The man crumpled onto the grass.

"He looted from the people," Girmay explained.

"How did you know?" I asked.

"We know," said Girmay.

We were playing cards with a warrior in a fur cape made out
of the pelt of a rare gelada baboon when we heard the BBC report
that Mengistu had fled. The Americans had secured him asylum in
Harare. Back in Addis Ababa, the survivors of his rump army
fought on. Girmay wanted to celebrate, so we found a local café. It
had a Gaggia espresso machine and men sat about drinking out of

big carafes of *tej*, Ethiopian honey mead alcohol that glowed yellow in the sunlight. On the menu, I observed with bliss, was an item identified as "*Wat* What is Not Hot."

I was swiftly being seduced by Meles. I was impressionable and flattered by being allowed in on the battle plans of a rebel army. When he spoke to me, he had this winning way of offering me a cigarette, then discussing the task that "we" had in the guerrilla struggle, hinting that he meant me as well as his party and forces. In fact, both the Tigrayans and Eritrean People's Liberation Front had a whole set of foreign disciples who hung out in the rebel areas. On a previous assignment I had visited the EPLF base of Orota, a maze of underground bunkers in a rocky hillside, and on the walls of the room where I stayed were pasted the business cards of every left-leaning Western politician I could think of. Inside rebel areas, various other foreigners worked as doctors, or cameramen, or writers of journalistic panegyrics. Their names were legendary, but when I actually encountered a couple of them they struck me as dilettantes who were somewhat at loose ends.

I also fell under the spell of the ascetic, authoritarian code of the fighters. Tigrayans were among the poorest people in the world and they accepted white man's grain in food convoys, but this had not made them indolent beggars. They built roads, fought battles, and devoted themselves to a political ideal with a sense of purpose I had never witnessed in a rich society at peace. How fortunate they were, I thought, to have a purpose and a struggle for which to fight.

By Sendafa, we arrived within artillery range of Addis airport. Under pressure from the Americans, the Tigrayans were holding off the attack, allowing Israel to complete the airlift evacuation of fifteen thousand black African Jews, who had been in Ethiopia since antiquity. I lay on my back in the grass, watching the planes of Operation Gideon take off and land.

As soon as we entered the air base of Debre Zeit, south of Addis, I dropped by the post office and found a working phone at last. On a hunch, I tried the Addis Hilton and was put straight through to Jonathan.

"Oh, there you are, you lazy sod," Jonathan said. "I've been so *bloody* worried about you. Where the hell have you been?"

I started explaining. Jonathan told me to hang on a minute until he got his notebook. Then I jabbered away for two whole hours, pure color.

I was relaxing over the first cold beer for a long time in the bar of the only hotel in Debre Zeit when the guerrillas brought me a British aid worker and his wife. They had been too late to evacuate from the fighting. As they attempted to cross the front line, somebody had opened fire on their car and their little boy had been hit in the spine by a bullet fragment. The rebels ran an effective team of battle paramedics and these were called to patch up the boy, although there was nothing to do but wait for the city to fall. While this was happening, the British couple looked at me suspiciously. I could not think why. In the hotel lavatory, I caught a glimpse of a strange, desperate-looking creature in the mirror. It was the first time I had seen myself for two months. The face was dirty, weather-beaten, hairy, and sunken-cheeked, with staring eyes and cracked lips.

The guerrillas took me to an ammo dump built into a hillside, on the road to the capital. Here we found hundreds of stacked cluster bombs, bullets, and missiles—the gifts of America, the Soviets, Chinese, North Koreans, and Israelis. There was enough weaponry to exterminate the entire population of Ethiopia several times over. I began photographing and we had been in the dump for only a few minutes when there were several detonations among the bunkers on the hillside. They were either booby traps going off or we were under mortar attack. Swiftly, we withdrew on foot to a nearby hill and my guides got on the radio. One of the magazines must have been ignited and the explosions intensified. For a while we watched the fireworks going off. We delayed too long. Without warning, the hillside rumbled and seemed to split open like a volcano, sending a huge ball of fire mushrooming into the sky.

We all scampered away across a field. It had been freshly plowed and the soil stuck to my boots in big clods. I didn't hear a sound except my own breathing, although rockets and bombs were raining down on all sides of me, bursting in plumes of mud and smoke. I arrived at a dry riverbed with steep sides, leaped in, and crouched against the face closest to the blast. Shrapnel bounced off the stones on the opposite bank of the trench. The sky was filled with missiles, moaning and fizzing like Catherine wheels in the air, then slamming into the fields with crashes that made the earth shudder.

I yelled for Girmay. After some minutes he appeared crawling on his belly with the bodyguards. During what seemed like an hour, although it could have been less or more, I chain-smoked and pressed as hard as I could against the dry earth. I am no practicing Christian but I whispered the Lord's Prayer and found it comforting. I had this sense that if I gabbled it again and again, the words would protect me from harm, like a force field. I glanced at one of my guards and saw he was praying too. He was a handsome boy, maybe fifteen. An intimacy had grown between us in recent days because he had followed me everywhere with his rifle, even when I had to take a piss. Since this was one of those movie moments between bouts of action, when the protagonists think they're going to get killed and reveal their true selves to each other, I asked the boy, "Do you believe the angels built the churches at Lalibela?"

The boy frowned quizzically. "*La-li-bel-a,*" I said slowly. He nodded. I flapped my arms, trying to look like an angel, and then mimed the act of hammering a chisel into the stone. He giggled and nodded again.

"Please God," I thought, "if you let me survive I'll go to communion." As dusk closed in the explosions began to die down. There was nothing for it. If we remained here we might be captured by a roving government patrol, or another dump might explode. We girded our loins and made a mad dash back across the field toward the car, which was miraculously untouched, passing the curious sight of peasants standing outside the houses of their burning village with occasional explosions all around them.

Barely had we got back to Debre Zeit when we were told to report to the commanders. They looked gravely at me.

"Do you happen to have a map?" one of them asked, his voice sounding sheepish. "You must understand that we are afraid of getting lost in the Addis Ababa." Few of them had ever been to the capital. If they had, they had defected in the mid-seventies, more than fifteen years before. All I had to offer was the map out of my old backpacker's copy of *Africa on a Shoestring*. It identified only a few street names, restaurants, and cheap hotels. But they were delighted at this and sent it off to be enlarged on a commandeered photocopier, then distributed to all tank and infantry officers in the advance units.

Girmay and I were assigned to a T-54 tank that joined a column rumbling north. We chugged back up past the hillside ammunition dump, which now glowed in the darkness. As dawn broke we entered the suburbs of Addis Ababa. From all around us came the swishing sound of small-arms fire, while farther up ahead were the thunderous booms of heavy guns firing toward the city center.

Several times, the armored column got into a traffic jam. I'd use these halts to jump off our tank and knock on the nearest door with a demand to use the phone. I reached Jonathan, who by this time had barricaded himself behind his room furniture at the Hilton. "We've done it, lad!" He kept yelling. "It's brilliant! It's brilliant!" The bullets were flying up there. He'd had a line open to London for twelve solid hours and now he was filing to the world desk like a maniac. I was having the time of my life. Khartoum to Addis Ababa had been an eleven-hundred-mile, two-month odyssey. My report

was splashed in the London *Evening Standard:* I SEE THE REBELS
TAKE ADDIS ABABA, REUTERS MAN RIDES IN WITH TANK CONVOY.

We reached the city center. Rumbling up the hill in a cloud of
black diesel smoke I saw the statue of Lenin with ropes attached,
already being pulled down by a crowd. Meles, the rebel leader, was
making his gesture to anybody in the outside world who might fear
he was a true Marxist. Our tank climbed farther up the hill, the
caterpillar tracks churning up tarmac, then scaled the two flights of
steps to the palace gates and smashed through them. It was a wonderful moment. We all whooped with joy at the sheer excitement.

Girmay and I jumped off the tank, followed by our teenage
bodyguards. With a triumphant roar the guerrillas waved and sped
off across the grounds toward the din of fighting. Desperate skirmishes were still in progress among the outbuildings and wooded
palace grounds. Mo Amin and his second soundman John Mathai
jogged past. I stood there, trembling and gazing into the thick
smoke swirling among the trees. And at that second I saw emerge
out of the haze a raffish figure, dressed in shades, a red beret, and
bomber jacket.

I thought he might be a Libyan. His skin was much too light
for a Tigrayan. When he took off his shades I saw his dark, fanatic's
eyes. The deeply creased forehead created an air of a man who had
suffered troubles in his life. This impression altered the next second, when he gathered his face into a smile. His eyes glittered and
his expression became one of brotherly warmth. When he spoke,
what startled me was his posh accent. Unmistakably, he had been
educated at one of England's finest schools.

"I'm on my way to Mengistu's office. Would you like to join
me?" We shook hands.

"My name is Carlos Mavroleon."

Impressive, I thought. But utterly unconvincing. It sounded
like the alias of a mercenary. The man carried a small Hi-8 video
camera of a type used at the time for home movies. It was as if he

wanted to give the impression of being a journalist, and it was an unconvincing act.

The real object of his interest was the AK-47s my escort guards carried. Carlos exclaimed with delight. He grabbed one out of an astonished rebel's hands, stripped the rifle down, then expertly reassembled it.

We sauntered toward the palace. I smoked one of his Marlboro Reds and it was the best damn cigarette I'd ever tasted. I had important questions to ask Carlos, but he engaged in breezy small talk. It was as if our encounter in the aftermath of battle on the grounds of a bloodthirsty dictator's palace was entirely normal. Who was he? Why didn't he ask where I came from? I sensed that it would be rude to tell him.

In the garden we found a lion Mengistu had left in a cage, starving to death. Inside it was quiet and, after several minutes, we found Mengistu's private study. On the mantelpiece was a photo of Mengistu posing with a grinning, backslapping Fidel Castro. On his private desk were a bust of Lenin and Bob Marley's LP *Exodus,* which he had evidently been listening to in the hour before he had fled the country. His high-backed red leather chairs were decorated with the hammer and sickle. On the bookshelf were a few Marxist-Leninist tomes, together with titles such as *The Kings and Queens of England,* ex libris the emperor. This had once been Haile Selassie's inner sanctum, and in sixteen years of occupancy Mengistu hadn't bothered to clean out his predecessor's kit.

I watched as Carlos systematically looted the dictator's private effects, cramming trophies into his pockets. A Lenin-statue paperweight, some medals, an ornate lighter inscribed by North Korea's Kim Il Sung. He rifled Mengistu's desk drawers, pulling out papers, condoms, and sundry unidentifiable drugs.

Years later, I see Carlos as a restless romantic, who had lived both on a grand scale in the wide-open spaces of the world and, tragically, on the point of a needle. He was both a saint and a damned soul. He had lived many lives. The son of a Greek shipping tycoon and a Mexican mother, he had a cosseted early childhood in wedding-cake Chelsea houses and the Mediterranean. He went to Eton, but toyed with Communism, shoplifting, and finally absconded from school. At sixteen, he ran away and overlanded through Turkey, Iran, and Afghanistan, until he came to the Swat Valley in Pakistan. Carlos lived for the next two years among the opium poppy fields of the Golden Crescent, learned Pashto, and got hooked on heroin. By the time he returned home, ill with tuberculosis, he had read the Koran and converted to Islam, taking the Muslim name Karimullah, "Blessed of Allah." At the same time he began to drop LSD and attended a London comprehensive school. He won a place at Harvard and when he arrived in Wall Street it was the 1980s. Carlos liked drugs and he already had money. But by themselves drugs and money did not hold enough interest. Soviet forces had invaded Afghanistan at the end of 1979 to end a power struggle within the Marxist ruling party. In New York, Carlos became a fund-raiser for the mujahideen anti-Soviet resistance. He tired of observing the war from the sidelines and in the mid-eighties he abandoned Wall Street, traveled to Peshawar, and persuaded the mujahideen group Hezb-i-Islami to allow him to join up as a volunteer. He rose to become a platoon commander and proved to be a courageous fighter, mainly on hit and run attacks and ambushes on convoys. I am told there is video footage of Carlos at an antiaircraft gun, yelling at his men to open fire as a Soviet helicopter gunship circles in the sky.

His aim in life was to exist by the strength of his personality, not the privilege of his upbringing. Afghanistan became the Soviets' Vietnam; Kabul's rulers fell into disarray, while government forces deserted. At last, in 1989, the Soviets withdrew. Carlos had discovered a purpose in Afghanistan. In war he had discovered a thrill that displaced heroin. Since his soldiering days were over, it was natural that he became a journalist. At the age of thirty-two,

Carlos picked up a TV camera. A year after Afghanistan on that day when we had our encounter in Emperor Haile Selassie's palace grounds, his pictures were still amateur. He had no idea about the news business and he didn't yet have any buyers for the footage he had carelessly risked his life to obtain. Carlos was once again testing his strength of personality and displayed the best attributes of a stringer: he had flown four thousand miles without an assignment, immersed himself in a story about which he knew nothing, and would struggle until he improved his camerawork and got a good story.

I had redrafted the perfect first paragraphs of my report on Ethiopia countless times on the advance toward Addis Ababa. Now that it was time for me to file, I barely was able to write a word. I was paralyzed. At the Hilton, Jonathan and a team of Reuters correspondents debriefed me for color, quotes, and analysis, tapped it all out on their laptops as I spoke, and shot it immediately down the open phone line to London.

After we had done I went down to the hotel lobby. Girmay and my escort were there, waiting to claim me. First, we went out to buy offal at a butchery and returned to the palace grounds to feed the starving palace lion. For two nights, we slept together in a heap with the other rebels ("Don't call us rebels now," said Girmay, "we won.") at the palace and ate sloppy lentils and *injera* bread. We related stories of our journey and congratulated one another on having made it. I told Girmay about my half brother and after a couple of phone calls we quickly discovered that he was safe. I was resolved still not to see him and disturb his life and mine, though the urge to do so was almost irresistible.

Girmay nudged me and said with a pleased look, "Even I look you like my brother." Yet we both sensed a barrier had suddenly gone up between us, ending the intimacy we had won in times of danger. I realized our visit to the Hilton had in some way polluted our friendship. Apart from Carlos, to me the journalists appeared

both cynical and vulgar in comparison to Girmay and his bright-
eyed comrades, but the hacks were my own kind. I clung on until
the commanders said it was time for me to go. Girmay and the
bodyguards hugged me. Then we parted and the fantasy evapo-
rated. I had dreamed of being a guerrilla, sleeping rough on the
open road, fighting for freedom for my lost brother, with a pen
rather than with a gun.

Back at the Hilton, I took a room and bathed, turning the
water dark brown. For two months I hadn't even taken my trousers
off. The story had died, so I joined the other hacks down at the
pool. In a flash, back among my peers, I forgot my devotion to the
guerrilla path. The airport had reopened and Addis Ababa's status
as love capital of Africa was restored. On the pool sun beds were
sprawled a crew of blond air stewardesses from Lufthansa, dubbed
by hacks the Let-Us-Fuck-Them-Hard-And-Not-Say-Anything
girls.

Addis Ababa means "new flower." Emperor Menelik founded
the city in the nineteenth century so that his wife could take the
hot spring waters. It was situated at high altitude, the climate was
cold and rainy, and it was so poor that the shanty hovels crept up to
the gates of the imperial palaces and the Hilton compound. Right
now I did not let the poverty worry me and enjoyed the euphoria
instead. I met men drinking at the bar who had just walked out of a
prison they had called "End of My World," where they had languished for eight years until that very day. I met Bald Sam and saw
he was happy. He'd heard the British SAS special forces were in
town, protecting the British embassy. "Cool aid," he exclaimed.

The clubs were full. In brisk order I had a one-night stand
with a German communist, who had supported the Mengistu
regime, then found myself in the free-world bed of an American
embassy honey trap. I let her ply me with Chianti at Castelli's, the
best restaurant in Africa, while she milked me for notes on the
rebels. Then she took me back to her apartment, which had a walk-

in fridge stocked with duty-free food, and fucked my brains out. Life this good, I thought, should be forbidden.

A week later another ammunition dump exploded inside the city. This time it was definitely a booby trap. Together with Bald Sam and Richard Dowden, a London newspaperman, we borrowed a Nigerian diplomat's car and raced toward the site from the west, along the Bole road, but on the way I saw a white Mercedes take the turn and head directly due south toward the dump. Traveling in the vehicle was the BBC correspondent Michael Buerk, who had shot the famous Ethiopian famine TV footage with Mo Amin. Also in the car were Buerk's cameraman Nick "Shirts" Hughes, the soundman John Mathai, and Colin, a BBC East Africa correspondent.

As we got close, the dumpsite erupted again. First we saw the sky blanch an incandescent white. Our car lurched off its front wheels, even as we drove toward the explosion. Tin roofs flew off houses in the force. Then the wave of sound arrived but I suppose the noise was too loud, because I forget if there was a bang. A red mushroom cloud billowed hundreds of feet in the air. Out of this coiled missiles trailing smoke wakes far into the sky. Then debris began to rain down, little fragments battering the car roof. Bigger stuff fell close by. I saw a chunk of concrete the size of a car fall from the heavens onto a house off to one side of the road. We yelled obscenities as Richard, who was at the wheel, maneuvered the car into a three-point turn and accelerated back to where we had come from.

At the Hilton, the piped music played in the lobby. I pressed the lift button. The doors opened and there was Buerk, shivering, his shirt caked in blood. I stepped inside, and as we began going up Buerk told me that one of the big explosions had hurled Mo's soundman, John, through the air and into a wall, killing him instantly. The rest had survived only because they happened to be standing behind another wall that had sheltered them from the blast. We trooped down to the hospital. Mo's left arm was mashed up like strawberry jam and he needed blood. "As if Mo hasn't had enough blood out of us already," somebody joked.

When we loaded John's body onto the plane that also evacuated the injured Mo, I saw he didn't have a mark on him. He appeared to be asleep. I pictured his body flying through the air in the white heat of the explosion, his arms flapping, like an angel, so vulnerable, before hitting the wall. He was a portent of what was to happen repeatedly in the coming years, a warning of the costs of testing the gods. I thought about what Jonathan had said, that no story is worth dying for. He had been sincere enough, but it was meaningless. Editors said it on the phone to cover themselves. Hacks chanted it in turn, and then drove into a gun battle. Perhaps it was a voodoo mantra to ward off the evil eye. This job was all about risking your life to get the pictures, the scoop, or the cover shot. If you *nearly* died for a story, editors sent you herograms. Your friends slapped you on the back. You were in the chips. You got an award. You got none of these if you were safe and ten miles down the road. Everybody parroted the line "no story is worth dying for," I think, to confer an air of professionalism on the job of combat journalism. The paradox was that you could plan all you wanted, but in the end, if you wanted to win the scoop, you had to be first on the spot where the news was happening. Often, there was no way of knowing how dangerous a place was until you got there.

Julian had said, "You're only as good as your last story."

"It's a numbers game, simple arithmetic," Jonathan warned me before I'd come to Ethiopia. It went in one ear and out the other. I had beginner's luck, which is really the ignorance of losing. I was swept up and borne along by a life more exciting than I had hitherto known. I had no cause for which to die. I did hope to make the world a better place, but never thought it might cost me my sanity, legs, or life. I wasn't interested in money. I think it was really rather like the games of "chicken" we had played at school. See how long one could stand as the thrown knife blade came ever closer step by step. I look back now and see how foolishly I longed for scars to make me wise.

After John Mathai was killed I returned to walk among the exploded ammunition dumps. Like a vulture, I could always find some bones to pick clean in the aftermath of a tragedy out of which to concoct a pathetic story. I trod carefully among a congregation of bodies so incinerated that their carbonated, fused forms resembled obsidian. High in the branches of a eucalyptus tree I caught a glimpse of an angel: a severed hand, with the fingers spread in benediction. I remembered the promise I had made in the dry riverbed. Early next morning I climbed Entoto, the mountain above Addis Ababa, and entered a round church where monks chanted in a cloud of incense and twirled their wandlike dancing sticks around them. The service was in Ge'ez, the antique language of the Ethiopian Orthodox Church. Despite this I somehow understood the sacrament. The priest approached with a crucifix for me to kiss. I bowed for his blessing.

My parents at their wedding celebration with the Sultan,
Zingibar, Southern Arabia, January 1951

The Zanzibar Chest

My mother knew the story of Peter Davey. When she married my father in Aden, before they left for Africa, they lived briefly at the house Davey and my father had shared as bachelors. It had polished black floors and cool, arched verandas in the colony's Arab quarter of Sheikh Othman. When my mother used to sit at her dressing table, she would see out of the corner of her eye in the mirror something flicker behind her. She sensed a presence in the room but when she turned around there was nobody there. She asked my father about this, and he smiled.

"It's Peter. Do you mind?"

My mother said no, she didn't.

After I discovered Davey's diaries in the Zanzibar chest at home on the Indian Ocean coast, my mother insisted that I take all of them away with me. At first I did nothing with them because I was in no state of mind to do so. I flew to London. After Africa, England was neutral territory. That summer, I was moving from place to place. I wound up in a concrete council block in London, in a flat that belonged to the junkie friend of a friend who had been dispatched to a rehab clinic to get off heroin. Outside it was summer, but the streets to me were like a Sniper Alley, dead open ground observed by empty, smashed windows. I ventured out on corner shop forays and retreated for days indoors, living off orange lentils, potatoes sprouting eyes, curling cheddar, and Heinz baked beans. In the days, foul-mouthed youths held shouting matches up and down the gray walkways that stank of urine on the other side of my door, which they kicked as they passed. Late at night the phone rang and I'd pick up to listen to slurred, pleading voices. On the radio I heard Portishead: "*Oh these sour times . . .*"

I lay on the junkie's unwashed sheets, missing Africa. I'd wake in the dead of night with a jolt and believe I was home, when the noises of crickets and frogs cease and the silence is intense. I slept. I woke. I looked around me. I saw my life in a suit-case on the floor. All that had passed was like a half-remembered dream. I thought perhaps if I concentrated enough on the idea, I could persuade myself that this mattress, this gray morning, the groan of a passing black London cab, these things were the only real things in my life. Perhaps I had always been here, in this place.

A memorial service was held at London's St. Paul's Cathedral on October 8, 1997, for all those recently deceased who had been awarded the Most Excellent Order of the Companion of St. Michael and St. George. Dad called his CMG medal, awarded for his services in agriculture in the Aden Protectorates, "Call Me God." His other medals, the OBE and the MBE, had been the "Other Buggers' Efforts" and "My own Bloody Effort."

My mother flew in from Kenya especially for the service and on that day I went along with her and my aunts Beryl and Mary. The three of them wore hats, with nets and alarming appendages. Aunt Mary, whose eyes always made me feel Dad was looking at me, cupped her hand and whispered down the pew, "I feel his pres-ence here now." The sermon was about the fight of good over evil. The blessing encouraged us to "Go forth into the world in peace; be of good courage; hold fast that which is good; render to no man evil for evil; strengthen the fainthearted; support the weak; help the afflicted; honor all men; love and serve the Lord."

As we emerged and descended the steps afterward, bells pealing, the City was bathed in sunshine. Mother took in the scene happily.

"I remember all this was bombed flat in the Blitz," she said.

Every conversation in London for me at that time was like chalk dragged squeaking down a blackboard. The day after the memorial service I walked with my mother in Holland Park.

"You used to have such an interesting life. But I think you've become really quite boring," she said to me. I felt this was her way of trying to persuade me to return to Africa. She was a widow and she wanted me home.

My mother could say the most surprising things, producing them seemingly out of the blue. She did this now, as we walked and I complained how completely at a loss I felt about what I should do next.

"Don't be so silly. You found the copies of Peter Davey's diaries, didn't you? Do you think Dad didn't mean for that to happen? Of course he did. It's as if he's sending you a 'zing-zing' message." "Zing-zing" was an expression she had adopted in the 1970s. It was her code for telepathic good vibes.

"Davey's is the story you must follow," she went on. "Davey's the golden thread leading you through all of this. Why not go to Aden? Follow the story?"

The next night my father appeared in my dreams. He did not resemble the European man I had known. He had become an elderly Muslim. He nodded at me but did not speak. His beard and his hair were dyed henna red. He was an al-Hajj, one who has completed his duty of holy pilgrimage.

* * *

My mother and I had encouraged Dad to write his memoirs. When I read his draft I was dismayed by the way he had restricted himself to the part he had played in the twentieth century's history of tropical agriculture: irrigation schemes, the vagaries of sesame, hybrids of cotton, the diseases of camels, and surveys of wild grasses. There were no lurid details, no confessions, no dwelling on the tragedies of which he had suffered his share. I shook my head.

"This will never do." I pestered him with questions about his long life before I was born. After Oxford he might have become a tea planter in Ceylon, or a rancher in Australia, or a cocoa manager in the Gold Coast.

"Why did you choose East Africa?...Tell me what went through your head as you rode on that steam train at night on the railway to Lake Victoria your first time, with the sparks from the engine flying over you?... Put some juice and color into it. Tell me about your love affairs!"

Dad chuckled and gently waved me away. He was a doer rather than a writer. Well into his eighties he threw himself into his work with the physical vigor of a man four decades younger, trekking off into the bush for weeks at a time. I picture him in his straw hat, sitting with a circle of rheumy-eyed old warriors under an acacia tree, transfixed by a debate on cattle and rain, while a pot of tea brews on the campfire. Some of what he did endured but most of it withered or was swept aside or destroyed by politics. He lived long enough to be philosophical about the ups and downs and said, "One day honey, one day an onion. Or some say life is like a cucumber: one day it's in your hand, the next it's up your arse."

I recall asking him as a boy, "Dad, where are all your friends?" I thought he should have them constantly around him, as I did at school.

"I'm afraid that they're all dead," he said.

"Why?" I asked. Dad counted off his fingers one by one. They had come down with blackwater fever and a battery of other tropical diseases. They got shot or chopped to pieces. They crashed in cars and aircraft, or committed suicide, or were gored by buffalo or elephant, while not a few had expired from quantities of gin and tobacco.

Dad rarely spoke about Peter Davey. When I asked about him he usually buried the subject within a few sentences. I remember how with his big hands he smoothed his now snow-white hair down onto his scalp, looked off into the distance, and grunted like an old bull.

From the day Dad saved Peter Davey's diaries from being lost in the hill country of southern Arabia in April 1947, they had accompanied the family through all its bad and good fortunes. After my parents married in Aden in 1951, the diaries were put in a tin trunk and went with them to East Africa. They moved with the family in the story I have already told here. First they were kept at En'neker-aka, my father's old farm on the slopes of Mount Kenya. They were snatched from there before the fires of the British colonial forces consumed the empty cedar house during the Mau Mau rebellion. They were transported to Langaseni, my family's ranch on the slopes of Kilimanjaro, where they remained in safety for seventeen years. When the ranch was expropriated by the government the diaries had to be rescued once more and sent to our new home in Devon, in the southwest of England. It was here as a young boy that I first heard of Davey because my mother told me his diaries were kept locked up in the old black tin trunk that sat in the farm office. In 1980, when my mother was reunited with my father in Africa and Devon was sold, Davey's papers were moved yet again, this time to the beach house on Kenya's coast. By this time I had forgotten all about the diaries' existence. But my mother told me that in the months before his death, Dad had got them all out and sat at his desk on the side veranda of the beach house each day, studying them, page by page.

I photocopied a letter asking for help and sent it out to the two hundred Daveys listed in the phone directory for Sussex, where his family had lived at least up to the 1940s. I drew a blank. Starting with a couple of old addresses my mother gave me, I built up a web of British colonial contacts. I joined the Anglo-Yemeni Society. A woman wrote to say that she wanted to swap notes because she spent her free time traveling the world recording imperial cemetery inscriptions. "It's quite nice to see their names on the page," she said. I spent many enjoyable hours talking to Nigel St. John Groom, a former British political officer who had succeeded Davey soon after his death in the very same places where he had served. Despite his easygoing modesty, Groom was an Arabist and historian of note and he had a meticulously detailed memory of many of the characters I wanted to learn more about. On a string of afternoons, while his kindly wife, Lorna, kept us going with pots of tea, cakes, biscuits, and cucumber sandwiches, Groom spoke of everything from the ancient frankincense trade to the Arabic and English characters in my story and the Aden Protectorates came alive for me in that living room on a leafy London street. I saw Sir Wilfred Thesiger, the great explorer who was the third white man to cross the Empty Quarter. He had known my father—but not Davey—in Arabia and Africa and I visited him at his Chelsea flat. We ate at a restaurant called Foxtrot Oscar on a street corner and when the waiter asked Wilfred what he wanted to drink he said, "What's that sweet brown stuff?" "Coca-Cola, sir." "Yes, that's it." Halfway through lunch Wilfred turned to me and said, "Who did you say you were?"

I was invited to lunch at the Travellers' Club in Pall Mall, where I met veterans of Aden and a sultan. Plenty of British had been in Aden. "Yeah, I was there. 'Orrible place, and full of fuckin'

Arabs," a cabdriver told me one night. In dozens of letters I attempted to track down people from Aden in the thirties and forties who were still alive. I received a handful of replies, in wobbly handwriting. They were modest and apologetic, despite the extraordinary lives they described. "I am old. Hope you can decipher the script!" Another explained that he and his wife could move about only with zimmer frames. "We are not in the pink of health." A third wrote with grim humor about the doctors having to chop out "various offending bits." Yet another telephoned and said, "I haven't much time." I told him hastily that I wanted only an hour or two to pick his brains. He replied that I hadn't understood what I meant. He was surviving off one lung. "I haven't much time."

I flew to Aden, now part of the Republic of Yemen, and checked into the Crescent Hotel at Steamer Point. My first evening, I leaned on the balcony and looked out across the harbor toward the Prince of Wales Pier. This had all been the European Quarter, but now the dwarf replica of Big Ben stood with its hands ripped off. Voices in unison rose from a guttural camel belch to the sustained tenor of an air-raid siren. Muezzin blared from a dozen minarets strung with fairy lights. Their calls to prayer echoed from the barren slopes of the jebel behind. Aden was my namesake. My parents gave me the name Aidan in tribute to the place because they had fallen in love here (though my godfather Judge Birkett Rudd insisted on the Irish spelling). Aden had been a central scene in my imperial family history. My ancestors all knew Aden. I imagined the generations of them who had passed through on P&Os, mail boats, and battleships: *Amapoora, Victoria,* the *Rawalpindi,* the *Usambara . . .*

I found a taxi driver named Omar lounging about on the pier. He had spent much of his life in the British merchant navy before returning to Aden in middle age. He lived in a private hell, he told me, because the land was dry. He was too old to return to the sea, and he couldn't get a drink anywhere. When I asked Omar to show me around, his trip down memory lane turned out to be a tour of bars emptied long ago. It was all oddly familiar.

"This was the Union Club," said Omar, his Kipling trooper's voice trailing off almost into a sob. I had heard all about it already. In the Great War, Grandpa had fought in Aden against the Ottomans. He recalled "frightening moonlit compass marches among the high sand dunes and thorny scrub inland, probing Turkish defenses for something to demolish ... A battle every Saturday, return to quarters, attend any necessary funerals, and then try to get to Aden and dine at the club." Omar took me back to the Crescent, where Dad and my mother used to dance the rumba. Finally he took me to the site of the Blue Gardenia. It was now a laundry, but in the late fifties and sixties it was here that British soldiers had drunk themselves into a stupor during the Aden "troubles," when they had fought the Arab terrorist groups that brought the colony to the brink of chaos. In 1967, on the day our last soldiers flew away in their Marine helicopters, the British said that the sun had set on the empire.

At independence, Aden became the capital of the People's Republic of South Yemen. The first president was Qahtan Mohamed al-Shaibi, a former protégé of my father in the agricultural department, but he was soon removed, and a succession of coups and assassinations followed. The country became so extreme in its communism that even the Soviet Union became exasperated. For years it was a haven for terrorists, and not only those from the Arab world. Omar took me to the Ching Sing Chinese restaurant near the port. The proprietor told me that after the revolutionary takeover, Carlos the Jackal used to eat here and that his favorite dish was the sweet-and-sour mangrove crab.

With the collapse of communism, the south went bankrupt,

both economically and morally. It united with the northern Republic of Yemen in 1990. But the socialists were reluctant to relinquish power to their new allies and old regional tensions that had existed since long before the British arrived resurfaced. In 1994 civil war broke out, which led to the military defeat of the south and imposition of northern power in all aspects of life in Aden. "Aden used to be the greatest city in the Arab world apart from Cairo," mourned Omar. "Now it is a ghost town." We drove out of Aden to the ruins of the state brewery, recently blown to smithereens by Islamic fundamentalists. Omar explained dolefully that under the socialists alcohol had been allowed, together with miniskirts and go-go dancers. But all that was history now.

As I spoke the museum official sat at his desk, smoking. He was a handsome man with honey-brown skin, a straight nose, and sleek white hair. All the while, he opened and peered into his desk drawers. He whispered commands to juniors, one of whom brought me a glass of black tea. Or he made arabesque doodles on a pad of paper. Then he seized my letters of introduction again, frowned, spluttered, and slapped the pages.

He asked if we could speak in Russian. He had been educated there. I had to disappoint him. I wondered what code of protocol I had violated by the letters, which he now stared at aghast.

"These people are dead! Gone! Since then we have had wars, revolutions, governments! *Revolutsii, voiny, pravitelstva! Istoria!*"

"You're saying I was born too late?"

He grunted, now scribbling at his doodle. It had taken the form of a dagger.

"Perhaps. And their grandsons are not interested. But you?"

He paused to study me over the smudged bowls of his glasses.

I must have looked harmless but I found myself tongue-tied when I tried to explain why I was truly here. He then waved me off. I was free to go where I pleased. He gave me names of other officials I might find along the road, whom I determined there and then to avoid like the plague.

We fell silent. I drank my tea as he scribbled. When I rose to leave, I saw his arabesque doodle had undergone a metamorphosis; it was now a machine gun.

I exited through a hall of carved stone from ancient cities that had flourished on the desert's margins before the reign of Solomon. Men then had believed their world was permanent, but all that remained of their laws and religion were these columns of Himyaritic and crescent moons, bulls and clashing ibex etched into stone. Alabaster funerary heads with eyes of lapis lazuli watched me go. In the Holy Koran is an epitaph for these ancients, who in their pride ignored Allah. *And they wronged themselves, so we made them as but tales, and we tore them utterly to pieces.* I was after a story that I feared might have sunk into the sands within the span of only the generation since the British had left.

The entry in Davey's diary for November 10, 1938, presented me with an unsettling paradox—he recorded meeting my father off his ship that afternoon at the Prince of Wales Pier. In the diary, both Davey and my father are younger than I am as I write this, but the meeting that day took place more than six decades ago and both men are now dead.

In the photographs Davey is a handsome Anglo-Saxon, blond, square-faced, with a powerful athletic body. He was a good sportsman and his school records describe him as having "a most dangerous swerve" on the rugby field. On the flight to Aden I had read my father's words that Davey was "a most likable man." Davey was his best friend at the time—possibly the best friend he'd ever had. I heard many other opinions about Davey. He was thoughtful. He could look particularly contemplative when he smoked a pipe. He was generous and brave. One man told me Davey was arrogant and short-tempered. Another claimed that he had been a fool. In Aden I met a Yemeni who told me Davey was a special man. "If you closed your eyes when Davey was speaking Arabic," the Yemeni said, "he spoke it so well that you would have to believe it was a Bedu from the desert . . ."

Peter Christmas Davey spoke Arabic well because Arabia was his home. His early life was spent on Perim, a waterless volcanic island in the Strait of Tears, the Bab al Mendeb, where the Red Sea narrows to a sixteen-mile pinch before opening out to meet the Gulf of Aden. Today it is a desolate spot: the haunt of Somali pirates and feral cats. Flocks of birds migrating to Africa on the Aziab wind that blows from Russia in the autumn then return north on the springtime Kharif, a rolling poisonous blast of heat and gray sandstorms. Davey's father was a manager on this remote outpost in its last years as a coal bunkering station that rivaled Aden as a place for ships to refuel. Perim had been in British hands since Napoleon had invaded Egypt. On the death of Davey's father in 1936, the island station was abandoned.

But Davey never forgot the exotic world beyond the station's cordon, the wicker furniture and the cricket matches played against passing ships' teams. He remembered Arab fishermen and pearl divers, teak dhows with lateen sails passing with cargoes of goats, dried shark, mangrove poles, French guns, and whiskey. Mecca-bound pilgrims disembarked at False Bay to be washed and dusted against tick typhus. There were picnics on the beach and moonlight swims, when the boy saw the lambent flashes of phosphorescence dancing on the waves, which the Arabs said were the sparkles of mermaid necklaces that vanished if you tried to pluck them from the ocean.

While his father stayed on the island, Peter and his brothers moved back to England with their mother so that they could go to school. They lived in Burgess Hill, a tame English village hidden from the sea and the chalk cliffs of the Seven Sisters by the dramatic sweep of the Sussex Downs.

Davey commenced his diary on October 6, 1932. He was a month off his eighteenth birthday and about to leave school, on the eve of his departure for Arabia. He wrote in the young man's slang of the time, of flicks, topping sports matches, grand yarns, and being so fit he could "push a house down." In these years he was dedicated to his diary. His hand was copperplate neat. He pasted in photographic snaps and his entries were like letters, describing the life of an English youth overseas in the 1930s. He took the train from Calais to Marseilles. The night before his ship the *Maboja* sailed for Aden, he stepped out to explore the old port, a maze of alleys ponging of cabbage and sour wine. He rounded a corner, hearing scratchy jazz coming from the Bar des Anges Noires. Inside, Nervis gangsters in red sashes propped up the bar. In the peculiar schoolboy French only the English know, he asked where one might see "un flick." Minutes later he found himself in a darkened room. The silent film had him rooted to his seat. After fifteen minutes, the tape flapped off the end of its spool, the lights went up, and the horrified young man paid up and ran for his life.

East of the Straits of Messina, the deck games and fancy dress parties started. Peter appeared as a gaucho, a chimney sweep, or a schoolboy. He posed in photos with sunbathers on deck, or after picking up a pith helmet at Port Said. The gossip was all about Mrs. Bailey, a woman married to an Indian army officer, who seduced a young man, barely a schoolboy. For the duration of the voyage, everybody knew her as the Bengal Tigress. The moment she stepped ashore in Bombay, she would become plain Mrs. Bailey again, and the husband would be none the wiser. The *Maboja* churned on south down the Red Sea, passing the island of Perim. On his first night in Aden Davey attended a party as a devil and met his American employer, a man named Klauder, dressed as Queen Victoria.

Davey's first job under Klauder was in the hides and skins trade. He learned how to select and grade skins in warehouses where the rawhides were stacked, hard, flat, and stinking of dried blood and salt, as Yemenis bellowed, urged, and pointed. Bargaining was done by grasping a trader's hand and covering it with a white handkerchief. Then one clasped the other man's fingers, each one signifying a price, until a deal was struck. Klauder was a drunk and he was going bust. So Davey moved on to whatever he could turn his hand to. He did some freelance journalism, cabling dispatches to the *Times* on Mussolini's invasion of Abyssinia. Or he was a guide for ships' passengers briefly in port, whisking them around Aden's sights. When the British governor learned that Davey was fluent in Arabic, he enrolled him as his aide-de-camp. Davey changed into dapper whites and handled protocol at Government House. His charges were the sultans from the Protectorates, who came down to Aden to pick up their annual stipends of guns and bags of silver dollars. Off the ships he met imperial officials and VIPs, like Sir Geoffrey Archer, former governor in Sudan, Uganda, and Somaliland, where he had smashed the Mad Mullah's rebellious dervishes. Davey wrote of Archer:

"When I talk to him I experience the feeling one gets when one walks out of a very stuffy room full of tobacco smoke into the open air and is greeted by a heavy buffeting wind, which pushes one back a step but which exhilarates and invigorates."

From my hotel in Aden, I could see inland to the black and rugged hills. Davey had sat in his bungalow in Crater each evening, looking at the same view, reading the works of desert explorers and filling his head with romantic notions. When at last he was told he could visit the hill protectorate of Dhala, he prepared for the trip feverishly. Come the morning of his departure he cranked the metal handle of his box Ford motorcar so hard he rubbed the skin clean off his hands.

In 1939 Davey finally won a position as Political Officer, thanks to his skill in Arabic. His new role, to broker peace between the feuding tribes so that some sort of development could begin, meant that he and my father were to spend a great deal of their time together over the next eight years. The foundation of their great friendship was that they accompanied each other on long trips across the Protectorates, suffering hardships, danger, and revelations together. At the start, they shared a common sense of purpose, that theirs was a mission to replace barbarism with civilization. Lord Belhaven, one of their contemporaries in Aden, believed that "if we did not make peace among these people sunk in hopeless anarchy, the only peace in the land would be the peace of death." In time, their ideas would change.

An hour's drive east of Aden is a river delta called Abyan. In the rainy season, a wall of red water roars down the dusty riverbed. The flash flood carries with it uprooted trees, rocks and soil, rubbish, fish, and sometimes the bloated corpse of a cow or a human, the whole lot of it as wide as the Nile and thundering down toward the ocean. Most of Abyan was a howling desert when my father and Davey first rode up in 1939. The floods passed uselessly down to the sea, leaving little behind for the delta's inhabitants except fevers bred in puddles of water. Abyan's clan feuds were over who among the tribes should harness the floods to irrigate their farms. But the quarrels had become impossibly tangled and complicated. One chieftain had a remembrancer, whose sole job was to recall if such-and-such a man was friend or foe and, if so, what was his debt in blood. Nobody, in fact, could properly remember why or when the first shot had been fired. And nobody among the British knew what to do about it. In the fat political file on Abyan held at the British Secretariat in Aden was a note that observed, "There is no way in which any of the disputes can be settled, until everyone in the district is dead."

I picture the scene of Davey and my father riding up on their horses to an Abyan village of mud towers. A line of warriors armed with silver-banded rifles is standing before them, chanting. Their indigo torsos glisten. A man shoulders his gun and puts a shot inches above my father's scalp in ceremonial greeting. Later, as night falls, I see my father and Peter sitting there. There are black tents beneath the stars and the horses are tethered at the edge of the light of the fire.

I had been invited to Abyan by Ahmed al-Fadhli, the son of the sultan who had presided over my parents' wedding. After the British abandoned Aden in 1967, Ahmed and his family had been forced to flee to Saudi Arabia. For a while they had fought a guerrilla war against the communist government in Aden, but this ran out of steam. In 1990, north and south Yemen had united to become a single republic and the new government in the highland capital of Sana'a had invited Ahmed and the other sultans' families home again. His accommodation in Abyan was a pleasant caravan, equipped with air-conditioning and surrounded by banana groves and the grass huts of his family's former slaves, now his friends and neighbors. I used to sit on the steps of the caravan in the cool of evening and watch the life around me. In the background was the thump-thump of irrigation pumps. Children with jet hair and brown bodies, as sleek as otters, swam in the water tanks. Ahmed's solitary horse, a delicate Arab gray called Saleh, grazed on the sward outside the peasant huts. On weekends, the son of the sultan came to stay and spoke to me about his schemes to help southern Yemen recover from the revolutionary years.

"I'm going to establish a newspaper," Ahmed said one day. "Would you like to be the editor?" I said that I would, if the idea ever got off the ground. On another day Ahmed announced, "I'm going to build a railway from Aden to Sana'a! What do you think?" I said from what I knew it was hard to make money out of railways these days.

When I met new people in Abyan with Ahmed, I produced from my leather satchel a selection of old photographs and passed them around in the hope that they would help bring back memories. I had the bundle of papers from the Zanzibar chest with me and I would read aloud from these. The survivors I tracked down treated my sentimental heart gently, by singing the praises of my father and showing me the dams and canals he had ordered built. Over glasses of sweet black tea they would reminisce.

"Hartley is still here. We know what he has done."

An old man who had been one of the sultan's former slaves told me my father had worked alongside the laborers. To prove it, he took me to a dam works and showed me what he claimed were my father's fingerprints in the cement. They showed me a canal they said was named Harteli. It was even marked on the map. One day, we were out driving among the farms, my portly host Ahmed behind the wheel, me in the passenger seat, various others in the back. Suddenly Ahmed slowed to point excitedly out of the window.

"You see that? See, see that?"

I looked out at the fields, the mud-tower houses like termite colonies and the hills beyond. I could not think what I was supposed to be seeing.

"Dwarf Cavendish!"

I puzzled over this for a moment. All I could think of was a stunted aristocrat. Ahmed beamed, while I smiled dumbly back.

"Bananas!" he said.

"Dwarf Cavendish bananas. It was your father who introduced them. Before, there were no bananas! But now, we have the sweetest bananas in the whole of the Middle East!"

"You should taste our papaya," chipped in a man in the back-seat. "And our grapefruits," he added.

Ahmed recalled how hundreds of farmers had taken part in building a succession of great sand barriers that would divert the floodwaters leading off from the wadi and into the fields. By and by the rains arrived in the highlands and the flood came in a roar. The first spate crashed against the first barrier with such force that it looked as if it would sweep it away. My father, standing on top of the dike, saw a spout of water shoot up in a geyser from its base. The story went that the sultan's *naib* saved the day. He drew his sword and in one stroke decapitated a working ox. He then commanded a slave to take the head, dive into the water upstream from the barrier, and plug the hole with it—and this, mysteriously, succeeded.

After that, the Arabs nicknamed my father Wet Foot. They said that wherever he walked, water followed him. I decided that remembering he had a "wet foot" was a good epitaph for Dad. His achievements could be observed in the flow of water, orchards of fruit trees, a canal named after him. Later at a farmer's house we sat talking. Little children peeked at me wide-eyed from behind a curtain leading to the woman's side of the house.

"It is not about politics, you understand?" said Ahmed. "It is people."

In the 1950s and '60s, long staple cotton from Abyan fetched some of the highest prices in the world market and made its people rich. Production and the market collapsed after the revolution. My friends in Abyan said it was their ardent hope that the British would return to help them revive the agriculture of the delta and, as part of their efforts, they decided to take me to meet all the top local officials. On one occasion I was even filmed by state TV meeting the local governor. I must have looked like a poor ambassador for Britain in my dusty jeans and sandals. Another day, my friends took me to see a man they called "the sheikh" in the delta's seaside village of Zingibar.

"You must meet the sheikh," said one of my friends. "But don't ask him too many questions." I asked why ever not. My friend looked anxious.

"Like the rest of us, the sheikh lived in Saudi Arabia after the revolution. He grew up there, but then he went to Afghanistan to fight the Russians. I think you know the story, yes? While over there, he acquired some strange ideas. I'm afraid we are a little scared of him."

The sheikh was my age, tall and aristocratic, and he dressed in the Saudi style. I greeted him and held out my hand. He did not shake it and spoke to my friend who introduced me, gesturing for us to sit down on a sofa. He sat on the other side of the room, on another sofa. I wanted to ask him about his years in Afghanistan, but did not get a chance to do this. At one end of the room was a TV with the volume turned up loud, broadcasting a Middle Eastern channel. The sheikh stole occasional glances at me, but otherwise he avoided eye contact. I sensed that he was uncomfortable, almost as if he were in physical pain. Glasses of tea were passed around and we slurped this while watching a news item about a suicide bombing in Tel Aviv. After an hour of this, the sheikh rose, said something to my friend, put on a smile, and walked out of the room. My friend leaned close to me.

"The sheikh is very happy. It is good. Very happy."

He didn't seem happy. As we left I got the sense that the sheikh had his pained look because he could barely bring himself to sit in the same room with me, a Christian foreigner. As a "sheikh," however, he simply could not refuse to show a visitor hospitality.

* * *

My grandmother, in the months before she died in her nineties, recovered memories of her youth in startling detail. It might be a fragment of music she had heard played one afternoon, or a stained-glass window she'd stood beneath in a church as a girl in Esher. She'd be hunched, tiny, and shrunken in her chair, clutching my hand, tartan rug over her knees, tick-tock from the ship's clock on the mantelpiece, sucking a chocolate, faintly humming a single note, when her liquid green eyes brightened for an instant and ... we are entering the doors of a splendid hotel in Monte Carlo and a man says to her: "Mademoiselle, you have dropped your handker-chief. Allow me ..."

And that's how it was with the survivors I met in Abyan. I'd sit with them talking for a few hours, wading through the synaptic junk of sixty years. Suddenly, their faces would light up as something came back to them. Encounters that had been stored away like old negatives in an attic were revealed with the clarity of new, glossy photographic prints. I heard entire conversations quoted back to me. But the recollections were not entirely what I'd hoped for.

"Ah, your father. He was always on a horse and used to wear these things," said one old man, performing a curious curtsey.

"Leather chaps?" I asked, drawing a blank stare. I tried a different approach.

"And you are sure his name was Hartley?"

"Arsey?" returned the old man, unable to pronounce the word. "I knew no Arsey. His name was Davey."

I used to join the Yemenis in chewing the vegetable amphetamine qat. These sessions would begin after lunch, when the men of the village gathered in a host's large reception hall. Every one of them carried a rifle, which he left leaning against the wall outside. "Englishmen carry umbrellas," said my Abyan friend Ahmed, reflecting a charming yet possibly outdated view of the former colonial rulers, "just in the same way that Yemeni men carry Kalashnikovs." During the Hour of Solomon, when the qat drug made men withdraw into thought and calm, I would sit back to read Davey's diaries. For hours each afternoon I let myself become lost in the neatly written pages, the photographs of young men in baggy shorts, bare-chested tribesmen with the eyes of hawks and raven hair, maps in crayon and ink, sketches of tribal artifacts, a stingray's tail, ibex, and ancient hieroglyphics.

When I asked my Arab hosts about him they exclaimed, "Ah! Davey!" A story would follow: always the same story. The old men roared about him for hours. Once they all leaped up and began acting out scenes silently, like mummers, with their daggers drawn and their guns raised, while their grandsons looked up at them wide-eyed.

Davey will always be young in my eyes, in pursuit of adventure and with a clear sense of duty. He is a man I envy. He skips lightly among the rocks as the bandits' bullets splash all about him. He rejoices in the strength of his body, his knowledge of language, and his ability to survive in the desert. At first, his diaries are a maze of names and places and customs and notes on everything from Bedu dialect to cipher codes. Only as I progressed down the road in Yemen did they gain meaning. I began to sense that themes from past and present were playing alongside each other, as in a musical refrain. I shared his intimate thoughts, the loneliness of his life. The immediacy of his entries, describing events that day in the place where I now sat all those years later, gave me an intense sensation of physical proximity. Below one entry I found a fingerprint smudged in ink. I opened another page written in a desert camp. From along the spine fell grains of sand. It was as if, for a moment, I was at Davey's shoulder as he wrote by the light of the fire in the desert and imagining the scratch of his pen across the page made my spine tingle. I began to believe that Davey could have been my friend as well as my father's. I felt that he might have understood me. I believe now that I began to see far more in the diaries than the sum of what was written in the words themselves.

I read how Davey and my father, with their Government Guards, rode out east of Aden along the desolate shore where the rollers foamed up the legs of their horses. At dusk they halted at a lone hut on stilts where they joined a party of fishermen around a driftwood fire.

> One of the men gave us a letter from an Englishman who asks the finder to pass it onto his wife. The letter had been placed in a bottle and tossed overboard from a ship in the Gulf of Aden. Unfortunately we were unable to decipher either the sender's name, or to whom it was addressed. It is not clear that the wife lives in Aden, or even when the bottle was thrown into the sea . . .

They curled up under sheepskin coats to sleep on the cool sand. It was a black moon with a clear sky. They woke long before dawn when the dome of the stars had rolled over to new constellations. Voices carried in from where the fishermen were already casting their nets. The sea was on fire with phosphorescence as stingrays and sharks trailed comets of light through the waters. Before leaving the coastal plain the Arab Government Guards dismounted and tossed rocks onto each of a string of cairns, cursing at each stop. The rocks marked where a giant pagan king had been ridden down after Khalif Ali, the Sword of Islam, had defeated his army. Each cairn represented the stride of Ali's horse, and the last, much bigger one was where the giant king was cut down. They passed a shallow well producing sweet water. Beyond that lay a grove of acacia with jasmine-scented blossoms droning with honeybees, like a plum orchard in spring. From there they trekked up a pass between desolate volcanoes. Black lava tinkled like porcelain beneath the animals' tread. The sun rose and they walked until it was too hot, then unsaddled and tethered the horses, brewed tea under an acacia tree, and slept until the shadows lengthened and they could mount to ride some more until dusk.

I felt great contentment when I read Davey's words: "*I have my horse tied up a few yards away and when I am bathed and changed just after sundown and feeling cool and well, I feel that I want no other life than this.*"

*Foreign correspondents and Tigrayan guerrillas invade
Mengistu's inner sanctum during the battle for Addis Ababa,
May 28, 1991. I am the one staring at my feet.*

Feeding the Beast

"When you don't know whether to do something or not," my bureau chief Jonathan once told me over a Tusker, "just think about what you want to look back on when you're an old fart. I always like to think of myself in my rocking chair, blanket across my knees, cup of cocoa next to me, and a little smile comes to my lips when I think of what I did when I was young ..."

Just prior to the commencement of Operation Desert Storm against Iraq in January 1991, I was on assignment in Djibouti. The tourist brochures said it was the *terre des extremes,* but all I saw were packs of Foreign Legionnaires hanging out in the red-light district. I had met a girl named Khadija, a striking Somali with huge black eyes, smooth skin, and shining black hair. She was a rich, educated Francophone. We fell for each other and for a year or so afterward we met in a string of weekend breaks in Khartoum, Cairo, Addis Ababa, Asmara. We drenched ourselves with sweat making love in my hotel room with the TV volume turned up loud. She was perfumed like sandalwood and tasted very sweet. Her face formed into a delicious expression of lust, with her large-lashed eyes closed and her big red lips in an O over her brilliant white teeth, and at the climax CNN burst into life with its "da-da-da-dah-dee-dah" signature. I had to stop and sit down and listen to this. The first bombing sorties had been launched and we were getting live coverage from CNN correspondent Peter Arnett (ex-AP, ex-Vietnam). Peter said, "The skies over Baghdad have been illuminated!" This panting, naked, beautiful girl was waiting for me and Iraq was drowning in a storm of Tomahawk missiles.

On the flight home to Nairobi, when we were diverted to Khartoum to evacuate Americans and Europeans as fears mounted of a pan-Islamic backlash, I knew that as a stringer in the backwaters of Africa I wasn't even going to get near the big story of the Gulf War.

I threw myself into my work. Often I emerged from the Nairobi Bunker to see that it was already two A.M. By that time, sleep was the last thing I wanted. My head was on fire after a liter of coffee and fifteen hours of staring into a VDU screen—gang rapes in the slums, a ravine bus crash with a death toll of sixty, an Antonov bombing in southern Sudan, the rescue of a round-the-world sailor from a remote Seychelles atoll: *the latter day Robinson Crusoe had survived for weeks on coconuts and turtle flesh . . .*

Feeding the beast was not only about stuffing endless morsels of news into the mouth of the Reuters system. The hard work, the competitive pressure, the continual reminders of the world's troubles made me want to go out and drink, fuck, and behave badly. The only place to take the edge off my mood was the Florida 2000. I hurried over broken pavements and smoking dustbins, past snotty-nosed kids clutching glue bottles and men hunched over offal sizzling on fires, and up to the bar entrance. I scaled the stairs toward the muffled beat and entered the red hell of a thousand girls.

Dancers jammed a floor of flashing disco lights. Propped at the bar, heads lolling, clutching beers, groping women, were white aid workers, bush pilots, turbaned Sikh lawyers, and black civil servants in cheap suits. On a raised platform naked black girls swathed in white ostrich feathers danced a disco version of *Swan Lake*. A woman grabbed at me.

"You ever had a black girl?"

"I'm broke."

"Well, what about the shirt off your back?"

Africa may have been in crisis but there was a bull market in the skin trade and for half the press corps this was heaven.

A middle-aged wire reporter was at our normal drinking spot along the bar.

"Life can't get any better than Africa," he said brightly. "No matter how old I get, the girls are always going to be eighteen."

And the girls were beautiful. They didn't like what they did. One girl told me the smell of whites reminded her of chicken feathers in the rain. But I suppose they did it because they were liberated from poverty, female circumcision, beatings, lives of peasant toil and endless childbearing.

"I'll do anything," one said. "I'll fuck you without a condom for more money. Deluxe service ..."

One offered to move in with me at the Ski Chalet for a discounted monthly retainer. They knew what AIDS was but it didn't stop them. They used condoms, visited witch doctors, or believed the epidemic was a Caucasian conspiracy against Africa. We were at ground zero of a global epidemic. But here they were, laughing, drinking, ambushing johns on the way to the loo. The turnover of girls was so high that after six months only half the faces were familiar. Some died off quickly. Others were refugees from regional war zones who moved on when they secured asylum in Europe or America. Every week saw a new intake of fresh teenagers from the rural areas. Only a few days earlier some of these girls had been in black Islamic robes with just their eyes exposed. Now they wore microminis and braided hair. The Somali girls went mad. They chased the dragon in the lavatories, fucked on the dark stairwells, sold themselves in pairs. They didn't care a bit. Some girls had kids at home. They hoped for a better future, not for themselves but for their uninfected children. I swear to God you could smell the AIDS in there. And here was I, careful to avoid dirty hospital needles, afraid when an injured guerrilla had bled over me as I helped load him onto a Red Cross aircraft, who filed news reports by day about the frightening epidemic only to seek the company of prostitutes by night. The truth is, they were congenial company.

"A couple of drinks, then I'll go home," I told myself. Yet I never seemed able to get out before dawn. I walked back to the Bunker, where I lit a cigarette to smother my alcohol breath and reported for my shift.

My emotional life was becoming complicated and rather strange, which was quite usual for a hack who never stayed in one place for more than a fortnight. My foreign-correspondent cousin Donald Wise had married five times during his life and he used to quip that he'd been up the aisle so often that wedding bells reminded him of an alarm clock. Julian, on the other hand, got over the problem of the need for intimacy by sleeping with all the women he could: married, single, black, white, brown, hacks, tourists, aid workers, bored housewives, hitchhikers, guerrilla fighters, the old, the barely legal, rich, poor, the bunny boilers, the leatherettes. He manacled an American TV correspondent up against a set of iron stair banisters. She didn't seem to mind, despite being naked, when he shot a roll of film of her and went out for the rest of the day. Julian fucked anything on legs—and one poor female didn't even have those. Julian was the European version of my Zambian friend Buchizya.

When Bald Sam and I were strolling down a Nairobi city street one day and a car exhaust backfired, we both dived into a ball on the pavement and people looked at us most oddly. The gang of young correspondents was changing in subtle ways. We adopted a grim form of gallows humor that we deployed against each other whenever something nasty happened.

"I've been making notes about what to say at your funeral," Julian told me at one point. After that, whenever we argued he joked that I should behave myself because he had included me in his will. After Julian was released from a fortnight of detention in a Khartoum cell at the hands of the military Islamic fundamentalist government that often punished offenders with floggings, firing squads, and beheadings, some might have advised that he go to a shrink for a debriefing session. All he got was the merciless ribbing of his friends. "Must have been hell," I said. "No pressed shirts or Armani aftershave and starved of Lufthansa girls."

Julian used the violence he witnessed to train his mind. He was a compelling man around whom incidents of every kind crowded, so you could be sure of a story or an adventure of some sort. His sharp mind showed up the dull-witted and his energy left his friends exhausted. He always had the most recently reviewed books or literary magazines in his bag in the most remote, unpleasant places. He browsed for expensive African artifacts on his trips and if he could he arranged his assignments to West Africa so that he flew via European capitals, where he took in the theaters and art galleries. In high spirits he'd impersonate the orangutan king in the Walt Disney *Jungle Book* cartoon and sing: "Now I'm the king of the swingers, the Jungle VIP . . ." What Julian craved most was love.

Julian, Eric, and I purchased our marijuana, known locally as *bhang,* in big brown paper bundles, and there was so much of it we sieved it through the fire grate. We occasionally laid our hands on pharmaceutical cocaine purchased from a dealer named Frodo in one of the sleazy districts of Nairobi. After the embassy cocktail parties, we knew the time of evening had come to descend into the city's sinks and stews. We used to drive into that shabby district of

South C where Frodo, maestro of special effects, waited to introduce us to Señor Escobar. We called ahead to order "one crate of Coca-Cola" and Frodo, scary but charming, was waiting with a five-gram bullet-shaped lozenge, which had passed as easily through customs as it had traveled wrapped in a condom in the alimentary canal of one of Frodo's Nigerian smuggler mules.

But what was this? Why are you on crutches, Frodo?

"Blaadifackin' hell Julie," wailed Frodo. Frodo always called Julian "Julie." Etiquette demanded that we sit down to sample our purchase and Frodo shaved off some of the crystal, chopped out three lines, snorted, then pushed the mirror toward us. If home was the Ski Chalet, Frodo was our instructor on the black diamond run. In the early days he had sold us the real *pulva*, but these days it was more often as not pig laxative mixed with smack. Frodo began his tale.

"I smoke crack for two months in Amsterdam, Julie. Beautiful crack. Then I buy a Jaguar and ship it to Mombasa. Beautiful Jaguar. I pick up the Jaguar in Mombasa. It's evening, huh? I have this beautiful crack, so I say to myself 'Frodo, I have my crack, I have my Jaguar, I have all blaadifackin' night to drive to Nairobi. Let's go!' So I have my crack pipe in one hand and I have one hand on the steering wheel, okay Julie, when a blaadifackin' truck hits me right in front. My beautiful Jaguar, she is finito, my leg, she is finito and you know Julie? Those police bastards are accusing me of being dangerous driver!"

We had a neighbor named Peter, who lived in a circle of tents in a forest of wild African olives. One night I visited his camp where a high-octane party was in progress. Gathered in the mess tent was an eclectic mix of old Africa hands, New York models, travelers,

hacks, and hangers-on. We stood among tables piled with wild animal bones, tribal artifacts, old fashion magazines, and photographs
with a view of the sunset over the Ngong Hills. Other guests
perched on stools around a campfire and nearby warthogs snuffled
in mud holes.

I became aware of a woman on the edge of the campfire light.
I stole glances in her direction to make out the features of her face
in the shadows. I felt strangely elated by her presence and at the
same time curiously fearful that she might vanish before I could get
close to her. The evening progressed, but as the fire burned down to
its embers I remained like a fool unable to go over and talk to the
woman. The next morning, I returned to Peter's camp. The fire was
ash and the woman was gone.

That day, events in the Indian Ocean island of Madagascar
turned violent and it looked to us as if President Didier Ratsiraka
might be toppled in a popular revolution. I headed for the Bunker
and within hours Jonathan had dispatched me on a flight to the
Malagasy capital, Antananarivo. I boarded the aircraft still thinking
about the woman in the firelight. We skimmed down over the Gulf
of Mozambique and I cursed myself. I considered a trip into a war
zone routine stuff but lacked the courage to say hello to a beautiful
woman.

Madagascar was frozen by *ville morte*, or "dead city" protests
against the dictator. Crowds of thousands upon thousands, all in
straw hats in the bright sunshine, gathered in Antananarivo's main
13 May Square to hear speeches and to sing. The days passed and
my regret began to subside, buried under the frenetic news routine.
A week into the assignment, I was sitting among the crowds when
through the lines of people I saw a tall female walking toward me
with a camera. She was too far from me to get to but I could see
immediately that it was the woman in the firelight at Peter's camp.
A little girl selling oranges from a basket followed her about and
clasped her hand. The woman paused every few minutes to snap a

picture, took the little girl's hand again, and walked on through the crowd.

Splashed on the front page of the *Madagascar Tribune* next day was a picture of the woman, standing in the sun with protesters all around and next to her the little girl with the basket of oranges. "*La Tension Devient Insoutenable!*" blared the headline. The tension is becoming unsustainable. The protests were reaching a climax and the dictator seemed sure to go. The tension for me that day when I saw her became unsustainable too. I saw her in the afternoon after the protests in one of Antananarivo's markets. I watched, rapt, as she moved among the colorful crowds in their straw hats, lingering between baskets of land crabs, mud fish, and piles of grotesquely shaped vegetables.

We finally spoke when I followed her into a shop where they sold Malagasy guitars. She said her name was Lizzie. She had recently graduated from college in New York, and had boarded a flight for Africa in search of pictures for whoever would buy them.

For several nights I couldn't sleep. Outside, tumult unfolded on the streets. The Marxist president machine-gunned his people from helicopters. Messages from the Bunker piled up at reception unheeded. My GMT deadlines came and passed and my output flowed to a trickle, just enough to prove I had not absconded entirely. For all I cared, Madagascar could have sunk into the Indian Ocean. I used every excuse I could to accompany Lizzie around town. "Are you sure you don't have to file today?" she asked when she was going off to photograph a witch doctor's ceremony or some such thing and I'd said I would go with her. "I've already filed," I lied. She had a twinkle in her eye as she said, "OK, come on."

We became constant companions. I went back to the music shop and bought Lizzie a guitar. From that day onward it never played in tune. She said she liked crème caramels. I bought her one, then a second helping, just so that I could watch her eat. We slept together for the rest of the trip. In and out of bed I studied every inch of her body. The babyish down on her tanned skin. Her slightly buck teeth. The way her jeans hugged her buttocks. How her blue eyes went misty in a certain way. She had a special way of telling a story, with the American South faintly present in the soft, lingering vowels, and I loved the way she repeatedly whistled the theme tune from *Gone With the Wind.* Her threadbare clothes would have seemed slovenly on another. On her they appeared just right.

I often wondered why this girl with her necklace of cameras and rucksack had abandoned America so young to come to my home to take photographs. She came from a family of preachers and eye doctors and somehow this ancestry seemed to combine in a young woman who captured with her lens images that told stories of good and evil. I remembered that in Africa some tribes used to believe that a camera is a box with which to capture souls.

Remembering Lizzie's life as a photographer, I am reminded of how "dark" is an epithet that completely fails to describe Africa. Africa is bathed in light, and it's the mornings you recall more than the nights with their noises and vague fears. Lizzie chased the light, rising before dawn, waiting for sunrise, capturing color and shadow, black faces with their depth and warmth, trapping the crescendo of light on film before watching heat leach out all the hues and contrasts, the world become two-dimensional, and faces turn blank, blinded by the sun. Long before noon Lizzie used to come back to find me wherever I was and rest until the sun sank; color returned and she went off to capture images of the fading day. At evening, the light had such depth that one could observe the incredible detail of things, as if the continent was made of liquid glass. It peaked, then she put away her camera and settled down to watch as the orange ball of the sun melted into the horizon; all sense of space and distance vanished in seconds. In East Africa darkness falls like a black velvet curtain, and almost before you can adjust you look up to see the moon and wheel of the constellations.

Lizzie had joined a small, nomadic tribe of reportage photographers. They were from a handful of agencies with names you'd give to a weapon or a virus: Blackstar, Sygma, Magnum, Sipa. Reportage photography was the greatest journalistic genre of the twentieth century, and now it was dying with the onset of the digital age. The photographers, with their chemicals and darkrooms and rolls of film, were artisans from an obsolete industrial era. These were the last days when a journalist would struggle to get to a bush strip in the jungle and sling onto the taxiing aircraft her film in an envelope marked PRESS PHOTOS—USELESS IF DELAYED. They'd have to pray that by some miracle it would reach New York undamaged, process well, and make it in time for that week's magazine deadlines. The photographers were from a former era. They regarded color film as vulgar and newfangled. Their preference was for black and white. It allowed them to depict modern suffering as an art form, as seen in the classic sepia tones of *Life* or *Paris Match* or *Stern*. They dreamed of shooting a picture that would become one of the great images of the century, alongside the Spanish soldier falling at the instant of being shot; the liberation of Paris; Che Guevara puffing his cigar; the men who bare their chests before the Soviet tanks in the Prague spring. Seeing the world in monochrome extremes was exactly the lens through which I wanted to see the world at that time and, for me, the photographers made dying look beautiful, war seem noble, and chaos appear as monumental as a heroic statue.

To get a picture, the photographer had to be closer to the news than the writer correspondents, who even at the front line could sit behind a wall while asking some other sucker what the scenery looked like. The talents who burned brightest in this subculture were often barely out of their teens, that is, before age and experience wore them out, or before they fell victim to the highest death toll of the entire hack pack. They relished the danger. I remember how an American dropped his trousers for a group of us at the bar and boasted how he'd lost his left testicle in a Balkans mine blast, which he claimed hadn't prevented him from seducing a nurse during his recovery in a Budapest hospital. If they survived their twenties the photographers I met evolved into eccentric, alienated figures. To me, the hero of them all was Patrick, a French photographer who wore only black and slept in his cowboy boots. I heard how in the Mozambique war of independence Patrick parachuted into a battle with Portuguese paratroopers despite never having jumped out of an aircraft before. He was one of few survivors from a Haitian refugee boat that had sunk on its voyage to Florida. His third war injury, after Vietnam and Cambodia, was suffered in Panama, when U.S. Marines shot him in the chest. Friendly fire. Patrick knew he was going to pass out as he lay there in the street. Before that could happen, he dipped a finger in his own wounds and painted his blood group onto his forehead, for the medics when they picked him up.

Back home in Kenya Lizzie gave me a book of war photography. Across the inside cover, she had made a collage of her own snaps of militias toting weapons, scenes from a trauma ward, herself in a bikini on the seaside, starving kids, Sudanese refugee children, wildlife snaps, and Malagasy politicians. "Partner in dreams," the caption said, "I want to do EVERYTHING with you."

After Madagascar Jonathan gave me time off. Lizzie's twenty-third birthday was approaching and I announced we had tickets for the sleeper-train journey south through Tanzania. Once we got to Zambia we would sail up Lake Tanganyika by steamer, a decommissioned imperial German battleship that had inspired C. S. Forester's tale *The African Queen*. Before we pulled out of the train station, I produced a cake with twenty-three candles. I paid a group of urchins roaming the platforms to sing "Happy Birthday to You" and they warbled it like choristers. Lizzie clapped. But later, as we clanked across the bush with me enthusiastically pointing out of the window, she became listless. She doubled up with stomach pains. We disembarked at a bush station under a portrait of Chairman Mao and Nyerere and waited most of the day for another train to go back the way we had come.

Back in the city, we visited a doctor. It was nothing serious but as we emerged from the surgery Lizzie told me she had decided to return to America without delay. Africa for her was suddenly too far away from home. As we drove through the shabby streets to the airport, I realized the girl was vanishing from my life. We both maintained our composure at the check-in desk, but my heart was sick as I sensed happiness slipping through my fingers as surely as the countdown of minutes would have ticked by on the African airport clocks, had they not all been broken. When it was time for her to go, she passed through the cordon of armed police in battered white helmets. She lingered on the other side of a smudged glass partition and gazed back at me. The tears rolled down her cheeks as she waved, turned, and walked away, her camera bag over her shoulder, then was swallowed up among the travelers.

My warrior ancestors experienced life in the four corners of the world, mastered exotic languages, immersed themselves in foreign cultures, and returned home with stories to tell—if they ever came home at all. In 1991, while kicking my heels in Africa, I had missed Operation Desert Storm, the biggest war story so far of our generation. I no longer cared. I had decided that what I was looking for was a war that I could call my own, a story that was mine, a complete experience that would define me as the son of my fathers and involve me as an insider, from the outbreak of hostilities to the victory parades and humiliation of the vanquished.

One day the bureau telex lit up with a message from our stringer in Somalia. "Mohamoud Afrah—never heard of him," I said as I peered over Jonathan's shoulder as the message clattered out. There were several stringers like Afrah in the region. They could sleep for months or even years before there was a story worth waking up for. For a decade, Somalia had been sunk in a war of extravagant barbarism. As the new year arrived it became the latest of our bouquet of conflicts to bloom to a climax—all to be buried in the headlines by the Allies' military build-up against Saddam in the Gulf.

> TKS YR STORY AFRAH, WHAT GIVES? GA
> IT VERY HOT BETWEEN HOME AND PUBLIC TELEX
> OFFICE STOP MAY BE DIFFICULT TO SEND TOMORROW GA
> OK AFRAH TKS STORY STAY SAFE BIBI
> BIBI
> ZCZC NNNN

Afrah managed to contact us regularly over seventy-two hours, but finally all lines to Somalia went dead and for years afterward if you dialed the national code 252 all you heard was electronic ether, ghostly distorted voices and lonely Morse signals repeated like pleas. An entire nation of people was lost, beyond reach, tumbled into an abyss.

Jonathan and Mo Amin called us in to discuss strategy. Since Mo lost his hand in the Addis ammo dump explosion he had acquired a prosthetic limb. It was a bionic device connected to the nerves in his stump that rotated 360 degrees and had a crushing handshake. He maintained his arrogant swagger when he limped around the Press Centre but he looked haggard. We sat down to study the maps and considered how the Somalis might react if we flew in unannounced. "Never go in to meet a defeated army," cautioned Mo. He told us a story about two European journalists who had boated across Lake Victoria to meet Idi Amin's retreating troops in 1978 and promptly been murdered. "On the other hand," Mo said, "the winning side always loves you." But who had won?

"You're going to go in with Hos," Jonathan said finally. "I want you to take care of him and go very carefully." Hos Maina was our Kenyan photo stringer. He was in his early thirties and already he was a veteran of a string of dangerous stories. Some time before I joined Reuters, Hos had been in a car crash, which injured him so severely that a priest was called in to read him his last rites. He had fought hard to recover, to live for his wife and children, but he was half-crippled. Still, he was determined to return to work and went through endless, painful physiotherapy. Hos was the man whom I had seen on my first day in the Bunker, when I'd thought he was a drunkard with a big bruise on his wide forehead. He stumbled as he walked, slurred his words, and stuttered.

"M-m-m-m Hos Main-er-n-n-n," he managed to say when we met, extending a limp hand. "M-m-m-m the fuc-fuc-fuc-*photographer.*"

The fingers on Hos's right hand were semi-paralyzed and flipperlike and it hurt me to observe his contortions as he crammed film into his camera. He took pictures by pressing the shutter release with his stronger left thumb. Management had wanted Hos out for a long time and he survived only thanks to Jonathan. Black cripples don't have a good time of it in Africa and if Reuters gave him the push, Jonathan figured that he'd end up on the streets—or establish a kiosk studio in a slum doing family portraits if he was very lucky. Jonathan kept him, and for all his handicaps, in the end it was because Hos was a nice guy and, as I was to discover, because he had a good sense of judgment. When Hos learned I was from a colonial English family, he nicknamed me Johnny, which is what the Mau Mau guerrillas used to call British soldiers in the 1950s rebellion. His grandfather, he stammered, had killed several of us.

* * *

Hos slept the whole flight with his mouth slackly open until he woke as we came in for the descent. From the air, Mogadishu was a white castellated city—all gleaming, set in reddish sands and thorn scrub, bordered on the east by coral beaches and a turquoise ocean. Looking out of my aircraft porthole, I saw districts roofless and destroyed liked the pitted cavities of rotting teeth. A battle was in progress as we went in to land and the cityscape was shrouded in dust and smoke. The pilot banked and dropped the Cessna's nose, feathering his props, bringing us down silently, and taxiing to a halt before a dark concrete warehouse. The door opened and we climbed out into a blast of heat and a smell of dust and burning bone.

Speeding toward us were battlewagons bristling with militias in aviators' goggles, long synthetic wigs, youths peering into the spiderweb sights of multibarreled antiaircraft guns. The vehicles were decorated with antelope horns, festive tinsel, and plastic flowers, the cabins were sliced away, and the paint jobs had been blowtorched off and sprayed over with militia graffiti.

"Fu-fu-fu-*fuck*," said Hos.

The savages yelled at us and sounded as angry as devils, until it dawned on me that they were giving us a warm welcome. This was just the way Somalis spoke, and I imagined the fighters also must have been pretty deaf from the relentless gunfire. They bellowed for us to jump onto their convoy and whisked us away, all the while shouting at us, at one another, and at bystanders. A youth in a flaming red wig plucked my sleeve and asked me if he could be my guide. "I am not a normal man," he assured me. I shrugged, "Okay." As we swung out of the airport gates I saw a big graffito sprayed over the Mogadishu airport sign. It said WELL COME TO THE NEW AFRICA but it might as well have been: "Abandon all hope ye who enter here."

* * *

Somalia still filled a space on the world's atlas, with its pink frontiers etched by European imperialists a century before. Those arbitrary borders had marked a separation between it and the rest of
the world, but now even the fantasy of what the space inside the
pink lines should mean was gone. Schools, law and order, taxes—
gone. All that was left was land and people and guns. I heard gunfire from an alley off to one side.

"Let's go down there!" I yelled.

"N-n-n-n-n-n," Hos moaned. "N-n-n-n-n-no!"

"Oh, come on, Hos."

Hos shook his head and said again, "N-n-n-n-n-n-*no*!" Suddenly the boom of a grenade going off filled the alleyway with dust
and debris. Thanks, Hos, I thought.

We hurtled up the hill, swerving to avoid debris, smashed
cars, and corpses, running dead traffic lights, and going along
whichever side of the road we pleased. When the trucks came to a
halt we got down off the trucks and moved from house to house on
foot. We were on a street running toward the Indian Ocean when I
looked down to see that my feet were ankle deep in brown leaves. I
thought of walking along the banks of the Isis in Oxford on October days, beneath chestnuts and beach trees shedding their branches.
But there is no autumn on the equator. Hos was looking down too.

"What and why and fucking how?" I said. Then I realized.
They were banknotes. Millions upon millions of banknotes.

"M-m-m-m-*money*!" said Hos with a big smile on his face.
He took a picture of a group of old men stuffing it into sacks.
The soiled bills spilled out of blasted doors between marble pillars.
It was raining money in the ocean breeze. We turned a corner and
the bills were replaced by wafting blue, green, and pink sheets of
paper out of ransacked ministries. Gangs were blowtorching the
bronze statues of Somalia's national heroes off their marble

plinths. Down fell Ahmed Gran, who had defeated Christian Abyssinia in the sixteenth century. *Crash!* went the poet and anti-British guerrilla fighter "Mad Mullah" Seyyid Mohamed ibn Abdullah Hassan on his rearing stallion. Hos clicked away. The gunmen smiled. Looters manhandled a yellow sofa, an old iron boiler, and a grandfather clock onto the back of a diesel truck. Holes were being opened up every few meters along the road. Men were pulling out the copper wiring and pipes. I saw men slaughtering a camel. It bellowed as they cut its throat and hacked it to pieces with pangas. The fire-ruined Catholic cathedral, once Africa's largest church, was roofless and the clock tower was cleft down the middle and about to topple. Inside, Jesus was headless on his cross and a militia man, cradling an M-16 and with a personal stereo system clamped over his ears, was doing a jig across a floor spangled with shards of stained glass.

The city was a fragment of what it had been but the atmosphere was electric. The militias had liberated the nation not only from dictatorship but also from modern civilization. A Dionysian orgy of destruction was now taking place across Mogadishu in which everything was smashed within the space of hours: priceless Muslim artifacts from the museum and the mosques, hospital equipment, factory plants, power cables, computers, libraries, telephone exchanges. The Somalis thoroughly enjoyed themselves and I got a contact high off them. On days like this in the news business I grew to understand how easy it must be for normally ordinary people to want to participate in riots and football match hooliganism.

A queue of civilians was huddled at a roadblock before a gang of rebels. As each person was waved through, another came forward and began uttering a litany of names. My guide with the flaming red hair said the people were reciting their clan family trees. The genealogies tumbled back generation after generation to a founding ancestor. It was like a DNA helix, or a fingerprint, or an encyclopedia of peace treaties and blood debts left to fester down the torrid centuries. I was thinking how poetic this idea was, when *bang;* a gunman shot one of the civilians, who fell with blood gushing from his head and was pushed aside onto a heap of corpses.

"Wrong clan," said my flaming-haired friend. "He should have borrowed the ancestors of a friend."

The eye of the maelstrom was the People's Palace, home of the dictator president Mohamed Siad Barre. At the gate, the carcass of the president's pet lion lay in its cage. The beast's hide sagged around the bones of the skeleton and its eyes were black holes. On the red carpet of the great entrance hall a looter had planted a coil of shit, like the visiting card of a burglar in a rich man's home. On the staircase I met a corpse.

"How do you do, Adan Darah?" our Somali guide chuckled. "The press would like to ask some questions ..."

In life Adan Darah had been the president's bodyguard. Now he resembled a cartoon character that had been bashed, with his squinty eyes, tongue out, canaries circling his head. Except the birds were fat bluebottles buzzing around the concave dent of his smashed, dead face.

Hos and I began moving down a corridor, trying all the doors until we came upon one that wasn't locked but it wouldn't open. Weight pressed against the other side. A cadaver? I barged with my shoulder and it gave way. I found myself in a room knee-deep in envelopes. They spilled from cupboard shelves stacked to the ceiling. There must have been ten thousand envelopes, with postmarks from across the Western world. They had been sent over the period of a decade, but I was the first to open any of them. Each letter began in exactly the same way: "Your Excellency. I am writing to express my concern about the detention of ..." For what reason did the dictator's aides fail to open the letters? How did they recognize they were from supporters of the human rights group Amnesty International? Why had they carefully put them away in cupboards and not thrown them away? I saved a handful of unopened letters. Years later I have them here on my desk as I write and I still have no answers to those questions.

That night we sat in the garden of a blown-out hotel, sipping grapefruit juice and watching the red, green, and white Morse of tracers in the sky. The man with flaming red hair told me he could summon up the jinn, spirits that would do his bidding. "And I can fly," he added. Now, Marco Polo never made it to Mogadishu by air or across the oceans, but he claimed that griffins flew in its skies. Perhaps this was indeed what the Bible called the "land shadowing with wings," beyond the rivers of Ethiopia. Flying across this wilderness of orange and glittering white, a land extending from El Uach, the Wells of God, in the south, all the way north to Cape Gardafui on the tip of Africa's Horn, I understood why the wartime British officers isolated down there had called it the Shag, or more floridly the Furthest Shag of the Never-Never Land. Today, Somalia is almost entirely lacking a history. It might have been the legendary land of Punt, though we can't be sure, where the ancient Egyptians sent their expeditions to trade for aromatic tree gums used in the rituals of the dead, for panther skins, ivory, and slaves. To the Greeks the coast was cursorily described as a land of troglodytes. History gains a foothold in the eighth century, the date of the first tomb inscription in Mogadishu, when already the port was Islamic and probably home to a cosmopolitan mix of Indian

Ocean peoples. In the fourteenth century Moroccan traveler Ibn Battuta found it to be a flourishing port, big enough to have hundreds of camels slaughtered daily for its inhabitants and ruled over by a sultan. Islam seeped slowly into the furnace of the interior where even after their conversion the nomads remained wild, superstitious, and warlike. Nineteenth-century explorer Sir Richard Burton had many names for Somalia and the Somalis, from "the land of give-me-something" to a nation of "turbulent republicans."

The Somalis themselves made a joke of their bitter history. They said one of their clan ancestors had migrated from Arabia as a fugitive after stealing the Prophet Mohamed's slippers from outside the mosque in Mecca. I liked that about the Somalis: they saw even their own origins as a joke. One desert village I visited several times over the years is called Dhuusa Mareb. The name is pronounced in a way that sounds as if you're clearing your throat ready to spit, and it means the Unending Fart. Dhuusa Mareb is huddled about a salty well, where youths in loincloths, their black skins flecked by spatters of white clay, pull up splashing leather buckets from the well to quench their camels, before vanishing back into the void for months. It is utterly remote, the wind howls, and I can picture some maddened nomad giving this place its name in a moment of lonely despair.

The Somalis were as tough as nails, they were as exasperating as the camels they loved, the women were beautiful, and their bloody sense of clan honor entangled them in feuds of Byzantine complexity. A legend told how when the warriors of a certain clan discovered they had no enemies to fight, they divided up their ranks and killed each other for sport.

The Somalis called me a heathen, or *gal*. "Gal! Gal! Gal!" crowds of children would yell as they ran after me. They showed off what devout Muslims they were if anybody was watching but when out of view of their neighbors would happily share my salami sandwich, drink beer, and debauch themselves with as many women as they could lay their hands on. The Somalis were black, but I came to learn they seemed to reject this fact and blithely called Bantu Africans "slaves." They rejoiced in making enemies of the world, and regarded themselves as nothing less than the kings of the earth, when in reality they were a nation of paupers.

As a correspondent, I suppose my job was to excite the sympathy of the world for this forgotten and reviled people, but all I can say now is that I have felt it a privilege to observe a people who shot themselves in the foot with such accuracy and tumbled into the abyss in such style.

We must share some of the blame for why Somalia became such a burned-out, smoking hole. What we can make out in the murk of the Horn of Africa's past is that it is a story of the steady, southward advance of the Somali clans against all others. The imposition of arbitrary colonial boundaries arrested their migration, at least for a while, and whereas elsewhere in Africa frontiers tended to lump unrelated tribes together, such boundaries in this case scattered a people who had one common language, culture, and religion. The colonial history is anything but edifying when one considers that, for the British, their piece of Somalia was taken over to grow livestock for export to Aden but ended up being used mainly for big-game hunting, which ultimately led to the local extinction of elephants. The French took a piece out of pride, so they would not need to send their ships to British Aden, while the Italians grabbed a piece thinking they would settle their excess peasants in this inhospitable land, culminating in Benito Mussolini's noted ambition to provide his subjects with a banana a day—to be grown in Somalia.

The foreigners colored their maps the way they wanted, but they never pacified this vast, empty land. Another remote town I know has the name Galkacaayo, "The Place Where the White Man Ran Away." Galkacaayo marks the spot where the dervish army under Seyyid Mohamed ibn Abdullah Hassan defeated a colonial force. The seyyid outwitted colonial armies for the first two decades of the twentieth century. He was unafraid of the aircraft that bombed him or the maxim guns that scythed down his troops. "I like war," he wrote to the British once in red ink. "You do not. God willing, I will take many more rifles from you, but I will not take your country. I have no forts or houses or cultivation, no silver or gold for you to take. I have no artificers. The country is desert and of no use. There is wood and stone and many ant heaps. But all you will get from me is war, nothing else." The seyyid claimed that he could overhear what men said seventy-five miles away, that he turned British bullets into water, and that the searchlights of Royal Navy ships in the Gulf of Aden were the eyes of Allah come to bless him. The colonials were never able to kill him and only the perfidy of a white man's disease—influenza—finally finished him off.

I. M. Lewis, an anthropologist I used to go to see lecture in London, wrote that though the Somalis "have been colonized they have never really been conquered" and that "by the establishment of international frontiers the great movements of the clans have to some extent been arrested, but the pastoralists' inordinate pride and contempt for other nations remains unchallenged."

When Somalia became independent in 1960—it was hardly won, but rather given after Europe finally washed its hands of the country—each of the five points on the white star in the center of a sea of blue represented one of the divided Somali territories: the former British and Italian Somalilands, Djibouti, Kenya's Northern Frontier District, and Ethiopia's Ogaden.

The infant democracies that were born across Africa as nations and gained self-rule in the 1960s were quickly strangled when power went to their leaders' heads. Somalia's elected president was assassinated in 1969 and military chief General Mohamed Siad Barre stepped into power on that same day my mother and her children were waiting in the "Scratchy Belly" hotel in downtown Mogadishu.

Siad took time to evolve into Saturn, devourer of his own children. He, like Africa's other dictators, adopted a childish political philosophy, "scientific socialism" in this case, but his initial efforts may even have benefited the nation. Like a black Atatürk, he had the Somali language set down in Roman script to replace the traditional Arabic. His five-year plans, literacy campaigns, and even the imprisoning of dissidents and poets actually worked in an odd sort of way.

The events of the 1970s onward tell a hopeless, bloody tale. Somalia's strategic position at the mouth of the Red Sea attracted the interest of the big powers. Africa's Horn became a cockpit of the Cold War, with guns supplied in quantities enough to exterminate several generations of local people. Siad was aided by the Communist bloc and later, after the Marxist revolution in Addis Ababa in 1974, America became his friend. He gained popularity at home when he attacked his neighbors in an attempt to claim the northeast of Kenya and Ethiopia's Ogaden, but lost it all when his forces failed miserably. Somalia went bankrupt in the 1980s, when the United Nations subsidized the dictatorship by turning a blind eye to the plundering of humanitarian aid deliveries. The last of America's Cold War weapons deliveries were made to Somalia in 1989, a year before Siad's reign collapsed. After the Berlin Wall came down, Somalia was what one diplomat described as "devalued real estate" and the regime imploded. Siad gave all the top positions in government and the military to his wives, children, and in-laws, and as he lost swathes of territory to the rebels he became known as "the mayor of Mogadishu."

An insomniac, Siad survived off cigarettes and espresso. Nobody knew what went on behind his black shades, which were said to have mini X rays in the lenses, but he couldn't have been more explicit when he said, "I arrived by the gun and I will only leave by the gun." When crowds at a Mogadishu football stadium jeered him as if he was a black Ceaus,escu, his soldiers simply opened fire on them.

During the fight for Mogadishu that erupted in late 1990, he had barricaded himself in the Presidential Palace with his artillery. Day after day he fired into the city, demolishing whole districts. When his ammo ran out, he fled Mogadishu and made for his clan homeland in the southwest of Somalia, where he intended to regroup.

As we got deeper into 1991, Somalia slipped further into war and insanity. I had a Somali friend named Yahya who had been a protocol officer at the U.S. embassy until the evacuation of foreigners. He used to tell me that the Somalis were in the process of committing what he called "geno-suicide" and that this all-out war of everybody against everybody else had produced a grim paradox.

"If you have nothing you starve," he said. "If you have something you are attacked. Either way, you get killed."

Western powers and other African nations might have stepped in to save Somalia after the dictatorship's collapse by supporting the establishment of a transitional government. Africa's leaders, however, were too busy exterminating their own populations to care about Somalia, while the West had been too absorbed with the Gulf War. Somalia was abandoned to its own devices.

Onto this stage walked a new breed of men who presumed to be the legitimate leaders of a nation. But war, not peace, was all they could offer. Peace was their worst nightmare. Correspondents of our generation had grown up in the Cold War. Nothing like Somalia had ever happened before and at first we had no idea what to call the frightening new strongmen. After discussing revolutionary China, Jonathan and I decided to christen the Somali militia leaders "warlords" and the name was taken up by everybody in the news business. They were ruthless murderers and their terrifying reputation was only enforced by the childish gangster names they awarded themselves. Each of them claimed the national presidency, though President Siad, now dubbed Big Mouth, was still in command of his rump Marehan clan army and was laying waste to the central regions, supported by his son-in-law Morgan, who wore a long pirate's beard to hide a harelip. I recall my first encounter with the Plunderer, known as Bililiqo in Somali, in a glade of flame trees. He brandished a spear and asked for medicine for his tubercular cough. When I met General Hussein of the Darood clan alliance on the banks of the Shebelle or Leopard River, he gave me a lecture on Clausewitz while perched on a pyramid of cardboard boxes, each one stamped in big yellow letters BANANAS. The scariest militia leader of all was Mohamed Farah Aydiid, or Mister Proud, a former police boss, international heroin smuggler, and now chieftain of the Habre Gedir militia. Thanks to Aydiid, Big Mouth was finally routed in two major campaigns and he fled into exile in April 1992 to Nigeria, where he promptly died. The prospect of sudden peace persuaded Aydiid to launch an offensive against his remaining rivals in Mogadishu.

The militias made up a Scrabble game of acronyms—USC, SPM, SNM, SNF, SSDF—and they called themselves National, Patriotic, Democratic, or United. But these militias were simply tribal family gangs. "When it comes down to it," Carlos Mavroleon, who had joined us in Somalia, observed, "this is no different from the turf wars between the Crips and the Bloods in South Central LA. Only these fuckers have heavy artillery." The clan militia rank and file were the *moryaan*, tough nomadic boys from the bush who swarmed into the farming areas and towns with fuzzy Afros glistening with rancid sheep's fat. They reminded me of a passage from T. E. Lawrence's *Seven Pillars of Wisdom*, in which he describes how the history of the Arabs is one of the migration of Bedu from Yemen to Syria: "We see them wandering, every year moving a little further north or a little further east as chance has sent them down one or the other of the well roads of the wilderness, till finally the pressure drives them from the desert again into the sown." The difference in Somalia was that war had brought about this huge social change overnight. A few years before, the Somali nomads had fought with spears and knives over grass and water for their camels, and for whatever honor might be derived from killing. As clan militias today they battled with Cold War–era weapons for modern infrastructure such as roads. One militia controlled the seaport, another militia the airport, and so on. Across the desert the war moved fast. Militia gangs fought along the crumbling tarmac roads, hurtling around in battlewagons. There was no front line. Nobody held any territory. The warlords couldn't stop a gunfight from taking place outside their own front doors. They ran rival radio stations in the north and south of Mogadishu. Both had identical signature tunes, broadcast simultaneously, and called themselves Radio Mogadishu. Their time checks were always different, and always wrong.

The correspondents saw incidents of violence that were often too comic or odd to include in news reports but for years they became stories we swapped over drinks, shaking our heads in disbelief. I was at the airfield in the southern port of Kismayu with Hos when, without warning, a MiG-17 erupted out of the acacia scrub, screamed low over us, opened up with its cannons, and strafed the tarmac farther down the runway. I scurried for cover as the old fighter circled and returned for a second pass. It opened up again, missed everything, then vanished. Seconds later, a plume of black smoke rose over the horizon and the boom of the MiG crashing followed. That was the end of the Somali Air Force.

A few days later I was at the main airfield back in Mogadishu. A crowd of gunmen was waiting for the aircraft that would bring in that day's supply of the amphetamine vegetable qat. I was hoping for a lift back to Kenya, as the aircraft always returned to Nairobi empty, since there was nothing to export from Somalia. The atmosphere was always tense when the Somalis were waiting for their drugs to arrive. As I waited, I saw three militia boys clambering around on a MiG and one of them managed to get into the cockpit. From the shade of a hangar, a lieutenant yelled at the kids to stop fooling around, but they took no notice. Seconds later, the youth in the pilot's seat hit the ejector button. The cockpit canopy blew off, instantly killing another boy who'd had his nose squashed up against the glass. The kid in the pilot's seat shot into the air and returned to earth with a dull, bone-shattering thud. The third militia boy on the MiG was left perching on one of the wings, looking sheepish. More yells erupted from the hangar and the lieutenant stormed out with his AK-47, flipped the button to automatic fire, sprayed the surviving teenager off the wing, and walked back into the shade, shaking his head in disgust.

The militias had little use for tanks, which were costly and complicated to drive, service, and indeed fire. They adored antiaircraft weapons, which they aimed horizontally into civilian districts, together with surface-to-air missiles. The best weapon of choice was the "technical" battlewagon. This was a Toyota 4x4 with the cabin sawn off and a weapon mounted on the back: an old Soviet 23mm antiaircraft gun, an artillery piece, or some of Stalin's Organ rocket tubes. I once saw a rocket pod scrounged from the wing of a MiG-17 welded onto the back of a technical that in theory would launch a cluster of twelve missiles at once. The owner told me proudly that his machine was called the al-Abbas, a name inspired by the Scud variants Saddam Hussein had fired at Israel during the first war against Iraq in 1991. Dramatically, after a couple of attempted launches, the entire vehicle somersaulted backward, killing most of the crew and sending al-Abbas's inventor back to the drawing board.

One day Carlos and I were with a crew of militias operating a mortar on the Green Line, a swathe of mashed rubble that ran from the Old Port to the inland desert dunes. The crew elevated the mortar tube and fired off several bombs at random.

"What the hell is that?" Carlos asked.

"That's a 'To Whom it May Concern,'" one of the crew said with a smile.

At the other end we heard that the civilians called all arbitrary flying projectiles "Yussuf," because they went *suf, suf, suf* before slamming into houses, schools, or marketplaces. Traditionally, feuds could be settled only by the payment of blood money for lives lost. The life of a man—a *waranleh*, or spear carrier—was valued at one hundred camels. Women were worth half that. In these days of mortars and AK-47s, you could not even see the attackers. Assuming they were from the rival lineage of clans, there was no way to keep track of blood money debts. I had seen an elder totter into a rubble-filled street and wave his walking stick to stop a fight between families. But without the payment of compensation, there was no question of ending the bloodshed. In any case, the Somalis were beginning to enjoy it.

Aydiid was barefoot, sporting a Muslim cap and spotless white safari suit. He reclined on a rococo chair, sipping sterilized car battery water (the only cold drink in Mogadishu that didn't give you dysentery).

"I am not a *warlord*," Aydiid whined in his cleft-palate voice. My use of the term incensed him so much that later he had his lieutenants say they'd kill me if I persisted in using it.

I tried to detect the signs of evil or psychosis in Aydiid's face. I wondered if I should really be afraid, sitting this close to him. I should watch my step, I thought. Yet he normally looked like a harmless old fogy. This was the banality of evil dressed in a Muslim skullcap. Only when he glanced at you out of the corner of his eye, he seemed in a mood to kill.

His well of hatred had been filled to brimming. Under Siad, he had spent years in jail and a man who served with him told me he had woken one day to observe Aydiid eating a bar of soap. On his release Aydiid was immediately appointed ambassador to Delhi, probably to remove him from the domestic scene. As ambassador he used his diplomatic status to traffic narcotics. He became a middleman in big construction deals with Italians, in which both the socialists in Rome and the Somali leaders negotiated backhanders sliced out of the economic aid program. A quarrel over who got what kickbacks in a project to construct a desert road led to Aydiid's decision to become a guerrilla leader.

Aydiid sucked in hard when the subject of Ali Mahdi came up, who had unilaterally declared himself president, but regained his composure after a swig of battery water.

"He must pe silenced."

"How?"

"By bolitical means." He pronounced his *p*'s as *b*'s and his *b*'s as *p*'s.

"That sounds like fighting will go on."

"Not really."

A salvo of Stalin's Organ rockets was launched outside with a terrific roar.

"So you will sit down and talk?"

When hell freezes over, he might have said. Aydiid spoke glowingly of the prosperity he would usher in after victory. There were minerals to extract and bananas to export to Europe. He raised a finger as a mortar bomb demolished a house nearby.

"Most imbortant of all, we have a thousand miles of peaches. Peautiful, white peaches. All the tourists, they want to come to Somalia."

What Aydiid ultimately wanted was to get rich. The problem with Somalia was that in reality there was little to fight over. Angola had diamonds, Sudan had oil, and Liberia had rubber—

Somalia was nothing but a desert sprinkled with camels, ringed by a shark-infested ocean. Very quickly, Aydiid realized that his main economic resource was his own population. After the factories, statues, and useful machinery had been looted and shipped to Dubai for scrap, Aydiid turned to plunder whatever the peasants possessed. I saw the body of a Bantu former slave on Jubba River who had been roasted over a fire until he revealed where his farm's grain store was hidden. After he'd done this they cooked him until he was well done. Aydiid's allies were from nomadic clans who rounded up the poorest tribes, such as the Bantu, the descendants of plantation slaves, and forced them to toil on the old Italian irrigated estates along the Shebelle, or Leopard River, producing bananas for export to Europe.

Inevitably as the food ran out across Somalia, Aydiid and the others woke up to the opportunity for riches presented by the resulting famine. The warlords realized that if large numbers of people began dying, the foreigners would lavish money on Somalia and do all they could to import aid by sea, air, and land. Aydiid's men cultivated as many deaths as possible and positioned themselves so that they were first in line to offer "security," transport, and housing when the foreigners arrived. And then they robbed everything they could lay their hands on. It was an evil but simple plan.

By February 1992, after five months of fighting in the city, the Red Cross said thirty thousand people had been killed or wounded. On our tours of the city we used to pick up the wounded all the time and deliver them to hospitals like the Digfer, where a brown track of drying blood flowed up the stairs and down the corridors. There were not enough beds and casualties lay all over the place, moaning and sometimes screaming. I remember a little boy lying in a corridor with all his skin burned off. In the hospital courtyard were piles of amputated limbs and bloody bandages. The warlords were using weapons that came cheap and could be fired by amateurs but that had incredible power. The damage made by a high-velocity round derives not simply from the hole it makes. The shock of the bullet damages tissue in a wide circumference around its path, shattering organs. Picture the mushiness of thawed vegetables out of a deep freeze. If bullet hits bone, bone either smashes or deflects the bullet, which pinballs around the body, cutting a path through the innards. I've seen a dead man with no visible mark on him but for an entry wound in his left calf. The bullet had zigzagged up his leg and into his guts and lungs. Normally a bullet exited the victim and took a cone of flesh with it as it continued on through a wall or into another bystander.

An air bridge had been set up by the Red Cross and UN importing intravenous fluids, plasma, and other supplies for the trauma wards. But Raymond, a wonderful American surgeon for the International Medical Corps, told me the quantity of IV fluids being flown in did not equal in volume the amount of blood being spilled on the streets.

"Imagine an Olympic swimming pool, full of blood," Raymond said. "That's how much IV we need."

I could get out of Mogadishu any time I wanted, as long as I made it to an airstrip. In three hours I was in Nairobi, in twelve I could be in London. Almost all the foreigners in Somalia had already been evacuated on the eve of Operation Desert Storm. As the fighting in Mogadishu peaked, the U.S. ambassador had gathered scores of foreigners in his compound, posted his diplomatic staff on the walls with rifles, and transmitted a Mayday calling for help. A flotilla of U.S. ships steaming to the gulf was diverted and raced to the rescue. A squadron of CH-53 Sea Stallion helicopters had taken to the air from the ships as time ran out and had flown all night to reach the U.S. embassy before the compound was invaded. As they lifted off, gangs of Somali looters were already scaling the walls.

I met a residue of colonial-era Italians who had refused to leave. They lived with young Somali women as graceful as antelopes in large, cool villas, staying on as if nothing had happened to disrupt their old ways, dismissing with a laugh and a shrug the fact that they faced starvation by candlelight. I got to know one Genovese, a heavy smoker who'd had his larynx removed. He spoke through a device that he pressed against his throat, which produced a metallic sound like a robot. Batteries were hard to come by in Somalia. When they ran out he came up to me, gasping, silent, pleading to me in hoarse whispers to restore his powers of speech using whatever I had to power my shortwave radio and torch.

I found the last Englishman in the whole of Somalia at the British embassy. At the door of the building, the ambassador's chauffeur in his peaked cap greeted me, snapping smartly to attention and saluting. He announced that not only had his boss vanished, but the embassy limo had since been looted.

Inside, I found an elderly man. He was a familiar, paternal old colonial. He wore patched khaki shorts and sandals, glasses on his nose. The thin hair was plastered back onto his tanned skull. When I entered, he was sitting on a packing crate, sorting scattered papers from the trashed office floor.

We shook hands and he said his name was Brian Bowden. When I told him my name, his eyes brightened. "Hartley. Was your father up here once?" I said that he was. Bowden exclaimed. "Well, *well!*" The last time he had seen me, he said, I was a towheaded little boy of four. I was taken aback. Bowden motioned me to a packing crate. "And how are your parents?" I said they were fine. Bowden chuckled. "I remember your father…" And immediately he launched into a desert tale that drew a perfect portrait of Dad.

Dad and Bowden, it turned out, had become friends many years before. Bowden, a water engineer, had fallen in love with a local girl and never left northern Somalia. As the civil war got worse, he had, with his wife and five children, fled to the city, where he got a slot doing paperwork at the British embassy. Since the collapse, Bowden had stayed in Mogadishu.

"It's been a bit scary, especially with these automatic cannons going off. It's been dodging bullets to find water."

Daily, Bowden woke at five and joined the city's residents as they picked their way through the bombed-out warrens, foraging for food and the odd bucket of water. Looters had invaded his house twice, stealing anything they could carry, including clothes and the furniture. Still, at eight sharp Bowden reported for work at the looted embassy, as he had done every day before the slide into chaos. Turning up to work gave Bowden's formless life the illusion of purpose. He sat on that packing crate, sorting the scattered papers into piles, being especially careful with the confidential documents. It was an act of loyalty to a nation that had forgotten him. He said, "Last week we had a circular signed by the ambassador expressing his thoughts. He told the staff their salaries are being paid in the UK." He was obviously impressed. Then he added, "But we need the money here, not in London."

Despite this, he did not resent Britain, which had yet been great when he had been posted to Somalia. In his mind it was still great. She couldn't possibly abandon an entire nation, half of whose population were her former colonial subjects. She could certainly never leave her own embassy staff to die of starvation or flying bullets.

"It's been long enough and I personally would say the ambassador should come back," he shrugged. "But that's diplomacy. They're probably waiting ..."

For what, he didn't say. In the end I was no better than the British. Africa is full of tribes, which care for their own people in times of distress. Bowden was from my tribe. He stood before me, my father's long-lost friend, a malnourished old man. There was nobody else to save him.

"You must leave," I pleaded with him.

"No," he said. "I am caught. If I go, I go as a refugee, even back to the UK," and smiled weakly. "Here is the only future I can see right now."

Perhaps he simply could not leave, to return to a cold island he may never have liked, one that had become a foreign country after three decades. Bowden loved Somalia and he had found love there. He asked me for nothing when I left, but rose to shake my hand and warmly asked me to pass his regards to my parents.

When I later told my father about this friend, the way Dad shook his head filled me with bitter regret that I hadn't forced the old man to accompany me to Kenya with his entire family. Back in Nairobi, I dropped off some letters Bowden had asked me to pass to the British High Commission. There, I asked a diplomat about him.

"Bowden!" The diplomat rolled his eyes. "He really is a nuisance, that man. Hangs about the embassy and pesters us all the time."

I asked why the British were doing nothing to help him. The diplomat explained that under government regulations, a citizen must cover the cost of his own repatriation, even from a war zone. Bowden was destitute, he had no surviving relatives in his native Devonshire, and he had a black Somali wife and five children. The government could not under these circumstances evacuate either Bowden or his large mixed-race family.

Bowden hung on for months. One day, he borrowed cash from a Somali loan shark to pay wages to the embassy staff since they still had no way of getting to their salaries, which accumulated untouched in a London bank. On his way from the moneylender to the embassy, he dropped by his home for a few minutes. A gang of armed thieves that had got wind of the loan were following behind. They smashed the door down, forced his family to watch as they beat him to a pulp, and when he was dead they made off with the cash.

*   *   *

The world remained deaf and blind to the news we filed out of Somalia in 1991. Reuters and the other wire agencies wrote reams of copy charting the destitute nation's descent into the abyss. Julian bashed out angry pieces for the *Financial Times*. Bald Sam spent evenings drawing up proposals for foreign military intervention. Across the months, our exasperation grew at the acres of newsprint about Charles and Diana's marital problems, the aftermath of Iraq, and now the Balkan crisis, while little filler "blobs" appeared in the foreign page columns on Somalia. The outside world shrugged at news of her plight and said there was nothing to be done until the Africans decided to wake from their own nightmare. We were on a zero play nonstory.

It took me weeks to track down our Mogadishu stringer Mohamoud Afrah, who had been in telex contact with us before vanishing when Somalia collapsed. When I found him it was down a dusty alley strewn with donkey turds and wrecked cars. Afrah was urbane and charming, a squirrel-like, silver-haired hack of the old school whose speech was laced with newsroom slang. Reuters was his sideline. His main purpose in life was a weekly column called "Talk of the Town" on his small newspaper *Vigilance*. The printing presses had been blown up and now he was writing a book about the liberation of Mogadishu from dictatorship.

As I stepped into his home I found it dark inside but for needles of light that came from the tin roof pierced by bullet holes. Afrah said he hadn't fired a weapon in thirty years but he showed me the vintage Tommy gun he kept in his study, beneath a bright oil painting of a Somali odalisque and a shelf of volumes with Charles Dickens, Solzhenitsyn, Achebe. We sat down to talk as a pot of rice simmered away on a charcoal fire. When I offered him a cigarette he accepted.

"Ah, smokers of the world, unite!"

He asked if I recalled the day the communications to Somalia went down, so that he did not file. I said I did and Afrah then told me he had spent hours trying to dodge a street battle to reach the public telex booth. As he entered the building a rocket impact destroyed part of a wall. Afrah and the telex operator scurried up to the third floor, but a burst of machine-gun fire sent them rushing into the basement, where they spent the next forty-eight hours without food or water until the shooting died down.

Afrah told me he was a Somali, as opposed to a man from such-and-such a clan, who loved the city culture of Mogadishu. He knew all about his nation's history, but he had no language to describe the present phenomenon of Somalia's collapse. Later, the aid workers came to call it a "complex emergency," jargon for the simultaneous arrival on the scene of the medieval Four Horsemen of the Apocalypse: war, famine, pestilence, and death. But Afrah pulling on his cigarette that day had no idea what was going on.

We took a stroll down to his local café, a lean-to of corrugated iron in the sand. They brought us bowls of liver and sorghum chapattis, which we ate with our hands, while Afrah told me what he wanted to do.

Until now, he had insisted on staying at home. He had nowhere else he wanted to go. The street fighting was getting so bad, however, that he and his son now planned to flee. His wife, Mana, was already camped at the Red Cross, across the Green Line in the north of the city.

One time the militias parked a tank outside with the barrel pointing toward the house. "They asked me what clan I was from. I told them I was from the clan of journalists. They said which one is that? I told them that it was an extinct one." They went away after he gave them money. Afrah was a prisoner. He told one of the *moryaan*, "There are too many Hitlers in Somalia today."

"Who's Hitler?" replied the boy.

That night I climbed the stairs to a flat roof veranda on Afrah's house and listened to the sounds of the city, quiet and without electricity. The luminous speck of a satellite drew a line of orbit across the sky. I wondered if the world up there even had a notion of what was going on here.

I awoke to the pips of the World Service, my body numb from last evening's qat. The fears that held me tight in the darkness lifted as if by magic with the dawn. Slipping on my sandals and *maweis* sarong, I padded into the corridor with its cool, perspiring coral walls. Afrah was sitting at his open door. His eyes and face were shades of silver and metallic gray in the first light. He was staring out at his future. He covered his face with his hands, sighed, and rose and turned to see me watching him. I understood in that instant our situation. Afrah wanted to flee, but was not free to go. I was a foreigner, so hooked on Somalia I never wanted to leave.

But I did leave Afrah, and then one day the fighting swept across his city district and we lost him for the second time. We looked, but he had vanished off the face of the map and movement in Mogadishu was very dangerous. Months later, we were having a buffet lunch back at the Bunker in Nairobi to welcome a visiting London manager. Waiters in starched white uniforms served canapés and chilled wine. On the walls were cartoons of famous Reuters correspondents drawn with big heads, men like Ian Fleming and Frederick Forsyth.

The door burst open and there stood Afrah. He had a crazy Mad Hatter smile, his silver hair stuck up and his shirt collar was frayed. After grabbing a glass of cheap wine and a cigarette, he stood there snickering to himself as we gathered around him.

The manager, who had heard about Afrah in London, treated him with boardroom jocularity. "So then, what have you been up to?" Afrah regarded him with a grin and said he'd been living among the sand dunes of a beach in a hut made from plastic sheeting, scavenging for food. As his tale unfolded, he became a ventriloquist from hell, imitating the repertoire of battle from the *suf, suf, suf* of an incoming mortar bomb to the pop of small-arms fire.

Afrah spat as he spoke and the corners of his mouth became flecked with foam. The manager clutched his wineglass and stared at the carpet. I looked up at the famous Reuters correspondents, wondering how Afrah fit in to all this. No Reuters official history will ever mention Afrah, his loyalty to the agency, his news, or who he was. In fact, in the instant that the manager turned away to engage in chitchat in safer, more corporate territory, our Mogadishu stringer was all but forgotten.

Afrah told me that after I had left him the last time, a militia tank had returned to his house and blown it to bits, with his son Abdulkadir in front of it. The old man buried his child at the doorstep, where he fell.

"No one can replace him," said Afrah. "Life will be empty without him."

People run away from hurtful memories in many different ways. Afrah went traveling. Before he vanished he gave me his war diary for safekeeping. On the first page, he had written, "In writing a diary on the civil war a number of problems present themselves. Mostly this centres on whether you will still be alive to see it published."

Afrah tapped out his diary on an ancient Olivetti typewriter. While battles raged around him, he wrote underneath his dining table, which was piled with mattresses and carpets, to give him some shelter against the rain of lead that tore into the roof. I picture him sitting there, the burning dot of his cigarette in the dark, dust in his gray hair, listening to rats and cockroaches scuttling across the floor. He made himself "as small as possible." He saw himself as a prisoner, as Anne Frank.

Beyond the range of the guns life went on. People greeted one another with the words "Are you still alive?" One of Afrah's friends was a sheikh, who ran the mosque next door and refused to abandon his religious duties. Five times a day, the muezzin call to prayer crackled out of a loudspeaker, even above the din of Stalin's Organs. Each close explosion made Afrah's ears sing until he went half deaf.

When Afrah's son was killed by the tank blast, the old reporter dug up what little cash he had buried in the dirt floor of his house and, typewriter in hand, fled with his sheikh friend on a perilous journey across the front lines. In the northern suburbs, they visited the Keysane Red Cross hospital, where Afrah's elderly wife was working in safety. There was no room for them to stay and so they left her and had finally come to rest on the ocean beach, where the only sounds were the waves and the wind.

Afrah's beach days formed a pause of calm between the noisy, tragic bursts of survival. He went fishing with a lawyer he called the Professor and caught tuna. He made a few coins as a public scribe, tapping out letters on his Olivetti or sending petitions to the warlords. The Professor held lectures every evening on the white sand. They dined off a table made from a Goodyear tire sign balanced across a couple of jerricans. There were heated debates about everything including whether they, like the Japanese, could use seaweed that they found along the tidemark as a condiment.

Among the stories Afrah's diary told was one about Ibrahim, a boy from a tribe of untouchables, who had fallen in love with Halima, a daughter of a proud nomadic clan. Halima's father refused to allow the marriage to go ahead.

"War, famine, and disease can cause anarchy in a country, but they cannot change what people feel," he said.

The girl went to the old men around the Goodyear table to plead for their help. Without delay, the sheikh told the group to reassemble behind the ruined Lido Beach Club. Halima appeared in her traditional robes, while Ibrahim dressed in white cotton, wore camel-hide sandals, and carried a spear and shield. The sheikh married them and they fled. Minutes later, Halima's father drew up, cursing, in a battlewagon.

"Too late!" The old men laughed. "Too late! Love has won!" And they sauntered back to their Goodyear table.

Eventually the beach came under mortar attack and the old comrades were forced to scatter. There was no way out by sea for Afrah and his wife. They had to come by air, but for that they needed visas. For months Jonathan had been trying to obtain passes to Kenya. By good fortune, not long after Afrah had fled the beach, the documents came through and he and his wife got a Red Cross plane out. First they stayed in Mombasa. "It's on the ocean, like home," Afrah said. And just like at home before the war, his wife cooked him rice and spaghetti with camel meat and bananas.

Then one day Afrah vanished again. Months later I got another postcard from him in Kathmandu. Finally he came to rest in Canada. He sent me another postcard of a moose against a snowy landscape after his immigration papers came through. "I told the magistrate to take his vacation in Mogadishu to see for himself what a nice place it is," he wrote.

Africa's wars have scattered Afrah and his brothers to the four corners of the earth. There are Somalis in Alice Springs in the Australian outback. A family of them inhabited the departure lounge of Moscow's Sheremetyevo airport for more than a year, since no third country offered them refuge. In the high summer of 1994 outside the Russian town of Titovka, near Norway's frontier, the bodies of five Somalis were discovered frozen solid in the melting ice like a herd of mammoths. They must have started trekking westward on foot in the middle of winter when a blizzard engulfed them. They carried no luggage. How the Somalis have suffered, always on the run. One woman told me her grandmother had been a refugee at the dawn of the last century, fleeing from the cavalry of Abyssinia's Emperor Menelik. On the long walk through the desert one of her daughters died of thirst and she cried so much for so long her eyelashes fell out and never grew back.

I hope Afrah has found a true home in Canada, for if he looks back over his shoulder he will see that the vibrant town of his childhood has been destroyed.

"The city has names that lay a quick, chilly touch on your bones: Bermuda Triangle, Yaqshid, Yoobsan, K4, Sinai, Bakaaraha, Karaan," his diary recorded. "And every night I have the vision of myself lying dead in one of those places."

Our Nairobi stringers were an eclectic bunch. Buchizya had by now abandoned Dar es Salaam and joined us at the Bunker. A very personable black American named Jonathan Ewing had become part of the team, though Jonathan the Boss never remembered hiring him, only saying "no" to his requests for a string, then sending him on assigments anyway. There was also an English bloke whose only experience was reporting on horse racing, and a Kenyan girl who wrote the stock market reports and scandalized the evangelical secretaries with her tales of what she liked to do to other females in bed.

Jonathan had a pressing problem in his plans for coverage of Somalia, which was what to do about photography. Hos Maina was our only regular picture stringer at the time. We had to keep this a secret from the Reuters bosses, but during the last few months it had become increasingly clear to us that Hos shouldn't even have been out there covering the fighting at all.

"Look at him," Jonathan said to me once while we were crouching behind a wall. It was in the Bermuda Triangle, or some other fucked-up district of Mogadishu, and Hos was shambling about trying to set up a photo, horribly exposed to the line of fire, as he stuttered and groaned at a gang of militias. Jonathan shook his head.

"For Christ's sake, it's not funny," he said. "The poor lad's more likely to spit at a gunman than plead with him not to shoot."

That Hos was black frankly made him even worse off. At long range the Somalis might mistake him for a fighter. Up close, the Somalis hated most people, and held in contempt Bantu Africans like Hos, a Kikuyu Kenyan. And finally, the militias were turning very nasty toward journalists. In the good old days of conventional war the members of the press were somehow more immune than they became in the era of stateless conflicts. In the early months of Somalia's implosion fighters had posed and camped it up with big smiles when Hos pointed a camera at them. These days, a year or so later, they cocked their guns at him and started yelling that they didn't want their pictures taken.

I felt bad about the state Hos was in. He seemed trapped inside himself. One day Hos said to me fluently, "You know, I didn't always used to be like this." I sat up at that and asked, "How do you mean, Hos?" He relapsed to his stammer. "F-f-f-f-ighting and f-f-f-f-ucking. N-n-o m-m-*more*."

I remember Jonathan coaching Hos on how to speak fluently on certain chosen topics before a senior editor visited from Europe. He told Hos to put together a portfolio of his pictures too, to prove that he was still up to the job. The danger was that if Hos was not allowed to go to Somalia, the managers would have cause to make him redundant. We knew they would not think twice about it. If Hos were to bumble on doing his job, perhaps covering a bit of Somalia but mainly other less lethal stuff in Kenya, we needed a second stringer. What Jonathan wanted ideally was a hungry Caucasian freelancer who aspired to nothing in the world so much as to cover bang-bang stories like Mogadishu without expecting to get paid anything more than pocket money for it. That way Jonathan could expand coverage without stepping on Hos's toes or his salary.

*   *   *

I picture Dan on the day he entered the Bunker. He was barely twenty. The long rains of 1992 were coming to an end and he was on vacation from college in California. A cultural hybrid like so many of us, his background was American, English, Romanian Jewish, but his heart was in Africa. I already knew his father, Mike Eldon, an intense and urbane man who was the manager of a local company. Dan's mother, Kathy, was an American journalist based in Kenya who had helped me publish my first magazine article as a teenager. When I met Dan he told me he was bored of America and wanted to get into news. I decided it was time to return the favor Kathy had done for me.

Dan's room at home was cluttered with all sorts of junk, like monster masks and teen idol posters. He had been taking pictures since he was a small boy. Laid open on his desk were his diaries, big volumes illuminated by a riot of snaps, bits of life's flotsam, quotations, and tarot cards. The inside cover of one diary was inscribed with the words, "The journey is the destination." I flipped through the books and saw how Dan had already thought about his own mortality. The tarot death card La Muerte and the skull and bones card La Calavera repeatedly turned up in the collages. Dan had drawn "Mr. Death" lurking behind himself in photos and he depicted scenes of his own fictional assassination. But Dan's journals also told a story of an idyllic youth spent in Africa, posing with cheetahs, on safari with pretty black and white friends. Dan showed me his latest photo project on a tribal circumcision ceremony in the Rift Valley. The images were of youths in white face paint, wide-eyed and trying to look brave as their childhoods were sliced away in a rite of passage that made boys into men. They were very good and I told Dan to report to the bureau as soon as possible with his portfolio. Jonathan took one look at his photos and hired him on the spot at fifty dollars for every picture that ran on the wire.

* * *

On Dan's first day in Mogadishu, Bald Sam and I took him down to the Green Line. Dan got cheeky to a teenager who thought the rocket-propelled grenade launcher in his hands entitled him to the respect of all. The youth lost his temper and pointed at Dan, ready to pull the trigger. Dan retreated, Nikon at his eye, the shutter release clicking on automatic. The grenadier wore a T-shirt that announced I AM THE BOSS and jabbed his RPG-7 into Dan's ribs. Behind us, the street cleared. Bald Sam slapped his forehead and rolled his eyes.

"Get me away from this guy," Bald Sam exclaimed.

I urged Dan to put his camera down. He ignored me to my alarm and opened his photo bag, from which he fished out a rubber monster mask I had seen in his room at home and slipped this onto his head. It had warts and wrinkly skin and green hair and when Dan stuck his pink tongue out of the mouth hole the little gunman brought his tirade to an abrupt halt with a yelp and a giggle. The moment of tension had passed and Dan pulled the mask off and let the gunman muck around with it.

And so Dan became the second stringer under Hos. His forays into Somalia increased and the place began to bring him under its obsessive influence. His photographs showed he had a tender eye. Don't misunderstand me, he was there for the same reasons I was. To see how it looks and feels. But sooner or later a foreigner had to form a view about the savagery of the Somalis. Were they victims, or were they to blame for their own fate? Most of the foreign correspondents concluded the Somalis were despicable for what they had done to themselves. Dan was different, I suppose because he was young and easygoing. He always treated people decently and looked for what was redeeming about them.

Dan gave me a photo collage from our trips together, captioned with the quirky phrases we had coined on the way. "The bishop don't come round here no more" appears under a photo of a kid holding up an M-16 in the cathedral ruins. What Dan says in a dedication fills me with sorrow today. "To Aidan, with mixed thanks for giving me my first exposure to the horror. Dan Eldon, August 3, 1992."

Mogadishu was so dangerous and out-of-this-world that Reid Miller, the veteran AP correspondent with the shrapnel paperweight, used to say, "I wouldn't even send my first wife there." Downtown resembled Pompeii with every wall patterned by bullet pits and floral explosion bursts. The trees, bullet-stripped of leaves and limbs, stood like charred totem poles. There were no street signs anymore, key landmarks had been razed to the ground, universities were no longer places of learning but militia strongholds, and factories were refugee camps. We hurtled through city streets and one moment there were crowds at roadside tea kiosks, piles of grapefruits, and wheelbarrows of meat, the next we were turning into an alleyway and our guards were clicking off their safeties. A roadblock appeared up ahead. *Pop pop* went a couple of rounds over our heads and we came to a halt as a gang of teenagers surrounded the vehicle. Our guards were piling out of the car with their AK rifles, yelling. It was all so arbitrary. Pull the trigger now, get murdered in the car, get hit by a stray round. Accelerating away from the roadblock, I tried to disappear into my seat. The back of my head tingled. I acted cool, though, so as not to appear scared in front of the guards who were laughing their heads off. And as we sped along Dan in the back softly started in on the song he always came out with at such times, a jolly number called "I Whistle a Happy Tune" from Rodgers and Hammerstein's *The King and I*:

> *Whenever I feel afraid, I hold my head erect,*
> *And whistle a happy tune,*
> *So no one will suspect*
> *I'm afraid...*

Dan knew and I knew how important it was not to show your fear. The words of the *The King and I* song went on to say that when you fool the people you fear, you fool yourself as well. "You are as brave as you make believe you are." But when fear subsided I felt this delicious exhaustion and it wasn't long before I wanted to do it again. Maybe it was simply about glands and hormones but I could have sworn then that I had experienced multiple spiritual epiphanies and moments of ultra-clarity.

Some of the correspondents used to sleep at a villa as guests of an American team of doctors and nurses. On a bad day they had three hundred casualties and the medical staff could be sucked into eighteen-hour shifts in the operating room. Each evening, by the time we got back to the villa my shirt was soaked with sweat. The journalists and medics set up a bottle of whiskey and started chewing their qat. As the Jack Daniel's drained away we all tried to put the world to rights.

Before the lights went off with the generator I used to lie on my bed drinking, reading, and writing letters to my mother, to Granny, or to Lizzie.

"Month after month and nothing seems to change," I wrote. "The fighting goes on and still the Somalis celebrate in their violence. It's as if they don't hate each other anymore, they just like killing because it's become a habit."

Outside in the villa courtyard, the guards chattered as they played dominoes with knucklebones on the asphalt. Gunfire roared in the distance. On the walkie-talkie, a bored Trinidadian UN official clogged up radio traffic with calypso songs, mock weather reports, and descriptions of what he'd eaten for dinner.

Hos shuffled about the room, struggling to get things done

with his crippled fingers. We'd talk about the colonial era and the Mau Mau rebellion. I told him my father's first farm house on Mount Kenya had been burned down.

"Johnny, it was my grandfather who torched it," Hos laughed. He found it even funnier to hear that it was instead the British who had done it. I remember one evening Hos said that when we had a spare weekend we should go together to visit the place where Gikuyu and Mumbi, the African Adam and Eve, met beneath a sacred fig tree up on Mount Kenya. I looked forward to that trip, but we never did make it.

About midnight, full of qat and whiskey, I'd file my overnight story on the satellite, perhaps inspired by an evening firefight, aid-worker tidbits, or eavesdropped radio traffic. The overnighter looked forward to the next day and kept the story alive, ready to be freshened up in the morning. The news went on twenty-four hours, never ceased, never went quiet. Always the beast to be fed. After the lights went down I knocked myself out with a final dose of whiskey and slept with a Beretta pistol purchased from the cook, in case I woke up startled in the dead of night with clammy, clawed feet scuttling over my face. Mogadishu was alive with rats and I heard it said that while you dreamed they blew on your bare feet to numb them before sucking the blood out of your toes.

Life in the city operated on at least two separate dimensions. There was the fighting, with trauma wards, feeding centers and warlords. Then there was the real city of Mogadishu, with its Indian Ocean culture, revolving around the teashop, market, and mosque. The domestic soap opera of life carried on, war or no war, and the two cities existed side-by-side, almost independent of each other.

Bakaaraha market was a teeming emporium where you could

buy anything from an alarm clock that played the Muslim call to prayer to weapons and, probably, a few pounds of radioactive materials. "Guns R Us," Carlos called Bakaraaha, where you could fire an AK clip or a .45 into the air while browsing for the perfect piece. I was walking in the market when a group of girls ran in front of me and swept off their shawls. Their ears and necks dripped with gold stars. Their feet and hands were patterned with henna. They darted into a door and flashed their eyes at me. I cantered after them in pursuit, past an armed guard, and into a shop housed in a metal cargo container where gold bangles, necklaces, and filigreed pendants shone in the gloom. I came away with an Empress Maria Theresa silver dollar as big as a tin-can lid, originally imported to Egypt by Napoleon Bonaparte on his way to defeat the Mamelukes at the pyramids in 1799 and thereafter used in the trade for slaves and goods down the Red Sea and Indian Ocean coasts.

We often ate lunch at the Lido Beach Club where I had played as a child. The establishment had seen better days, and some of the older correspondents recalled how it had once been packed with beautiful whores who wore blond wigs. These days the wall at the entrance—there was no door and no roof—was a sign of an AK-47 in a red circle with a line through it, indicating that patrons had to leave their weapons outside before sitting down to eat. Years later I've still got the snaps taken at some fabulous seafood Lido lunches with Dan, Hos, Jonathan, Bald Sam, Eric, Julian, Carlos, and all the other hacks. Replete after succulent lobster, spicy rice, and watermelon juice, before heading back into the heat and the fighting, we used to strip off and run across the blinding white sandy beach and dive into the clean blue waves. Some people warned us about bull sharks, the six-foot, three-hundred-pound psychopaths that rode in on the surf and could bite off a man's leg. Bull sharks are attracted by the refuse tossed into port waters and so they had always been a problem in Mogadishu, probably even when the traveler Ibn Battuta had visited in the fourteenth century and remarked that hundreds of camels were butchered daily on the beach. The more prosperous Mogadishu was, the more rubbish it produced and the more sharks. In 1991 the beaches were still stained with blood and puddles of animal guts glittered bluishly in the sun. But the economy had collapsed and as the city slid toward starvation, the sharks disappeared. I swam frequently, and after a few months I was fit, I got a deep tan, and my shaggy hair was bleached blond by the sun and salty water. I might almost have been on vacation.

Carlos announced one weekend that we were all going fishing off Jezira beach. He had organized a boat, with tackle and bait, and out we went. We bobbed about on the blue, each one of us with a hand line over the side. We sat in the sunshine chatting and when one of the lines went tight we pulled it up and out flapped a bright coral fish, a grouper, a snapper, or a mullet. We later sat on the sandy beach and built a fire of aromatic acacia wood in a long trench. When it had burned down to coals we raked them flat. Then on top we laid a large kingfish, caked in a paste of salt, oil, and lime juice. It turned to a plaster-like cast as the fish baked inside. When it was ready, the fish was grasped by its charred head and tail and set down on a cloth. The salty crust was chipped away and the brown and white flesh divided up in chunks. It was moist, sweet, and slightly gritty from the sand and coals.

I strolled at dusk with Carlos during the holy month of Ramadan through the ancient quarter of Hamarwein, down narrow alleys behind the old port among closely packed coral towers stained white and sienna. We fasted out of respect for the Somalis, denying ourselves both food and drink during daylight hours. There were no gunmen in the quarter and past us down narrow alleys slipped old men in skullcaps murmuring "peace, peace, peace," raven-haired girls in gold earrings, and women in diaphanous *bui bui* robes revealing nothing but their henna-decorated ankles. In the mosque at the hour of *maghrib*, sunset prayers, a youth's voice was singing *hadith*, the vesperlike tales of the Prophet. I sat outside the mosque entrance to observe the men come and go. Here Carlos gave me his camera, removed his sandals, and bent to wash his feet, then his hands, then rinsed out his mouth, sucked in, and blew out water through his nostrils, scrubbed his ears and neck, and finally stood up with his face and the black fleece of his hair glittering with dewy droplets. He entered the doors into the cool where I was not allowed. In a while, I heard a collective sigh and I peered in to see Carlos sitting on his thighs, in a line with the other men, praying.

We were invited to friends' houses to celebrate the festival of Id al-Fitr, when the new crescent moon was sighted to signal the end of fasting. Guests left their guns outside, leaning against a wall. Shoes were removed. Incense and myrrh burned. We were invited to sit down on colorful, machine-made carpets. Kneeling in a circle, eating with our right hands, we shared sweet pastries and dates and watermelon juice, the first hit of sugar and liquid since before daybreak. This was followed by fatty broth, and cardamom rice and bananas topped with piles of goat meat, bones, chicken with fierce green chiles, and sorghum chapatis or slabs of coarse bread baked in the fire's hot coals. There was no sense of rank or division at these occasions. Men ate side-by-side, just as they had prayed together. The talk gave way to loud wet noises as eaters crunched and sucked on bones and split skulls, then fell back greasy-fingered and replete.

Afterward, a murmur of expectation rippled around the room. Men looked at one another, raised their eyebrows, and blew out one cheek like Satchmo blowing his horn. Youths entered with bundles of emerald leaves. Each man got his bunch and, satisfied, lay back and tucked his legs under him and an elbow propped on a cushion. Thus seated, the chewer then plucked at the baby rhubarb shoots, popping them into his cheek, forming a bolus of pulp to be masticated and sucked.

As the juices flowed into my system, my limbs began to tingle.

Ever so delicately, I fell under the vegetable's spell. The days and weeks slipped away and my old life seemed a distant thing. The explorer Sir Richard Burton believed that qat was the same plant as lotus, to which Ulysses lost half his crew because as they chewed they forgot all their ambitions to return home. I had begun to chew every day and in the afternoons I'd climb to the tops of shattered buildings, sucking at the pulp, and stare out at plumes of smoke rising from the Bermuda Triangle or Medina districts, wherever was taking hits in the predusk mortar duel. The tableau was more sublime to me than the cityscapes of Florence, or Paris, or Manhattan. I'd hear the muezzin pipe up from a dozen mosques for *asr*, afternoon prayers, caressing the broken lines of the city with Kufic arabesques of sound. The amplified cries to God, impact explosions, sea breeze, softening light, and my heartbeat wove together.

During my time off at the Ski Chalet in Nairobi, the normalcy of family life was a comfort to me. My parents were regular visitors, my brothers came to stay, and my sister, who lived with her husband and two boys across the valley, rode over on horseback some mornings for a coffee before I went to work. I assumed they knew what was going on in my life because they read the papers. In fact, my mother clipped my reports and pasted them into a scrapbook, while Dad used to fire questions at me about regional politics. It made me proud that the work I did apparently won his approval. The truth, as I later discovered, was quite the contrary. Dad had appointed me as executor of his will. At some point, however, he wrote to his lawyer without telling me to say that because I might be killed before he died somebody else should handle his estate.

Granny wrote to me from England, "I do hope you won't be sent to famine countries for that means you will have inadequate food and water ..." The last time I saw her at her home in Sussex, long after Grandpa died, I was on a Reuters training visit to London. There was snow outside and the living room was freezing. We sat on the radiator together and she held my hand and mumbled with her eyes closed. She served my supper on a Beatrix Potter plate that I had been given on my childhood visits to Sussex, the kind that revealed Peter Rabbit as one ate up one's custard. Granny had been asleep by the time I closed the door of her flat.

"Thank you so much for all your help when you came as I can do so little now. Sickening! Aunt Beryl has brought in snowdrops and one daffodil and it is so lovely having the spring and warm come. But goodness what a mess in the Middle East and Saddam still there ..."

The warlords had swelled like ticks on the blood of the conflict. After laying waste the land, in the opening months of 1992 it became clear that they had created a famine. For months, Red Cross situation reports—known as SITREPS—had warned of a human catastrophe. The United Nations sent a Sierra Leone official, James Jonah, to broker negotiations between the warlords. He accorded them the respect due proper leaders and by doing so conferred an undeserved legitimacy that later came back to haunt Somalia. The warlords enjoyed red carpet treatment on an expenses-paid trip to New York and used the time to order fresh weapons while paying lip service to international demands. A truce was declared in Mogadishu on March 3, 1992. After an absence of thirteen months, the United Nations reestablished a diplomatic presence in Somalia in April. Mohamed Sahnoun, a former Algerian foreign minister, was appointed the special representative. Finally, the world cranked up aid and food shipments. Among the

Somalis, violence immediately shifted from interclan bloodletting to looting emergency humanitarian supplies. They swarmed over relief shipments and convoys, the charity goods found their way into markets, and the clans used the profit to buy more guns. Gunfire and explosions remained a part of the daily city routine, but hospital casualty wards were under less pressure. Apart from hospital triage rooms, the city's main barometer of security was the seaports and airports. The militias routinely looted a Second World War–era Dakota DC-3 from Nairobi that attempted to fly in each day with emergency vaccinations, essential drugs, and high-energy therapeutic foods called BP-5 and UNIMIX, used to revive starving infants. The gunmen smashed the vaccines and ate the UNIMIX. From November 17, 1991, the port had been totally shut down. The Red Cross delivered grain by floating barges up to the surf-lined beaches of villages to the north and south of Mogadishu. By February 14, the Red Cross had delivered three thousand tons but declared this to be a "drop in the ocean." Two days after the truce in early March, the first UN food ship attempted to enter the port, but came under mortar fire and had to sail away again. A few yards from the port entrance, children were dying. Only on May 3 did the MV *Felix,* chartered by the UN, finally discharge a cargo of five thousand tons. The warlord militias focused their efforts on being first in line when the mercy boats arrived and if they couldn't control the seaport they would resort to shelling it. I saw the night sky light up like day when they hit a string of fuel tanks, which exploded in a fireball hundreds of meters high, setting light to a warehouse full of grain that would have been enough to feed the city for months. "There's no business like aid business," Gutali, one of Aydiid's cousins, told me that season.

When a ship was unloading the seaport fizzed with gunfire day and night, so inevitably we tended to spend our time there—along with most of the population of Mogadishu. It was a place surrounded by mobs of heaving rags, rolling eyes, and angry mouths. Rival clan gangs competed to control the fortified port perimeter. Inside the docks it was like a circus with various freelance gangs killing one another: militias, the private armies of grain and sugar merchants, stevedores, and unemployed members of the defunct police forces in tattered uniforms. Worst of all were the cripples. My guards were hardened killers, but they went pale with fear when they saw a squadron of these deformed creatures barreling across the tarmac toward us. They charged in wheelchairs, on crutches, or on trolleys like skateboards—paraplegics, victims of polio and land mines. One had the swollen legs and the gourd-sized testicles of elephantiasis. They bristled with guns and grenades and we would have to speed off before they could skid to a halt or drop their crutches to take aim at us.

My first glimpse of the famine was on a road trip to the inland town of Baidoa. We were all qat-stoned and my translator Sharif was gabbling nonsense in my ear. We were going for the land speed record down the empty highway, slicing through a forest of myrrh trees. Receding behind us was the city, where the insanity could almost be held in your hands, but up ahead a terrifying question loomed. A granite peak a thousand feet high stood like a gate to another kingdom. We hurtled forward, slowing down only for camels crossing, or wild pig, or when the road was clogged with smashed technicals and sun-dried corpses hanging out of the cabins. Four hours out, I got a blurred glimpse of crouched figures in the shade of thorn trees—brown rags, slack breasts, and callused feet in the greenish gloom. Long teeth, white tongues, sunken eye sockets, alien heads, rib cages showing the crocodile-skin ridge of vertebrae poking up through the back. We slowed down to avoid hitting emaciated figures tottering down the highway in a herd. The air reeked of shit and wood smoke. The driver honked his horn as the wraiths crawled to get out of our path. Coming alongside, we stared. They stared back. Our mouths were full of qat. They proffered open hands. We wound up the windows. They scratched at them with feeble claws.

When I saw a prone figure on the roadside ahead, I said okay, that's enough, we're stopping. I got down from the car and approached the figure, black and Giacometti thin. His breath was coming in short, crackling sighs. His eyes were rolling back into his mummified pharaoh's face.

"Get him in the car."

Sharif spat and talked to the guards.

"They say no." Sharif gestured to the others.

"In the fucking car. Now."

Sharif began arguing loudly with the gunmen. Sharif and I lifted the starving man out of the dirt and dragged him to the car. As we folded him onto the backseat floor, the guards raised their feet to avoid touching him and glared at me. My gunmen were Aydiid's men, Habre Gedir and their allies from powerful nomadic clans. The dying man was a Rahanwein, from a clan of farmers. The farmers raised sorghum and cattle off the black soil. The nomads kept camels—and there we have the great divide between Cain and Abel. Drought shriveled up the land in the two years before the dictator had fled. The farmers survived the thin spell on grain stocks saved from the fat years. But when the civil war erupted the nomad militias knew Somalia's central farming provinces of Bay and Bakool were convenient battlefields since a man could live off the land if he was aggressive enough about it. Roads through the crop zones became the main axes of fighting, as the opposing militias fought high-speed technical skirmishes. Fighters on both sides looted all the livestock and grain they could, and each time a militia advanced or withdrew a new wave of hungry gunmen would go through. Seven harvests came and went and famine was the result. The man was dead by the time we rolled into Baidoa.

The town's main street was a spaghetti western set with camps on all sides of igloo huts constructed from twigs and bits of plastic. I saw men and women standing about in flowing robes and thought they had great dignity. They had walked here with nothing but their children on their backs, their milk pots, and their herding sticks. On the street we found a shelter resembling a bus stop where bodies were dumped to await removal. We dropped our corpse at one of these and went to find a place to sleep.

Since Unicef had established therapeutic feeding centers in June, several charities had set up shop in Baidoa. Aid staff raced about in 4x4s with flags planted on the bonnets, their armed guards in the back. I knew an American nurse named Rose. Her charity had opened a center in town and she had invited us to stay. I learned that bandits from Mogadishu were following the aid operation into the interior and the charity's compound was therefore defended by local armed youths against the gangs roaming the streets outside. On the flat roof of the villa was a sentry position constructed with sacks of baby-milk powder instead of sandbags. It was the guards on the charity payroll, however, who posed the most danger. Their daily dilemma seemed to be whether to accept their working wage or fleece their employers at gunpoint. It was a question they never properly resolved, so they either protected or extorted, depending on their mood. In turn, the foreigners spent nearly as much time quarreling with their volatile guards over salaries as feeding the dying. Eventually, the gunmen killed an Irish nurse.

Once inside the high, broken glass–topped walls of the compound, the charity workers were the usual collection of oddballs: kindly old mums, hippies in cotton print skirts, Filipinos with beatific smiles, all devoted to the Lord. Among them, Dan noted, were svelte young females whose pictures would definitely sell newspapers. Rose wore a Somali woman's diaphanous headscarf. Her hands and feet were patterned with henna, in the style of a Somali bride. None of them spoke of their wish to save the world, which was certainly a relief. A few drinks around the dinner table revealed that they were not unlike journalists in Africa, being fugitives from emotional distress at home, divorce, bereavement, career burnout, boredom, or simply themselves.

The media had covered famine in Africa repeatedly since the catastrophe of Biafra in 1968 and the hunger story had become a separate news genre. TV broadcasts aimed to stimulate moral outrage and claimed that individual viewers in the rich world didn't have to remain mere spectators. News went out hand in hand with charity appeals that told people they could "do something" to save the children pictured on their screens. After the media circus of the 1984 Ethiopian famine, it got harder to shock people into responding. We were told that Europe and America had come down with "donor fatigue."

In this state of affairs there was no way to sell the story unless you could expose suffering on a scale rarely or never witnessed before. I once traveled with a British TV cameraman to a village in Sudan where the crops had failed. Our guides ordered the kids to parade in front of us and display their swollen bellies and thin limbs.

"I'm sorry," said the cameraman. "They're not thin enough."

The Africans looked at him astonished.

"I can see they're hungry. But to the viewers they just don't look that far gone." The journalist had to get thin ones. If he didn't, he would not be doing his job. He had been sent to find thin ones. He turned to the Africans and enunciated in a voice both loud and slow, "NOT. THIN. ENOUGH!"

There was no shortage of thin people in Baidoa, where in town alone four hundred people a day were dying. Baidoa looked like a concentration camp without the barbed wire.

The peasants who had initially starved in their villages had been sucked into Baidoa by the magnet of news that the foreigners were dumping food in town and along the highways. Somalis gave the 1992 famine the epochal name of the Time of Swollen Feet because the peasants had to trek so far to reach the feeding centers. I saw how tough their feet were when I found a skeleton the maggots had picked clean but for his hard soles. Many died on the road but when they reached the feeding centers they were so weak and without proper shelter or hygiene that multitudes swiftly fell victim to disease.

Rose's feeding center was a big white tent, a sort of marquee. Her charity's logo appeared on the roof and on a flag fluttering on tent poles, so that it was highly visible. It looked like a trade show display but apparently it was so the camp didn't get bombed in an air raid.

Inside the luminescent, yellowish glow of the tent's interior, I saw rows of small creatures sprawled across the blue plastic ground-sheet. They didn't look human, but rather like the crew from a crashed Martian spaceship with their oversized heads, bulging eyes, and plastic tubes in their noses and arms, crapping watery puddles. Slack-breasted, listless mothers sat or lay with them.

"That one's circling the drain," said Rose pointing at a child. "You know, like a spider in your bath?"

The nurses constantly used such language in the camps. Another term the nurses used was DBT—Dead By Tomorrow.

Our villa was next to one of the camps in the town. Perched on the wall of baby milk sandbags, I used to gaze down into the mass of humans. The days were quiet, but the nights were eerily so. A chorus of hacking coughs heralded dawn, as a few fires built by those with strength enough to gather twigs were lit to cook the dried animal skins and bones they had found out on the plains. By eight, the survivors of the night tottered on spindly legs around and around until they flopped down panting in the heat. The hours of light passed and cold came again as darkness fell. I walked into the camps at evening and saw hungry children with night blindness brought on by vitamin A deficiency stumbling about, crying for their mothers.

I'll always have in my mind those children's eyes. As severe hunger took hold of them, their eyeballs turned red and rough. Next, a process the doctors called "melting and wasting" set in. The eyes foamed with mucus. They sagged and formed ulcers that burst in welters of pus. If the kids survived, their sight was scarred for life with blemishes like opals or moonstones on the pupils.

I saw every starving person as a symbol of the civil war. As the body wasted away it began to consume its own self. I crouched next to the dying and asked them to tell me what they had endured. In Somalia victims were the main interviewees and gave us vox pops on their own deaths. The stories were all the same. Militias looted our granaries; the rains failed; we started walking; we arrived here and now we're waiting for food. I spoke to Abdullahi, who had had a wife and nine sons and daughters. Two had died on the trek, and five more were lined up next to him on the ground where I met him, his healthiest son immobile, with the skin on his knees splitting apart to reveal jutting bare bone and cartilage.

Abdullahi obliged me with an account of his hunger. He told me the initial ache—a point at which I'd never been past—was replaced after a few days by burning thirst. Among kids low-calorie intake caused marasmus, giving the Martian-headed skeletal look. Protein deficiency produced that swollen-belly effect known as kwashiorkor. I'd press my finger into the flesh of a baby's arm and see how it left an indentation from edema. I saw the peasant children's black glossy hair turn sparse and reddish blond. Their teeth fell out and they displayed *cancrum oris*, a condition in which oral bacteria eat ulcers into the cheeks like gunshot wounds until they slough away. It was hard to get the ones who lived beyond these stages to make any sense. They became zombies with staring eyes, no longer individuals. Inside their sagging guts they were cannibalizing the spare parts of their own bodies, eating up their fat reserves, then the protein of the muscles. It reminded me somehow of a hyena caught in a trap, chewing off its own leg, or the way a slug turns itself inside out when doused in salt. Electrolytic balances went off-kilter, immune systems crashed, and batteries of diseases poured in. If victims survived all forms of illness their terminal release came with total organ failure. Running on empty.

The way people died, and why and how, was far more complicated than we were able to comprehend. Even within the camp, there were those who suffered only a little, or escaped it altogether, or even thrived off the very misfortunes that killed those surrounding them. Crowds of healthy children used to run after me, yelling and laughing. Among them were other children, who did not follow you except silently. Some stayed behind sitting and took no notice at all. It was to these last children that the cameramen were drawn.

We went about browsing for pictures, interviews, vignettes of the dying and the dead. The humanitarian SITREPS gave me just the bare bones. "UNICEF nutritionist reports that from an informal rapid eye assessment (the eyeball test) approximately 50% of children require intensive feeding ... Measles widespread as are dysentery and malaria ... UNOSOM pays gravediggers (food for work by day, rather than per grave) who report 200 deaths per day (unconfirmed by expatriates) ..." I was ignorant of the Somali language, so what might have been descriptions of beauty, struggle, courage, suffering, were lost on me. I pressed my translator Sharif for the nuances I knew he wasn't giving me. But Sharif's English was limited and he was an ex-policeman, not a poet. He barked questions as if he were interrogating a criminal. The refugees gave us long stories, full of gesture and expression. When one of these dying men had finished, perhaps giving us his deathbed valediction, Sharif would shrug. "He says he doesn't know."

I didn't ask the famine victims' permission if I could record their terminal moments or call Dan in to take a picture. Mo Amin said we were not exploiting them because we would help by exposing the truth to media audiences. This made sense at least in the abstract, because people suffer secretly, in this case die of hunger, only in places where they are robbed of their freedom to speak the truth.

I sat beneath a tree next to a man, asked his family members waiting beside him for his name, age, life history, and scribbled down some detail of color as he rattled his last. The only way successfully to convey the tragedy of famine was to depict the death of an individual. But the challenge was to make audiences appreciate that naked, black, Muslim Africans were worth caring for. We experimented in any way we could to tug the heartstrings with novel effects. I found a TV soundman on his knees, poking his furry microphone boom into the face of a Somali spread-eagled on the earth. The man lay silent, until with a faint exhalation he died. The soundman held on for a few more seconds, then switched off his machine and got to his feet. "I've been wanting to do that," he said. "I've captured the sound of death on tape."

At dawn we accompanied a truck that did the rounds of camps to collect corpses. This daily trip gave one an accurate figure of fatalities in town over the previous twenty-four hours. We'd find a row of bodies waiting in a neat line. Night deaths were high due to hypoglycemia, or low blood sugar, which led to a crash in body temperature and hypothermia. The dead were naked but for a string of beads tied with a thong about the neck and a blanket or cotton shift. Workers swung the corpses up onto the back of the truck where the reporters sat and we drove on. Once we had a full load we drove outside town to a derelict military camp filled with rusty guns. Here teams of women washed the corpses with tenderness, then for shrouds wrapped them in their blankets. What I respected about the people in Baidoa was that every famine victim who died was an individual and I never saw them tossed into mass graves, as I would later in other parts of Africa.

I watched a person die and however strange I felt about it I still had to sit down and tap out a news report if I wanted to do my job well and beat the competition. My only pleasure, if that is the word, was knowing what distress I could cause somebody over the morning papers next day somewhere overseas—and what disturbed me was that clearly people were not disturbed enough. These days I wish I had responded with more dramatic personal gestures. I could have run marathons, chained myself to the railings at the Houses of Parliament, and donated my salary to charity. I made no sacrifices. The more weeks I spent witnessing the famine zone on Reuters expenses, the more my wages piled up in my bank account. I told myself we were like doctors and we should not become emotionally involved with our subjects. It was the same for the other hacks like Jonathan, Sam, and Julian, and I suppose Dan, Hos, and Carlos were using their camera lenses as shields. All my energies to articulate the horror of what I witnessed were being poured into the stream of reports I sent to Reuters. I sold my angry observations, if you like, for a cheap price to benefit a news service. I was not at the same time able to pass on to the wire my sense of personal distress, the bruises of being a witness. That's what I feel now, but at the time I detected no serious shift in my state of mind.

Except, come to think of it, I could barely stay awake in the days. I yawned in the face of a nun showing me a children's feeding unit. I dozed in the passenger seat of my battlewagon, head lolling and dribbling, as we bumped down a dirt track past villages of abandoned beehive huts. I could be taking notes on a saga of a group of peasants who had walked for days in search of food. Instead of the tale changing my life, as it should have done, I was overcome by tiredness. I fell asleep at my work desk, in the middle of meals, as soon as I sat down in a comfortable chair. I see now that the narcolepsy helped me get along because it tuned me out from what I had seen. But somehow I ingested what I saw on a deeper level, like sounds heard in sleep.

One's physical urges were a different matter. The starving peasants lost their appetite for sex, they aborted fetuses, and their dugs dried up. But healthy people, including me, maintained or even increased their appetites for food, sex, and laughter. At the end of a dusty trip to an outlying village of skeletons, I would have ravenous hunger. It was as if we were feeding off the weakness of the poor. At the charity house there was a Gaggia espresso machine and coffee never tasted so good. On the road we had huge meals at roadside tin shacks run by plump maidens. They served bowls of sorghum pancakes, bananas, slabs of greasy roasted camel meat, a bottle of cloudy brown oil, and glasses of thickly sugared black tea. My Somali partners poured the liquid in their glasses and some oil onto their pancakes, mashed it all up with their right hands, and shoveled the mess loudly into their gobs. All this might take place while a group of dusty little peasant children stared at us from a few feet away. Among the reporters I saw two TV men who had so overindulged themselves that they had decided to diet and were guzzling slimming yogurt drinks while filming the skeletons. An American TV correspondent took early morning jogs with his shirt off and a heart monitor on his chest along a road past a famine camp with the night's bodies laid out for collection. It was as if an aerobics class had been transported in a time machine back to medieval London during the Black Plague.

In the summer of 1992, the UN secretary-general Boutros Boutros-Ghali, complained that while the West lavished aid and attention on the "rich man's war" of the Balkans, it allowed the blacks to starve en masse in Africa. The leaders of the West have little problem with letting Africans exterminate one another or leaving them to go poor or hungry. But to be accused of racism makes these presidents and prime ministers flush with guilt and in this case promises of action were not long to follow. Overnight dozens of charities descended on Baidoa, joining the handful that had been there from the early days like the Red Cross, Goal, Irish Concern, Unicef, and the International Medical Corps. The militias could not believe their good fortune. Aid workers hired fleets of vehicles to these new foreign outfits, which stamped their logos on the car doors and planted flags on their bonnets. They hired hundreds of guards, cooks, and mechanics. Money was no object. It was such a circus that Dan and I in a mood of cynicism rigged up our car with a flag and the logo of a phony aid group on the side: DESPAIR—BECAUSE WE DON'T CARE!

The charities did begin distributing large quantities of grain, but it was all so late in the day because the majority of children under the age of five had by that time already died. In late October Sean Devereaux, a Unicef worker who became a friend of mine before he was shot in the back by the Somalis, told me, "Whoever was going to die has already gone." The toll was in the region of three hundred thousand peasants, most of them small children. By the time the skeletal figures appeared on the world's TV screens, most of the individuals filmed were dead. The chubby-faced kids with milk dribbling from their lips months later were the ones not thin enough to make a news story before the food arrived. All the news bulletins, the air bridge of food, the celebrity visitors, and the battering ram of Western military hardware would come too late. "If only we had intervened before November [1991]," the UN envoy Sahnoun wrote later. "Because of that delay we now pay the price." Sahnoun called for an investigation into the failure to act promptly. This honesty riled UN headquarters so much that they sacked him from his post in Somalia.

Squadrons of hacks flew in on day-trip charters, took pictures, filed reports, and then flew out again. They obediently trotted out the story that the UN and overseas charities had magically put a stop to the famine overnight. Next in the parade came the politicians, the movie actors, and the rock 'n' roll stars. Hos and I flew to a refugee camp on the Somali frontier with UN "goodwill ambassador" Sophia Loren and forty Italian paparazzi. On arrival at the dirt airstrip, a fleet of gleaming UN vehicles whisked us off to a line of tents. A procession formed behind Sophia as we filed into a shelter crowded with starving kids. The idea we wanted to convey was of Sophia "working" as a UN envoy in her pricey outfit and diaphanous scarf. Her famous big eyes were hidden behind brown-tinted glasses and I noticed how her makeup was melting in the heat. A semicircle of cameras whirred and clicked as Sophia fed a skeletal infant by holding a spoon to its lips.

"Again?" she said in a little girl's voice. Two "feeds" more and the dying child was handed back to its mother. Sophia swept off between sprawled bodies with photographers treading at her heels. I dropped behind and went to look for something else to do. But Sophia kept crossing my path, advancing through the tents with the stampede of photographers zigzagging after her. After they had stormed through one time I found Somali nurses fussing over a naked starving child whose leg had been stamped on by one of the marauding photographers because it had been too weak to crawl out of the way.

The UN officer who had arranged the trip was a friend of mine and he pleaded with me not to tell the story of the kid whose leg had been stamped on as its use would stop people contributing toward the famine. And so reluctantly I wrote: "'... It's a tragedy on a biblical scale,' said the Oscar-winning star of classics such as *Two Women* while holding a skeletal infant in her arms."

I asked my friend what his agency was doing with Sophia Loren.

"I know," he shrugged. "We discussed Madonna, but she's just too sexy for a famine. Pity really."

It was time to get out of Baidoa. I joined a Red Cross friend driving into the bush with a Somali veterinary team to deliver livestock drugs to the nomads. We dumped the vehicle and marched off the road to look for the nomads' *bomas*. To walk again gave me animal joy. I fell into pace with the Somalis. I listened to the sound of our footfalls on the dust. The bush was a beautiful mix of colors. Red termite hills the length and shape of elephant trunks, yellow and green myrrh trees, and flowering desert roses as pink as my mother's plants in the garden at the beach house. Doves and hornbills flew overhead and, from a treetop, a go-away-bird jeered down at me. I imagined my father was walking beside me, with great swinging strides.

We came at last to a family *boma*, a pastoral idyll. There was a flurry of excitement as we approached. Children ran up first, then the young men with warrior strides, whistling through their teeth, wielding spears and carbines, their bodies covered in ghee and their hair in coiffed helmets. The women held back, shouting huskily. Then elders, seeing the veterinarians' familiar faces, henna-haired with their rosaries and walking sticks, came out to greet us.

At dusk, bleating sheep and goats and camels, their wooden bells clonking, came home to their thorn enclosures. A clear-eyed youth, his hair glittering with ghee, milked a camel and brought me the pot foaming over with the warm liquid. I said how much I liked the nomads' camels and one of the elders replied, "If you know so much about camels, what is the part of it that looks like a man?"

Allah provided the camel to the bloodthirsty poets who inhabit the Shag of Somalia and it remains one of the three subjects of poetry, together with war and love. The Somalis have more camels than any other nation on earth. Camels outnumber Somalis. They provide the nomads with their staple diet of milk and meat, their leather is as thick as a car tire, they are pack animals, and even their hair can be used for weaving. The camel is the ultimate symbol of wealth even for the nomads in modern Somalia.

I considered the old man's question. I knew a Somali joke that the camel was the last animal created by Allah. He was tired as he stuck the animal together with the head of a giraffe and skin of a lion. As it shuffled away, God looked at its bum and saw in his fatigue that he had overlooked giving the camel a penis. He threw the organ of a man at the camel so that it stuck onto the groin, but pointing the wrong way.

"Old man, the bit that pisses backwards," I replied. He laughed, said yes, and invited us to the fireside.

The sun set and then the velvet curtain of equatorial night fell. Only in a wilderness such as this could I see the stars so clearly and for one who has lived under the brown, light-polluted skies of the city this has always moved me to wonder. The old man saw me lost in my thoughts as I gazed up and he cheerfully told me to tell him what picture I saw in the Milky Way. "Look," he said. "There are the tracks of a herd of camels across the girdle of the stars …"

For all the horrors of Somalia's towns that year, I knew that the tranquil scene I was part of that evening was more typical of what was happening around myriad campfires across the Horn of Africa. Life continued, almost undisturbed, and the Somalis welcomed us that night rather than shooting at us because they were bound by the age-old rules of hospitality to strangers, something Westerners have all but lost. And the nomads were genuinely happy to see us because the vets had brought drugs for their livestock, which was the thing on which their well-being depended. Sitting among that family, I longed to stay in the bush and not return to the towns of Africa where people were killing each other. I decided that my father had led a better life than I. He had chosen to live among simple people out here, whereas in the noisy years of my twenties I had grown fascinated with all that was wrong with the world.

In July 1992, a man named General Imtiaz Shaheen appeared with a small group of UN officers and Pakistani soldiers to monitor the "cease-fire" in Mogadishu. It was an impossible task and Aydiid was furious because he feared they would undermine his ambitions for power and interrupt his plunder of humanitarian aid. Peace in Somalia remained the exact opposite of what Aydiid wanted and his Habre Gedir clansmen, ensconced in the city villas, Shebelle River plantations, and the other symbols of wealth they had taken as the spoils of victory over their enemies, had no intention of relinquishing it all for a cease-fire. The Pakistanis were therefore unable to carry out their mission and were confined to one end of Mogadishu Central airfield.

Shaheen was a good man and one who didn't give up easily, but he could do little except hold cricket matches and have his white-gloved orderlies serve splendid curry lunches to the hacks and aid workers on the airport runway. The cricket pitch was marked up in the dead ground from which unexploded ordnance had been carefully removed. Shaheen's Pathans played us, a mixed team of Brits, African colonials, West Indians, Aussies, and Kiwis. I used to go off to daydream in remote fielding positions on the perimeter where I could observe the Somalis racing to and from their skirmishes in the seaport. Somalia was in a stalemate and the blue helmets vs. hacks and do-gooders' cricket test series might have continued indefinitely had it not been for a nation that knew nothing of cricket—the United States of America.

I sat on the seawall at the Mogadishu harbor with Sharif the translator and our Somali guards. It was pitch-dark. I made out the throb of helicopters. Dan roared up in a Land Cruiser and I yelled at him to get out and take cover as the silhouette of a chopper hovered overhead. Flares blossomed in the darkness, floating down on little parachutes. I heard a noise like *shhhh*. Then again *shhhh*. I realized these were bullets zipping over our heads and I pressed down on the concrete and noticed that out on the black water an armada of warship lights was strung along the horizon.

The Marines of Fox Company scurried ashore, soaked with sea spray from their invasion on Zodiac dinghies. The press had swarmed into Mogadishu as the date for the operation drew near and the first soldiers on land were set upon by photographers and cameramen. The initial casualty was a Special Forces man in night-vision goggles. He clutched his eyes in pain as the flash bulbs popped off. The U.S. Marines shouted and crawled in the dirt on elbows and knees. Banks of TV satellite equipment and technicians dressed as surfer dudes obstructed their invasion. They took one look at our rabble of dodgy-looking reporters and Somali gunmen, all of us chewing qat, and arrested us. I found myself on my back, staring up the barrel of an M-16, yelling questions at the camouflaged face behind it. "What's your name? Where are you from? How does it feel to be here?"

"Lance Corporal Eric Chavez. Aztec, New Mexico. We're just here to feed the people and it feels great! Now place your hands on the ground in front of you. Sir!"

This was the first day of the UN Task Force (UNITAF) landings for Operation Restore Hope. Most of us inside Somalia wanted to believe it would prove there could be what President Bush had called his New World Order. To be truthful, I saw it as a new civilizing mission, similar to the imperialism of my British forebears in that it would bring to an end starvation, war, and dictatorship and replace it with peace, justice, and proper government. The American-led army, with troops from more than two dozen other nations, was the only large-scale Western military intervention ever launched in Africa for purely humanitarian reasons. These were what the UN secretary-general had called his "battalions for peace." I and many others, black and white, in Africa that day truly felt that after a generation of watching things get inexorably worse we were able at last to see the light at the end of the tunnel, no matter how distant it might be.

Jonathan and I strolled around the seaport, after the Marines had moved on through the docks. The ground was littered with leaflets dropped on the city by Psy-Ops aircraft, with cartoons depicting American soldiers and Somalis shaking hands in peace. We found ourselves standing at the entrance to a metal cargo container. We heard a scuffle inside. Three armed and scowling cripples emerged from the darkness, carrying their guns, limb stumps, swollen testicles, and crutches and limped off into the darkness. Jonathan and I looked at each other and laughed.

"It's all over," I said. "This is the end of the story. Do you remember the first weeks when we came here at the beginning of all this? Do you realize Dan is selling T-shirts proclaiming the end of war and famine?"

"And it's thanks to us that all this is happening," Jonathan replied happily. "All those fuckers at Reuters who quibbled over our expenses and never showed any interest in the story, look at them now. The U.S. Cavalry's come riding over the horizon and here we are, top of the news schedule. We're the biggest story in the world. We did it. We got out of it alive and there will never, ever be another story like this again on our patch. You might never see one like it in your lifetime . . ."

First light seeped in, revealing a flotilla of ships like a city of steel on the ocean. Widening out from the shore, the beachhead filled up with hundreds of vehicles, hovercraft, and tanks. Galaxy and Starlifter transports swarmed onto the tarmac. The sky darkened with helicopters and fighter jets. The Somalis welcomed the Marines with garlands of bougainvillea. In return, the Marines handed out candies and gum. The city was festooned with imaginative pictures of Aydiid and President Bush shaking hands. Correspondents drove ahead of and alongside the Americans, shooting acres of film. When the U.S. Marines arrived at the derelict U.S. embassy compound, the Marines played the part by advancing on their bellies in the dirt, leaping from behind one wall to the next. "It feels good to see a flag going up, rather than down," said a Marine colonel as Old Glory was hoisted up the pole on the chancery. Particularly, he said, because this flag was the very same one that had been taken down from the U.S. embassy in Beirut after the 1982 suicide-bomb attack that had killed 241 Marines.

When U.S. forces came ashore the warlords appeared to lose all power and their ragtag armies seemed to melt into the bush. The same day foreign forces landed, the grain started arriving again in aircraft and ships. "You watch, we're going to see an amazing transformation here," an aid worker said shaking his head. "You're going to see the Americans build bridges and highways out into the desert. When they finish doing that, what are they going to do then? They'll have to build cities out there. Pretty soon, they'll run out of things to do." I saw visions of street lighting, hamburgers, public libraries. Cobra attack helicopters airlifting in ballot boxes. We were blinded by the light glinting off the metal of all these planes, hovercrafts, tanks, trucks, ships, guns, and helmets.

Days later, when the U.S. Marines advanced inland toward Baidoa, the first truck of food I saw being delivered to an outlying village had a Cobra providing air support, with a ground convoy of Humvees and armored vehicles. When we got there, the peasants looked terrified. After the soldiers left, I waited for thirty minutes and then, as if by magic, a gang of militias emerged from the bush to steal all the food.

"That's A-W-A for you," observed one of the correspondents.

"What's that?" asked a Marine captain.

"Africa Wins Again."

In the days before Christmas, President Bush flew into Mogadishu Central airfield to visit his troops. As he made his speech I found myself pinned down in a cross fire between gangs in revived fighting along the 21st October Road, within mortar range of the spot where Bush was addressing his men and women. That night, militias fired mortars out to sea toward the anchored U.S. Navy ships where Bush slept. It was hardly a good omen.

We had expected U.S. forces to sideline, detain, or even kill the warlords. None of these things happened. Instead, Aydiid and his rivals were invited to another series of peace conferences in Addis Ababa, Nairobi, and New York. "The warlords are the players, so we have to play along," my friend John Fox, who "watched" Somalia at the Nairobi U.S. embassy, told me at the Addis Ababa summit. Encouraging the militias to form a government was like appointing the Mafia to run Manhattan. One evening the UN threw a lavish cocktail party at the Addis Hilton and the warlords, all in their Muslim skullcaps, helped themselves to whiskey out of half-pint glasses, scooped caviar from a giant ice swan, and ogled the buttocks of the Ethiopian waitresses who served the canapés. Fox cast his eye around the scene and sighed. "At last I get to do what they taught me in the foreign service and have drinks with a room full of mass murderers."

Mogadishu had swelled with so many press that we Somalia old-timers sourly called it a gang bang. Reid Miller of the AP called it a "goat fuck." For this reason Reid and I together helped set up the Hotel al-Sahafi, Arabic for "The Journalist," because we needed to find enough room for our crews of reporters, photographers, and TV people. Most of Mogadishu's hotels had been blown up or turned into refugee camps and we couldn't cram into the American doctors' charity guest house anymore.

The al-Sahafi was a three-story white concrete block, completely empty when we first found it, which the proprietor, Mohamed Jirdah, furnished and opened within three days of striking a deal with us. He served kingfish steaks with cooked cucumber, which was great until we'd eaten it month in, month out. The air-conditioned rooms were cold enough to hang meat in and the hotel overlooked the K-4 roundabout that linked the airfield and seaport roads. Journalists were crowded four to a room at the al-Sahafi. The hotel's flat roof was a forest of aerials and dishes. Passages were stacked with TV equipment. Fleets of 4x4s waited outside.

As usual, the stringers had been big-footed, as in trodden on by the more senior staff correspondents from places such as London. All the top Reuters shooters had swooped in from the Balkans and the Middle East and made Dan put down his camera and toil away as their minion. Photographers shouted at him over their T-1 transmitters as he scuttled about mixing chemicals and bringing them coffee. He took it all in good spirit and co-opted the Somalis to play along with his antics, like wearing plastic Viking helmets at dinner or blaring Edith Piaf at full volume from the dining-hall speakers. On the side Dan sold the U.S. Marines postcards and souvenir booklets of photos with Americans feeding Somalis. As a student, Dan had paid his way through college by selling T-shirts on the California beaches like an African hustler. His T-shirts now said I RESTORED HOPE IN SOMALIA. The Marines were like souvenir-hungry tourists and sent them home to their families. It was a feel-good operation. Another T-shirt had the silhouette of a Cobra attack helicopter. Dan loved Cobras. His business expanded so fast that he was soon filling bulk orders for entire Marine companies, cash or barter. His room piled up with whiskey, combat uniforms, and goods to be traded on the growing military black market.

Dan still got so revved up from chewing qat that he ran around like a child howling after a plate of Vindaloo curry. One day he was mixing chemicals ready to process film. He was a sight, wearing his *maweis* sarong and a Somali bucket hat of woven sisal, with talismans hanging from his neck and wrists. A TV network producer who had flown into Mogadishu that morning pitched up in new Banana Republic safari gear, with his rucksack and bottle of mineral water. One of the common clichés produced by journalists and the U.S. military at the time was that Somalia's war was fueled by qat and that "qat-crazed gunmen" were destroying the nation. The United States tried to outlaw it and this TV producer evidently assumed the drug was not that different from crack cocaine in the Bronx. He regarded Dan with alarm as the kid strode around like Groucho Marx, jerking his head. "Hey you, what are you on?" he said with a scowl. Dan smiled. Green pulp oozed out between his teeth. "Fifty bucks a picture. You?"

* * *

I knew violence wouldn't entirely end in Somalia just because the Americans were there, but I reasoned the news would go off the boil now as foreign forces got on with cleaning streets and mending peasants' teeth. For the first time even Africa's small wars seemed, well, simply small. A big story might come around in a journalist's lifetime as seldom as a full eclipse. I wondered how long I would have to stick around in Africa before another conflict erupted. I wanted to become what is known in the business as a fireman, reporting only the big stories when they happened, like Bosnia, Chechnya, or Northern Ireland, and never kicking my heels in a backwater.

This new ambition to climb the greasy pole of Reuters was partly due to competitive envy. Julian's paper was promoting him to a position in the Middle East. I didn't want to get left behind and plotted to go one better. Jonathan said he would try to get me a string in the Balkans, where I could cover the wars in the breakaway republics of Bosnia and Croatia, as well as unrest in Serbia's ethnic Albanian Kosovo region.

"Yeah," I told Julian. "The Balkans." It made me feel good to get one over Bald Sam, too. A senior news editor in London also said he would help but expressed shock that I should want to leave Africa.

"Are you sure?" he asked. "I never imagined you could tear yourself away from the fleshpots."

I waited, but Reuters gave me no definite answers for some weeks. One day in early 1993 I heard Lizzie was flying back to Kenya. She had been taking pictures of cowboys on the rodeo circuit for a year. I had all but given up ever seeing her again but events in Somalia had finally persuaded her to return.

At another UN conference of Somali warlords in Addis Ababa, I bumped into a man named Omar Jess in the Hilton hotel garden. Jess was one of Aydiid's lieutenants, a bearded gangster with a Muslim cap squashed onto his fuzzy head. He said he hated my guts for what I had written about his militia and got straight to his point. "We don't like your kind of journalist. Come to Somalia again, and we'll see how long you survive." UN forces were powerless to stop the assassination of foreigners. Sean Devereaux, the British aid worker with whom I had visited the famine camps, had bickered over an armed protection "contract" with Jess militias and for that he had been shot dead in cold blood. Fate now took its course. Jonathan told the senior Reuters editors about Omar's death threat, and quite to my surprise the agency came back with a request for me to prepare to depart for the Balkans.

"Why are you looking so miserable?" asked Jonathan. "I thought this was what you wanted."

Somalia had moved into a completely new phase, but I wouldn't say the U.S. Marines had ushered in a renaissance. I remember the beach where they had landed next to the airfield. Girl U.S. Army soldiers in bikinis with M-16s slung on their shoulders sauntered along the white coral sand. It was to be my last visit to Somalia. The soldiers were far from home, but this was like a location for a weird beach-party movie in which the chicks all carried guns. Sunburned grunts played ball or surfed on inflated tire tubes in the turquoise waters. The waves smelled of Jet A-1 fuel. I turned to look from the back of the hut behind the beach dunes, to Mogadishu Central airfield. To the sides of the runway were warrens of tents, sandbags, howitzers, helicopters, and transport aircraft taking off and landing, giant fuel and water bladders, PX stores and hangars. And beyond the airport base ringed by coiled razor wire and observation posts was the rotting city, what the Marines called "Skinnyland," and it was a million miles away.

It was going to be useless to resist the posting to the Balkans after all my efforts to lobby Reuters. By then, Lizzie had flown back into the city. I looked down and saw Lizzie standing there, also in her bikini, snapping away at the cavorting Americans with her camera. Always working. She looked so beautiful. I went over to her and we sat on the beach together.

I asked, "Are you sure you don't want to come to the Balkans with me?"

"I've come a long way to get here already, Aidan," she replied. Then she turned to look at me and said brightly, "Stop worrying. You never know how things will turn out."

This was early 1993. On the beach we all assumed the Marines had installed a shark net. Surely they knew about the sharks. The cable out at sea that we thought marked the line of the shark net turned out to be a fuel pipe. Soon after the mission started a French woman diplomat was savaged waist deep in the waves and died of shock and blood loss. A Russian pilot on an Antonov transport flying freight into Mogadishu Central took a swim directly after landing. He was hit, as if by a truck, as he waded in the limpid water. The Marines then put up a NO SWIMMING sign with a skull and crossbones on it.

In May, the United Nations took command from the U.S. Marines. The UN Mission in Somalia (UNOSOM) aimed to continue protecting relief operations. But under the new Security Council resolution 814, peacekeeping troops were being given Chapter VII rules of engagement, which permitted them to disarm the clan militias and police the cease-fire, "taking appropriate action" to prevent the resumption of violence. UNOSOM's commander was a Third World figurehead, General Cevik Bir of Turkey. Real command was in the hands of two Americans. The first was Admiral Jonathan Howe, a retired U.S. Navy submarine commander who was the "civilian" special envoy. I met Howe before leaving Mogadishu; he was a gaunt figure with skin so white that under the Somali sun he appeared translucent, like a salamander. The other was U.S. Army Major General Thomas Montgomery, ex-Vietnam and ex-Pentagon, who later compared Mogadishu to the movie *Indiana Jones and the Temple of Doom.* He was Bir's second-in-command, but as commander of U.S. forces in Somalia, he reported to his operational chief, General Joseph Hoar at U.S. Central Command in Tampa, Florida. In Mogadishu, Montgomery was tactical commander of the one thousand–strong Quick Reaction Force of Tenth Mountain Division, left behind by the Americans to bolster the main body of ill-trained, broadly ineffectual Third World contingents.

Lizzie and I hitched a ride to Mombasa on a C-130 Hercules transport aircraft with troops from the Australian contingent going on R&R. The Aussies drank beer in the hangar before takeoff. When we got airborne a rugby game erupted with a six-pack of cold brew for a ball. The C-130 was a civilian charter, one of the "Air America" outfits run by pilots who had flown guns to the Contras in Nicaragua in the eighties and graduated to Africa's complex emergencies. To entertain us the pilot swooped down to skim the desolate shoreline. The cargo loadmaster, in his ten-gallon hat, lowered the back bay cargo door so that we could see the waves below. I looked behind me to see the Aussies in their shorts and RESTORE HOPE T-shirts, all facing the surf break vanishing behind us, standing on imaginary surfboards, whooping.

Julian and I had borrowed enough money to buy the Ski Chalet. He wanted an anchor in Africa and it helped me to know that I had my own home to return to from the Balkans. As I packed up to leave Celestine the gardener and I set about planting two hundred indigenous trees, from wild figs, podocarpus, and euphorbia to African olives. We ripped out the patterned beds of Christ thorn and bougainvillea and replaced them with gardenias, creeping jasmine, and tuberoses that would breathe perfume into the night. We planted a vegetable garden of maize and potatoes and cabbages.

Celestine looked at me with silent reproach, not knowing what on earth I was up to. I told him to stop looking depressed and to care for Lizzie and the house and garden in my absence. I told him I was going to the war in Yugoslavia. He wasn't particularly impressed. "How long will you be gone?" I told him I didn't know. "Why are you going?" The idea of leaving home to go overseas when I could stay and earn the same salary struck him as nonsensical.

"So, this is it," said Jonathan, holding out his hand. The rest of the boys were in Somalia. "See ya." Eric, who was now based in his beloved South Africa, gave me a lucky charm, a 5.56 bullet casing he had picked up at the site of a homelands massacre. "Keep it on you and stay safe, brother."

I hated leaving my family, particularly Dad. At the age of eighty-seven, his strength was draining like water from his mind and limbs. Despite this it remained almost impossible to persuade him to have his hospital checkups and he disagreed with the doctors.

"My heart is *supposed* to beat that slow," he said. "Like the rhythm of a Tibetan Buddhist's drum."

On the aircraft I split open my medical pack and popped a codeine tablet. With my nose pressed against the iced porthole, I stared at my receding Africa.

Warrior in Southern Arabia greeting Davey, who took this picture. The tribesman's comrades mass behind him in the distance.

GOING NATIVE

"Experience is an art to be studied rather than a haphazard process," wrote Lord Belhaven, the political officer and contemporary of Peter Davey. To see the Kaur escarpment for the first time, he wrote, you should approach it at dawn. I caught my first glimpse of the Kaur at the head of the pass, as the car roared through a lifting yellow mist. It was a table of rock spanning the horizon. As the sun rose it turned amber, then violet, with streaks of slate-blue cloud hanging above. At the foot of the escarpment was the village of Loder. My mother had told me to look out for a cluster of stone forts on the edge of the village, where the sultans had sat in their windy towers, "eating colored jellies loudly and with relish." The towers were in ruins. In Loder I found two brothers who had once worked for my father and Davey. Alawi, the elder of the two, was half blind. The younger, Abdallah, painted his eyes with kohl and laughed a great deal. He pointed at the escarpment and beamed. "We used to leave here at dawn, with your father and Davey, and run up that thing!"

In those days it had taken hours to climb the Kaur, however fit a man was. I noticed with regret how we climbed in a matter of minutes along the modern road blasted into the rock. From the summit, I looked back over the lava fields to the Indian

Ocean. Before my parents left for Africa, my father brought my mother to live up here when she was pregnant because of the healthy alpine climate. He had persuaded the Arab peasants in the area to plant fruit trees and European vegetables for sale to the ships in Aden.

"We grew such wonderful fruit," said Abdallah. "Plums, greengages, apricots, apples, pears—everything from England!"

We visited the market in the nearby village of Mukeiras to see if we could find the legacy of this. There was no fruit at all on sale. Mukeiras was a filthy street of concrete hovels and rusting machinery. It was a scene devoid of exotic charm, and I felt depressed about what had happened. But then I witnessed the extraordinary sight of a man walking through the market with a cloud of bees trailing behind him. Abdallah told me the man had hidden the queen bee in his turban and had brought her to Mukeiras to sell. The swarm followed him like a trail of smoke or a veil wafting in the breeze.

By now I had become immersed in Davey's account of day-to-day life in Arabia. I stood in Mukeiras and imagined him and my father as they rode through here and on across the plateau past wild fig trees and barley fields divided by low walls, through a maze of valleys guarded by fighting towers of mud or stone. Woad-blue warriors like Greek statues cantered up to meet them shooting their salutes and old men with indigo-flecked beards entreated them to halt for meat and milk because it would shame a man—or, as the Arabs put it, "blacken his face"—if they were unable to show hospitality. They had to dismount and wait for a sheikh to solemnly order one of his few sheep to be slaughtered and prepared with wheaten bread for the visitors. They rested as youths anointed them and rubbed their legs with sesame oil. Davey was more relaxed about these stopovers than my father. He wrote, *"It was past midday when the food of boiled mutton and wheat bread was placed before us; poor Brian loathes sitting for any length of time and got very impatient at the endless wait . . ."*

A thin drizzle and mist swathed the plateau at dawn each day and the riders wrapped themselves in their big sheepskin coats. They descended the northern escarpments into Wadi Beihan, shedding heavy clothes until they panted against the hot, dry winds of the deserts spread out below them. This was the Ramlat as'Sabateyn, on the margins of the Empty Quarter.

I was following in their path sixty years later. When we reached the desert we stopped the car and I saw the sands were crossed by the hieroglyphic tracks of beetles, the arabesques of snakes. A lizard sprinted away from me with tail and head raised against the searing heat. The desert was clean. I felt like we were the first men to set foot here. But not far from the road I found a menhir, carved with stars and planets. Davey wrote, *"Getting away completely by myself, I got the most amazing sense of utter desolation stretching away all around me. Nothing but stones and stones and stones. Its utter starkness affected and impressed me in some way."*

I understood why some men are drawn to the desert and what attraction it had for Davey. The Empty Quarter, like the oceans and polar caps, is a void that challenges us. It must be traversed, survived, and conquered in the mapping. "We carry our deserts with us through the world," wrote Lord Belhaven, who was an ardent traveler. "... And there is none more deadly than the empty heart, when the springs of hope are left behind."

The valley of Beihan was, I imagined, little changed from when my father and Davey first saw it. To me, it even seemed oddly familiar. The cob tower houses set among date palms. Turbaned figures or female forms in pleated long robes at work in green fields surrounded by orange sands. A donkey next to a well. The scenes were pictures from my first school Bible.

While my father remained on the move, Davey used Beihan as his main base for nearly eight years. It was here that he wrote most of his diaries. In Beihan he had found what he needed: a life worth setting down. The valley is really a confluence of gorges cut into the jagged, black rock massif thirty-five miles long. It has been inhabited for thousands of years and the cliff rock faces are decorated with inscriptions from the pre-Islamic era that Arabs call the Time of Ignorance. Beihan had been a major center of power in what the Romans called Arabia Felix, "Arabia the Blessed." It had once grown rich off the taxation of the trade in frankincense, which was transported on the backs of camels on the land route from the Indian Ocean coast to Gaza, via the rock-hewn city of Petra. I saw script in Himyaritic, the ancient language of southern Arabia, in columns stating laws governing the taxes on trade, hieroglyphics of ibex and mounted riders, or rude jokes scrawled in a forgotten demotic. I saw grooves worn into the boulders where the ancient traders had tied up their camel caravans. Midway along the valley, where the gorges meet, is a hill named Raydan, shaped like a pyramid with a solid egg of granite for a summit, which is covered with strange zodiac signs and red hand imprints. Beihan's past had remained amazingly intact until now, as it was suddenly being destroyed. Oil had brought Yemen new wealth and the government was using the money to construct roads. In a single day I saw a team of bulldozers demolish a three-thousand-year-old toll gate constructed with great stones to make way for a new tarmac highway.

At the mouth of Beihan the valley opens out to the shores of the Empty Quarter. I was mesmerized by the sand void, which appeared like an ocean. The dunes ranged from pinkish to blue. Their crests divided shade from light perfectly, the lines like billowing silk, the motion of serpents, a woman's thigh. Its appearance changed constantly through the day, pulsing in and out of focus. The horizon was as clear as a scar or lost in a mist of dust. The desert and mountains made the valley a world all its own. At a meal

I saw a man hold a sheep's thighbone up to the light after having gnawed off all the meat and gristle, studying it intently. When I asked him what he was doing, he showed me a groove along the bone. This was like a map of Beihan, he told me, which revealed all the news going on in the wadi. The way he described it was as if it were like surveillance TV. The man gave the example of a guest who had been eating at his house the previous week.

"He looked at his bone and shouted that his wife was with another man. He jumped up and ran off home to find that it was true!"

"And did he catch his wife in the act of having sex with another man?"

"No," the man laughed. "His son had come home for a visit."

Life here, as in Abyan, runs to the cycle of floods that roar down the valleys twice a year. I knew that winter was bitterly cold, when mists rolled in from the sands. Now in the spring, lightning flashed in the night sky from the highlands. Farmers built great sand barriers to deflect the spate into their fields, before the flood dissipated into the desert. After the rains came the locusts. Summers were intensely hot and dry, when flies crowded the eyes and mouth and sandstorms rolling in turned the noon sunshine to twilight.

I was brought to the bedside of Shoban, who had taken care of Davey's horses. He was laid up in the local hospital. His son sat with him. When my guides announced who I was, he frowned. "Harteli? Is he alive?" They said it was his son. This sank in slowly. Shoban's eyes were baby blue and liquid. He was blind, bald, smooth, and thin. The doctors were worried about his blood-sugar level and whether he could survive an operation. Shoban was dying.

Here I was at the bedside of a man who had personally witnessed the events of a story played out on the edge of the desert half a century before. I hoped for an eloquent valediction, so I asked him what he remembered. He shrugged.

"It was so long ago."

I told him I had read about him as a young man in the pages Davey had written.

"He was always writing. He was writing even when he talked to you."

I asked about the horses. Shoban brightened at this. The old man had ridden alongside Davey and had cared for his horses all his years in Beihan.

"Davey loved his horses as much as his eyes," old Shoban said, pointing to his own dead pupils.

He asked if "Harteli" were still alive. When I told him no, he thumped the bedside, as if to say: another one gone.

"Where are all the horses your father took to Africa?" he asked. "Harteli wanted me to go with him, but Davey told me to stay. Harteli went to Africa with some fine stallions and mares. Where are they now?"

I pictured the horses, gone feral like mustangs on the plains of the abandoned farm below Kilimanjaro.

"They bred well. You should see them," I told Shoban. Then I asked him where were the horses of Beihan. He was more honest than I had been.

"None left. Not one." To the communists horses represented the sultans, the feudalist ethos of the *faris,* the chivalric code of knights, or they were considered reactionary, backward, not mechanized. Two Beihan horses made it to the market in Mareb, where they were sold to Bedu. The rest were turned to donkeywork, driven until they collapsed.

"What has changed between life in those old days and now?" I asked Shoban.

"Honor," he replied. "Honor is the same, but the times have changed. Honor is not like clothes, which grow old and have to be thrown away."

"And where has honor gone?"

"Down, with the value of the Yemeni rial," quipped Shoban's

son. The group encircling the bed laughed. When it was time for me to leave, Shoban gripped my hand hard and would not let me go at first. My father had done that the last time I ever saw him.

When Davey arrived in Beihan, the sultan of the valley was a mercurial man named Sharif Hussein. From the descriptions I read by my father and the British political officer Nigel St. John Groom I learned that Hussein was generous, and sensual, with a soft cultured voice, and he struck a heroic, erect figure, with an eagle's eyes, flowing raven hair and beard. But he was also a despot. When he lost his temper his eyes narrowed into slits, his voice cracked and he neurotically tugged the gray hairs out of his whiskers. If he felt his power was under threat he would brood and begin devising a conspiracy to have his way, and if necessary he did not stop at having his opponents or rivals murdered. Groom told me that one could never impose an idea on Sharif Hussein. You had to make him think it was his discovery, and then praise him for his sagacity.

Like the Seyyids, his family, the Ashraf, claimed descent from the Prophet Mohamed. They had migrated to these southern shores of the desert with their horses and exploited their religious influence and warrior skills to rule loosely over the aboriginal inhabitants. In Beihan, these include a tribe of red-skinned peasants who farmed the valley's upper reaches. Jews had also settled here, as early as the first century when, after the destruction of the Temple by Titus, they had wandered south into Yemen. In a walled village near Beihan called Habban, the community of Jews kept what they claimed was the key to the gates of Jerusalem. Legend said this was also the place where in the fourth century, emissaries of Helena, mother of Emperor Constantine, found the bones of the magi who had adored the Christ child. They carried them to

Constantinople, so the story goes, whence they were removed first to Milan and finally in the twelfth century to the cathedral in Cologne where they still rest.

Beyond the mouth of the wadi, out in the sands, were rival Bedu clans who lived in sable tents and raided one another for camels and sheep, and to settle blood feuds. The sharif's family lived in tents decorated with bright colors and cowry shells. But Hussein wanted to become more than an influential tribal chieftain. He dreamed of establishing a dynasty that would rule over the whole of southern Arabia, like the house of ibn Saud. It was his father who had sown the seeds of this ambition, when in 1904 he had sent the British governor in distant Aden a white oryx, requesting a treaty of protection.

Hussein's brother Awadh had no political ambitions, but roamed the desert and went by the nickname King of the Empty Quarter. Davey's photographs show Awadh squinting in the sun with sunken cheeks, a tangle of unkempt hair, and great bare, cracked feet. He wore a turban and loincloth, with a *jambiya* dagger sheathed in silver and studded with carnelians and rose-colored glass stuffed into a belt of .303 rifle cartridges. Awadh knew his place in the world, which he believed to be flat. Once a visiting Englishman had persuaded him to look through a telescope at Jupiter when the planet's four moons were visible. He looked again some minutes later, by which time one of the moons had vanished. Awadh got up abruptly and walked off into the night, troubled by the Copernican universe. Well might Awadh have been horrified. He was happy with the world being flat. The modern era was about to arrive with its cars, oil, and revolutions, the end of the nomadic way of life.

Speeding out into the desert I felt a thrill, even though it was an asphalt road strewn on either side by rubbish, spilled oil, burst tire rubber, the bones of roadkills. Our way was marked by cross-barred telegraph poles that could have been headstones along our road. Beyond were the sands, clean and fresh like the ocean. The desert was hung with a curtain of moist mist slung from one end of the horizon to the other. I marveled that there could be so much condensation in the air, even out here.

But then, rising up, I saw the real cause of the fog. Angry flames burned from tall chimneys belching smoke into the blue sky. The desert was rutted with tank tracks from recent wars. Down-wind from the wells, fires had rained down black filth on the clean sand. The road we drove on became slick and greasy with crude. Orange flames glinted on the dark join between land and sky and as we drove closer the chimneys became a complex of streetlights and prefabricated buildings all fenced in.

Burton called this desert the Empty Abode. In 1852 he became the first Englishman to attempt a journey to remove "that opprobrium to modern adventure, that huge white blot," from the maps of Arabia. By the time he arrived at the holy city of al-Madinah disguised as a pilgrim, he had dropped the idea. Eight decades passed before there was another attempt. Bertram Thomas, political officer and wazir to the sultan of Muscat, set off from the Indian Ocean coast in 1930 with an escort of Bedu and became the first European to emerge on the far side. Harry St. John Philby, adviser to the Saudi king, cantankerous, mean, and pro-Nazi, entered the Sands the following year. He quarreled with his companions so bitterly that they contemplated murdering him before heading home. He was so resentful to be second after Bertram Thomas that he returned and drove all over it in a Buick. The next European to cross the desert was Wilfred Thesiger. Doting on the beautiful youths that guided him, he made the Bedu the heroes of his story. Men had long ventured deep into the Sands, of course, and there was nothing empty about them. Like Polynesians who navigated across the ocean in canoes, the Bedu could find their way across the Sands for weeks as if by instinct and make it to a well hours from dying of thirst. As Thesiger ended his second crossing, foreigners were already invading the region, this time to explore for oil. And so, less than a century after the challenge of the desert was first taken up by Burton, humankind had destroyed all that was fearful and awesome about the Empty Quarter.

The nomads who lived in this harsh land wove no moral message into the landscape. Their drama was survival, which can seem mean only to the person who has never been starving or dying of thirst. And after they had lost their fear of death, they sought out the cheapest of things to gratify themselves. Strip lights, car horns that blared tunes, machine-made oriental carpets. But when you see a nomad transformed into a settled creature, his Land Cruiser parked outside his concrete bungalow, which has metal girders sticking vertically up from the roof in case he can one day afford to build another floor, you have to wonder about what had happened to the beauty of Arabia.

My father was an agriculturalist, a farmer and a man of the land. He was not by his nature a military man like so many of our ancestors. On the outbreak of war, he and Davey were forbidden to join up in the forces in England or East Africa because the handful of officers in Arabia were needed on the ground. Davey was forced to sit out the entire conflict in Beihan. Dad, on the other hand, was ordered to lead a gang of Somali spearmen to seize the Italian-held island of Socotra.

There was no battle. When my father's ship, the *Chantala*, approached the island's steep shores, he saw the Italians boarding a dhow sailing ship. The British didn't bother to pursue them as they got under sail to flee, even when they opened fire on the *Chantala*. My father and his spearmen landed and, not to be discouraged in their hunt for Italian fascists, they set off on a trek around Socotra's granite mountains. Along the way they met shark fishermen, traders in the red cinnabar resin tapped from the dragon's blood tree, and troglodytes—but no Italians. Back on the mainland Dad raised a camel corps of scouts from the Subeihi, a tribe known as the Children of the Rising Sun. The force camped on the Strait of Tears coastline, sending warnings of the arrival of Italian Caproni bombers from Somaliland to the antiaircraft batteries in Aden. They transmitted their messages using a radio powered by a stationary bicycle that had to be pedaled in order to run the dynamo.

On the evening of June 18, 1940, the scouts were camped by the lagoon of Khor al Umeira. The camels had been turned loose to browse. A pot of ginger coffee bubbled on the fire. Dad lay on the beach, watching a group of fishermen hand-line for mullet. Suddenly, with a loud throbbing sound and not far out, a submarine surfaced. As Dad stood up in his Arab garb, the crew clambered out. They stared at each other. Waved at each other. Then the crew began speaking Italian. Clearly, they assumed the scouts were simple Bedu and nothing to worry about. They strutted about, filled their lungs with fresh air, blew out the tanks, and cleaned up the ship. Meanwhile, Dad sauntered behind a dune where the transmitter was in position, the bicycle was pedaled furiously, and a message was sent to Aden.

The boat was the 231-foot *Galileo Galilei*, flagship of Mussolini's Red Sea submarine fleet. As soon as the scouts' message was received, a hunt was launched. The *Moonstone* caught up with the *Galileo Galilei* a day later and one of its salvoes hit the conning tower, killing most of the officers and the senior ratings. When an Allied party boarded the stricken vessel and went below, they discovered the crew's survivors were paralyzed, lying in pools of their own vomit and raving madly. The explosion in the conning tower had released methyl chloride gas from the sub's air-conditioning system, poisoning anyone still alive. My father was later told that the submarine had been sunk, but due to operational secrecy he never knew the details I discovered after his death. Even though it was wartime, I believe he would have been horrified to hear of the Italian sailors' suffering.

Meanwhile Davey sat in his Arab mud tower in Beihan, listening to Churchill on the wireless following the Nazi invasion of Russia. "Awful and horrible things are happening in these days," the prime minister said. "Here then, is the vast pit in which all the most famous states and races of Europe have been hurled and from which, unaided, they can never climb ... And this is just the beginning. Famine and pestilence have yet to follow in the train of Hitler's gang. We are in the presence of a crime without a name ..."

During the blitz, when his mother's letters described air raids and dogfights over her house on the Sussex Downs, Davey wrote in his diary how she would *laugh if she could see me, sitting under the shade of a thorn bush reading her letters.* Davey rarely had any English visitors. One of the few was an RAF pilot named Murray, who used to fly in with a Vickers Vincent biplane each month to pick up mail and drop off supplies. Murray had flown Spitfires during the Battle of Britain and said the biplane was like driving an ice-cream van after having been at the wheel of a Rolls-Royce.

The truth was that Davey increasingly found his fellow Englishmen awkward company. A man who came to survey airfields showed him snaps of his wife, said he could ride, and got thrown off one of Sharif Hussein's horses. "All these fellows like doing anything once for, as they say, it gives them something to write home about." The majority of the Englishmen disliked the Arabs and hated the heat and the camels. An official with whom Davey traveled was Baylis:

> *a decent enough fellow but like all strangers in a strange land, he struck a note of discord. He quarrelled with his camel man, no doubt justifiably, but I somehow, unjustly, blame him for bringing out the worst in them. Anyhow I am glad they have gone and we have returned to tranquillity again. But I am afraid Baylis will go back convinced that he has plumbed the*

*depths of Arab mentality and will sum them up in two words.
"Mercenary swine." And most of his fellows will believe him.*

In Europe, the extermination of countless thousands was under way: Hitler's Blitzkrieg, the gas chambers, the cities being engulfed in flames and reduced to rubble. Civilization was a thin layer. But Davey's diary mentioned the war less and less after the Italian surrender in Ethiopia. North Africa, Burma, D-day, and the A-bomb all became increasingly remote from life in Beihan.

Davey was preoccupied with violence of a different nature in the valley where he had to keep the peace. *"A war is in process between sections of the Masabein. The normal Arab war—a rifle fired every two or three days at any of the opposition indiscreet enough to show themselves; the targets including women, children and dogs ..."*

He routinely had to deal with a story such as this. A village feud had erupted after a slave drove a donkey past the house of the neighboring sheikh. The sheikh's wife, at her window, shouted insults at the slave. Offended, he at once returned home, where he found his own master's wife sitting at her window. The slave demanded his right to be defended. A slanging match ensued. Within a day the husbands had become involved. A shot was fired. Attacks and counterattacks between the two families worsened, until they could leave their mud brick forts only by a system of trenches. All farming had to cease in fields within rifle range. And so the people, who lived in fear, went hungry. It was up to the young Englishman to bring about peace. That was his job, the axiom of British imperial rule. But how to bring peace?

* * *

Davey escaped death by a whisker on several occasions. While reading his diaries, I listed the different times he nearly died and with the benefit of hindsight it seemed as if he were marked by fate. Assassins poured fire down onto his party as they rode down a valley. Bullets passed between his legs as he flew in an aircraft over a rebel village. Bedu lost their tempers and cocked their rifles, calling him an "accursed" infidel.

> So I got up in a rage and stalked out, but with rather a ticklish feeling in the small of my back. One cannot threaten a whole village full of armed men without expecting reactions . . .
>
> All day fingers were on triggers as they moved . . . a quarrel erupted and apparently a fight was about to take place, when it was realised it was between members of the party over a cup of water.

It was clear to me that it would only be a matter of time before his chances ran out.

One March day Davey heard an aircraft fly north over the sands. That afternoon Murray flew in with the news that an RAF plane had ditched in the desert. The Vickers Vincent pilot had intended to chart a course for Aden but, incredibly, he forgot to turn his compass round, mistook south for north and so flew toward the Empty Quarter until he'd run out of gas. Murray took Davey up in his machine and they flew out over the sands for four hours, but saw nothing. The next day a Blenheim bomber spotted the ditched aircraft near the Abida salt mines at Safir, when the men were camped under the silk of a parachute. Murray was now joined by another RAF Vickers Vincent, piloted by a man named Reid and carrying two crew from the Blenheim that had spotted the men. The team set off from Beihan.

I thought I was to fly in Murray's machine but as I was making towards it, was called back by Reid who said I was to go with him ... The spot where the men were was well out into the desert. A landing T was spread out on the ground and Murray, without making a dummy run or taking a closer inspection of the ground prior to landing, did a half-circle and came down touching about half way along the emergency ground. Then, seeing his mistake, he tried to take off again but was too heavily laden. His machine hit the top of a dune, bounced about 30 yards into the air, came down on another dune, bounced again and turned completely over with its wheels in the air and facing the direction from which it had come. We all the time were circling steadily round. Finally we saw two figures standing beside the wrecked machine, neither of them Murray, waving to us.

The aircraft returned to Beihan, where Davey immediately saddled up his horse and was joined by Sharif Awadh. Ordering a string of camels to follow loaded with water skins, they cantered out of the wadi, skirting the line between the hills and the sands, watered at a last well, rushed on across a gravel plain, past ancient ruins along the caravan route, and entered the enormous dunes of al-Rozeyd. The wind played strange tricks with the sand, which was coarser-grained at the top of the dunes and soft powder in the valleys. They moved down a pass between the sand mountains and finally entered the Wadi Seyla, where they spotted the black form of the crashed aircraft.

The men nearly wept at the sight of us. Murray was dead, killed by petrol fumes, jammed in his cockpit with the wind-screen pressing into his mouth. I went over to look at the poor fellow where he had been laid out in the sand a little distance from the machine; I saw no sign of any injury ... Sharif Awadh and I with a small party of Ashraf went about the

*melancholy task of burying Murray. I took a signet ring off
the little finger of his left hand and a bunch of keys out of his
pocket.*

They buried Murray in a sleeping bag, put a wooden cross on
his grave, and took a photograph of the site to send to the man's
widow. On the way home to Beihan they traveled by moonlight
with the sand cold underfoot. The camels took swipes of 'Abal and
'Alqa bushes, swinging their long-necks as they went. When Davey
passed by the crash site a few weeks later the cross had already been
swallowed up by the sands and the Bedu had looted the wreckage.

Davey woke each day on his charpoy bed to the bellow of the
muezzin. He heard the squeak of the wooden pulleys at the well-
heads, the braying donkeys, and the indigo beaters. Dust crept in
the shuttered window of his room, with its table and shelf of old
packing cases and goat-hair carpets.

He had reached the age of thirty and he was lonely. For company he had his horses, a room full of saddles and books, guns and
Haddab, a saluki Bedu dog with which he went after desert hares
and bustards. While swimming at Gold Mohur beach in Aden, he
looked at the other men with their wives and children and it made
him melancholy.

*January 9, 1942—At times like these I see the narrow and
constrained life of a bachelor in the wilds of the protectorate—not that I would change it for anything.*

In the early days he had looked forward to his trips down to
Aden, when he saw my father: together they played polo, went out

drinking, journeyed out to Abyan to shoot duck, threw New Year's Eve parties at their house in Sheikh Othman. But Aden and the company of Englishmen were losing their grip on him. When my father went on leave to Kenya he wrote:

> *November 29, 1944—I do not have many friends there and Aden becomes, more and more, a place of strangers. I think the only time I ever feel lonely is in Aden, particularly now that Brian is away ... Living as I do, I cannot see that I have much chance of meeting and marrying the very rare type of English woman who would prefer to live months on end in wild country with no proper comforts, with no other European female or male companionship and without even the means of getting to civilisation except by aeroplane or by horse or camel ... Very rarely does one find an English woman who is prepared to put up with all these disadvantages and who is yet feminine and attractive. I do not like the missionary type nor the tough type. On the other hand Arab women, many of them, are attractive physically, intensely feminine and loving and even faithful ... From the physical point of view I must have a certain amount of sexual intercourse if I want my equilibrium and without either drying up inside or taking a liking to boys, which is not uncommon among unmarried Englishmen abroad.*

When traveling the valley, Davey and his companions stopped as guests at villages for the night. On these occasions Awadh would often "marry" a widow on the spot. Next morning, he would divorce her again. He urged the Englishman to also take a local woman. In Beihan, the sharif often had performances in his courtyard of wandering minstrels, snake charmers, and clowns who fought with axes and swallowed swords. There were also gypsy girls, the Shahad, in green and black dresses, who danced to the music of a vulture-bone flute and the tambourine. As they stamped their feet, the silver bells and coins dangling from their wrists and necks jingled. They spun like dervishes, rolling their heads so that their hair swung in wide circles. At a meal after one of their dances, a girl named Fatuma clambered astride Davey's thighs as he rested on his haunches. She balled rice in her henna-decorated hand and popped the morsels into his mouth. Her face was painted with crimson and yellow turmeric paste. Her raven pigtails glistened with rancid butter. She was barely thirteen.

In the year 1944, there is a sudden proliferation of incredible detail about Arabia in Davey's diary. Davey begins to write about vanished parts of that Arabia: local dialects, folklore, customary laws, plants, histories, even local idioms for lovemaking.

> *Steppes or desert Arabs allow a certain period of courting between a boy and a girl before marriage. They will go out herding camels together and sit together in their encampment. A young girl who has still not married cannot discuss her marriage with her future husband: all this is left to her father or brother. If she is of mature age or has been married before, a suitor may speak to her direct and she can decide her own fate ... As amongst Europeans, Arab marriages are sometimes love matches and sometimes concluded by one party because the other has money ....*
>
> *The tying of the marriage knot is performed by a Qadhi or some other responsible learned man. He sits between the bridegroom and the Wakil of the tribe—her father or brother or some close relation. He reads from the Quran.*

* * *

Finger nails are supposed to be poisonous. A woman wishing to get rid of her husband will roast the parings of finger nails and then pound them up with human hair into dust, after which the dust is mixed in the man's food. This is considered sufficient to poison the unfortunate husband to death.

A woman wishing to obtain the divorce of her husband, she having a lover who desires to marry her, will do all she can to prevent her husband having sexual intercourse with her. She will also go to her family, run away from her husband if necessary and ask them to cooperate with her by persuading her husband to divorce her. The father of the woman will go to the husband and explain the situation and will try to persuade him to accept a certain sum of money to be decided by the husband: anything from a few dollars to over a hundred dollars . . . Very often the husband will accept the inevitable, take the money and divorce the woman who will immediately be claimed and married by the triumphant lover who all this time has been lying doggo waiting for the miracle to happen.

Davey had found what the other British officers called "a sleeping dictionary." A girl. He was in love. It took him nine months to confess her existence to paper in his own journal. The entry seems absurd in its brevity, in among all the feuds, politics, and desert journeys.

November 30, 1944—The day after tomorrow I leave for Beihan, God be praised, where is all I care for in this Protectorate and with her the Sharif and my horses.

That "all I care for" was hardly believable to me, mixed up as it was in the same breath as his friendship with Sharif Hussein and his beloved horses. It took him another three months to mention her name. At last I discovered it was Sheikha.

I dearly hoped that Sheikha was still alive and that she was still in Beihan. I wanted to know what she had done with her life since Davey. When I first arrived in the valley, a man who served me tea, a former cook of the sharif's, had told me she could be found in her family's village. I thanked him for telling me.

"You're welcome," the man laughed. "Come back and I will show you what I cooked for Sharif Hussein!"

The news that Sheikha was alive made me nervous. What would I say to her? It kept me up that night as I bedded down at a village flophouse, in a room full of men contentedly munching on their leaves and sucking water pipes, their heavy-lidded eyes fixed on a satellite TV soccer match between Saudi Arabia and Iran. They cradled their guns; one levered off the back of his watch with a dagger and stared with stoned concentration at its contents, while others slept with sheets drawn over their heads like shrouds. I finally drifted off and dreamed of Sheikha and saw her face for the first time. When I woke in pitch-black among snoring men I felt extraordinarily contented. The next day, I discovered that the cook had been wrong. Sheikha had been dead for four years and my heart sank.

I asked people what Sheikha had been like. One man cupped his hands in front of his chest, elbows out.

"She was well built: a nice body, with good breasts."

In the 1940s, a time more liberal than today in Beihan, Sheikha would have lived without a veil over her face. I found it difficult to picture her looks. I had no photos of her. And I had no way of comparing my imagined Sheikha with the Arab women I saw around me, for females in modern Beihan were in purdah. They wore black, shapeless gowns with gloves and hoods so that not a morsel of skin was exposed. Even their eyes were concealed with a gauze material. They were completely out of sight.

In one house I asked my host, a Bedu with kohl-ringed eyes and hands the size of plates, what he knew about Sheikha. When he opened his mouth he was fluent in English, spoken in a Yorkshire accent acquired while operating a crane in a Sheffield steelworks. He said he knew nothing about the woman. "Nother cuppa tea?" As I pressed him, perhaps a bit rudely, I was interrupted by a woman's voice. It came from around the corner, in the passage. The Bedu crane operator's wife had been quietly eavesdropping on our conversation. Staying out of sight, the woman declared Sheikha had been her close friend. My crane worker looked stunned at this and went to the door. For some minutes he stood there, yelling answers and questions back and forth between his invisible wife and me. He became increasingly agitated and, just as the conversation with the woman in the passage was getting interesting, he abruptly terminated the interview. "That's enoof now." I wanted to talk to his wife, not to him. I rose and made for the passage. As I rounded the corner, I glimpsed a dark-robed figure slipping behind a curtain. My host smiled. "Tea? Biscoots?"

Sheikha bint Mohsin was a cousin of Sharif Hussein and so also a descendant of the Prophet. Like Davey, she was thirty years old, but she had already had a son by her first marriage. When that husband died, she had married one of Davey's bodyguards. The old men told me Sheikha had lived right next to the house where Davey slept and stabled his horses. Her house was of smooth mud and golden straw at the edge of the village. The other, lower house where Davey had stayed has since been demolished and a new one built with metal doors and window shutters. In the street a donkey and a camel stood ignoring each other in the sun. Beyond were the fields.

At her family house we were welcomed by a man with clean desert features, his eyebrows and hair dark even in old age, and a strong nose and intelligent sharp face. He was Sheikha's brother. We entered a sunny courtyard and walked through an open door into his main reception room. The walls of the room where we sat were hung with portraits. Taking pride of place was a picture of my host, looking much younger in a turban. There were also pictures of his sons, with big mustaches, dark glasses, and flashy seventies shirts with big lapels. The old man told me one had been a MiG fighter pilot until he was killed in a crash. There were no pictures of women on the walls. By now I felt I had been warned against asking the man about his sister. My guide told me he might be offended. I waited for him to open up to me voluntarily, but he didn't. And so Sheikha's old brother and I sat staring at each other, sitting on our cushions, as the minutes ticked by in awkward silence.

After some time the tension was relieved by the appearance of a figure at the door. She was a little girl of ten, with eyes of agate, brown skin like an antelope, and with pigtails, gold earrings, and an embroidered green dress. She noticed me only after she had walked halfway into the room. She gaped at me with wonder, lisped a little *salaam aleikum,* then ran away again. A few seconds later she reappeared at the door, this time with a smaller brother. The girl stuck out her tongue at me. From offstage a woman's voice called out strong and hard and this time they disappeared together. To me the little girl was a vision of Sheikha. As we left the house my guide pointed down the slope from the earth tell on which the village perched. It was the cemetery. Somewhere in that plot, beneath a nameless mound marked only by a rough flat stone at her head and foot, Sheikha lay among her people.

Everybody claimed to know how Davey and Sheikha had first met at the well outside the village of Darb, at the mouth of the valley, when Davey was watering his horse Mashur.

"'I want you,' is what he said to her at the well," an old sheikh told me.

The truth is that there might have been several encounters before any conversation took place. I imagined them being silent to begin with. I couldn't work out how a British man would be able to meet a woman in Arabia. During my travels, I saw the women glide by like black wraiths. They even turned their backs on me.

Sheikha used to come to him after dark. She padded barefoot between the towers and crossed the dunes from her village. She wore flowing black robes, which covered her face except for her dark eyes. The clothes enveloped her entire figure but stroked against her body so that her shape was outlined. Dragging behind her was a long train, deliberately used by women for this purpose, to obscure her tracks in the sands. Once she had knocked at Davey's house and was safely inside, she dropped her veil. Her eyes were agate. Her neck was as thin and as graceful as a gerenuk's. In the hour before coming she had squatted over a tray of smoking frankincense. Her body and clothes were perfumed and so was her long black hair, which she used like soft fingers, stroking and whipping her lover's skin. In Davey's notebooks I found the following entries:

> *A dancer lowers his or her head and allows the hair to fall over the face, and at the same time the head is rolled and turned so that the hair flies round.*
>
> *A term used in sexual intercourse, when the woman (on her back) raises her legs and places them over the shoulders of the man who is contacting her.*
>
> *As above except the woman's legs are over the man's arms by the elbows.*
>
> *Sexual intercourse when the act is committed with the woman sitting in the man's lap. The man also sits.*

Sharif Hussein learned of the love affair late, probably at the time Davey confessed it to himself in his diary. The news shocked him. He was secretly annoyed, but he decided he might be able to benefit by the arrangement and so he kept quiet about this. He assumed that Sheikha could be a useful tool to influence the Englishman. For however much he liked Davey, his priority was to enhance his own power in Beihan as well as in Aden. Who can know what the sultan thought of what happened next.

> *Saturday, February 24, 1945—Beihan—I have decided on two momentous decisions. I am determined to marry an Arab girl, which means that I will have to profess the faith of Islam.*

A woman had a right to divorce her husband. When Sheikha's husband learned that Davey was in love with his wife, he shrewdly sold her to Davey for two hundred silver Maria Theresa dollars. The lovers then agreed to marry after Sheikha had, according to custom, lived for three months from the day of her divorce. Admitting the affair to his diary allowed him finally to express in writing his feelings of love and excitement. "*We have both become very, very fond of each other,*" he wrote. During their night trysts, they talked until the early hours. They made love until the first call to prayer bellowed out from the village minaret. She was downcast to leave him even for a day.

The worry of what the sharif and the governor would think preyed constantly on Davey's mind. He predicted that the marriage would cause a scandal among both Arabs and the English. Sharif Hussein dismissed this and put Davey's mind at rest. He said the marriage and Davey's conversion to the only true religion, Islam, would bind them closer together as friends.

Davey remained worried about the reaction from his British comrades and superiors. No English political officer had ever converted to Islam or married an Arab woman in the Aden Protectorates. Which would be regarded as the bigger transgression—the religious conversion or legitimate sex with a desert Arab, a mother and divorcée? The governor in Aden was a devout Christian. He dreamed of retiring to become a vicar, with his own parish in England, which he later got. Before Davey had met Sheikha and was in Aden with my father, the governor had come once to snoop at their house during the siesta hour. There were women there and it caused what my father described as "an inconvenience." But the governor tolerated his officers having any kind of sex they wanted so long as there wasn't a scandal. Once he asked my father, "Do you like boys?" Davey said he might as well have been a pagan for the Christianity he practiced. By contrast, he promised to himself to embrace Islam properly, knowing that he would be closely watched in the valley. He ruminated that his political officer's reputation could only be enhanced among the Arabs by his conversion. This, then, was the way he thought he might convince the Arabs to listen to him in his efforts to negotiate peace in Beihan.

The decision had to be taken while considering whether or not it would mean his status as an Englishman would be undermined by "going native."

> I am fully aware that the thought of an Englishman marrying a "native" woman is repulsive and put that way it sounds repulsive, but I feel that I know Arabs and like them as well as my own kind and I am prepared to take the chance. If we don't hit it off divorce in Islam is very easy . . .
>
> Either I must keep a mistress, which I have been doing for some time but which is bad, very, for one's prestige and unnatural in tribal Arabia where marriage is so easy, or I must marry locally . . .
>
> Anyhow I have quite made up my mind and cannot turn back if I do not want to let Sheikha down.

Davey would like to have heard what my father thought, but Dad was off trekking to the valleys of the Hadhramaut. It was a four-hundred-mile walk, sometimes across country never previously visited by a European. The people of Hadhramaut were starving, thanks to the effects of the war in the Far East where many of the Arabs had their businesses, so my father ultimately stayed there for several months.

March 21, 1945—How I wish Brian were here.

By the time my father and Davey met again, events had taken their course. "I am not sure what I could have done to help him," my father later wrote. "His devotion to Arabia was to be balanced against his love for the young woman Sheikha for whom, without doubt, he had converted to Islam." Dad was not prone to the racial prejudices of the time. He had been in love with the African girl Binti Mwalimu on Lake Victoria. But he was pragmatic and would have advised Davey against marrying Sheikha because he was as aware as Davey of the trouble it would cause for him.

He had learned about it from his favorite uncle, Ernest Hartley, who had been given the social cold shoulder in Calcutta when he married my great-aunt Gertie, because she had Parsi and Armenian blood. My father did object to Davey's conversion to Islam, which he suspected had been embraced at least initially by his friend only so that he could marry. The Arabs called nonbelievers who converted for a woman "Muslims of the night," but they would rather a man was a Muslim, whatever the motive. What Davey previously thought about religion he described on a safari two years before, when he and my father reached the top of the Kaur escarpment and were resting.

Standing at the top we watched two vultures sailing out from some crevice in the cliff face below us into the void and

gliding and mounting without effort until they were specks
in the sky above us. We were passed by a Seyyid ... I asked
him politely from whence he came and after he looked at me
as if I was a particularly repulsive form of insect for some
seconds, he replied that he came from Allah and then he
began exhorting me to become a Muslim. I became rather
annoyed at his attitude and retorted that I would turn Mus-
lim only if I saw Arab Muslims helping each other and
existing at peace. At present, I said, it was the Christians in
the Protectorate who worked for peace and not the Muslims.
He would reply to none of our questions on ordinary affairs
and so we pushed on and he continued down the pass.

Another odd detail is that Davey wrote to his mother almost
weekly. He often exclaimed how he missed his family, fearing for
his mother in the Blitz and his brothers in the military, and he
never forgot a birthday. But my father told me that when he spoke
to the family later it became clear that Davey had never mentioned
a word of his conversion to Islam or his marriage to Sheikha. I
think he feared that nobody, not even his closest friends or his family, would understand what he was doing.

Back in Beihan, the conversion ceremony took place in Sharif
Hussein's meeting hall, in the presence of the elders. The sharif
took his hand and asked him to repeat his words. *La illahi ila Allah!*
"There is no God but Allah ... and Muhammad is his Prophet!"
The elders mobbed forward to shower Davey with compliments
and kisses on his hand. Part of his conversion was the adoption of
a Muslim name and he chose Abdallah, which means the Slave of
God. In the week before Davey's conversion, the sharif had
coached his friend in the genuflection and prayers of the mosque.
On the eve of the ceremony, Davey was circumcised.

A few days later, on March 28, 1945, Davey and Sheikha were
married in a simple wedding. To pay the bride price, Davey had to

sell his prized stallion Kubeyshan to the sharif for 250 silver dollars. The qadhi held his hand over the clasped hands of Davey and Sheikha's uncle, her eldest male blood relative. They repeated the qadhi's words and it was done. They set up in a new house, each of them buying in goods dictated by custom: he the carpets, water skins, and coffeepots, she the rope of the camel, saddle bags, pillow cushions, and wooden food bowls.

Even now Davey did not tell the governor in Aden. He went to great lengths to pose as the lonely political officer when Englishmen came up to stay at Beihan. Each evening when they were visiting him, he dined with them in his old official house and pretended to turn in for the night. Then he slipped out and sped across the dunes on horseback until he reached the house he had taken to settle down with Sheikha. He was back at dawn to shave, wash, and eat breakfast with the British again.

The marriage coincided with several events that Davey saw as disturbing portents. There was a terrible sandstorm. Under cover of this Bedouin raiders from across the frontier, in the territory of Britain's foe the Imam of Yemen, invaded the valley and killed two women who got in their way. Davey summoned the Imam's representative from across the frontier and he arrived, small and fat and in a sweat with an escort of soldiery, to discuss compensation. The talks ended without result and a war threatened. News came that a large RAF Hudson aircraft carrying Government Guards crashed on takeoff from the valley's airstrip. By the time Davey and Sharif Hussein reached the site they found twenty bodies pulled from the wreckage.

The rains had failed and as the weeks passed, no life-giving spates of water coursed down the wadi beds and all the planted seed died in the ground. In the months that followed animals began to die, even the camels that need not drink for a full month collapsed, their teeth bared and their necks arched back. Davey was horrified to see the Bedu had nothing to eat except soup made from the rawhide of dead livestock and pounded bones. The Arabs packed up their camps and began to move to high ground in the hope that they might find grazing and water. Davey began to travel too, fleeing in his case the heavy clouds that he felt were hanging over his head. Even as the holy month of fasting arrived he was forced to leave Beihan. A rash of feuding had erupted in the wake of famine across the Protectorates and Davey had much peace work to do. Before he left he was completely unable to console Sheikha, who wept so bitterly that in the end he agreed that she should accompany him.

> *Sheikha hates it even when I leave for the day and I know that she is not going to like being away from Beihan but she says that she would be unhappier if I left her behind so I do not know what to do. I know myself that I am only really happy when she is with me.*

They set off, Davey on the bloodred horse Mashur, Sheikha on a hired camel, a great beast that had carried its owner on the Hajj pilgrimage to Mecca. Following behind were the horses' groom Shoban, Haddab the saluki, an escort of Government Guards, and all their belongings loaded on ten baggage camels. They climbed the narrow gorge at the head of the valley back onto the plateau. When they descended the Kaur on the southern side, Sheikha entered a world so alien it might have been the Sussex Downs where Davey's mother lived. By now, a road had been built as far as Loder and a big Ford motorcar was waiting there to take them to Aden. Sheikha clambered aboard as if she had done so all her life and Haddab cantered alongside. Davey had planned to leave her at Abyan to wait for him, but she fell ill with stomach pains and could not eat when the fast was broken at evening. He decided now to take her to Aden, where he could find a doctor. On descending the pass to the coast, she saw the ocean for the first time. This, to her, resembled the desert she knew so well, except that this one boiled and she stared at it for hours. Then they drove to Aden, racing along the harder sand of the beach to beat the tide until the dark rocks of the colony rose up before them.

The doctor examined Sheikha and declared there was nothing wrong with her. It may have been the strain of the long camel ride, or her dislike of the plateau villages and strange women, or because the month of fasting was hard on her. But Davey fussed and worried over her like a man who suspected she was pregnant. Sheikha recovered when she saw the house at Sheikh Othman. She discovered the overhead fans and electric lights, whose switches she turned on and off, off and on like a child. She ran from one room to the next, looking at my father's engravings of English hunting scenes hanging on the walls. She loved the way the water gushed from the taps. And the way her bath was warmed by a fire-heated drum outside in the garden of pomegranates, figs, and mangoes. She gathered up her long robe and stared down at her reflection in the black, polished floor. She was like Bilkis, Queen of Sheba, who approached Solomon across a courtyard of glass so that he could glimpse her feet.

When men look back on how Sharif Hussein gave in to tyranny, they say it happened at the same time that motorcars arrived in the wadi. The British in Aden had used cars since soon after their invention.

Across the frontier in the Imamate, however, the first car arrived in the highland capital of Sana'a in the 1920s, a present to the ruler Yahya from Benito Mussolini. There were no roads, so it had to be transported in parts by camel from the port of Hodeidah to Sana'a, at eight thousand feet, where an Italian engineer assembled it. But now that they had a car, they needed a motor road, so on the Imam's orders all the peasants along a chosen route were forced to construct one back to Hodeidah. At first the car sat neglected, looked on as an infernal Christian contraption. But Ragib Bey, an Ottoman qadhi who had learned to drive while serving in the embassy to the czar at St. Petersburg, turned the court. Once the Imam rode to mosque in a car, all his feudal lords decided they wanted one too. Davey had unwittingly become part of the story as a young man when he was sent to deliver the first car to the Imam's lieutenant in the town of Taiz in October 1935. Philby drove his Buick into the desert a year later.

Sharif Hussein evidently grew to believe he too needed a car. The political officer Groom likened the sharif to Mr. Toad in *Wind in the Willows*. The sharif's enthusiasm to own a motorcar became an all-consuming and ultimately doomed obsession. He persuaded the RAF to fly a jeep up in a transport aircraft. A driver was appointed who had not the faintest idea what he was doing. He drove the jeep in a straight line, regardless of whether there was a track or not, ignoring all obstacles in his way. On the first day it tipped into a ditch and the gearbox broke. For several weeks it had to be driven in reverse, that being the only gear that worked. When my father was next up in Beihan he visited the sharif's stables with Groom, where they found the horses standing about with coat-hanger ribs. My father was aghast, Groom recalled.

"They are in a disgraceful condition!" he exclaimed. The sharif replied that his horses were starving due to a shortage of barley. Since his new toy had arrived, the sharif had lost all interest in his stables. He had not even ordered the horses to be exercised. My father gloomily predicted that from now on, the sharif would become estranged from the subjects he knew so well from when he'd ridden out on his horse. Then his people could greet him and he them in return, and talk awhile, and observe how things were in the valley.

"But now you will not even hear them," my father said. "Instead you will throw up dust in their faces and drive on without stopping."

* * *

For almost a year Aden had been ordering Davey to take his home leave in England, but he had avoided it on the excuse that he had delicate political negotiations to complete in Beihan. On September 26, 1945, Mashur, the horse to which he was devoted, fell sick.

> *He was standing with his head hanging down but ... I thought he had a cold only. When I turned in for the night ... I rubbed him down with a cloth. By midnight he was dead with a heavy discharge of white froth from his nostrils. I have been much distressed over my loss today and then this morning I received a bomb-shell from Seager that I was to come straight to Aden in order to proceed on leave. How can I go into Aden leaving Sheikha here ... I have sent an urgent wire asking permission to arrange my private affairs.*

But they both knew that he would be forced to go and home leave was six months long. Sheikha was happy about returning to Beihan, but it would be bittersweet homecoming. "*She knows this will be my first move towards leaving for England. I woke up yesterday morning to find her crying.*" There was an air of inevitability over what was about to happen.

By the time Davey and Sheikha returned to Beihan from their travels across the Protectorates, months had passed. In their absence, the sharif had built himself a new tower that gleamed with whitewash. The reception room was the widest anybody had ever seen in the valley. He sat on a raised throne with a spittoon at his feet. Now his followers formed something like a medieval court, complete with advisers, tribesmen, dancing girls, and refugees from the Imam.

Davey discovered that his soldiers at the garrison were selling their rations and other bits and pieces of government property. He reacted by banning them from leaving their quarters until investigators flew in from Aden. The troops nearly mutinied, but Davey stood at the gate of the compound, bringing his rifle up to his waist, and threatened to shoot any man who attempted escape.

At about the same time, Sharif Hussein asked Davey if he could build a fort on a prominent rock at the head of the valley. This was within view of the Yemeni frontier, and reports of the tower building got back to the Imam's officials, who threatened to break off all peace talks with the British in Aden. To be diplomatic, Davey asked Hussein to cease construction. Sharif Hussein lost his temper and delivered a letter to Davey for the governor, declaring his resignation as sultan of Beihan. Davey lay low for a day or two. After much mediation, Sharif Hussein dropped by Davey's house. They reconciled and the sultan took back his letter before Davey could deliver it. All seemed to be quiet. Aden ordered Davey again to take his home leave in Britain. Davey was so exhausted by his work and the constant politicking of his job that he admitted to himself he was ready for some time away.

> Although I shall hate bidding au revoir to Sheikha, I shall be very glad to get some leave as I am feeling heartily tired and really want a rest—mentally—from the eternal affairs of the Protectorate.

Home leave meant returning to England. That Sheikha might join him was not even discussed. Her dislike of leaving Beihan even to travel on the plateau and down to Aden ruled out the idea. For his part, even if he had not kept the marriage a complete secret, he did not discuss it with the British in the colony.

> I am thankful to say that Sheikha has wisely decided to stay at al-Himma with her mother and brothers while I am on leave. She will not find life too lonely there surrounded by her family and I shall be more satisfied in my mind about her.

Sheikha wept when she saw Davey fly away. Davey's saluki dog Haddab sat down next to her and howled. They both knew he was gone for good.

A Punjabi regimental band was playing "My Nut Brown Maiden" in the breezy hall at Government House. Men in whites, ladies in hats, babu clerks asking after the health of the King Emperor, this was how the governor liked it. Not Englishmen going native.

> *Wednesday, March 6, 1946, Aden—the Governor has issued an ultimatum to me: that either I divorce Sheikha or I shall be transferred. This is the hardest thing I have yet experienced in my life I think ... I have feared this all along but have been lulled into a sense of security as it is now a year since I was married.*

The governor threatened to post Davey to Africa. He would never be allowed to return to southern Arabia. As far as the British were concerned, and the governor's deputy Seager in particular, Davey had compromised himself as a political officer by marrying a local Arab woman. The governor claimed Sharif Hussein had planted Sheikha as a honey trap for a lonely Englishman. To keep a mistress would have been acceptable, but what was intolerable was the legitimacy of the relationship. My father took a photo of Davey riding at Khormaksar that day. He is spurring the horse for a jump. He looks thin and tired. The ride may have cleared his head but even before he had saddled up he knew that he had no freedom to choose.

> *The subject is so painful for me that it is impossible for me to write in detail of the pros and cons but it is obvious that I cannot continue with Sheikha as life would be made too difficult for us both, officially and socially.*

Davey saw that the ultimatum gave him no choice. He could not bring himself to be exiled from the Protectorates, the place of his youth. But it was also unthinkable for him to leave the colonial service and live freely with Sheikha in tribal southern Arabia. He could not take her with him either to Africa or to England, where his family was ignorant of what he had done. Davey did the only thing he could.

> *Thursday, March 14, 1946, Aden—I divorced Sheikha today in the presence of Sharif Hussein and Sheikh Qassim Ahmed. I pray to God that she will take the news calmly and philosophically and that she will be happy again very soon. God bless her and guard over her always. I have been forced to divorce her and I feel as if I have been cut in half but I have no way out of it as God knows. May He heal the wounds in our hearts.*

Imagine this terribly sad business. Far to the north in Beihan on the edge of the desert Sheikha was longing for Davey, afraid she'd never see him again but ignorant of what was that very day taking place. And picture the brokenhearted Peter Davey saying out loud three times in the presence of a witness, *anti tallaq*—"I release you." The witness, of course, was none other than his friend Sharif Hussein. Sheikha would not learn what had happened until the sharif returned to Beihan to tell her the news himself. The sharif wept as he saw Davey sail away. He stood there waving a white handkerchief, muttering oaths, already sorry for his betrayal. In the process of using him, he had truly become his brother and friend.

For it was not only the governor who had destroyed Davey and Sheikha's happiness. Sharif Hussein was also to blame, a man who lived by conspiracies and whispered conversations. Originally, he had assumed that he could gain some sort of advantage by using his cousin Sheikha to manipulate Davey. To his alarm, Sheikha did not behave as he asked. Her priority was the welfare of herself and her child, Davey, and then Hussein, in that order. As time went on Sheikha was transformed from being a hidden voice behind the veil to a woman with real power. One minute the perfumed odalisque, every exotic, sensuous thing an Englishman in love with Arabia wanted, the next a sulking, angry creature demanding he should do this, or sack that person, or trust this tribal section rather than that one. Sharif Hussein grew aware that he was being usurped as the true Arab ruler of Beihan by a woman. His anger grew too much to bear.

After Davey refused to allow him to build his fort at the top of the valley, Sharif Hussein decided that he would go to the British in Aden and have the Englishman transferred away from Beihan. The day Davey and Sharif Hussein flew down to Aden together, the sharif went alone and in secret to Seager and the governor. They had already heard all the gossip about the secret marriage and Davey's conversion to Islam. Davey had been naive to think he could keep it a secret in a place like Aden. The British had not liked it but they had bided their time, waiting for an official excuse to deal with the matter. Sharif Hussein's tirade concerning Davey's refusal to allow him to build his fort, together with his evident paranoia regarding Sheikha, gave the governor and Seager the excuse they were looking for to end the marriage.

Anthony and Dan, Mogadishu, July 1993

THE SOUND OF
FREEDOM IN THE AIR

I expected Reuters to send me to Sarajevo. That spring of 1993, the Bosnian capital under siege by the Serbs was at the heart of the Balkans story. American stringer Kurt Schork had been covering Sarajevo for months and the rumor was that he wanted a break. I was wrong. Instead they sent me to the Serbian capital of Belgrade, where Slobodan Milosevic ruled in darkness; often literally, thanks to international sanctions that fueled million-percent inflation, power cuts, and shortages of all kinds. It quickly dawned on me that the Balkans wasn't my story and I respected the possessiveness of the stringers who had slogged it out here since the summer of 1991. Kurt, a former New York Port Authority bureaucrat who had cut loose in his early forties to go stringing in Iraqi Kurdistan, had graduated to Bosnia and barely drawn breath for twenty-four months.

My new bureau chief was a gruff Scot with whom I got on badly from the outset. I asked him when I would be going into the field and he didn't take kindly to that at all. He slapped me on the night shift, subbing copy and pulling together stories from all fronts of battle and diplomacy in the overnight Balkans wrap. Most of the office staff were educated Yugoslavs, a dying breed in the Serbia of the day, but they were too preoccupied by their own tragedies to be my idea of fun. We were all watched over by one female, let's call her Svetlana, a Serb with dyed red hair who gave me the shivers.

It seemed to me that Svetlana would have you believe the Serbs were the most persecuted people in Christendom. In my opinion she was typical of the times. Jesus, the Serbs got me down. I loathed their plum brandy, served by peroxide blondes in those curious white platform shoes all women in Communist Europe once wore, and their diet of pork—fried, smoked, sausaged, chopped, boiled. All conversations led back to the subject of the Battle of Kosovo against the Muslims in 1278, which the Serbs lost. And the defining characteristic of Serb culture was losing. Their museums were stuffed with medieval weapons and instruments of torture that boggled the imagination. Their paintings depicted brutal rapes. The sexual savagery was repeated in the hardcore porn the Serbs loved to watch on TV. Their polka folk songs. Their goblinlike language, all sharp Slavic consonants. Arcane tribal rivalries that in Africa so fascinated me seemed here impenetrable. Serbs made the worst Africans look angelic. My Serb Everyman is a bearded Chetnik gleefully whispering tales in my ear about faces being ripped off, buckets full of Muslim ears, disemboweled pregnant women, and how the enemy tattooed their names on the buttocks of captured POWs after gang-banging them.

I liked the dark-skinned Gypsies who had camped in the brambles below the Reuters office and greeted me every time I passed by day or night. But I felt terribly lonely in Belgrade. I used to walk across the bridges of the oily Danube, praying for NATO's bombs to fall. On sleeping streets, I came upon queues of the elderly and disabled people outside bakeries, which would open only at dawn to sell sanctions bread. At my apartment on Revolution Boulevard, I would find the landlady had left for me a bowl of apricots and cherries on the table. Among the cigarette butts in the ashtray might be one ringed with dark red lipstick, and then I would think of Lizzie. This would upset me as I sat there, knocking back codeine and plum brandy. I'd try to phone her, hang on to hear the crackle of Belgrade ether connecting to African ether, the monotone rings and then the answering machine with her recorded voice. When the codeine ran out I scored some new pills from a Serb gym instructor that kept me awake. What was in them was a mystery, but they were the kind of thing Chetnik snipers with hangovers used to steady the hand. I lay sleepless and wired, listening to the trams humming down iron tracks on the cobbled boulevard outside.

Lizzie wrote that she had flown to a camp of orphans in southern Sudan. A little boy with bright eyes, snot running down his ash-powdered face, dressed in a burlap sack and holding a bowl, had run up to grab her hand with his black, spidery fingers. He smiled at her. She took off her flannel shirt and buttoned him up in it. It hung off his tiny frame with the tails dragging in the dust. It was time for her to go and the aircraft propellers coughed into life. She took a last look at him. "Then he did a strange thing," she wrote. "He just plopped down on the ground with his bowl and his new shirt, which was more like a dress ... I started crying like a baby, thinking I had made him miserable by giving him the shirt and that one of the bigger kids was likely to steal it as soon as it got dark because the little guy didn't have any parents to keep an eye on him and I was sorry and this was a godless country and then the pilot ran up and told me to get on the plane because the rains were coming."

She was now headed for Somalia, where the United Nations had taken over command of the military mission in Mogadishu from the U.S. Marines in May. Almost immediately, a quarrel had broken out between Aydiid and UNOSOM. UNOSOM claimed that Aydiid had refused to disarm and tone down his verbal attacks against the foreigners on his "pirate radio." On June 5, Pakistani forces conducted what was officially described as a check at five of Aydiid's "weapons cantonments." One of these was at the radio station compound, which the Somalis feared might be shut down. Aydiid's followers converged at the site and overwhelmed the Pakistanis as they exited the station, oblivious to the danger they were in. Simultaneously, Pakistanis escorting a food convoy in the city were set upon by crowds of women and children. Some soldiers were ripped limb from limb, while others were shot. Eighty Pakistani blue helmets were killed or wounded.

The UN Security Council in New York reacted by authorizing UNOSOM to deploy "all necessary measures" to halt violence against its troops, including their "arrest and detention for prosecution, trial and punishment." Aydiid wasn't named, but UNOSOM chief Admiral Howe fingered him by issuing a Wild West–style poster with a $25,000 bounty. Wanted: Dead or Alive. Several nights later, American AC-130 gunships pounded Aydiid's "command and control facilities," mostly garages and scrap yards where the Somalis blowtorched together their technical battlewagons. Among the casualties was an eight-year-old boy incinerated while sleeping in the warlord's compound. Aydiid himself calmly remained in his house a five-minute drive away from the UNOSOM base. On the night of June 17, the foreigners launched an air and ground assault against Aydiid's complex of garages. Prior to the attack helicopters mounted with loudspeakers and spotlights warned the Somalis to evacuate. This allowed Aydiid himself to slip the net. After raining lead down from the air the Americans left it to the Third World contingents, the Pakistanis and the Moroccans, to go in on the ground. In the ensuing battle, a Somali mob set upon the invaders. The Moroccan Task Force commander was among the forty-five UNOSOM casualties. Mortally wounded, he refused a medevac and fought on with his troops until he bled to death.

My Nairobi friends were all in Mogadishu. Dan was getting big play in *Newsweek* and *Time* with his pictures of Cobras swooping low over militia tanks and running Somalis. During one of the AC-130 Spectre gunship raids, Jonathan, I heard, had crawled under a bed in the al-Sahafi hotel. Buchizya had tried to join him, but he was too fat to squeeze into the narrow space. My colleagues were sitting on a fantastic story in Mogadishu. I could have been there too, but I wasn't. I was stuck in a European war I hated and I cursed myself for it.

I heard that Lizzie had returned to Nairobi, but not to the Ski Chalet. I tracked her down to a hotel, where she had checked in under the name of the model Jerry Hall. It was a double room. She picked up the phone and we spoke for an hour. Another time I phoned the Ski Chalet and Dan picked up. "Good to hear your voice," he said. "Yeah, yeah," I replied suspiciously.

When the Scot finally sent me on assignment to Bosnia, I was shocked by the intensity of my reactions to a war in Europe. To be honest, it was because the bodies were Caucasian, not black; the starving POWs filling the cattle barns were white, not black; the bruised faces of soldiers were white, not black; the teenage girls weeping in fear as they fled a village being cleansed were white, in platform shoes and flares, not blacks in rags.

Serbs trying to argue why they had to murder Muslims would appeal to me as a European. "We Europeans must defend ourselves against the East," they would say. Or: "They breed so much faster than we Europeans. Unless we fight we will be overwhelmed." The idea that I had anything in common with Serbs was frankly preposterous. Yet I identified with their plight on a level that was more profound than I liked. Was it that the job was getting to me? Had I become inured to suffering in Africa? Or was it due to an involuntary impulse, one that caused me great shame, that these were white people? Trapped in my skin, I was a stateless colonial, a freebooting hack. Was the Africa I missed my home, or was this Europe my home, or at least the only one I deserved?

"You come from Kenya?" the Chetniks laughed. "Yet you are not black. Blacks are like monkeys."

I found temporary succor on a lonely road at the Bosnia-Croatia frontier. Flagging us down at a checkpoint, instead of hairy white irregulars there were black United Nations troops. I peered at them. Their features seemed very familiar, with lop ears and handsome Maasai faces. To Svetlana's consternation, I sprang from the car, grasping the hand of a soldier. I loudly greeted him in Swahili and he looked astonished at me, then gave me a gap-toothed smile. We had arrived in a peacekeeping zone under the command of the Kenyan army UN contingent. Over a cigarette, we swapped news of home. Back in the car Svetlana demanded in her screechy voice to know what we had been talking about. "Rain," I said truthfully.

The Kenyans' camp was in Knin, the capital of Serb-held Krajina that was famous only for its role in the war and its nuts and bolts factory. That evening, while Svetlana was with the shaggy Chetniks in the bar, I gave her the slip and went off to join the Kenyans for a beer. All were lads from poor backgrounds and they had never been abroad before. They had suffered casualties in a recent Croatian mortar attack on a bridge. The bitter cold of winter got to them. The primitive barbarity of the war shocked them, particularly the way neighbors turned on one another in what had come to be known as the crime of ethnic cleansing. But they remained cheerful. They were sending home extra money from their UN stipends. On R&R they went on shopping trips to Vienna, where they would pick up boom boxes, Sony Walkmans, dark glasses, Levi 501s—all the stuff their village neighbors would be impressed by when the soldiers went home. One sergeant named Lekitado confided to me that their spirits were constantly boosted by the attentions of local Serb women. Being the avid fans of porn movies—"darty filums," Lekitado called them—the Serbs expected my Kenyan brothers to be hung like stallions. In addition, the combination of plum brandy and that onerous crusade of defending Europe against the Oriental hordes had played havoc with the male Serb warriors' libidos.

Graham was twenty-seven and still looked a boy, but one with a face beaten to a bloody, bruised pulp. He had been ordered to wear his tattered combat fatigues, the same ones he'd had from serving with the British army in the 1991 Gulf War. I had met British mercenaries before. But here, the more I heard about Graham since Svetlana had announced we were being taken to interview him in prison, the less comfortable I felt about the story. I knew the public display of POWs against their will violated the Geneva Convention. When the Serbs said he might be shot as a spy, however, I saw this might be my only chance to save his life.

The prison turned out to be in one of Knin's hospitals. Serbs in white coats wandered about, except that now they were being employed not as nurses but as prison wardens. The Serbs told me to wait in a room where there was a bed and a gantry from which dangled a half-used bag of plasma. It appeared the drip tube had been hurriedly ripped out of an arm, because a needle and plaster dangled at the end of it.

Graham was brought in, but on the pretext that we'd get better light for pictures outside I asked if we could take a walk in the garden. The Serbs agreed and we were able to move a few meters away from Svetlana and the others. I didn't know where to start, so I asked Graham why he was here. He shrugged and told me his simple story.

On his return from the Gulf deserts, he was discharged from the British army. This was a young man who should have been born when his country had an empire and plenty of wars and causes to fight for overseas. He didn't want to march around in uniform without any genuine purpose. I could sympathize with him. But this was modern Britain, so instead of finding new adventures, Graham ended up in Brighton, on England's south coast, working in a bingo hall for elderly pensioners. From there, like so many veterans who are never thanked for fighting for their countries, he ended up homeless and on the streets. Graham decided life in peacetime was pretty much worthless, so he looked for a new cause. One day he fished a newspaper out of a bin in the street and read an item about the Balkans crisis. Then and there, he resolved to become a volunteer warrior.

Graham caught a bus from King's Cross, in London, to Zagreb. He had a little money on him and a Michelin tourist road map of the Balkans, together with a notebook and camera. "I planned to make some money selling stories to the newspapers," he told me. "I thought I'd have enough experiences to write a book of adventure." In Zagreb, Graham made his way across the city of cobbled streets to the offices of the Croatian HVO military and declared that he wished to join the international brigades. The Croatians informed him that the brigades had been disbanded. Graham ignored their warnings to go home when somebody in a Zagreb fast-food joint told him a bit about the war in neighboring Bosnia. Looking at his map, he saw that the Muslim rebels were holding out in an isolated pocket of land known as Bihac in northern Bosnia, next to the Croatian frontier. Graham bought a train ticket to the Adriatic resort of Split, telling the conductor and police at the station that he wanted a beach holiday. Going by his map, he then waited until the train stopped in its tracks close to the Bosnian border, jumped down, and vanished into the undergrowth until the train moved on down the line. It was high summer and Graham walked until dusk, when he found a lake to camp by. He did not dare to light a fire, but it was warm out and he just curled up on the grass to sleep. In the distance, he heard men's voices singing.

Next morning, he changed out of his jeans and civilian clothes and put on his British army fatigues. He set off walking and after some hours he began to observe the signs of war. Barbed wire, abandoned and burned houses, feral animals, and farmyards in which the grass had grown up through machinery. He carried on and presently he came to a plowed field. In the middle of this was a sign painted in large black Cyrillic letters. Graham wondered what the notice said. On the far side of the field he came to a hedge, which he climbed over, and dropped in a lane. He walked down this way until he came face to face with a group of soldiers at a checkpoint.

At this point Graham looked at me sheepishly and said, "I said I had come to fight for the Muslims. They looked very surprised. They told me two things."

"What was the first?"

"That the field I had just walked across was full of land mines. The sign said 'mines.'"

"And the second?"

"The second thing they did was to welcome me and say how interesting it was that I had come to fight for the Muslims, because this was a Serb military checkpoint."

The Serbs blindfolded Graham, bundled him into the back of a van, and drove him somewhere. Here they beat him during several days of interrogations. He said they refused to believe his story and asked whether he had been sent by his government. After a while they gave up asking him questions and just beat him. They put him through mock executions and repeatedly told him he would be shot by firing squad. Graham was in a trancelike state and clearly resigned to his fate.

The Serb wardens closed in and since this now felt like an official interview I quietly asked how he was. Svetlana had her tongue out and was listening intently. Graham spoke louder.

"The first week was rough because they said they were going to shoot me. Frankly they treated me better than I expected. You get the odd slap, but we're fed twice a day. Once a week, we get a chance to shave and shower."

I wondered if he needed anything. He asked me to get a message through to his parents in England, to say he was alive. I promised to get in touch with the British embassy in Zagreb. We shook hands and then he was led back into the hospital down to his ward-cum-cell, which he shared with five other captured Croatians. That was the last I ever saw of Graham.

Instead of filing a report I went off to find the local International Committee of the Red Cross office and reported his story. The ICRC in turn contacted the British embassy and promised to track down his family in England. I objected to the idea of making a story out of Graham because of the way he had been presented to me by the Serbs. The truth is that I was shocked by the sight of him and didn't know what to do. Svetlana knew this was a good story, and she went off to phone the Scot behind my back. I then had him on the satellite phone ordering me to file immediately. Never argue with the desk, they say, but I did, saying what I believed about the Geneva Convention. After a few minutes I relented, of course, and sat down to write.

Back in Belgrade, a letter from Celestine the gardener was waiting for me. It made me even more homesick. He thanked me for the wages, a pittance to be truthful, which I had arranged for him to be paid in my absence. "Dear Sir," Celestine wrote. "Get much sincere jubilant greetings from me. My pleasured gratitude accompanied with joy and great love is delightfully flowing to you. May the Almighty bless the work of your hands. I have received your outstanding help of ten thousand shillings. I was so happy I wanted to come to Yugoslavia to shake your hand, but lack of material has hindered me, so I am putting it on paper."

I required a distraction of an extreme sort if I was to stop pining for Africa. I found it in Andric, an Australian who was one of the thousands of ethnic Serbs who had returned to the Balkans on the outbreak of hostilities. He introduced himself as a photographer for the Australian Associated Press, based out of Sydney. "I didn't know there was such a thing as the AAP," I said. "It's part of the AP, but it's the Australian wing," Andric replied breezily. He struck me as being rather evasive about his working arrangements but my mind was laid to rest by the fact that we met several times in the Belgrade AP bureau, he had AP logos on all his equipment, and he showed me some of his front-page pictures in the international newspapers. He was a good photographer and the AP was Reuters's main rival, but what the hell. Andric cut a handsome figure with his gold earring, his mop of lush black hair, and his fetchingly wild personality. In sanctions-hit Belgrade inflation was a million percent and our dollars went a long way. Andric had rented the presidential suit at the Hotel Moscow and invited me to join him.

"Move in with me," Andric said. "Have some fun."

The rooms were full of rococo furniture and oil paintings of Slavic lords and Christian virgins being massacred by Muslims. MTV played at full volume. Andric had filled his lavish space with cases of beer, cameras, looted Bosnian road signs, and of course girls.

"Welcome to my world," Andric laughed.

I promised to consider his offer. It was tempting except for the strange, frightening people whom Andric described as his friends and who hung out at his rooms in the Moscow day and night. One was an American mercenary who never removed his shades. A second was a cultured young Serb who cried a great deal and told me he had been an artillery officer in the Yugoslav National Army in the fighting against Croatian separatists. He claimed his generals had ordered him to shell a target for weeks without telling him what it was, only to discover afterward that he had demolished the town of Vukovar in which so many civilians perished. A third guest was a Chetnik weekend warrior who worked in a Belgrade office and went off on Fridays to fight alongside his ethnic brothers in Bosnia. He carried a Scorpion machine-pistol and at parties he had a habit of trailing the red dot laser sight around the room, bringing it to rest on whomever's eye he wanted to catch. At times Andric would vanish for a few days on assignment. Once I was sitting in the sunshine at a terrace café drinking lager with Andric and the American with the shades and they were talking about accompanying a Serb night patrol near Sarajevo where Andric had witnessed the slitting of a Muslim sentry's throat. They laughed when he had finished his story.

Andric's parties at the Moscow Hotel were uproarious and they routinely degenerated into orgies. To these events Andric would invite all his weirdo friends and he had dozens of young girls who came and went. During one very noisy night the place was raided by Serb paramilitaries. When they saw the roomful of girls they put down their batons and pistols and entered the fray. At some point in the evening I blacked out. When I came around, I was on a bed, handcuffed to a naked teenager with short dark hair and very white skin. The chain between the cuffs had been passed between the bars of the brass bed where we lay. Andric entered the room with the keys to the cuffs, which he said the militias wanted because they had to return to duty. I stayed awake long enough to watch the young female slip on her clothes. I later got up and went to take a shower. In the mirror, I saw the girl had scrawled her name and number across my chest in lipstick. Back in the main room, a group was watching a Serb rock video of men in camouflage performing with their guitars and drums in front of a smoking howitzer. A woman walked toward me, took me by the hand, and led me back to bed.

Later, I called the girl with dark hair and white skin and we used to meet for long walks through the city. She was the daughter of a Serb colonel and wore crimson lipstick and fingernails and cheap clothes. She loved books and music and said she wanted to see an end to all the wars being prosecuted by Slobodan Milosevic in Bosnia and Croatia. One afternoon we joined an antiwar protest. When the police opened up with water cannon and advanced toward us in a clouds of tear gas, she led me down cobbled side alleys back to the refuge of my apartment on Revolution Boulevard. I decided to begin enjoying Serbia. My new girlfriend took me to Novi Sad to admire the Austro-Hungarian architecture, we slept in a peasant village and picked wild marijuana in a pretty country landscape.

"I've decided to move into the Moscow with you," I told Andric one day. He smiled and knocked back his plum brandy. "Good man."

Chance intervened again and, back in Belgrade, the Scot ordered me to drive immediately across the UN-patrolled demilitarized zone to Zagreb. Andric surprised me by asking if he could come along too. We set off in a Reuters car through the UN checkpoints west of Vukovar's ruins and entered Croatia. Andric was tense on the trip and I just assumed he must be apprehensive the Croatians would harass him if they discovered that he was an ethnic Serb.

"Fuckin' monsters, the Croatians," said Andric. "Ustasha fascist murderers. They're barely human. You'll see."

We checked into the most expensive hotel in Zagreb and

asked at the desk for directions to a decent bar. "Where we can meet girls," said Andric with a wink. The female receptionist smiled and told us the way to a bar called something like Hoop. Andric's Serb paranoia about the Croatians was starting to rub off on me as we walked across a wide cobbled square peering at the people around us. "Look at 'em," he said with a lowered voice as we passed groups of skinheads. "Told you." I decided the Croatians did look quite fascistic, like their Ustasha forebears who had sided with Hitler in the Second World War and helped massacre thousands of innocent Serbs. It was a relief to reach the bar, but as we entered Andric and I gasped with horror. There were girls, lots of pretty girls. But the men were all shaven-headed and every single one of them was at least seven feet tall. Andric murmured more expletives from under his breath as we sidled up to the bar and ordered a couple of beers. We drank up quickly, avoided speaking to any women, and hurried back to the hotel. "What was going on at that bar?" Andric asked the receptionist. She smiled again and said, "Didn't you like it? Croatia's Olympic basketball team hangs out there. That's why the girls go."

We regrouped for another beer in the hotel bar, where Andric revealed that he was in deep trouble with his employers at Associated Press. He said the suite at the Moscow back in Belgrade had turned out to be a lot more expensive than he'd expected. He had run up a huge bar and room-service bill because his weirdo friends and the harem of girls had all been signing for goodies on his behalf. He told me that AP went ballistic when he filed the expenses claim and the agency's accountants had ordered him to report immediately to regional headquarters in Budapest. "Now I'm broke," Andric said. "Can you help us out with the bill here? I'll pay you back soon as I get back." I said, "No problem, mate." Next morning, I picked up his hotel bill and lent him a wad of German marks. He departed for Hungary, or I think that's where he went. That was the last I ever saw of him.

At the Zagreb Reuters bureau, an urgent service message from Belgrade was waiting for me. The message quoted Andric's full name and revealed that he was a Serb impostor claiming to be from the Sydney office of the Associated Press. It said something like "Our colleagues at the AP advise Reuters that on no account should correspondents trust this man as he is not bona fide and has no permission to use the AP name." But Andric had vanished, leaving his vast bill at the Hotel Moscow and a pile of international newspaper clippings showing his rather good photographs.

I was on the Zagreb early morning shift when a three-belled urgent pinged over the World News wire. At that instant, I was settling down to pull together a wrap from the Sarajevo correspondent Kurt on twenty-four hours of Balkan killing. It was an anthology of mortar impacts, mosque demolitions, and infighting between factions.

I got up from my workstation and strolled over to the teleprinter. Three bells was big news. Only a six-belled bulletin was more important—a dead pope, assassination of a Western president, or a hike in U.S. interest rates. Three bells was most likely a bomb, a plane crash, a group death of some kind.

The two-paragraph first take described a helicopter attack in Mogadishu. Many deaths. A group of journalists had gone missing. My mind began racing with worry. More alarm bells rang out with rising casualty figures, vox pops, condemnations, and blind analyses. For several hours, my fears grew until the confirmation came through. Every day until now the bells had tolled and they were simply stories. Three bells and everything changed.

* * *

The words come back to haunt me once again. "Woe to the land shadowing with wings, which is beyond the rivers of Ethiopia … Go, ye swift messengers, to a nation scattered and peeled, to a people terrible from their beginning hitherto; a nation meted out and trodden down." For me now, this nation was Somalia. And like angels of death, the wings are gunship helicopters shadowing my journalist friends, the swift messengers.

Time among the swift messengers made me forget there was ever another life outside this. I thought because of the things we did together, I shared great intimacy with my colleagues, only to discover later that in reality I hardly knew them: whether they were married, where they had come from, or where they went after the stories died. We were thrown together like aircraft passengers on a long-haul flight, who share an intimacy for the duration of the journey, which then evaporates in a second on touchdown.

After it was all over, I discovered I had nothing in common with some old comrades other than our "when we" and "do you remember" conversations. Sworn friendships slowly died, revived briefly in stilted discussions over occasional beers. The silences between meetings became more difficult to end, until in time friends were no more than numbers in my old address books.

Dead friends are different. Death gives us a permanent loyalty. Our intimacy is frozen in memory at the instant they lost their lives. I mourn the old ages they will never have, but I will know them as young and beautiful for as long as I live.

And I can't separate them from the way they died, or where they died. At a sandy crossroads in a ruined city. On a lonely dirt track overhung with eucalyptus. In a seedy room where the muezzin is heard through high windows. Out beneath the black waves of the Indian Ocean.

* * *

The Somalia story had refused to fall off the news schedules. Reuters was obliged to cover it, but the managers were becoming alarmed at the story's huge price tag. Our team in Mogadishu was paying a fortune for housing, armed guards, and vehicles. This was in line with the wider picture, where all foreigners were being shaken down by Aydiid and his boys. The UN army had bribed rather than blasted its way into the city. Forget about the starving kids. It was the militia chieftains who had really lucked out.

The Reuters bosses had been uncomfortable about the cost of the Somalia story since the outset. They clearly hoped it would sink down the page. Instead of visiting Nairobi or Mogadishu to show an interest in our coverage, the Cyprus-based editor for Africa flew to South Africa, where the townships were convulsed with violence. What Reuters was ultimately interested in was the kind of financial journalism that garnered clients and enhanced share values, and South Africa has gold and diamonds and golf. Somalia has camels and war.

Jonathan had phoned me a few weeks before. He told me he had been driving to the Hotel al-Sahafi from a press briefing at the UNOSOM base when a mob dragged coils of razor wire across the road, mobbed his vehicle, and spat at the windscreen. The signs were that Mogadishu was heading for bloodshed from the very day the United Nations assumed command of the operation from the Americans. Jonathan put in a request for six extra flak jackets for the Nairobi Reuters team. Cyprus's reply was that they'd send two. "Can't you share?" The managers looked for other ways to shave costs. For months, the agency's top journalists and photographers had flown in to beef up Nairobi. Now they were all being pulled out, leaving Jonathan and his boys to soldier on alone.

In that phone call Jonathan told me that he had a sense of foreboding. He was exhausted. When Cyprus offered him some leave, he grabbed it. Before he left for London he called Dan and

Hos for a meeting. He told them that since there were no reinforcements coming in, they would have to handle the picture operation in Mogadishu by themselves.

Both Hos and Dan had tired of the big story. They wanted
out. Hos told Jonathan he was terrified about returning to
Mogadishu. Jonathan reminded them how much he had done to
promote their careers at Reuters. They owed him and he was calling
in his favors. So they struck a deal. Hos and Dan would share one
more month of Mogadishu—two weeks on assignment each. In
return, he promised Hos that he'd organize it somehow to get him
better pay and conditions. He promised to support Dan's applica-
tion for reassignment to a completely different sort of story far
away from the wars in Africa.

Dan went in for his final spell. A handful of journalists
remained in Mogadishu, far fewer than at the time of the Americans' arrival in December. Other Reuters journalists were already at
the al-Sahafi: cameraman Shafi, his soundman Anthony Macharia,
the talented young American text stringer Jonathan Ewing, and a
text correspondent named Andrew. Andrew was both the oldest
among the Reuters crew there and, as Jonathan's deputy in Nairobi,
also the most senior. I haven't mentioned him before because we
did not know each other well. Andrew distinguished himself over
many terrible months in Somalia and what he was about to endure
would have caused many men to snap.

July 12 was the date set for Dan's handover to Hos. On the
morning of that day, Hos flew into Mogadishu Central. He was
immediately driven by the Reuters guards to the al-Sahafi. Dan had
his bags half packed by the time Hos walked in the door and was
bursting to leave for the airport. Unfortunately his plans were about
to change.

UNOSOM forces had become increasingly alarmed at their
inability to capture Aydiid following the massacre of Pakistanis on
June 5. They had taken dozens of casualties in a chain of fruitless

attacks on the downtown Habre Gedir militia compounds. The Americans didn't seem to know whether to cast Aydiid's militias as dangerous Islamic fanatics or ragtag gangsters. They couldn't understand why the Somalis were running rings around UNOSOM but promised that victory and Aydiid's capture were imminent.

On July 7, four off-duty Somalis employed by UNOSOM's propaganda radio and newspaper *Maanta* were shot by carjackers, who dumped the bodies and stole the vehicle. It was typical of the sort of banditry one witnessed any given day in Mogadishu, but UNOSOM declared it to be an act of terrorism.

Two days later, Italian troops were routed at Checkpoint Pasta, outside a spaghetti factory on the Via Imperiale road heading north out of the city. A Somali mob of gunmen, women, and children attacked the Italians during a UNOSOM house-to-house weapons search. The Italians held their fire until they were overwhelmed by RPG and rifle fire. Three Italians were killed and twenty-three wounded. The survivors couldn't maneuvre their armored personnel carriers down the narrow sandy alleys. They were sitting ducks for Somali rocket-propelled grenades, so rather than wait to be fried inside their APCs they jumped out and fled on foot.

The Security Council in New York had ordered UNOSOM to "take all necessary measures" against their attackers after June 5. This didn't authorize the indiscriminate slaughter of civilians, but following the *Maanta* murders UNOSOM decided on a plan called Operation Michigan to attack a gathering of unarmed Habre Gedir clan elders at the house of one of Aydiid's lieutenants, a man named Qabdiid. The villa had a large room on the second floor that was appropriate for a conference.

UNOSOM knew the purpose of the clan elders' meeting that day was to force Aydiid to enter peace negotiations with UNOSOM. It was the latest of several clan conferences. Advisers who scurried between the Somalis and UNOSOM briefed Admiral

Howe on these talks, which were supposed to have his endorsement. In fact, a number of elders killed in the massacre had visited Howe only three days before.

A Somali spy for the UN attended the meeting. The signal for the attack to start was the moment he walked out of Qabdiid's villa. In previous UNOSOM assaults, Psy-Ops helicopters had been deployed with loudspeakers and searchlights to warn people to clear the area or surrender. This time, there was no warning. The helicopters in Operation Michigan hit the villa at three points: the roof, so that the ceiling caved in on the clan elders on the second floor; the stairs, which cut off their escape, and the main gate, through which U.S. troops had an easy entry to the compound where they moved about killing and photographing survivors.

I have imagined the scene over and over. The strobing blades of a dozen Super Cobra helicopter gunships and bubble-cockpit MH-1 "Little Birds" describe arcs of light against the dawn sky. They lift off and circle out over the surf-lined beach until they line up in formation, then turn back to head inland over the broken city and skim the rooftops until they come to hover wasplike over a square white villa. Suspended there, they open up and pour TOW missiles, 20mm cannon, and Gatling-gun fire into the building. The roof collapses according to plan. Most of the occupants are crushed. With the stairs blasted away, whoever crawls out leaps off the second floor. The firing continues until almost everybody inside the villa is either dead or broken. Black smoke billows from the blazing ruins. As the hourlong air assault ends, U.S. Army soldiers rope down from Black Hawks, enter through the demolished gate to deal with the survivors, and photograph the faces of their victims.

I interviewed Howe inside the UNOSOM fortress a fort-

night later. Even after months in Somalia his face was still salamander white. He avoided my eyes and seemed defiant. A fecal odor
hung in the room. Howe claimed a dozen or so people had been
killed in Operation Michigan. Most of them, he claimed, were
armed people "shooting back." He described it as a "clean, surgical
attack." However, figures produced by the Red Cross and city hospitals suggest that the number of civilians killed that day was between
fifty-four and eighty-five. Some of those killed were clan elders,
women serving tea, and children playing in the villa courtyard. The
day following the massacre, the legal adviser of the UN Justice Division in Somalia resigned after a memo in which she said that some
UN member states would regard the attack as "nothing less than
murder committed in the name of the United Nations." Howe himself promised that there would be an inquiry. As far as I am aware it
has never happened and certainly nothing was ever made public.

A crowd began gathering at the demolished villa. Qabdiid's
house was a five-minute drive away from the al-Sahafi, off the main
road to the UNOSOM fortress. When Scott Peterson, an American
photographer, arrived on the scene U.S. soldiers were still on the
ground. Peterson stayed after they evacuated and he was immediately
attacked by the mob. He made it back to the al-Sahafi with machete
wounds to the skull. There Dan and Hos met him and patched him
up while he told them what the situation was at the attack site.

When the assault started, Shafi was drinking tea with a
Pakistani commander at the UNOSOM base. Shafi was a Kenyan
of Pakistani origin, and he had friends at "PAK BATT, the Pak-
istans battalion." He dropped by to see them each morning to gossip about overnight violence and work out what he was going to
film that day. "We all raced to the top of the building to get a better view," Shafi recalled. "The Pakistani commander did not know
what was going on and seemed surprised by the American attack."
Evidently, nobody except the Americans, presumably including
Howe, had prior warning of Operation Michigan.

Shafi sped back to the Hotel al-Sahafi, where Anthony was waiting for him with the TV rig. They climbed up to the hotel's flat roof and began to film the attack. "We all talked about trying to get to the scene but we agreed that it was too dangerous while the gunships were firing." Andrew was also on the hotel roof and saw the helicopters hovering. One of them was dipped at an angle, pointing downward. It was firing at a ground target with its Gatling gun slung out below the nose. Andrew put on his flak jacket and jumped into one of the Reuters cars. Two armed guards carried AK-47s in the back and Abdi, one of the translators, had his Beretta .38. As the vehicle approached, the attack was still in progress. The gathering crowds hammered on the side of the car. Abdi had a relative who lived about 150 yards from Qabdiid's house. They climbed to the roof again and watched the choppers demolishing the villa. Andrew also saw the ground assault in progress and there was heavy automatic fire coming from the sides of the compound. The Reuters guards got closer to the site on foot and returned to warn him off. As Andrew emerged into the sandy street, the angry crowd surged around him and he was hit on the head and arms. He and the others bundled into the car and drove back to the hotel to file a news snap.

It must have been clear that to visit the ruins of Qabdiid's villa now would be very foolish. Shafi intended to satellite-feed the footage he had filmed from the Hotel al-Sahafi roof. He wanted to wait for several hours until the attack site had calmed down, then go out and film material for a 1600 GMT feed. Plans changed. Some fifteen minutes after the attack had ended, a group of Aydiid's officials appeared at the hotel. They wanted journalists to see "what the Americans had done." Dan and Hos knew the individual Somalis in this delegation, who promised to provide safe passage through the city.

At that instant, Andrew was struggling to send his three-belled urgent by satellite phone. Dan and Hos appeared at the door wearing their flak jackets. They shouted to him that they were going to the attack site and he barely took any notice. "There was no discussion of whether they should or not," Andrew said later. They had done it before. People knew the risks. He remained at his desk, fiddling with the computer. Each time he connected on the sat phone, the modem link-up failed. All this time he could hear a storm of noise outside. Andrew climbed the stairs up to the flat roof to adjust the sat-phone dish. From here he saw a swarm of U.S. helicopters wheeling about in the sky. Airborne hardware and the babble from radio traffic was shredding Reuters satellite communications.

Three vehicles of journalists set off from the al-Sahafi. The Somalis put one of Aydiid's officials in each of them. In the lead was the Reuters car, carrying Shafi, Anthony, Dan, and Hos. The second car carried AP reporter Angus Shaw and his photographer Hans Kraus, newly arrived from Germany. The third vehicle carried some Italians who turned back halfway.

At the attack site, the two cars parked outside the compound. The Reuters team entered through the destroyed gates and Kraus of AP followed them in. Shaw stayed in his vehicle. As the party approached the shattered building, a crowd of about a thousand Somalis went silent. Aydiid's men cleared a path into the compound. Bodies were being carried out of the ruins slung in bloodstained carpets and dumped into the flatbeds of two pickup trucks. A Somali showed Shafi a corpse. "He wanted to uncover the body . . . I could see the feet sticking from beneath the blanket, but he threw aside the cover anyway. The body was badly broken in the attack, with a lot of blood. There was a second body in the other pickup in the compound and then a third was carried out of the house in a carpet and shown to us. We saw four bodies in all."

The team stuck together and took pictures and ran the cameras for three or four minutes. An armed Somali gestured to the journalists to start moving on into the house to see more devastation and corpses. "We had only taken a couple of steps toward the buildings when the crowd attacked. They started throwing stones and pushing us."

Dan turned to Shafi.

"Let's get out of here! Run!"

Shafi yanked the sound cable out of his camera and yelled to Anthony to save himself. Shafi saw Dan, Anthony, and Kraus bolting out in a group. Hos had already vanished.

Outside the compound, the AP reporter Shaw heard gunfire and saw Dan, Anthony, and Kraus sprint past on foot. There was nothing Shaw could do and he ordered his driver to get going. Had he delayed a few seconds more, he would have been killed.

Back in the compound Shafi found himself trapped between the crowd and a wall. Women and children lunged at him, trying to snatch his heavy Beta TV camera. Among the sea of faces around him, some angry, others curious, he thought he recognized one Somali whom he had seen loitering at the al-Sahafi. He tossed this man the camera and then turned on his heels. When he got out of the compound he jumped into the back of a pickup truck he thought was the Reuters car. It was the wrong vehicle and Shafi found himself standing on a pile of bloody corpses. By this time our Somali bodyguards in the Reuters car had sped off through the melee. The guards had done as we always feared they would in a tight spot—they had saved themselves and forgotten about the people they were supposed to protect.

Shafi got down from the truck and started off running again. A crowd pursued him and he was struck on the upper back by what felt like a large rock. He fell sprawling to the ground. As he lay there Somalis rained more stones down on him. A man started beating him with a length of wood. Shafi later told me he thought to himself then: "Hell, I don't want to die like this. I don't know where I got the strength. I still don't know, but I managed to get up and just ran at the crowd, pushing people as I went." The mob suddenly parted. Shafi thought he had broken through, but instead he came face-to-face with a man aiming at him with an AK-47. "I thought I was going to die. I was running toward him and he fired, I don't know, I think three or four shots. One of them hit me in my arm. It burned a lot and I fell down, but I managed to roll over and get straight back up. That's when I saw Dan and Anthony."

Dan and Anthony were running away from the roaring crowd. They reached a junction in the road and turned down an alley. Shafi ran in the same direction until he saw a woman standing at an open, metal door. He sprinted toward her but as he got close she slammed the door shut in his face. He turned and headed back down the sandy alley Dan and Anthony had followed. At the junction, he saw Dan's flak jacket discarded in the dust. Shafi told me with tears in his eyes, "I was happy to see the flak jacket. For me it meant Dan was alive. He was smart. He realized he couldn't run properly with the weight of the jacket and he must have taken it off."

As he ran Shafi spotted a Land Cruiser passing by with its back door slightly open. He leaped in the back and found himself being stared at by several Somali men. Immediately, the vehicle sped off. Shafi begged to be dropped off at the al-Sahafi hotel. He looked out of the back doors as the car drove and hoped to come across Dan and Anthony. The men in the car said nothing. Even so, Shafi thought his ordeal was over. He was wrong. The vehicle accelerated past a turning to the hotel and raced on toward the chaos of Bakaaraha market, where a week earlier the decomposing remains of two Pakistani soldiers killed on June 5 had been found dumped on a pile of rubbish.

"You're going the wrong way!" Shafi told the Somalis in the car. Again he pleaded with them to take him to the al-Sahafi. "But they laughed. A man in the front of the car reached over and put his hands around my neck and began strangling me. I was trying to pull his hands away but he just held on." Shafi screamed. One of the men said, "Do you know what the fucking Americans have done here?"

Shafi whimpered that he was a Kenyan. The Somalis laughed again and said he was a Pakistani.

"You are Pakistani. You are a Christian."

Shafi gabbled the first sura of the Holy Koran. There is no God but Allah ... *La illahi ila Allah!*

In his mind, Shafi pictured the rotting corpses of the Pakistanis. "I began talking a lot ... pleading ... I said anything ... I thought they were taking me away to kill me." Blood gushed from the gunshot wound in his arm and only now did he notice that he had a gash in his thigh, probably made by a stone, and it was also bleeding heavily.

The Somalis fell silent. Shafi saw that the Land Cruiser had doubled back to arrive at the K-4 roundabout outside the al-Sahafi. He began pleading again and the driver slowed down and one of the men kicked open the back doors. Another of the men shoved Shafi so that he tumbled out of the moving vehicle and hit the road. As he cried out in pain and rolled, he saw the Land Cruiser accelerate away once more toward Bakaaraha.

Our stringer Ewing was the first to see Shafi carried in through the gates. Right away he slung him into the cab of a pickup and they ventured back out into the streets, speeding to the U.S. Army's 42nd Military Field Hospital. On arrival, the orderlies refused point blank to treat Shafi, saying he was a Pakistani.

"What are you saying?" Ewing yelled. "This man's wounded, he's my friend, I work with him and I'm a motherfuckin' American and I'm not leaving until you take him in!"

Ewing was usually a gentle and charming man but he could lose his temper with great effect and in this case it worked. Shafi was taken in.

* * *

A U.S. Black Hawk pilot, circling the attack site to assess damage, spotted a lone Caucasian fleeing in front of a Somali mob. He radioed back to base, to check that all American troops had made it safely home. The helicopter continued to circle while a count of U.S. troops was made. The pilot passed over the white man again. This time the mob had caught up with him. The pilot did not intervene. He could have dropped tear gas or stun grenades—the Black Hawks dropped them on journalists all the time for fun. All he did was request a second count. This was the story Dan's father Mike was told weeks later. He mused, "Why did this peacekeeper, *this peacemaker*, not intervene when he could have saved a life?" By the time the helicopter passed over Dan a third time, he was sprawled facedown in the dirt. Only then did the Black Hawk land in the street to pick him up, a dead American civilian.

Weeks after July 12 in Nairobi, I used an old bayonet to force open Jonathan's locked top desk drawer, which I knew was where he kept confidential documents relating to events in Mogadishu that we weren't supposed to see. In there I found Dan's postmortem report. It showed the front and back diagrammatic profiles of a man. There were several pen marks on different parts of the body. "Pronounced dead at the 42nd Military Field Hospital at 1245 hours, 12 July 1993," the postmortem recorded. "On the right cheek, two cuts of 1 inch and 2 inches ... a stab wound in the centre of the stomach above the navel ... a crescent shaped open wound to the bottom left of the navel ... an open blow wound to the left back of the skull ... one bruise on bottom left shin and cut on one finger ..."

Hos had been killed by two shots to the chest. He was probably the first of the group to die, based on the fact that Shafi never saw him even in the Qabdiid compound. With his car crash–induced stutter, Hos wouldn't have even been able to get the words out to plead for his life. He was thirty-eight and left his wife, Lucy, and three small children.

What I know about Anthony is that he broke free of the mob coming after him and Dan. As Dan went down, Anthony carried on running. The Black Hawk swooped over them at this point but the pilot was focusing only on the supposedly "one Caucasian male." Anthony made it to another junction that brought him onto the main thoroughfare between the UNOSOM base and the al-Sahafi on K-4 roundabout. Anthony's luck was still good, or his sense of direction in the maze of Mogadishu was truly special. It was only his second assignment to Somalia. This spell he'd been there nine days. The mob was still pursuing him and he began to lose speed, either because he had already been hit by flying rocks and was in pain or due to fatigue from running in the intense heat. He was in sight of the gray metal gates of the al-Sahafi—he had almost made it—when suddenly a Somali caught up with him and struck at his head with a long, sharp knife. Anthony fell and, like a stag pulled down by a pack of dogs, was overwhelmed by his murderers.

I barely knew Anthony. We had been together on assignment in Rwanda and I'd exchanged probably twenty sentences of conversation with him. He was twenty-two and came from a poor Nairobi district I'd dared venture into only with an escort during a previous year's riots. On his body was found his last monthly paycheck for thirty dollars, the price of one of my restaurant dinners in Nairobi. He also carried a letter to his mother, in which he proudly promised to buy her a sofa with his wages when he got home.

Back at the al-Sahafi, Andrew was still struggling to transmit his news snap and the helicopter interference still kept breaking the line. He eventually gave up on the modem and phoned his urgent through to Nicosia. By the time he'd finished the report one of our Somali guards was at his elbow. Andrew put the phone down and the Somali told him that Dan and Kraus had been killed. Fresh reports came in to say that two African bodies had also been seen close to the attack site. Andrew updated his story to say that two Western journalists had been killed and two Kenyans were missing.

A UN friend dropped by the al-Sahafi and offered to take Andrew to the U.S. Army's 42nd Field Hospital, by which time Ewing was already there with Shafi. Dan's body had been dumped in the facility by the Black Hawk. Andrew identified Dan and signed his death certificate. After he saw Shafi, he went to check for the other bodies at an adjacent hospital run by the Swedish military contingent, but they were nowhere to be found. From there, Andrew went to meet Howe and a group of U.S. military. The U.S. military liaison officer said he wanted to help. "If your boys are in trouble out there we'll go out and get them." When Andrew said they were dead and that he wanted UNOSOM to send out an armored column to pick up the bodies, the liaison officer seemed to lose interest. He said that by now, the streets were in turmoil and it would be suicide for UNOSOM troops to venture out on the ground. The Americans wanted to limit any PR damage to UNO-SOM as a consequence of the journalists' deaths. They asked Andrew whether he believed a trap had been set. They clearly wanted to avoid discussing the obvious truth, which was that the Somali mob had reacted to the U.S. helicopter massacre with spontaneous blind fury. Our colleagues were unfortunate to be the first foreigners they could lay their hands on.

It took Andrew and Ewing another twenty-four hours to locate the missing bodies, using the Reuters private army of guards and drivers. The Somalis had taken the bodies to the Bakaaraha market, where they were left on a rubbish dump. We later heard their intention was to use the corpses as sniper bait, in case UNO-SOM forces attempted to retrieve them. But the blue helmets refused to go near Bakaaraha, which was a labyrinth of alleys where foreign soldiers would only end up playing blindman's buff against Aydiid's scurrying militias. A Somali middleman appeared and said that for a fee he would retrieve the corpses. Andrew thought there was still a tiny chance that the missing men might be alive until the middleman asked for a sum of money that was small enough to indicate that he knew they were dead. On July 13, Kraus's body was picked up and taken to the military field hospital at the UNOSOM base. He had been shot after barely a week in Somalia. Andrew went to the morgue with the AP reporter Shaw to identify the body, and while they were in there news arrived that Hos and Anthony had been found.

A man named McIlvane, the deputy chief of the U.S. diplomatic mission to Somalia, met Andrew as he trudged back through the UNOSOM base toward the military checkpoint at the main entrance. McIlvane had heard that the bodies had been recovered. Without being asked, he offered to have the bodies cleaned up, to "minimize shock to the relatives." He also volunteered to have them choppered over to the morgue at Moga Central to await air repatriation to Nairobi. McIlvane said the United States expected $900 to be paid for each coffin. These were big, shiny aluminium boxes. Alternatively, the diplomat said Andrew could fill out paperwork that pledged to return the coffins "as soon as practicable." When the Reuters aircraft charter landed in Mogadishu with Mo Amin on it, they found it to be too small to fit all four coffins, so the bodies had to be removed, zipped into body bags, and slung one on top of another on the floor. The body bag flight touched down at Wilson Airport in Nairobi and the bodies were hefted awkwardly off the plane in full view of the gathered relatives.

On the morning of Operation Michigan, Jonathan was enjoying his leave in London. He was trying on a pair of shoes along the King's Road when the news was broadcast over the shop radio. I flew home as soon as I heard the news, abandoning the Balkans altogether. Lizzie returned from assignment in Nigeria.

A week of funerals followed. Dan was cremated and his ashes

were scattered at the southern end of the Ngong Hills. Anthony and Hos were buried in their Kikuyu villages outside Nairobi. Hos was laid out in an open coffin for mourners to file past and peer at the smashed face of what had once been a handsome man. AP flew the body of Kraus back to Germany. We became weary of funerals. The trouser legs of my only dark suit were caked with mud from gravesides and I gave up trying to get them cleaned. Hos's wife Lucy said, "Now I believe that God only takes the good ones." We sang "He's Got the Whole World in His Hands" and "Love Divine, All Loves Excelling" and in Kikuyu "Jesu ni Muriithi wa mburi ciake."

We had naively thought we were neutral in Somalia and therefore somehow immune. When I saw the Eldon family, I recalled Dan's collage that he'd given me after his initiation in Somalia less than a year before. There it was, the denouncement of me in their son's own hand written just eleven months before his death. "To Aidan, with mixed thanks for giving me my first exposure to the horror. Dan Eldon, August 3, 1992."

The phrase came back to me yet again. "No story is worth dying for." From among Dan's journals we later discovered a quote by Plato. "Only the dead have seen the end of war." The families wanted to believe their sons had died for a cause of some sort, in the line of duty, taking pictures of unfortunate people in the hope that it would somehow contribute to making the world a better place. In my gloomier moments I've thought that perhaps there was no higher reason for his death and that what we did was simply get paid shit money to get close to gunfire and hope for the ego trip of a front-page splash. Like our colonial ancestors, we were just meddling in the tragedies of foreign lands and this was always going to be dangerous. But in my brighter moments I believe that our colleagues were among the biggest heroes ever in the news business. They genuinely did die trying to draw attention to the plight of the suffering in forgotten corners of the world. Journalism gave us comradeship, a purpose in life, and some form of honor. Reuters was lucky to have had such people who had risked their lives and who in this case had paid the ultimate price.

The Reuters chief executive, Mark Wood, went on TV to describe it as the saddest day in the history of the agency. But life at the company went on unchanged. Wood, instead of paying his last respects at the gravesites, flew to Moscow for a champagne cocktail party to celebrate the opening of the agency's new offices there. Lesser editors did fly out to attend the burials with flowery wreaths and long faces. The presence of white men, sweating under the equatorial sun in their city suits, swelled the grieving relatives with pride. To the black Kenyans, their presence proved to them that their sons had been of some importance.

"Well, the truth is they were not on staff," said one of the editors when a few drinks had loosened his tongue after we had put away Dan. He said, "You know, they were only stringers."

Reuters had never noticed the distinction between staff and stringers when Dan, Hos, and Anthony's pictures scored so well around the world even days before their deaths.

One of the correspondents got up from the table to go and said to the editor, "You have just said what I hoped I would never hear."

That summer I believe all of us in the circle of survivors shared a sense that we were being stalked by some indescribable malevolence. We saw the writing on the wall and felt it was for us. Yet it was good to laugh sometimes. Jonathan showed me a condolence letter about July 12 from a British diplomat who had been a drinking partner in Nairobi before he'd been posted to Manila. "After the death of Aidan in December," the letter commiserated, "this must have hit you particularly hard ..." I suppose a part of me did die on July 12, 1993. But I decided the only way I could properly honor my dead colleagues—and the only way I could imagine being happy again—was to go back into Somalia.

* * *

The Reuters bosses said they could not tolerate any more casualties so they banned our travel to Somalia—for a week or two. July 12 had put Somalia back on the news map and the story ran out of control. Within days of my flying in from the Balkans, Jonathan got me back my old job in Africa and I had a UN Movement Control pass to board a flight into Mogadishu Central. On the aircraft I sat in the cockpit up front with Doug, a U.S. pilot who had served in Vietnam. He gave me some earphones and over the drone of the propeller engines I listened to all the military radio traffic in Africa's busiest airspace. The skies coming into Moga were alive with activity, with swarms of choppers, transports, and "the spy in the sky" Orion plane. As we came into land the ocean was azure and the city looked as if it had been hit by an act of God. The velvety heat enveloped me as I climbed out and I drank in all the smells—dried shark, the sea, aviation gas, shit, desert, burning rubber, and maybe even frankincense. I was back and I felt more at peace than I had for months.

At the al-Sahafi I moved into Dan's room. By day, there were leaden skies and it was almost cool. The muezzin called. At night, monsoon winds blew down the hotel's long corridors. It felt lonely and empty in the quicksilver light of the moon. When a patrolling helicopter woke me, I wondered if I should believe in ghosts. In the cupboard I found a pair of Dan's boots and a worn Cobra T-shirt that retained the kid's sweat smell. There was not much else: photos of the Somali girlfriend who had dumped him months before he died, clothes, film rolls, and notebooks. There was a press release by Madeleine Albright, U.S. ambassador to the UN, which she had given on her flying visit to Somalia nine days before Dan's murder. "In Somalia, we are blazing a new trail for the United Nations," Albright had said. "We are trying to do what has never been done before. And I would like to make this point clearly. Despite the monumental task ahead in securing and restoring Somalia, the

United States is committed to help the United Nations stay the course." Dan had scribbled two things on the page. One was a doodle of what looked like a be-turbaned Arab gangster, with shades and thick lips. He'd also written the words "silly cunt."

For a time life in Mogadishu returned to normal, with the hacks, soldiers, do-gooders, and Somalis all playing their parts: hit-and-run attacks, retaliatory strikes, summary executions, hostage situations, and barefaced lies. In any normal universe the bloodletting that culminated in July 12 should have created what is known in the tourist business as a "distressed inventory" for Mohamed Jirdah, manager of the Hotel al-Sahafi. Instead it attracted more bed nights than Jirdah had seen since Christmas. I saw lots of new faces together with all the usual suspects from the BBC to the VOA. The Hotel al-Sahafi had by this stage become our home away from home, by turns reminiscent of a school dormitory, safe house, lunatic asylum, or holiday resort.

It was only a matter of days before Lizzie appeared with her cameras. After the funerals, she'd said she wanted us to get out of Africa because it was no longer worth the risk. This was all just talk and we both knew it. Meanwhile, she had transformed during my absence in the Balkans. Her hair was stringy, her face more gaunt and tense. She wore Dan's old Cobra T-shirts, a necklace of Nikons, a khaki armless jacket with pockets and webbing, a baseball cap, red paisley bandana around her neck, green cargo pants, and Caterpillar boots. Her pockets bulged with film, batteries, cigarettes, duct tape, pills, condoms, gum, lipstick, tampons, and a couple of must-have bits of jewelry. The Southern belle had become an Amazon.

Of all the time Lizzie and I spent together, these months were the happiest. Mogadishu was our Paris: gunfire, flares at night, Huey rides, razor wire, heat, and deadlines. I'd look into Lizzie's eyes after a morning out in the city and see her pupils were dilated. We'd rush up to our room at the al-Sahafi, drop cameras and notebooks, and make love, half out of our clothes and still in our boots.

I asked Lizzie to marry me. She playfully said she'd agree only when I could afford a huge rock to go on her finger. She drew the size of the stone she wanted on a piece of paper. It was never destined to happen, because this was the only world in which our love breathed. One day a battle erupted outside. Bullets stripped off chunks of masonry and the hotel shook with mortar and grenade impacts. The window in front of my desk in our room was blown in by a .50-caliber round. We scurried to Mohamed Jirdah's basement laundry room, where we huddled in among the fresh linen. Lizzie and I sat holding hands, listening to the chatter and boom. By the time the battle died down we were so comfortable and happy we lay there for an hour together in that womblike space of white sheets and towels.

Our most romantic evenings took place on the cooling concrete of the al-Sahafi's roof, scanning Mogadishu through night-vision TV cameras so that it was all illuminated by green, ambient light. In the streets below, thousands of little oil lamps flickered among the tea stalls and clusters of refugees' blue plastic makeshift huts. Across this scene occasionally flashed the laser beams from an invisible USAF AC-130 Spectre gunship circling far above. The Reuters Rock Spider TV cameraman used to fire up enormous joints of Durban poison or Malawi cob to pass around. Reid produced bottles of Jack Daniel's. Photographer Duke came up with a freshly caught tuna and sliced it up into sashimi, complete with wasabi, soy sauce, and chopsticks. And Carlos set up his stereo and played a variety of obsessive, disturbing tunes like "The Revolution Will Not Be Televised" or Screamin' Jay Hawkins caterwauling about how "I put a spell on you, Because you're mine . . ."

I'd lie on my back next to Lizzie, staring up at Orion and the Pleiades. We'd stay on the roof until people traipsed off to bed. Then we'd make love, the both of us gazing over the shattered city, our skin caressed by warm winds and the jet-stream odors of invisible gunships.

*　*　*

Few foreign expeditions into Africa in the annals of history can have been more surreal than UNOSOM. Somalia was a failed state, with no government, none of the institutions that make a modern nation, not even a single proper school, laid low by famine and all-out war. And the United Nations, embroiled in a bloody feud with Aydiid's forces in Mogadishu, was expected to oversee democratic elections within less than two years. The foreign imperialists on this mission to civilize Somalia were no longer only white men like me and my British ancestors, but men and women of all races and nations. But for all their arrogance, I believe the British had their feet on the ground in a way that the UN did not. My father learned about Africa and Arabia during the course of a lifetime. He became intimate with his countries, traveling among the local people on foot or horseback, speaking their languages. UN officials stayed in Somalia a few months at most and few saw the nation beyond the razor wire and sandbagged walls of the main UNOSOM base. Soldiers pointed over the walls and said to me, "That's Skinnyland. Why the hell you want to live out there?"

When UNOSOMers came in and out of Somalia they were often too afraid even to drive two miles through downtown to Mogadishu Central airfield. Instead UNOSOM flew them by helicopter in a five-minute ride that cost six times the annual income of the average Somali. Inside, the base, dubbed "MogaDisney," was a sort of theme park to the New World Order. It hung with the whiff of fermenting shit and the cooking of two dozen nations whose national flags fluttered in the dusty winds. It was a modern version of the Tower of Babel. In area it covered the grounds of the former, half-demolished U.S. embassy, together with the campus of what had been Somalia's only university—now bulldozed. It was a weird oasis of pizza parlors, tarmac roads with street signs, ranks of prefabricated barracks and offices, a swimming pool, tennis courts, PX duty-free shops, a radio station, field hospitals, a mosque and a church, a morgue, and a private sewage system for fifteen thousand inhabitants. The soldiers were there to protect the elite civilian UN employees, men in white safari suits, women in high heels and city dresses, clutching walkie-talkies and driving between offices in air-conditioned limousines. The office huts were signposted with the names of the mission's various departments: JUSTICE, HUMANITARIAN, RECONCILIATION. Inside the civilian employees wrote reams of memos to New York. Edicts returned by satellite on how local councils were to be gender balanced, suggesting topics for discussion at seminars on human rights and timetables for multiparty polls.

Even amidst the fighting, the UN lavished money on projects to "empower" civil society, women's groups, and schools. Anything to pretend this was a society with hope. The problem for teachers was that pupils had grown up seeing only civil war. They had themselves become the most dangerous of warriors. Once Lizzie and I visited a school and found a group of youngsters at an English lesson. They solemnly read out dialogue from the blackboard.

"You! You are the fink who got me sent to prison for being a thief!"

"That was then. This is now. Let us be friends."

"No, I am going to shoot you!"

Much to the disgust of the UN's Justice Division, the Somalis established *sharia* courts in parts of the city and introduced the traditional punishments of floggings, hand amputations, and stonings. We saw a youth, sentenced for stealing a woman's scarf, have his right hand and left foot sawn off with a dagger while he was fully conscious. It took two minutes, he pumped blood across the walls of his cell, and he never even cried out.

We used to visit the UN base daily to attend press briefings. UNOSOM's spokesmen were made up of a U.S. Ranger, Major David Stockwell, backed up by a comic civilian double act of a diminutive Levantine and a stuttering West African. The hacks treated them mercilessly and behaved like a class of delinquents. "At 1000 hours QRF augmentation soldiers conducted a surgically precise operation ...""—we sniggered and jeered—"which took about twenty minutes, involved about fifty U.S. Army Rangers and six helicopters ... Three dead and five wounded ..."

At one of Admiral Howe's briefings, he was at the lectern declaiming in his high-pitched tone about some subject or other. I remember his observations were often strange, such as expressing his superstition that Sundays in Mogadishu always brought bad luck. As he spoke on this occasion, a Huey clattered off a nearby landing zone and drowned out his words for several seconds. Howe closed his eyes, and as the torrent of noise faded he opened them again and almost sobbed.

"You hear that? How I love the sound of freedom in the air!"

You might have been able to hear a pin drop in the press briefing room after he said that.

Howe appeared to loathe journalists because we didn't toe the line. He claimed we were the gullible victims of Aydiid's "Soviet-style" lies and manipulation. The truth was that Aydiid was too unsophisticated to convince anybody of his lies. He couldn't hide the fact that he was a savage, despite claiming his "dervishes" were fighting a war of liberation for the sovereignty of Somalia. For its part UNOSOM called the hunt for Aydiid a police action, using a Security Council mandate to use all "necessary measures" to thwart its attackers. That might have been justifiable except that some UN officials lied to hide the brutality of the operation while others toed a line of propaganda that was palpably absurd to reporters who went around and saw what was happening. On one famous occasion a spokesman at one of the daily briefings flatly denied that a U.S. Cobra-launched TOW missile had misfired and spiraled into a tea shop, killing a woman. At this point a TV cameraman got up and played the tape he had filmed of the incident. The UN also refused to give figures for Somali casualties. They didn't want us to reveal the extent of the UN's slaughter, particularly the numbers of women and children killed—which is not to say the women and children were innocent, since they carried guns too. But for every blue helmet death, probably a hundred Somali bystanders got wiped out together with a handful of gunmen.

On August 8, a Humvee was driving in convoy between Mogadishu Central airfield and the UNOSOM base, on a bypass road specially cut through the bush to the south of the city to avoid downtown. A mine explosion blew the vehicle to bits. Three American military police and a Somali-speaking interpreter were killed. Such was the force of the explosion that by the time correspondents arrived youths gathering at the scene had only bits of flesh and burned combat fatigues to hold up for the cameras. I remember how one youth picked up a strip of bloodied meat from the dust and ripped at it with his teeth.

The Americans observed the hand of foreign Muslim extremists in Aydiid's tactics. UNOSOM officers took us in for "deep backgrounders" in which they blamed Hezbollah, or the Iranians, or a Saudi terrorist emerging then just onto the scene, Osama bin Laden. The violence escalated. I watched in disbelief as American bulldozers demolished a block of residential houses to the east of the UNOSOM compound. It robbed Somalis of tall buildings from which to launch attacks and created a clear line of fire over dead ground for the machine guns along the walls of the UN base. In an echo of Vietnam, UNOSOM was destroying Mogadishu in order to save it. In reply, the Skinnies fired RPGs from flat rooftops at overflying Black Hawks. On September 9, Americans and Pakistanis clearing roadblocks from the 21st October Road came under attack. A mob of Somali women and children advanced in front of the gunmen and some of the females also carried weapons. The soldiers on the ground called in air support and within minutes a Cobra arrived, opened up with its 20mm cannon and machine guns, and slaughtered a hundred gunmen, women, and children. Some were mown down on open ground, while others were killed while trying to take cover in buildings and behind walls.

A second mine explosion wounded six Americans in the third week of August. Days later a company of U.S. Rangers laced with Delta Force flew into the city. By day, we sat watching them train in their helicopters like swarms of wasps in the sand dunes south of the city. By night, they launched their missions and fucked up like champions. Largely this was due to their Somali spies, who did all they could to plant misinformation to confuse the Americans. On the Rangers' first mission on August 30, they rappelled out of helicopters onto a villa roof, went inside, and arrested all the occupants at gunpoint. Howe told me this operation was a tactical success. The only snag was that the Rangers had arrested a group of United Nations officials, including whites and females. The Rangers carried out five more operations in the next two months. On one occasion they arrested a Somali senior policeman who was Aydiid's sworn enemy.

From the flat roof of the al-Sahafi the correspondents could watch the fighting in progress. One day, an American network correspondent looked down to observe one of his hired cars drive into an ambush on the far side of the K-4 roundabout. He saw the driver and guards get out of the vehicle and take cover as the bullets flew. While they were pinned down, the correspondent called his office in the United States on the satellite phone. His news desk patched him through to the Pentagon and whoever was in charge of Somalia that day called Mogadishu Central airfield. Within a few minutes a Cobra arrived at the scene, laid down a carpet of hot lead and wiped out the attackers. It must have been among the few times in history that a journalist called in an air strike.

The UN rules of engagement in Somalia, known as Chapter Seven, empowered foreign forces to make war to restore peace. Major Stockwell, the U.S. press spokesman, said it required a soldier "to have a gun in one hand and a spoon in the other." The U.S. Quick Reaction Force, backing up the Pakistanis and other Third World contingents, conducted cordon and search operations that invariably developed into firefights. The UN compound took regular mortar and rocket hits. It was presumed these were fired by Aydiid's militias, but one could not be sure. Increasing numbers of Somalis had grievances, from sacked sewage contractors to relatives of civilians killed in cross fire. And the Somalis could have been doing it for fun because they still got a thrill out of seeing what would happen if they pumped a few salvos of heavy ordnance into the UN base. There was an old water tower in the center of the base with a spherical tank on top. This got hit repeatedly and, quite clearly, the Somalis were using it for target practice.

True, the Americans had some awesome firepower. At the Mogadishu Central airfield an officer sauntered up to Lizzie and me. "Howdja like our country? Which one you say? Somalia! We're thinking of giving it back to the Somalis, but we want to fix it up for them first. We've got people here who are ready to blast this place off the map if they have to. Then put it back together again." On the tarmac were parked various USAF aircraft. One had an evil, red-eyed Roger Rabbit painted on the fuselage nose. Another pictured Yosemite Sam with pistols drawn. The cartoon images told me this was all an unreal, childish fantasy. There was an AC-130 Spectre with its howitzer and array of guns poking out of its flank. Painted on the hull was a skeleton blazing away with a cannon and the caption YOU CAN RUN BUT YOU'LL ONLY DIE TIRED.

And yet UNOSOM couldn't track down Aydiid inside his territory of several city blocks. The white sliver of the Orion spy plane circled above us twenty-four hours a day, eavesdropping on all the bandit radio traffic. They must have heard very little. A *Newsweek* piece about how hard it was to fight a Third World warlord had the title "When the Bad Guy Has No Phone to Tap." In contrast, the Somalis knew every UNOSOM move ahead of time. Confidential memos out of Admiral Howe's office constantly found their way to Aydiid's own generator-powered photocopier. A Somali walked off with all the CIA intelligence files on computer disks, which he found in a cardboard box in a hangar at the

Mogadishu Central airfield. At the al-Sahafi we monitored radio traffic day and night. Late at night I'd eavesdrop on military conversations and hear Somali voices suddenly cut in.

FUCK YOU AMERICA!

"Break break break—who's on this frequency?"

FUCKYOUFUCKYOUFUCKYOU!

The Somali enemy was as hard to apprehend as the swarm of angry bees that attacked a Tenth Mountain Division rifle company on the outskirts of Mog. The soldiers' response was symbolic of that entire wasted mission. They fixed bayonets and charged the insects, firing smoke grenades, flares, and live ammunition. As the weeks dragged on the Americans grew so frustrated by failure that they resorted to acts of childish nastiness. They would hover in their Black Hawk helicopters just above the streets to cause an updraft that peeled off tin roofs and terrified people inside their homes. A Somali came to me outraged because he told me a sandbag had been dropped through his tin roof from an overflying helicopter in the dead of night. U.S. Cobras repeatedly used a mosque and a Muslim saint's tomb on the beach south of the city for target practice, half-demolishing it. Or they amused themselves by flying into the bush and scattering herds of camels.

Late one afternoon I interviewed the admiral. His line on what was happening was typically surreal. He still forecast that democratic elections would be held in less than two years. Aydiid was still at large. By the time I emerged from Howe's refrigerated, fluorescent-lighted hut night had fallen. Trying to find my way out of the base, it was so dark I got lost in the maze of tents and huts. I finally reached a tarmac road. A Humvee with spotlights burning came by and I thumbed it down. By the reflected dashboard light I saw that the driver was sweating, terrified, as if he had seen a ghost. I jumped in first, and then asked for a lift to the front gate. As we drove he told me about the camps at night, where soldiers suffered dreadful nightmares. Some said it was the malaria drugs they were having forced down their throats and soldiers were becoming suicidal. At night, you heard the wails and screams as soldiers huddled in their flak jackets, gripped by hallucinations. The driver said he himself had woken to find a black angel standing at his feet.

The battle of October 3, 1993, when Task Force Ranger forces attacked the Olympic hotel in the Bakaaraha market during a meeting of Aydiid's lieutenants, is already so well known that there is no need for me to dwell on it for long. The American soldiers had rappelled down from their helicopters, arrested twenty-four "suspects," and attempted to escape back to the airfield. Two Black Hawks extracting them from the narrow streets were shot down by RPG fire. Another two were hit but managed to make it back to the airfield. The soldiers on the ground got pinned down for sixteen hours. An armored column of various Third World UN contingents had to fight its way in and out again. Tragically, eighteen Americans were killed and seventy-five were wounded. But city hospitals were at the same time crammed with Somali casualties. The bullets and shrapnel had ripped through flimsy mud and tin huts for many blocks all around. Foreign forces killed or wounded more than a thousand Somalis during the battle. I later heard American officers quote this figure with pride, which proved that "they" had a harder time of it than "us." Yet the majority of the Somali casualties were civilians.

The reaction was even more furious than it had been after the helicopter massacre on July 12, when my Reuters colleagues were murdered. On the morning of October 4, a Somali came in to offer a videotape for sale. The tape showed a group of Somali boys dragging the fresh corpse of a white man around a rubbish-filled compound. One of the boys jumped up and down on the body's chest.

Then they turned it over. A second boy stuck his M-16 up the body's rectum, looking at the camera all the time and laughing. The tape then cut to a crowd of Somalis of all ages, some of them wearing airmen's goggles and other clothes looted from the dead Americans. They were dragging a naked body by a rope down the street. Later, a second tape came in of a captured U.S. airman. The home movie camera focused on his swollen, handsome, terrified face. On the tape, a Somali asked whether it is good to kill innocent people. The airman gulped in pain.

"It's not good to kill people," he said.

I felt extremely sorry for the ordinary American soldiers who had come to Somalia initially to help people. Within months they had become entangled in a crisis created partly by the stupidity of their generals, politicians, and UN bureaucrats. After the battle at the Olympic, Mogadishu went dead quiet. I remember sitting on top of the al-Sahafi, watching a Huey fly over with speakers hung out the doors, playing rock music and a message to the captured airman, saying "We will not leave you behind . . ." Meanwhile, President Clinton dispatched his envoy Robert Oakley to negotiate with Aydiid's militia. The airman was liberated some two weeks after the battle at Olympic. At the same time, Aydiid declared a unilateral cease-fire. UNOSOM claimed the hunt for Aydiid was still on. Clinton ordered in a joint task force of air, naval, and ground troops. Yet even as we stood around filming the M1A1 tanks and Bradley fighting vehicles, it was clear that the Americans had struck a deal with Aydiid. Clinton announced U. S. plans to withdraw. Western contingents, the French, Belgians, Italians, and Australians, followed suit. These days, military spokesmen talked of "force protection." Put simply, this involved deploying all the firepower of the huge UN army to defend itself from the people it came to help. They just sat it out, waiting to go home, which they eventually did in March 1994. They left behind a smaller UNOSOM army of Third World contingents who lingered until 1995.

Even if they had wanted to, they couldn't have done the job. Both their troop strength and firepower were cut. "Force protection" was all this emasculated rump army was capable of. It was a holding operation to save face, although for a whole year before it ended everybody knew UNOSOM had failed. With it had gone any hopes that we could help the Somalis put their nation back together. UNOSOM had cost countless millions of dollars, the lives of 150 peacekeepers, and thousands of Somalis. Yet it had achieved nothing.

"If you flew a C-130 in a grid cross-country with its back bay door open, turfing one-dollar bills out the back, it would do this place as much good as what the UN is doing here," one UN official told me. "It would inject cash into the economy at no risk to us and the Somalis could spend their days usefully employed as well, picking up money."

The day the Americans evacuated General Montgomery gave a speech to the press. "I always carry in my memory faces in Vietnam of brave soldiers who made a brave sacrifice. Now there are faces from Somalia." He looked like a turtle under his helmet, with his mean, downturned mouth. On the runway I met the Marine major in charge of the withdrawal operation. He smoked a big cigar and told me he had taken part as a young officer in the chopper evacuations off the Saigon U.S. embassy's roof in 1975. "The last one was anything but orderly," he said. "At least this one's orderly." As the Marines pulled back from the outer cordon of Mogadishu airbase toward the beach, packs of Somali looters breached the coils of razor wire and poured onto the tarmac. I was sitting at a position on the inner cordon with some Marines peering down the sights of their M-16s and spitting quids of tobacco. "Look at them come! Hey Skinny! We knew you'd be hungry!" A Psy-Ops chopper blared warning messages in Somali over loudspeakers for the looters to retreat. Then the two-blade racket of Cobras kicked in overhead. A black sergeant drawled into his field radio, "It's like Kmart down here. Jockey fowerteen, Jockey fowerteen. We have a blue-light special in the third aisle of Mogadishu airport!"

The military press spokesman Major Stockwell perfectly summed up the Americans and UNOSOM efforts in Somalia: "We fed them. They got strong. They killed us."

The Americans left in a cloud of helicopters and a convoy of amphibious vehicles that plunged into the waves off the beach where we had swum and where they had first come ashore. That night they let off one last display of fireworks. We sat on the roof of the Hotel al-Sahafi one last time. Ship-launched flares exploded over the city, making it all seem like a giant film set. Lizzie sang softly. "My country 'tis of thee, / Sweet land of liberty . . ." There was a sustained burst of gunfire and copper-headed grenades rained down on our district, which I discovered next day had killed a house full of civilians. One of them was split clean in two as he slept on his open veranda. The same day a cholera epidemic took hold across the city. A few bags of chlorine to cleanse the wells would have prevented the spread of the disease, but Somalia was back in the dark ages now and nobody cared. My Somali translator Sharif got infected, and as I sat with him at the hospital, he lay in the open air with a drip in his arm, and the reflection of a departing aircraft passed over his staring eyeballs. Sharif said to me weakly, "Aidan, last night I dreamed that you and I looted a helicopter from the Americans. We were flying over the city. We were so free." He gulped. "It was such a happy dream."

A million schoolkids were being fed in Mogadishu up to the day before UNOSOM left. The day after, it was zero. The schools ceased to exist. The flotilla of warships that sailed away left nothing of value. No ideas had rubbed off on the Somalis. UNOSOM had simply put the civil war on mothballs. What UNOSOM did leave was a lot of waste. There were countless empty plastic water bottles. In the bases, on the roads, along the beaches, south from the airfield past the rusting windmills to Jezira beach: clear blue bottles wafting along on the breeze like vast shoals of lost jellyfish.

After takeoff from Kilometer 50 airstrip, I looked down at the plantations along the Shebelle River, where the Bantu slaves were still toiling to grow bananas for export to Europe. I saw that the snake of brown water had broken out of the straight dikes and irrigation channels built long ago by the colonial Italians. For the first time in perhaps a hundred years, the river was returning to its natural course, uncoiling across the red sand wastes of the Shag.

Re-entry to life in Nairobi was hard. Inside Somalia I had felt on top of the world and only when I left did I sense that the story was taking it out of me. I yearned for Somalia. I listened for news of it on the BBC World Service. I logged on to the wires to get news updates. I wore my *maweis* about the house, gestured like a gunman at a roadblock, chewed qat, ate with my hands, sat cross-legged on the floor in preference to a chair, and missed the muezzin's call in the hour before dawn. I fidgeted, and I found it hard to concentrate. I walked into rooms and forgot why I was there. I dialed numbers and could not remember what I was calling about. I threw red-faced rages about nothing. In my waking dreams I was always in the air. I was a fighter pilot, in a dark visor, listening to yells in my earphones, dive-bombing, strafing residential neighborhoods and peasant dwellings. I developed an obsession with numbers. That is to say, I saw mysterious significance in the digit 3. I looked for it on number plates, rings of the phone, gunshots, how many stairs I should leap up at a time.

I fell into a dark mood at home. I decided all I wanted was to be with Lizzie, and I felt an immense distance from those who did not share our world. Time spent with them was embarrassing; we had so little to talk about. Yet when Lizzie and I were together I was short-tempered.

"It's as if you only thrive when you have discord around you," she said. "As if you actually enjoy conflict."

I simply couldn't get used to normal domestic life. As one correspondent said, there was no common ground between Somalia and coming home to somebody complaining about the toothpaste being squeezed in the middle of the tube.

In the meantime we were dragging all the bloody insanity of the field back home with us, in our heads and suitcases. Duke brought home in his duffel bag the skulls of two recently killed conscripts from a Sudanese battleground. The skulls had good teeth and were like ivory, picked clean by ants. Duke put them on the coffee table at his house. When I stared at those skulls for long enough, I swear faces appeared to take shape. Nobody in Duke's family could sleep with dead men's heads in the house, so he stuck them on stakes at the bottom of the garden. "To scare off robbers," Duke announced.

Yet this being Africa, I didn't need to travel to see a famine or a slaughter, to witness a tragedy. It was before my eyes whenever I went to the shops or to pick up the mail in Nairobi. In Kenya, letters are delivered to a personal post office box. Mine was at the shops in Nairobi's suburb of Karen. Each time I went I had to dodge suburban neighbors inviting me to dinner parties, my creditors, vendors of pawpaws and gewgaws, AIDS-infected cripples and child beggars who used the pocket change I gave them to buy bottles of cobbler's glue to sniff their way to oblivion.

"Your car," a kid would say as I drove up. "I take care?" Always, the same conversation followed.

"If I give you this, you promise to buy food, not glue?"

"Me, I can't cheat you." But I'd see it in his rheumy eyes, slurred words, and snot-clotted nose.

My mailbox was in an alcove of the post office. It had a little black door with the number painted on it in white. Following long assignments outside Kenya I always had piles of mail. One day out of the blue I received a letter addressed simply to SOON. I wrote

WRONG ADDRESS, RETURN TO SENDER on it and popped it back in the collection box. In the following weeks, more letters began arriving for SOON. I sent them all back. But any number from five to twenty letters a week continued to arrive. After some time, I decided to open them. They contained filled-out mail order coupons and begging letters from African readers of an evangelical missionary society's magazine. On each coupon was written the words "Please write YES next to what you want." Then it said: "DO YOU WANT GOD TO CHANGE YOU?" dot dot dot. The coupons indicated that SOON Bible courses could be ordered from Bangalore, Tsuen Wing Street in Hong Kong, the British town of Derby—and my personal address in Karen, Nairobi.

I decided to write to SOON in Derby, enclosing a bundle of the letters and asking the missionaries to change their address. I wrote several times to Derby, then to the addresses I had for Bangalore and Hong Kong. I never received a reply. Meanwhile, the letters kept coming. Soon, they threatened. Soon. They were like premonitions. They kept coming. I began throwing them away. They kept coming. I stuffed them back in the post box as fast as they came. I revived a childhood hobby and started collecting the colorful stamps from two dozen African nations. In time I began opening them because the coupons were often accompanied by handwritten, begging letters. Brother Ackson Mbewe of Kasama, Zambia: "May God richly bless as you persevere and press on harder in extending the Kingdom of God Almighty ..." Balikouwa Lunkese Florence, of Sseguku Hill College in Uganda: "My best hobby is schooling but it's embarrassing that I am near to give up because my parents are bankrupt because of some few problems. I humbly request you to sponsor me because education is the key for the future ..." From Priscilla Kemunto in Kisii, Kenya; Bereket Metiku in Nazareth, Ethiopia; Narendra Kalyani in Arusha, Tanzania; Clement Baba Joseph of Jilo Junior Secondary School, Bimbilla, Ghana; Elijah O. Ajiboye of Ekiti State, Nigeria; Moses

Mushabe of Mbarara, Uganda ... They wanted religious correspondence courses, Bibles, pens, help with school fees or clothes. Some begged for TVs or computer games. Yet this sort of letter was very rare. Typical was this one I opened from Gilbert Kwao Forson of Ashanti, Ghana: "Greetings of love to you in the name of our Lord Jesus. The reason why I am writing is that I am short in the words of God. I ask you to give me the words of the Bible to enable me to fear God, so that when the Lord appears I will not perish. I end here. Hoping you will hear my cries ..."

Africans so poor that they had sacrificed a meal to set aside the money for the postage stamps had written to SOON because they had been promised imminent salvation. DO YOU WANT GOD TO CHANGE YOUR LIFE? Their pleas were delivered instead to me, a journalist who believed in Jehovah only in turbulence at thirty-six thousand feet. I tried to imagine the missionaries licking their envelopes in the SOON mail room in Derby, or Bangalore, or Hong Kong. In my imagination, they frowned and asked each other: "What in the Lord's name do you suppose has happened to Africa?" Surely, they must have wondered why their readers from the continent had fallen so utterly silent.

I never knew what to do about SOON. I built up a trunkload, and this was minus the ones I had thrown away, lost, reposted, or used to start fires. As I write this years later the letters are still coming. It is as if SOON were some elaborate message from a God who didn't want to waste on me the high-budget special effects he had deployed against Saul on the road to Damascus. Instead, God is a postman. He has sought to wear me down by attrition, sending me years of misaddressed religious junk mail containing the plaintive voices of myriad impoverished Africans. Today I look back and think that each letter is like one of the lost souls I have seen on the road in Africa. I tried to ignore the anonymous masses for so long, but in the end they have all come back to haunt me: the refugees, the injured, the starving, and the dead. And each and every one has a name.

"I feel that I want no other life than this. . . ."

EMPTY QUARTER

Peter Davey's passage from Aden to England was on a military tank landing-craft. The other passengers were all men returning home from war in the Far East. An atmosphere of exhaustion hung over the boat. Gone were the deck games, the fancy dress parties, or going ashore for little outings at Port Suez and Marseilles. Instead, a loudspeaker barked out orders. "Hands to mess!" Or: "All cooks to kitchens!" The waters of the Gulf of Aden were alive with phosphorescence. Myriad ghostly forms moved across the plain of shimmering white fire. Davey leaned over the railings, watching a school of porpoises race alongside.

> *The day seemed to go very slowly indeed although I am giving myself things to do: reading, studying Arabic newspapers, writing letters, skipping, walking up and down the deck and of course eating and sleeping.*

I can only imagine what went through Peter Davey's mind on the journey home. "I believe he contemplated suicide," Dad recalled.

Davey had not been home in six years, since before Dunkirk.

Back in Sussex, he never once revealed what had happened to him to his mother and brothers, both of whom were now in the army. He bought a horse, Shamrock, which he rode daily across the Downs. He went to the races or to horse shows. In London, he stalked alone around the blitzed ruins.

I have not felt wildly excited about coming home, but have a feeling of deep contentment, which I have never known before.

It rained nearly every day in the summer of 1946. Davey disliked the English cold and the gray and the lack of sunshine. He had been away too long.

When the pain gets too much the senses go numb. I think that Davey had the peace of one who needs to breathe again, to take stock, recover from his last bout of experience. He was rootless and washed away by fate, with a broken heart. It was the ideal time to travel.

While dining at Quaglino's with an old comrade from Aden, Davey announced his plan to traverse the Empty Quarter. It was a fanciful idea, which he never had a chance to put into practice. He had experience and accumulated knowledge. He threw himself into the study of the politics of the Middle East. The eminent people he met encouraged him to write a book. I wonder, would he have told his true story? The world around him was changing fast. At an Oxford conference on "Empire," he heard speakers press for the end of colonial rule. At the same time trouble was brewing in the Middle East with the imminent birth of Israel. Had he stayed home Davey could have shone among the ranks of colonial officials dealing with Arabia. People might have listened to his ideas. Instead, he returned quietly to Aden.

* * *

The last leg of my journey in Yemen involved a visit to the area of Dhala, a town in the high hills north of Aden. We left the coast after the afternoon's heat began to lift. A Yemeni driver with a New York accent, two armed guards with their AK-47s, and I drove out of the city along the coast road. Before turning inland we passed pink flamingos stalking the salty shallows. Men worked on careened dhows while, farther out, fishermen beat the waters around their nets. At a roadblock soldiers with the billiard-ball cheeks and alarmed eyes of the qat-stoned checked our papers and waved us on. Inland along the wadi banks farmers worked in the cooling day among irrigated fields of sorghum, cotton, lady's fingers, and groves of shady date palms. Burned-out tanks and buses from Yemen's recent civil war rusted on the roadsides. When we stopped to piss, the driver warned me not to step off the tarmac in case of antipersonnel mines. We bought bundles of qat, green oranges, and chunks of yellow sweet meat dusted in sugar at a roadside hamlet of kiosks constructed from oil cans beaten flat. Then we headed into the black basalt hills and climbed into cooler air. The route zigzagged up valleys that became ever steeper. I saw a Bedu encampment on a hillside; a group of men in a line were bowing and kneeling in prayer. A thick mantle of gray hung over the way ahead.

We rolled into Dhala at twilight. The town was like a dusty building site, with concrete stores the size of warehouses lining the muddy thoroughfares. We stopped in one of the cavernous buildings, where we were brought pancakes with fried liver and chiles. Later, we found a guest house in which to sleep. It was a long, gloomy room ringing with voices. In the air hung a rank smell of sweaty, sodden clothes. Men in turbans and robes squatted in clusters with their cheap black shoes removed, smoking hookah pipes and chewing qat. They were surrounded by bundles of trade goods and piles of discarded qat stalks. We slept hugger-mugger on mats that were not so much stained as stiffened with secretions of food, dirt, and human spit.

In the chilly morning, after more plates of liver, I took a look at the town. A few old stone towers with colored fan windows stood on a hill overlooking the maze of new concrete. One of these was another local sultan's white fort, long derelict like all the others I had seen in Yemen. Down the main street, a stinking brook bubbled through the dirt past kiosks piled with tangerines, halwa, bouquets of whole dried tobacco leaves, grain, dried locusts, honey packed for sale in small gourds, bundles of qat, and green and yellow pumpkins piled high on the roadside. At every corner men in black turbans and bright sashes sat chewing, spitting out chlorophyll-green pulp onto the greasy earth in puddles. The women were dressed in garish colors and had their uncovered faces decorated in herbal masks of fire-engine red, green, and yellow.

The mountain Jihaf rose above the town, its jagged profile that of a sleeping leviathan. People pointed out a white shrine built on a black spur that they said was the tomb of the prophet Job. At times I thought if I looked at the scaly horizon long enough I might see it breathe. Tower villages like little piles of cubes sat perched on hill spurs in the far distance.

For six decades, British officials and soldiers languishing in the heat of Aden looked forward to assignments in the cool hills of Dhala. But aside from the mountain air, Dhala is a melancholy place with a history stained by bloodshed. A few days before I arrived the corpse of a soldier from Sana'a who had quarreled with a local tribesman had been discovered in a ditch, missing its hands and feet. The place seemed cursed to me, just as certain houses feel cold as soon as you enter the door. The plains and rocky heights of Dhala existed under such misfortune perhaps partly because the "violet line" that had carved up Arabia between the Ottomans and the British snaked through the hills and valleys of the district. Dhala had fallen under British influence when the local Arab governor had signed a treaty under which Queen Victoria promised to protect his rule against the Imams of high Yemen. A dynasty was created and his descendants remained as suzerains of the town and the tribes in surrounding valleys. The Imams continued to covet the area and stir unrest. Meanwhile, the locals wished to be ruled by no outsiders at all.

As soon as Davey returned to Aden, he shelved all his plans to cross the Empty Quarter. He was immediately posted to Dhala, where there was trouble. At that time the district was nominally under the rule of Amir Nasir, an elderly qat addict and pedophile who looked like Buster Keaton and displayed no interest in the responsibilities of office. He spent his days as a guest of the sultans of Lahej, on the coastal plains, lolling about in fragrant gardens, chewing the emerald leaf, and gazing at his catamite, who rejoiced in the name of Turtle Dove.

The rule of Dhala was left to the amir's son and regent Haidara. He was a gaunt man who sat in a castle perched like an eagle's aerie on the summit of Jihaf and ruled over the pocket hand-kerchief–sized state with extreme cruelty. Haidara's castle had been built in stone with big cedar timbers from across the seas in Africa. A tall tower stood at each of the edifice's four corners. Beneath the floor was a dungeon, where the regent kept his rivals' children chained up as hostages. The people who got in his way were tossed over the castle tower ramparts onto the rocks of Jihaf. Following an audience with Haidara a man was forced to excuse himself and withdraw by crawling backward out of the room on his hands and knees.

Haidara was a keen horseman and rode a magnificent bay stallion, Wazir, who had a deep girth, strong hindquarters, and jet hooves. My father recalled his first dramatic encounter with

Haidara. The Arab ruler spurred Wazir to a canter down the rocky slopes from the castle toward my waiting father below as his armed guards loped along behind. That day he was dressed in a kilt of green and red, with a blue shirt and a big, brightly colored turban. At his belt he wore a dagger sheathed in gold and silver and a .303 service rifle was slung over his shoulder.

Tyrants can be keen farmers and my father and Haidara got along well enough while debating the merits of growing potatoes, onions, and fruit trees to supply the passing ships and local population of Aden colony. I think my father admired him for trying to ban the local consumption of qat, which Dad thought made men into lazy, impotent creatures whose habit robbed food from the family table. Haidara knew potatoes were a better commodity to grow because the British would buy them and he could get rich on taxation of the trade. He might have continued thus as an agriculturalist and despot, prospering from vegetables and throwing his own people off his castle ramparts. The British in Aden would never have interfered, had his overweening hatred for Christianity not got the better of him.

The root cause of Haidara's bitterness was not his devotion to either Islam or Arab freedom but a dose of gonorrhea that he had contracted as a youth from a prostitute in one of the brothels of Sheikh Othman. Haidara had allowed the disease to go untreated. As a result, he discovered years later that he was sterile and therefore unable to father an heir. This humiliation, he decided, had been brought down upon him by the immorality of the British authorities in Aden, which had licensed the whorehouse where he had been infected. In his half-crazy mind, he came to believe that he was victim of a Christian conspiracy to sterilize all Muslims. He was all the more bitter because he willingly swallowed the propaganda of the Imam of Yemen and his benefactors in Nazi Germany and fascist Italy that the British were helping the Zionists to dispossess the Arabs of Palestine. A community of Jews had lived in peace side-by-side with the local Arabs probably since even before the first century destruction of Jerusalem. Most of them were silversmiths, carpet makers, and stonemasons. But Haidara one day declared that he hated all Jews, and to prove it he had one of them arrested and burned alive.

By Davey's arrival in Dhala in October 1946, rebellion against Haidara had been fomenting among his vassal tribes for some time. Traffic to the town had been reduced to a trickle after a string of ambushes on the road from Aden by a fierce tribe of highwaymen called the Wolves of Radfan. Sometime before Davey's appearance, a small clan called the Shairis, who lived in a fortified village within rifle range of Dhala town, picked a quarrel with Haidara. The Shairis had languished in Haidara's dungeons. As usual, their leaders had been tossed over the ramparts. Finally, the year Davey arrived in Dhala they decided they had endured enough and refused to pay any more taxes.

Under the terms of his treaty with Britain, Haidara had a right to demand guns and ammunition from the British in Aden, which in due course the senior political officer Basil Seager gave him, so that he could squash the rebels. The Shairis fled en masse across the frontier to the Imam's Yemen, where they began plotting mischief. This put a fresh complexion on things. Seager worried that they would soon have an Imam-backed guerrilla war on their hands. He coaxed the Shairis home with promises of compensation and independence. It was the kind of secretive deal-making adored by Seager, who as I mentioned before was known as "Cloak and Dagger" Seager. When a charismatic young sheikh of the Ahmedi clan named Mohamed Awas saw what the Shairis had won by coming out in open rebellion, he followed suit and led his people in a fresh uprising. Haidara became apoplectic with anger at these developments and blamed the British. He withdrew to sulk in his castle and refused to emerge when summoned to meetings with officials from Aden. Within its walls, he began plotting to murder the nearest British officer that walked into his sights.

Davey had gained in experience and judgment since his early times as a political officer. On only his second day in Dhala, on October 23, 1946, already he had grasped that the crisis had got out of hand thanks to a mishandling of the situation by Seager. He also saw that the rebellion against Haidara had widened to include Mohamed Awas's Ahmedi, thanks to the British deal with the Shairis. Though Davey may have been disturbed by the choices of the British, he was ordered to follow a clear policy in line with Haidara. It is hard for me to read between the lines, but the pressure of his task clearly burdened Davey and he did not like this unfamiliar place. *"The house in which I am living is a disgusting place swarming with slaves and hangers-on, all wishing to hear what I have to say."*

He did not give away much of how he felt about returning to Arabia. The story of his conversion and marriage in Beihan was by now common knowledge in Aden. This made him friends among Arabs. But he was irritated by the persistent gossip among the Europeans and so, in the coming months, he visited the colony as rarely as he could manage. He knew his job was going to be hard. He took solace in the fact that the climate was good, and that he had a healthy diet with plenty of fruit and vegetables. Unlike the coastal belt there was no malaria in Dhala, where the days are cool, almost alpine, and the nights are cold.

Within four days of his arrival in Dhala, Davey rode out on

his newly purchased mare Zahra accompanied by a platoon of Government Guards with their camels to tour the troubled district. A classified official report called it a flag march, intended to display to Arabs of all persuasion who was really in charge. Davey set off west, crossing behind Jebel Jihaf and entering a system of vertiginous valleys. The watercourses ran with a clear, permanent flow and the valleys were well populated by peasants. Along the way, his unit came across a war party of 150 Ahmedi warriors, all well armed. They were enraged by Haidara's vandalism of their irrigation water channels upstream, which had robbed them of their corn harvest. Davey urged them to stay calm and to wait. His party passed on down the valleys, sleeping each night under the stars by the wadi's banks. At last they came to al-Hussein, the stronghold of Sheikh Mohamed Awas. Riding out to meet Davey on a scratchy-looking mare was the sheikh himself, who received him warmly. Davey took an immediate liking to the young tribal leader, taking him to be a man of substance, with great influence among the tribes.

I saw a photograph of the rebel sheikh in the Dhala museum, which had been set up by the communists following the British abandonment of Aden. The room was stuffed with guns and unexploded bombs in glass cases, but on one wall was a hand-tinted photograph of a beautiful, turbaned young man with huge dark eyes, thick eyebrows, and a pencil mustache. It was labeled "Mohamed Awas—A Hero of the Struggle." For days afterward I thought many times of the young sheikh from al-Hussein. Davey liked the sheikh and his home village. He wrote, *"It is a bright, cheerful-looking place with elb trees and bananas growing along the banks of the river."* The valleys had become steep gorges by now and cultivable land was so scarce that villages were built into the rocky slopes, high above the fields. There were citrus orchards, plots of qat and food crops, and beehives that produced a fine acacia-blossom honey.

Haidara meanwhile sat with a hundred followers in his

mountain castle and declared himself to be the only Muslim bulwark against the rule of the Christian invaders. He encouraged anybody with a grievance against the British to visit him and he paid them handsomely to spread unrest. In January 1947, the British got wind of a plot to assassinate Davey. He shrugged it off, and in his next report to Aden he urged Seager to do the right thing and remove the family of Haidara and the Buster Keaton lookalike Nasir once and for all.

> *In formulating policy government should, in my opinion, give prior consideration to the future welfare and happiness of the people of the district. In all districts where the treaty chief has power and influence for good or ill, the welfare of the people is bound up with the chief ... tribesmen are, literally, up in arms and the rest of the population seethes in nearly open revolt. For many years they have suffered harsh and tyrannical rule and they have just about had enough of it. Daily complaints reach me from all grades of society of overtaxation, unjust imprisonment, ruthless treatment of the population by hired soldiery, farmers being forced to sell their land, and similar actions, which cry aloud for redress. Not a single person wants him, not even his own relations ...*

Davey advised that the British had to choose between two policies. Either they replace the existing rulers of Dhala and establish a just system of government or support the status quo without question and suppressed the rebellious clans such as the people of Mohamed Awas. "Only by starting a complete new order can Government hope to improve the political and economical welfare of the people."

He delivered the report on a visit to Aden at the end of January. Seager responded by writing to the governor's office, calling urgently for Haidara's arrest or complete removal from the Protectorates. Seager wrote: "He must be winkled out and arrested or allowed, perforce, to emigrate to [the Imam's] Yemen. If he does react adversely, our case against him is complete down to the last crossing of the t's and dotting of the i's."

Davey swiftly persuaded Mohamed Awas to join in operations with the British. A small force was assembled in Aden, comprising a company of Government Guards and an armored car. Mosquito fighter-bombers flew up ahead to drop letters on Haidara's fortress, urging him to surrender. Reinforcements followed. On February 8, Davey, with a company of soldiers, two three-inch mortars, and a caravan of 150 pack camels, climbed Jihaf. Fighting erupted when Mohamed Awas and his followers attacked Haidara's men from the northern slopes of the mountain. The British then advanced to within range of the fortress and opened up with a Bren gun. A curtain of cloud swept across the mountain at dusk and the British forces spent a wet, cold night among the slippery rocks. After dawn next morning, the attackers opened up with mortars and advanced up to the fort walls under a smoke screen. The order came to prepare for a final assault after dusk. A thick mist rolled in again at twilight. As night fell, they advanced up to the fortress, only to find the great main doors were swung wide open. Haidara had fled, leaving nothing behind other than a Jewish hostage with a bullet in his chest, surrounded by piles of spent cartridge cases, ammunition boxes, and rubbish.

In the London Public Records Office I came across a sequence of photographs of a building belonging to one of Haidara's supporters. Davey is clearly visible, standing in front of the house. He scowls at the camera. The last photo in the sequence is of a massive explosion. Dirt and smoke plume into the sky as a herd of goats flees. The British next destroyed Haidara's fortress in an act of symbolic castration, using the Mosquitoes to blow it up with rockets.

A conference of tribal sheikhs was called. Despite Davey's

advice, Seager hoped that Mohamed Awas and the other rebels would agree to restore their allegiance to the Amir Nasir. Mohamed Awas, having aided government forces to expel Haidara, was horrified. He had clearly expected to be given his independence. Davey made two further marches into the hills controlled by Mohamed Awas to show the flag. The young sheikh responded with a hit-and-run campaign against members of Haidara's family. His forces looted settlements and seized farms that they claimed had been stolen from them decades before. The British had failed to bring peace to the hills because they still supported the brutal and arbitrary rule of an unpopular family. Despite his own serious misgivings, Davey was left with no choice but to go out and arrest Mohamed Awas and force his followers to submit to British-backed tyranny.

In this period Davey's diary entries fail to betray any emotion. He does not even remark on whether he felt his solitude had become lone-liness. His tone is deadpan. The last proper diary I found ends on the last Thursday prior to his death. It ceases abruptly, with an entry about having eaten lunch at a village and a beautiful red chestnut filly with skin like velvet that he wants to take for a ride. His writing is tidy, but he takes less care over the journal. It is a small "one day to a page" desk diary, cheaply printed up by Cowasjee Dinshaw and Bros. of Steamer Point, rather than one of the smart clothbound foolscap volumes he used as a younger man. White ants have eaten the pages right through. The last entry ends halfway down the page and is followed by several more blank sheets. The diary has no cover. Smudged on the first page of text is the unmistakable print of a muddy, bare foot. The entries are mainly lists and notes of cables sent in cipher to Aden. In what there is of the diary, Davey is not the man I thought I knew. No longer does he write of plants and laws. When attacking the rebels on Jihaf, he no longer hesitates to take cover but walks grimly on until the fortress is captured and he has demolished it. Undone by love, imprisoned in his Englishman's khaki authority, Davey is a ruined man, no longer either young or at liberty. My father is far away now, getting on with his dam building and cotton fields, still riding across the desert and entranced by the world they had both loved. Davey is sad in his colonial officer's house on the hill, over-looking a squalid village full of people who hate him.

The story that my father told in his papers I found in the Zanzibar chest was that after Davey was forced to divorce Sheikha in Aden, husband and wife never saw each other again. On my travels to Yemen I met a member of the Government Guard who had served under Davey, who told me that he had personally escorted Sheikha across the hills with a string of camels to Dhala some time in late 1946. I asked him three times to confirm the details of his story, to satisfy myself that he wasn't going senile.

I also heard from several elders in Dhala that the English-man, whom I thought had converted to Islam only so that he could marry a Muslim girl, had begun to appear at the mosque to pray each day. He certainly had no reason to practice Islam if he had no hope of seeing Sheikha ever again—unless he began to believe in the religion. People in Dhala also told me that one day a large dog appeared in Davey's house. "He threw it meat and took it for walks!" screeched an old man with pallid skin who wore high-top sneakers, tufted turban on his head and purple robes. The animal was very obviously Haddab, Davey's beloved saluki from Beihan, which had stayed by his side on all his long walks and run alongside the car when he and Sheikha had driven down to Aden. All the sto-ries I heard indicated to me that Haddab and Sheikha had become inseparable, so that the appearance of one could have been a sign of the other's presence.

This is what I'd like to think. Sheikha never believed that Davey wanted to leave her. In Beihan, they had talked many times about what they would do if the British demanded a separation. So when she didn't hear a word after he had left that day, she knew what had happened. Instead of forgetting about the Englishman, she waited like Penelope. This went on for more than seven months, then one day the message she was expecting came at last. It was brought by Davey's own orderly, calling her across the hills to Dhala. The bodyguard was the elderly Government Guard I had questioned so intensely. I imagine the story. Sheikha turned up in Dhala one day, dressed like a Bedu woman, walking alongside her camels with Haddab the saluki. She and her husband were over-joyed to be together again. The inhabitants of Dhala quickly learned that Davey kept a woman in his house. A few knew the truth about her. The only people who knew nothing were the British. Nothing should have come in the way of Davey and Sheikha now. But as the days turned into weeks, Davey and Sheikha became aware that seeing each other again simply under-scored how impossible was their situation. Even if her presence was revealed to the British in Aden, they would not necessarily care. They could live together, so long as Davey never made Sheikha his Arab wife again. Secondly, if Davey disliked Dhala, then Sheikha must certainly have detested it more. She had never before left the wadi of Beihan, except for her one visit to Aden with Davey. Apart from the novelty of the electric lights and the overhead fans in the house in Sheikh Othman, she had not wished to be anywhere other than her birthplace on the edge of the desert. And so she left.

Did it happen that way? "The box office would like that," said one of the old Englishmen I lunched with at the Traveller's Club in London's Pall Mall. I'd like it to have been true. But I'm afraid it didn't happen that way. Davey and Sheikha never saw each other in Dhala. By the time she heard news of him he was dead.

Dawn rays of sunshine spread across the slopes of Jebel Jihaf, where the domed white tombs of saints gleamed in the first light. Lower down, villages of gray angular towers bunched together on the mountain's spurs. As the sun rose, a blanket of mist lifted from the valleys like breath from a polished blade. Accompanied by my driver, bodyguards, and Ali, a teacher who said he was a direct descendant of the rebel sheikh Mohamed Awas, we set off into the hills along the same route that Davey had taken from Dhala to al-Hussein. A dirt track wound through barren hills where no trees grew except for stunted myrrh and succulents that bloomed with delicate pink flowers. Herds of humped cattle and black goats with corkscrew horns grazed the rocky slopes. Ali observed his home landscape with gloom. He said it reminded him of a passage in the Koran in which, because of man's wickedness, Allah transformed the lush green hills of Yemen into a wasteland of "devilish trees." To me it was magical, with its soaring mountain peaks shaped like javelins and pyramids.

Our vehicle picked its way down the rocky valley bottom and even in this dry season a clear brook still babbled along. Shoals of brown minnows scattered as we drove through cold, slow pools. Birds of prey circled between the canyon walls. A hammerkop, a brown bird with a head like a tomahawk, flew off squawking in alarm, while electric-green dragonflies hovered above the stream. Families working in fields of golden sorghum, maize, and qat stood up from their work to gaze at us silently. In a narrow valley like this, I thought, perhaps the passage of fifty years meant nothing. When we stopped to exchange greetings I asked the teacher how many strangers came here. He could remember only a band of Russian prospectors trekking down the valley years ago on a fruitless search for gold.

We arrived at al-Hussein in the early afternoon, just as Davey had. A cluster of stone houses perched on a rocky hillside above the river's course. The men of the village were sitting beneath the trees, where they were chewing qat after prayers and lunch among the fields. Several children clustered by the car, but the adults held back. They were armed with AK-47s and the atmosphere was tense. We called out our greetings. Then an old man approached and politely welcomed us. I told him right away why I was here. The old man looked astonished. After some seconds he motioned for me to sit on the riverbank. He introduced himself as al-Hajj Ali Awas, a surviving cousin of the sheikh. Yes, he said, he had personally witnessed Davey's appearance that day, those many years ago. Onyx-eyed children gathered in a circle around us. It was in this very spot, the old man said, that Mohamed Awas chewed qat with his retainers each day on a carpet spread beneath an elb tree. The party was here the day Davey on his horse with a handful of his guards appeared advancing up the gorge. From what the old man told me, combined with what my father had left in his own memoir, I could piece together exactly what happened next on that day, April 15, 1947.

Sheikh Mohamed Awas knew that Davey was out to arrest him. He had signed himself to a truce after talks with Seager and Davey in Aden in late March. Yet he remained angry at the prospect of being forced to show allegiance to the Amiris once more. A few days later, he burned and looted the village of Dakkan. He and Davey knew each other well enough. For six months they had been allies with a common enemy. Mohamed Awas might have voluntarily turned himself in at Aden, since he would have been released after a further round of talks, if only Davey had diplomatically asked him to do so. But for a proud tribal leader like Awas to be forcibly arrested on home ground and beneath his own fortified village involved an intolerable loss of face. It was an affront to his dignity and manhood. My father believed that the "balance of Davey's mind must have been disturbed."

Striding toward the group on the carpet, Davey called out his greeting:

"*Salaam aleikum!*"

The men on the carpet stirred. Their cheeks bulged with qat and the drug coursed through their blood. It can make a man edgy, quick-tempered if pushed, like the militias I got to know in Somalia.

"*Wa aleikum salaam!*" came the reply. The sheikh, as host, rose to his feet to receive the visitor and motioned for him to join the group on the carpet. His retainers remained sitting, their legs tucked under them, leaning on cushions.

Davey then shouted, "Mohamed Awas, you have broken your word on the keeping of the peace. I can no longer trust you, so I have come to arrest you!"

There could be no doubt now that the Englishman intended to humiliate the sheikh in front of his followers. Davey should have been armed. Instead he carried only a walking stick, one with a curved handle like a shepherd's crook. With this he advanced in order to hook the warrior by the scruff of his neck.

Mayhem erupted. The sheikh yelled, "Your mother lies!" *Ummak kadhab!*

From his belt Awas drew his silver-hafted *jambiya* dagger and sprang at Davey. The Englishman raised his free hand and knocked his attacker off balance. The blade sliced down and glanced off his arm. The sheikh lunged again. This time he thrust the dagger into Davey's chest. He plunged it in with such force that the handle snapped off. His fist slid down the blade. This sheared off all his own fingers. Only his thumb was saved when it came up against the ribs as he rammed the knife deeper into Davey. Both men, spurting blood, staggered backward.

On both sides, their followers were wide-eyed and snarling. Rifles and knives were raised and cocked. Davey's escorts, too slow to block the sheikh's knife blows, now had a clear shot at Mohamed Awas. One, a young guard named Nasir Salem, opened fire from a distance of a few feet. He aimed low, so that the soft-nosed bullet hit Awas in the stomach. The dumdum round fragmented inside the man's guts and blew out his entrails. Awas fell onto his backside without uttering a sound. He just sat there clutching his belly as his face drained to white.

Davey stumbled about in the open ground. Men on both sides

now opened fire. Lacking real cover, they kneeled or pressed themselves to the ground. At this moment the sheikh's armed slave, who had sprinted down from the fort when he'd heard shots, charged at Davey with his rifle. Davey's guards opened fire on him. The hail of bullets cut him down in his tracks. At the same instant that he began to fall, with the barrel of his gun feet away from his target, he pulled the trigger. The slave's bullet smashed into Davey's rib cage. It passed through his heart and killed him instantly. Tribesmen further out in the fields rushed in when they heard the shots. A hush followed. It was over.

Davey's escort quickly withdrew and fled back up the gorge to the nearest guard post several miles away. Dead and wounded lay sprawled about in the valley. Davey's body lay in the sun as the blood soaked through his khaki tunic. Next to him was the shattered body of the slave. The sheikh's retainers now rushed forward to attend to Mohamed Awas. With a rag they stuffed his guts back into the gaping bullet hole. They bound up the wound with a turban and twisted it like a tourniquet. Fearing the colonial soldiers were likely to return quickly, they then dragged him to a mosque. By the time they got there Awas was unconscious. When the tourniquet was loosened, the sheikh's guts poured out. He died swiftly.

Davey and the slave remained where they had fallen. My father later reported that Davey's head cloth, his treasured fountain pen, some papers, and other items had been looted from the corpse.

I believe Davey kept most of his kit at his bungalow in Dhala, or at the house he so rarely used now with my father in Aden. He might well have been carrying his current diary. If the looters took it, perhaps in a satchel with other items, they would have thrown it away. It was worthless to them, but how valuable I would find it now, to know what had gone through his mind in those very last days.

Rumors of the gunfight spread quickly, but a proper account of the incident reached Dhala by runner only two days later.

Rwanda

LAZARUS

When U.S. troops withdrew from Mogadishu in March 1994, all our hopes of a new world order vanished along with the flotilla of warships over the Indian Ocean horizon. Our region disappeared from the headlines the same day. America had been so humiliated in Mogadishu that overnight, all mention of Somalia became a blasphemy in the media and, by extension, the very concept of intervening to sort out Africa's problems was far-fetched beyond words.

Lizzie and I pondered this as we flew to the Kenya coast and checked into a beach hotel. That night we propped up the bar under fiberglass black marlin trophies and old photos of Ernest Heming-way who had come here to go deep sea fishing half a century before. This was our first holiday for a long while and we consid-ered the prospects of scuba diving, swimming, and lying about with good books and long cool drinks under the palm trees. Next morn-ing, in shades and sunblock, me in my shorts, Lizzie in her blue bikini, we sauntered down to a terrace overlooking the beach for breakfast. A breeze played in the casuarinas. Beyond the white sand lapped the limpid sea.

"Isn't the ocean perfect?"

Lizzie nodded with a smile.

As we ate, I switched on my Sony shortwave radio. Each of us had a newspaper to read. You will have seen those couples in restaurants, eating in silence while avoiding eye contact. That was us. For months we had dreamed of this time off. We had arrived at last, only to find that we had nothing to say to each other. My memory paints a picture of early days when we stayed whole afternoons in bed at the Ski Chalet, entwined, making love with the doors thrown open to the garden. Things had begun to change in the twilight days of the Somalia story. Time off had increasingly become the gaps between arrivals and departures. Our dreams were of assignments and stories. To engage Lizzie enough to put her in a good mood, I scanned the papers for a hot news item.

"The shit's hit the fan in Angola." She perked up.

"What's going on?"

"UNITA ambushed a train. Total mess."

"How many dead?"

Given a choice between a story and a beach holiday on a perfect ocean, we both knew what it would be. We found peace with each other surrounded by the imbroglio of an emergency. Perhaps stories were the way we avoided the subject of how unsuited we were to each other. The mango and coffee arrived as the BBC World Service's top-of-the-hour time pips came up on the shortwave followed by the Lilli burlero signature tune. Are you sitting comfortably for the 0600 hours GMT menu of crises, accidents, and summits across the globe? A deadpan Queen's English voice came on and, one by one, the correspondents queued up with their reports, delivered in urgent voices down crackling phone lines. I loved the World Service. There was no puff, no fat content. I always got a thrill hearing about a Sendero Luminoso car bomb in Lima; unrest in Russia; separatist rebel abductions in Bougainville Island; Hindus demolishing a mosque in India; a Hezbollah ambush in South Lebanon. Crises ticking over, rising to a crescendo, going off the boil.

Lizzie and I used to play a sort of game, in which we assessed news stories breaking elsewhere in the world and compared them to what was going on in our patch of Africa. We estimated what each was worth in terms of assignment contracts and how it might affect interest in the African news schedule; ultimately, what it would be like to be there instead of here. What the both of us half hoped for at breakfast that day was an African disaster, a mother lode of bylines, photo day rates, and expenses that would whisk us away from the prospect of taking things easy.

That morning, April 7, 1994, the top BBC news headline was about a plane crash in Central Africa. Rwanda's Hutu president, Juvenal Habyarimana, and Cyprien Ntaryarima, the leader of Burundi, had been killed while flying together when their aircraft was hit by a surface-to-air rocket and exploded in a ball of flame on the approach to Kigali airport. The presidents were on their way back from a conference in Tanzania on ways to stem the chronic bloodletting between the Tutsi and Hutu tribes in their respective nations. Nobody knows for sure to this day who brought the aircraft down, but whoever it was did not like the fact that the presidents were nearing a final accord that might finally bring peace to Central Africa.

I leaped up from breakfast and put a call through to Jonathan. Minutes later the mask and flippers and our diving holiday were discarded and we sped off for the local airport. We were almost happy as we elbowed our way through a crowd of tourists in Hawaiian shirts and sarongs.

In Nairobi, Lizzie and I packed our kit and rushed back to the airport where we boarded a charter headed for Entebbe, Uganda. With us were the young Kenyan Reuters TV cameraman Patrick and TV producer Michael, an overweight Israeli who had a habit of boasting about his exploits while in his troubled country's Defense Forces.

"You're in for a quick in and out, so don't you dare go walkabout," Jonathan lectured me before we left. He had been on the phone to the Reuters editors. He had told them he thought this story was going to be big, bigger than they realized. Their reaction underlined Jonathan's point that we shouldn't take unnecessary risks. "They regard this as your classic bongo story," Jonathan told me. "There's not going to be any interest in this unless they start raping white nuns. Cover the whites, get the nuns evacuated, and that's the end of it. That's what they want."

Small wars in the pocket handkerchief states of Central Africa were less likely than ever to get play after Somalia. In addition both Jonathan and I knew that at the best of times it was almost impossible to get more than one African story at a time into the world headlines. And in the month of April 1994, editors around the world were preparing for one of the most hopeful stories of the decade to come out of our benighted continent: South Africa's first multiracial elections, which would surely sweep Nelson Mandela to power.

At Entebbe we bought a sackload of near worthless Uganda shillings and hired a taxi to speed us west to the frontier. We zoomed past a blur of lake inlets, lush banana plantations, dripping forests, and villages deserted as a result of old wars and AIDS. As night fell the road turned into a dirt track and we bumped up to a barrier made out of an iron bar. In the dying light we strolled past the barrier and ran into a gang of men in combat fatigues. They were crouched on the ground, listening to their radio. Over the pop and wheeze of the airwaves, we heard an agitated Bantu voice. The fighters were silent, with heads bowed as they listened. When the voice had finished I asked them what had been said. They replied that it had been a call for the Hutus to kill the Tutsis.

The latest spasm of killing in the Rwanda war had started in October 1990 when a force of exiled Tutsis, the Rwanda Patriotic Front (RPF), had invaded from Uganda. I had covered the conflict on and off since the first days of the invasion. But it was Buchizya who had become the expert on this war and he was on backslapping, beer-drinking terms with most of the Tutsi exiles in Kampala. The Tutsis had been thrown out of the country in a string of pogroms since 1959. The RPF's ultimate aim was simply to come home. To achieve this, they had to overthrow the dictator Habyarimana, who had resisted the repatriation of exiles because the country was so overcrowded, or, as he put it, Rwanda was like a glass that was already full. The rebels would have won within a year or two had they not been prevented from doing so by France's deployment of its troops to protect the capital. The RPF also caved in to diplomatic pressure to concede to a United Nations brokered cease-fire. The subsequent Security Council resolution 872 deployed the UN Mission in Rwanda (UNAMIR), an observer mission of twenty-five hundred troops, to oversee a complete cessation of hostilities and preparations for multiparty elections. An RPF contingent had even been deployed in the parliament building in Kigali to guard their politicians and begin the plan to integrate rebel forces into the Hutu government army. The process had dragged on and been delayed but all things considered it was progressing relatively well until Habyarimana's aircraft got zapped. Stunned silence followed. Then on the evening of April 8, as we arrived on the frontier, fighting erupted along the line of trenches in the hills a few miles to the south of us. Artillery boomed out and blue flashes lit up the horizon.

Several more cars of journalists arrived in the following hours, but it became clear to most of them that this was the wrong place to be. The guerrillas had launched an offensive, and to reach Kigali overland from here would mean crossing government forces' lines during full-scale fighting. The majority of the correspondents quickly agreed that the best thing to do was go back to Entebbe and charter an aircraft directly into Kigali, where, according to the BBC, widespread killings had erupted.

Buchizya was somewhere on the road behind me and I knew I had to stay with the RPF guerrillas until he arrived. Apart from anything else, I could communicate easily with the RPF because they were mostly Anglophones. In Kigali, I would have to speak French and I didn't fancy trying out my C-grade schoolboy's Français on armed Hutus. Besides, I knew Jonathan even now would be packing off other correspondents directly to the capital.

Lizzie and I stood together in the headlight beams. I knew she had to try for Kigali if she were to score an assignment. A car appeared to carry the noisy pack of journalists away. We hurriedly kissed. A roar of laughter emerged from the vehicle. "You're sitting on me!" *Pppght!* "Oh no, who farted?" Lizzie climbed in and slammed the door. "Open the windows! I'm suffocating!" I stood beneath the banana trees and watched as the car bumped away down the muddy track and the rowdy, happy voices grew fainter until they and the headlamps were swallowed up in darkness.

At that moment I had a sensation of looming blackness that I'd never before experienced. I felt afraid that Lizzie and I would never see each other again. What happened in the weeks, months, and years that were to follow proved there was more than a grain of truth to my fears. In this life, we should dread all things unexpected. For now, Lizzie's image as I'd last seen her in the halo of light from the car's headlights hung before me like an icon. The only way I could fight my fear was to join her as soon as I could. I swore I'd make it to Kigali even if I had to walk.

The guerrilla HQ was a collection of mud huts among tea plantations gone wild. Tutsi officers and truckloads of fighters came and went, watched miserably by a handful of UNAMIR military observers deployed here to police a cease-fire now in tatters. Forgotten and superfluous, they sat about having childish arguments over rations and whose turn it was to use the bucket of cold water with which to bathe. To fill the hours of boredom, we got the Austrian officers to shave our heads and played poker with the Uruguayans and Nigerians.

Small units of guerrillas were punching through the trenches and sprinting for Kigali, where a beleaguered company of their troops was now holding out in the parliament building. Patrick and Michael the Israeli were busting to push on to Kigali and so I quipped, half joking, "Hey, what about walking?" The TV boys took that as a challenge. "Okay," I said, "we'll walk." "You can't possibly walk," said Paul Kagame, the RPF's taciturn commander-in-chief. "Oh yes we can," I argued. "Look at us: we're fit young men and we've all had military training." It was a barefaced lie; though he had served as a conscript in the Israeli Defense Forces, Michael was so fat he wheezed as he walked up a hill. Patrick was a kid who knew nothing about guns. My only soldiering had been in the Combined Cadet Force at school, I was a smoker, and my only shoes were a pair of scuffed moccasins.

A couple of days passed and then, incredibly, I got a message back to say that Kagame had relented and the order was that we were to join a supply column moving out the next evening. We stripped our kit down to the minimum and at dusk we joined a group marching toward the front line north of the town of Byumba. In charge were two officers, Lieutenants Frank and Emmanuel. In the fading light, I saw a platoon of guerrilla officers and *kidogos*, child soldiers, herding three hundred Hutu peasant men they had press-ganged into being porters. The members of the column trotted in single file, boxes of ammunition, rocket parts, food, and medical supplies balanced on their heads. Both sides were trading mortar fire between hills but as night fell we slipped down the slope to a valley bottom.

Lieutenant Frank, a dapper chap with a mustache and a shot-off thumb, whispered, "Be ready for ambushes. This area is infested."

For two hours we walked without speaking down a valley, passing abandoned farmsteads and banana groves. Empty ammunition boxes and bullet casings littered the path from the fighting that had preceded our arrival. The government army lines were in a string of trenches on the heights above us and at one point they must have heard or seen us moving below them. Gun muzzles flashed and the launch of an occasional mortar bomb erupted with the sound of a train as it roared through the night mist. They were firing way over our heads, but every few minutes the valley fell silent as the enemy listened for us. A whispered message passed along the line. "Tread carefully and make no sound." Another one made me smile. "Nobody light a cigarette." We were clearly with the professionals. We tiptoed along for what seemed an age and held our breath when a porter lost his footing on the muddy path. His burden of rockets clattered to the ground. In an abandoned village nearby a dog barked, but no reaction came from above, and minutes later the column was on the move again. We entered fields of bananas and under their leaves it became so inky black we edged forward like blind men, expecting to bump into horrors at any second. Further into the night we encountered a ragged group of wounded. They were returning north, the only place where they could get medical treatment. The badly injured cases were on stretchers and as I passed one prone figure, clutching his stomach, I heard him sigh ever so faintly in the dark.

Finally, an hour before dawn, we scaled a hilltop where we collapsed among foxholes dug in among banana groves. I slept almost where I fell, but was roused at first light by mortar fire. Within minutes we were up again. I was stiff, my feet were blistered, but at the same time I felt very alive. The supply column formed up again, men stamping the sleep out of their limbs, their breath steaming in the highland dawn. Incoming was landing in the earth and banana groves as the rebel guides hissed and herded the porters down the safe side of the hill toward the south. In the daylight the enemy on their hilltops would be able to see us moving. As we trekked down one valley we saw many families on the move. We passed a group of peasant women who clapped their hands and pleaded with us to take them along. We never stopped. A little farther down the way we passed a different group of peasants who glared at us in silence, their eyes full of fear and their faces contorted with open hatred. An hour on we entered a hamlet of burning huts and in the path in front of us we came upon the body of a young man. An eerie silence hung over the land, where even the birds had fallen mute. I saw a dead cow, a broken cooking pot, one shoe. Another human corpse. If we didn't see bodies we smelled them and at one point Frank said rather dramatically, "You smell that? That's the perfume we have got used to while fighting this war."

Even at a time like this I knew what a good quote was, so I took out my notebook and wrote that down. We advanced at a trot for two hills, then rested for a few minutes. Then two more hills and stopped again. On one rest, the rebel officer Emmanuel took a sachet of white powder from his jacket pocket and poured some into my open palm. "Glucose," he said. "To keep up your blood-sugar level."

I sensed we were being watched by unseen eyes. It was early afternoon when a heavy machine gun opened up on us from a hill-side, sending us scuttling for cover in the valley bottom. We didn't stop for a second. Some miles on, despite quantities of glucose powder, the pace got the better of Michael. He collapsed, and two porters had to donate their ammunition loads to others in order to carry the fat white man along on a stretcher. He lay there, out cold with his arms swinging limply. To anybody observing our column, he must have appeared dead. "The government military spokesman claimed that white mercenaries in large numbers were assisting the rebels," BBC radio's Focus on Africa program broadcast that night. "On the Byumba front, several mercenaries were reported killed."

We halted in the evening, occupying the garden of an abandoned house with distant views of Kigali. Dog-tired after yomping up and down steep hills, we collapsed in our blankets on the cool grass. The next morning, I woke up to see a *kidogo* boy soldier sitting nearby between the rows of vegetables and gnawing at a carrot. I got up and went over to crouch next to him and picked one myself. I never consumed a carrot that tasted so good. The boy and I passed a raw cabbage between us, taking out big bites. Then we rubbed mud off onions onto our trousers and scoffed those too.

"We must have meat," I announced. "For our strength. And because we got here."

Frank, who had lived for years on beans and maize porridge, readily agreed it was a good idea. We hobbled on stiff legs for twenty minutes down the road to a huge redbrick church with a spire that dwarfed the tiny settlement around it. A woman was lying on the church steps. Black, drying blood trailed from her skull. We knocked at the rectory. The door was opened by a nun and without a word she motioned us into a stone-floored parlor, where we sat in high-backed wooden chairs. A pastor entered and sat. I can't explain why now but we did not bring up the matter of the dead woman on the church steps, nor did the pastor volunteer any information on why she was there. He had seen the first column of rebels advancing on Kigali at the double.

"They rose up out of the ground shrieking." He had wondered if they were devils. "I did not know who these creatures were. They were covered with mud, from head to foot."

The priest hastily agreed to sell me two goats. I then noticed the white trainers he was wearing. My own moccasins were coming apart and my feet had begun to bleed. When I explained what I wanted, he took off his shoes immediately and gave them to me, refusing to take the money I offered him. The trainers were a perfect fit, with Velcro flaps instead of laces and chunky soles that would come in handy for the steep, muddy hills.

Back at our camp at the abandoned house, we slaughtered the goats and while the *kidogos* chopped them up and started roasting them I decided to take a look around. The house had been looted, but as I walked from room to room I could see that the thieves had not bothered to steal anything that was fine or cultured, like the books. I could also see that the owners were bourgeois, religious people. The words GOD WATCHES OVER THIS HOUSE were woven in a banana-leaf tapestry that hung over the fireplace. On the floor of the living room, I found two *kidogos* flipping through the vanished family's photo albums. They turned the pages reverently and took out pictures and put them into their own pockets. It was as if they were searching for the happy family histories they had missed as refugees and orphans.

When the goats were ready we sat in a circle while the greasy, fatty meat was handed around. Frank kindly gave me the honor of choosing morsels of liver and kidney, which I wolfed down. Then I started on a nicely charred leg and the stringy bits of meat stuck between my teeth and the fat dripped down my chin. Offal, brains, tongue, bone marrow; every part of those beasts was consumed, even the hooves and the hairy skin. Replete, we lay basking on the grass, picking our teeth and watching after-rain butterflies dance about in the sunshine. Patrick, Frank, and I played a game of Kenyan poker, using matches for bets. Men removed shoes to study blistered feet, cleaned guns, dozed. That garden was a little envelope of peace and I felt the air of contentment one has after having eaten a large Sunday lunch with good wine.

The highland chill descended with evening and we slept together in a pile, our sweaty bodies packed close against the cold. One of the *kidogos* made little whimpering noises in his sleep. I woke in the stillness of the night when there was no wind and I smelled a familiar odor. At that instant I realized that the family had never fled their home. They hadn't had the chance. They had been here with us all the time. Sure enough, next morning we found them beneath the carrots and cabbages of the wonderful vegetable patch, rotting in their decent clothes not twenty feet from where we had slept.

We trekked on in a wide curve to the western outskirts of

Kigali, until on the evening of the fourth day we camped for the last time before entering the city. Our resting place was a farmstead of wattle-and-daub huts, where we lay in the afternoon sunshine on the hard-beaten earth. A woman appeared. Nobody spoke as she brewed us some tea. At that moment none of us cared much about the story. What was on our minds was first, how we were going to find our next meal and next how to get out of here alive. There was no way we could return from where we had come and in front of us now we could hear the rumble of battle. Emmanuel and some of his men spread out to search the hamlet. One appeared a few minutes later and came toward me with his eyes wide open.

"Found anything?"

He tossed me a glossy color magazine called *Fuckarama*. On its cover was a heap of Caucasian men and women engaged in an orgy. An abandoned African village at war was hardly the place to unearth hard-core pornography and I shook my head in disbelief. *Fuckarama's* main feature was a blonde apparently being gang-raped. The final photo in the spread had her eyes fixed on the camera in what looked like a drowning scream of panic. I looked up. Lieutenant Frank was peering over my shoulder.

"Are you crazy? That's bad luck, man," Frank said. "Before you see fighting man, wow. You must be crazy."

I got up and stumbled off toward a corrugated-iron latrine hut. I opened the door to find a dead man's pair of bare feet poking up out of the stinking hole. Farther on down the path in the emerald filtered light of the banana grove, I dropped my trousers and squatted. My heart pounded. I stared up through the jungle into the sky. "What if there is only this?" As if in reply, my bowels loosened. How was it that I came to be stuck inside this strange, involuntary body? It seemed to me that there was no heaven or hell, right or wrong. There was only this.

* * *

The Tutsi guerrillas were winning the war. At least, they were clearly winning territory. For the Tutsis, this was nothing new. From the years that they had been forced into exile by the Hutus, they had become mercenaries or fought for their own survival. They had done nothing but struggle in a succession of conflicts: in Tanzania, in Uganda, in Congo. Only since 1990 had they been in Rwanda. Many Tutsis had been in exile since childhood or birth.

"Are you happy to be here?" I asked Emmanuel. His face creased with a frown.

"I don't know," he replied.

As we walked a cultured guerrilla named Gerald told me how the Hutus had crucified his father on the summit of an anthill. For three decades, he had wandered the earth. Now he was returning home to a land that had become alien to him. With each step that he advanced toward rescuing his Tutsi people, another village of them was being wiped out. He was unclear as to what victory would bring, except an end to the war that had given form and purpose to his entire life.

Next day, we marched on to an industrial quarter on the city's outskirts. In a deserted factory, one of Frank's soldiers who had grown up inside Rwanda found a phone that worked and called home, to be told that his family were dead. Later, after darkness, we joined a convoy of vehicles and drove along a series of tracks that cut through no-man's-land between the opposing forces with our lights off for an hour. Finally, we reached the parliament complex in central Kigali where the guerrillas' main positions were stationed. Dawn heralded a helicopter attack, when several rockets were fired into the building.

We said farewell to our Tutsi escorts and made our way to the football stadium, which was under UNAMIR guard. Hundreds of Tutsis were camped on the pitch, huddled beneath plastic sheeting slung over the goal posts. As we watched, mortar bombs rained down into the field, into the body of a Ghanaian UN soldier, into a family of Tutsis. Over at UNAMIR headquarters, it was sheer panic. The Hutu extremists had disarmed and then butchered ten Belgian blue helmets guarding the woman prime minister, Agathe Uwilingiyimana, a Hutu who was murdered for being too moderate. She was Africa's second ever female prime minister. She was also pregnant. Her killers disemboweled her. UNAMIR headquarters had listened in on the walkie-talkie network as the European soldiers pleaded for help and screamed before they died too. Belgian forces stayed long enough to evacuate the expatriates along with a French force that flew in for the job. French and Belgian troops in the eighties and nineties always seemed to be rescuing their citizens from postcolonial meltdowns in Gabon, Zaire, Chad, and the Central African Republic.

The order then came for the Belgians to evacuate themselves. Before they left I saw a Belgian remove his blue beret and stamp on it in disgust. Finally, it was decided that the Bangladeshis, some Ghanaians, and most of the civilian UNAMIR staff should escape too. That left a slimmed-down force of Ghanaians and a handful of officers. In the Hotel Meridien, I tracked down the UN's special envoy, a fat-cheeked Cameroonian named Jacques-Roger Booh-Booh. He seemed to be in a state of paralyzed terror from the look on his face. His mission was collapsing.

We joined a convoy of vehicles headed for Kanombe airport. We sped down deserted streets, at every junction stopping for a few scary minutes at checkpoints manned randomly by one side or the other. GUINNESS, said a billboard, IS GOOD FOR YOU. The terminal building was gloomy, the floors crunchy with shattered glass. Hutus hung about: in the departure lounge, on the baggage carousels, in duty-free. In the foyer stood a statue of a gorilla made, the label said, out of soap. A giant Ukrainian Ilyushin 76 transport landed and taxied down the tarmac. The Bangladeshi soldiers, carrying their weapons and in full battle dress, broke ranks and made a rush for the aircraft. A fistfight erupted between them as they struggled up the lowered back bay ramp.

Patrick, Michael, and I avoided the melee by following Booh-Booh and the other civilian UN staffers into a side door. A Ukrainian loadmaster, reeking of alcohol, helped me strap myself into a canvas seat. Chances were the pilots were just as drunk. A big, rolled-up carpet lay on the deck in front of me. A carpet? It later turned out that a man had been smuggled onboard hidden in the rug right under the noses of the Hutus. We waited while the Bangladeshis piled on with their kit, almost to the fuselage roof, crying and praying. Mortar bombs began to rain down outside. Then night fell. We were so heavy on takeoff that the fuselage hardly tilted up. I prepared for death from several causes: excess cargo, vodka-soused pilot error, Stingers and SAM-7s. *Deliver us from evil,* I prayed. The temperature dropped as we gained altitude and the chill entered my damp crotch and sweaty clothes.

It was April 26, 1994. Nelson Mandela had just been voted in as president of South Africa.

Central Africa had been in crisis for years. My previous experience of the violence in Burundi had proved to be a foreshadowing of what was about to take place in neighboring Rwanda. In late 1993 Jonathan had pulled me out of Somalia for a side trip to Bujumbura, capital of Burundi, days after another president, Melchior Ndadaye, had been murdered. Ndadaye had been elected in the first democratic elections Burundi ever held, an event inspired largely by the collapse of French influence in Africa and demands by the United States for pluralism across the continent. On that occasion I had been with Mark Doyle, a big, gruff BBC man, and he was the one who came up with the idea that we should see the massacres from the air. We had seen army Gazelle choppers swooping off to attack the rebels, so we went to the defense ministry and boldly approached a lieutenant colonel for assistance. Without hesitation, he had written a note for us to whomever it concerned: "*Mettez a la disposition des journalistes étrangers—Agence Reuters et BBC—un helico de liaison . . .*"

Burundi exploded as a direct consequence of Western pressure for democracy, for this tiny state since independence had been ruled by a military dictatorship of the Tutsi minority. In 1993 the Hutus, who made up 85 percent of the population, naturally elected their own ethnic candidate, while the military consisted almost entirely of hard-liner Tutsis. It was another example of a Western one-size-fits-all solution to an African problem and Burundi became a catalyst for at least a decade of crises in the region.

Out of the bubble cockpit we saw smoke from fires all the way to the horizon. Crowds of peasants in their brightly colored clothes swarmed to the tops of hills as if the Deluge had returned to engulf the world. The pilot took us down to rooftop height over a deserted village and outside one hut we hovered over a family of corpses, five of them, sprawled in the dust. The black smoke coiled away and the cockpit's interior was cool. We floated from street to street, and in my helmet earphones I heard the pilot's exclamations. "*Mon Dieu,* my dear God, here are some more . . ." We advanced down the main street almost at walking pace with the skis a few feet off the ground. Suddenly a group of men carrying spears and machetes rounded a corner. The pilot throttled up into the sky by twenty feet and we bore down on them. I had them in my video viewfinder and Mark gabbled into his microphone. We hovered over the group, flattening the grass around them, but instead of running away they jumped up and down and waved their Stone Age weapons at us.

The next day I had driven through southern Burundi's hills with a French journalist who was unfazed by the emptiness of the roads. At one point we stopped to piss and as soon as I opened the car door we smelled it. The French correspondent raised his face to the breeze with dilated nostrils and snuffed the air.

"Ha! Now I can smell a story, and very close by it is too!"

I looked at him, wondering if he was mad. As I got my notebook and video camera out of the car I saw my hands were trembling violently. On one side of the road was a steep bank, on the other side of which I could hear a steady hum. The Frenchman remained standing next the car, smoking his cigarette. I clambered up the slope. At the top of the bank I found myself on the edge of an open field ringed by trees. The humming sound came from the center of the field. I walked toward it. A million flies. The corpses were in a pile, about two days gone. Fifteen, twenty. It was impossible from a distance to count properly in that tangle of limbs. Whoever executed them piled them up two or three deep. I held up the video camera, pressed the record button, and walked in a circle around the heap. They were like obese men too bloated for their soiled, moist jeans and stained shirts. They were bursting at the seams. I had that familiar feeling of eyes observing me and I turned to walk back to the car. When I replayed the tape later I saw that I had forgotten to turn off the camera. On the tape you can hear me breathing heavily and the sound of my footfalls suddenly speeds up as I break into a run. I scrambled down the bank. "We're going," I urged. "Right now. Drive, drive, drive!" The Frenchman flicked away his cigarette and we started off, me peering through the rear window.

"What was it?" he said.

"I'm not sure."

The track curled around past an abandoned Roman Catholic mission. Twilight was closing in and up ahead were huts burning with leaping red flames. As we advanced, the fires were being lit by whoever the killers were. A mile on down the track we were forced to halt. Carefully laid out to block our path was a line of bodies. I remember there were six males, and two of them were young boys. We got out of the car and walked up and I crouched to take one's hand. It was still warm and floppy. Fresh blood oozed from their wounds and they looked as if they were asleep. I was sure that this roadblock made of corpses was another indication that we were being watched and that whoever was observing us clearly didn't wish us to proceed. It was now very nearly dark and I was losing any sense of space and distance. The blackness of the hill loomed; the red flames closed in around us and the dead men. By now I was trembling so badly I could hardly keep still to light each fresh cigarette off the butt of the last burned-out one. We got back in the car. The ignition kicked into life. The French correspondent turned us around. We sped back down the track where we had come from. We could hardly see but my companion kept the car's headlights off.

A minute later we saw them silhouetted against the horizon of fading orange light. Our watchers. Moving on foot, they must easily have heard our engine returning their way. I saw three figures sprinting down the ridge toward the mission buildings we had passed. Above them were flames. Below them was the track where they would cut us off. We glided past the first figure as he reached the track, so close that I saw the outline of his face. Through my open window I heard him hiss. We hurtled on down the hill. About thirty yards on, two sharp reports. I looked back. The road curled around near the spot where I had filmed the heap of bodies and we were safely out of sight.

We reached the asphalt fifteen minutes later. Up ahead our lights picked up the profile of a vehicle parked across our path. We stopped, got out of our car, and greeted a group of men in uniform. The Frenchman said we were priests and that he was sorry, but we were lost. Which way to the town? In the beam of the headlights I could see the officers smile. They politely gave us directions and waved us on. Nearby, a group of soldiers sat on the porch of a looted trading post, knocking back bottles of beer. They waved.

That we had witnessed the handiwork of the army killing peasants in the valley was obvious, but they seemed not in the slightest bit ashamed.

Burundi had been bad but nothing would prepare me for what I was about to see in Rwanda. The memory of Rwanda sits like a tumor leaking poison into the back of my head. History is supposed to explain why events happened as they did. But how do you account for the evil we saw in the green hills of that nation in 1994, where one day we saw a mother with a baby tied to her back gleefully using a machete to hack up another woman also carrying an infant?

Rwanda was so brimful of hatred that even quarreling over the origins of it caused bloodshed. Everybody blamed everybody else. Some blamed the history of the African tribes. Some claimed that tribes didn't exist at all and that they were imagined by the whites, whose fault it all was. Like everything in Africa, the truth was somewhere in between. What was certainly clear is that Central Africa's history was a succession of ghastly experiments carried out by crackpots. I stumbled across some clues in a book called *In the Heart of Africa.* This was a 1910 account of Duke Adolphus Frederick of Mecklenburg's shooting safari to the Ruanda-Urundi, at that time part of imperial German East Africa. Duke Adolphus, who appears in waxed mustaches and a spiky helmet on the frontispiece of his book, pursued eugenics as a hobby. The duke went on safari with calipers with which to measure brain capacity in the skulls of blacks. With this information, he figured he could judge how far up the evolutionary tree the Africans had climbed. He also studied the width and flatness of the Africans' noses.

Duke Adolphus had arrived in Africa following the great

British imperial pioneer Sir Harry Johnston, who established Nyasaland and the Uganda Protectorates. Johnston's two-volume survey of Uganda, which he brought under the protection of the crown, sat in my father's library as I grew up. In it Johnston noted: "Summing up the experiences of many African travellers, together with my own observations, I should venture to say that there is a prognathous beetling-browed, short-legged, long-armed—'ape-like'—type of Negro dwelling in pariah tribes or cropping up as reversionary in better-looking people, to be met with all down Central Africa."

Johnston photographed his specimens, getting them to bare their filed teeth or squat in their nakedness on tree stumps. After one of his pygmies died, Johnston boiled the flesh off the skull and sent it to London for scientific scrutiny. There were still pygmies in Rwanda in 1994 and they were horribly ill-treated, but these complex people known as Twa were held in such contempt by their African brothers that they were regarded as barely worth exterminating.

On the other hand Duke Adolphus and his contemporaries were almost polite about the Tutsis. He wrote, "Wa Tutsi are tall, well-made people with an almost ideal physique." It seemed natural to him that they should be the overlords in their mixed society. The British explorer and empire builder Ewart Grogan observed that Tutsis "would have been conspicuous for character in a London drawing room" if they had their faces bleached and necks put in high collars.

The Tutsis were traditionally cattle keepers and in the hierarchy of old tribal Africa this way of life made them nobler than the more populous Hutus. The Hutus Duke Adolphus came across were peasants, cultivators of bananas and sweet potatoes, "whose ungainly figures betoken hard toil, and who patiently bow themselves in abject bondage to the later arrived, yet ruling race, the Wa Tutsi."

The "Hamitic myth," or belief that Tutsi-type peoples originated in Abyssinia and invaded Central Africa to become the ruling caste, was promoted in the nineteenth century. For centuries, Abyssinia was known in Europe as an isolated Christian empire, the home of the fabled Prester John surrounded by barbarity. John Hanning Speke, who discovered Lake Victoria for the British, wrote in his "Journal of the Discovery of the Source of the Nile" what he called his *Theory of Conquest of Inferior by Superior Races,* that Abyssinia dispatched slaving armies and that one of these was "lost sight of in the interior of the continent, and, crossing the Nile close to its source, discovered the rich pasturelands ... where they lost their religion, forgot their language, extracted their lower incisors like the natives, changed their national name ... and no longer remembered ... Even the present reigning kings retain a singular traditional account of having once been half white half black, with hair on the white side straight, and on the black side frizzy."

The Germans appointed the Tutsis to be their lieutenants in the imperial project, but the kaiser lost his African empire as part of the reparations after the Great War and Belgium assumed control over what is now Rwanda and Burundi. Belgium stuck closely to the efficient administration developed under the kaiser and the Tutsis continued to receive better treatment thanks to their straighter noses. In time, they were educated and therefore dominated the nationalist movement for independence in the 1950s. Stung by such ingratitude, the Belgians organized the Hutus and ensured that when self-rule came in 1959, festering racial hatreds were unleashed between the two groups. In Rwanda the Hutus, who outnumbered Tutsis by four to one, rose up and overthrew the feudalist rulers, killing thousands and forcing many into exile. The Tutsis who stayed home were culled in a succession of pogroms. Bertrand Russell described a round of massacres in 1964 as "the most horrible and systematic human massacre we have had occasion to witness since the extermination of the Jews by Nazis."

Across the frontier, Burundi was in some ways Rwanda's mirror image. There, the minority Tutsis still ruled with ever greater brutality over the majority Hutus. It was the big people against the little people, a bit like the little-enders and the big-enders in *Gulliver's Travels*.

And yet what was bizarre, almost funny, was that Tutsis and Hutus were quite clearly the same people, who couldn't be stereotyped at all easily. In 1993 I had interviewed President Habyarimana, the Hutu supremo, and I saw that he was a very tall man, with very light skin and hair that stood straight up as if he'd stuck his fingers into an electrical socket. Like my idea of a Tutsi, in fact. Some Tutsis I saw were fine-boned and tall, with straight noses and light skin. Some were short and dark. But while the Hutus felt uneasy about the possibility that they were inferior, the Tutsis genuinely believed in their own superiority.

"You see that?" asked a Tutsi woman as she turned her profile sideways to me in Bujumbura. "Only Tutsis have noses like that. And you see this?" She performed a double-jointed maneuver with her thin fingers. "A Hutu can't do that. Only a Tutsi."

In 1994 the Hutus murdered Tutsis in very special ways. I saw tall massacre victims with their feet chopped off because the Hutus clearly wanted in a literal sense to "cut them down to size." They chopped off their fine tapering fingers and their straight noses. They tossed them in rivers so that they "could float back to Ethiopia, where they came from." But in the villages peasants also murdered one another because they saw that they could. I met a man who confessed he killed his neighbor because he had coveted his cow.

The Hutu government army had contained the RPF invasion in the north for more than forty months. Yet they were now losing fast. Suddenly the truth dawned on me that there was a mad logic about it. The point was not to win the war but to wipe out the Tutsis. Time and again, Hutu forces held a position long enough only so that the slaughter of civilians could be completed. Then they fell back, driving the remaining population before them into exile, taking their nation with them on foot, robbing the RPF of a people to govern. The RPF did not so much advance as get sucked into the vacuum of death the Hutus left behind. It seemed as if the Hutus wanted life in Rwanda to appear in their own image, which was, as Bald Sam put it quoting Hobbes, "nasty, brutish, and short."

After evacuating to Nairobi Jonathan told me to drive to Arusha, in Tanzania, where the Organization of African Unity was holding cease-fire talks between the warring sides in Rwanda. I turned up in my crumpled suit and tie and found gangs of fat, shiny men all gathered in the Kilimanjaro Hotel banquet hall, pigging themselves on free food and booze. The atmosphere was a million miles away from the panic unfolding a few hours' drive down the road. The OAU was little more than a club for dictators. For decades, the organization had stood by and done nothing about the slaughters in Central Africa. Indeed, Africa's leaders applauded one another for the horrors they perpetrated. They had, for example, made Idi Amin OAU chairman, then given him a standing ovation when he entered a summit sporting a cowboy hat and six- shooter pistols.

Predictably, the Arusha talks collapsed within hours, leaving only a military option. Lizzie was inside Rwanda by the time I left Arusha and to my relief Jonathan ordered me back into the field. I hitched a ride with a Canadian Royal Air Force C-130 Hercules. Both Hutu and Tutsi forces had surface-to-air missiles and as we crossed over the brown serpent of the Kagera River marking Rwanda's eastern frontier, the pilot dropped the aircraft to skim us over the hills at treetop height. We veered from side to side and the engine roar drowned out the sounds of vomiting from an Italian belted into the webbing opposite me. We barely descended as we glided onto the tarmac. The Hercules taxied with churning propellers and the loadmaster pressed a button to lower the back bay ramp. I peered out through the rippling propeller exhaust and saw Lizzie standing in a group of black and white faces on the runway apron. A plume of dirt kicked up from the tarmac behind the aircraft. The loadmaster yelled into his microphone. The plane swung in a circle, straightened out, and accelerated back down the runway for takeoff again.

"What's happening?"

"Sighting rounds!"

"What?"

"Firing at us!"

The loadmaster strapped himself into the webbing next to me and we were off, returning across country with the same sickening acrobatics as our incoming flight. "Damn," I thought. "I don't want to go back to Nairobi. I want to stay in Rwanda."

The UN closed Kigali airport after that, so to enter Rwanda I had to go in by road. Lizzie and I linked up again on the eastern frontier. Our reunion was in a square of UN tents erected around a pyramid of maize sacks on which was written DONATED BY THE USA. The guerrilla army was advancing down the eastern border and an exodus of Hutus fled before it across the frontier into Tanzania. A vast camp of Hutu refugees was taking shape around the square of tents, turning green plains to red mud. We commandeered a bivouac and inside while Lizzie sat down to check her cameras I filed a first report. She looked up.

"I felt so proud of you when I heard you were walking to Kigali. Nobody else did it."

"Thanks," I said. I congratulated her on her *Newsweek* double-page spread of Belgian and French paratroopers evacuating the Europeans from Kigali. Later, I looked back and wished I'd said what was really on my mind.

"Thank God you're here. I was worried sick about you, I thought you might die. I thought I might die ..."

The deserted border post at Rusumo Falls was a high bridge over the Kagera River. On the Rwanda side of the bridge machetes, knives, axes, guns, and clubs lay all in a pile several feet high. The fleeing Hutus had dropped these before they fled into exile, where after all their murders they could demand UN rations and escape justice. I drew from the pile of weapons a hefty, two-handed wooden club, spiked with a bouquet of six-inch nails. I took it back to the camp and gave it to Lizzie. Be my Valentine. She said thank you and later she set it in the corner of our bedroom at the Ski Chalet, where it seemed to throb with evil.

The State Department in Washington announced that "acts of genocide" were being committed in Rwanda. To me this phrase was meaningless. It was either a genocide or it wasn't. Washington refused to say that what was happening in Rwanda was genocide, plain and simple.

This infuriated me. At Rusumo Falls I met an American who said he was from the State Department and I took him down to the bridge.

"Look," I said, pointing down at the river. "See for yourself ..."

Our long-haired Reuters cameraman, the Rock Spider, was filming the scene. A human form bobbed down the brown river below the bridge. It sped up toward the falls and as it sank over the lip where the curtain of water becomes translucent it stretched out its arms in the sign of the cross until it crumpled into rocks and foaming white rapids. Seconds later it appeared in stiller water below the bridge. Here the body got stuck in a circling eddy, where it was caught in a logjam with other corpses. Some were fresh, some bloated, some clothed, some not, some children, some with their black skin bleached white by water, or sloughed off completely, some tied at the elbows, some of them waving up at us. After a short interval, another corpse arrived after its journey down the falls, bumping into the body I had fixed my gaze on and together they broke free of the logjam and floated on into the slower water that flowed to Lake Victoria.

The American did see. He knew what was happening in Rwanda and he also had a good idea of the scale of the killings. The Rock Spider stopped his filming, lit a huge joint, and passed it to the State Department official.

"Not for me," the official giggled nervously. "I get tested." And without looking again at the bodies in the river he walked away off the bridge.

On May 17 the UN Security Council passed resolution 918 to deploy UNAMIR reinforcements with the mandate to protect civilians. But Rwanda followed hard on the heels of Somalia and the United States and other powerful UN member states had no stomach to reenter the hornet's nest of an African war with an aggressive military mission to impose peace. Washington endorsed a limited UNAMIR mandate to save civilians, since it was now a race against time to rescue Tutsis trapped behind Hutu lines west of the capital. UNAMIR had no chance of deploying without the armor, logistical support, and airlift that only America could offer and by the time these were provided two months later the genocide slaughter was complete.

Inside Rwanda the hills were deserted and along the roads were all the abandoned huts and discarded possessions of fleeing Hutu refugees. As usual, we were going in when everybody else was trying to get out. I managed to get a vehicle from some Tutsi guerrillas who knew me, and Lizzie piled in with photographers Sebastiao Salgado and Gilles Peres of Magnum. *Snap, snap, snap* went the photographers, all in a line. Up ahead, a truckload of bloated Hutus blasted by an RPG: *snap, snap, snap.* Go on for five minutes. Heap of corpses seething with maggots, partially eaten by dogs: *snap, snap, snap.*

We found the road was controlled by RPF forces all the way to Kigali, where I was overjoyed to find Carlos and the gang—including Jonathan, Buchizya, Eric, Bald Sam, Duke, and the Rock Spider. We also found that 450 UNAMIR soldiers had stayed on in the capital. Canadians, Ghanaians, Senegalese, Uruguayans, and a few others made up our thin blue line. Each day they tried to evacuate Tutsis from Hutu territory. It was a curious story as to how the UN men, notably the Senegalese, came to be heroes. They had begun by evacuating the pretty Tutsi whores they knew at the Kigali By Night club in the days before the fighting. Then the prostitutes' families, then their friends and their families and so on. Meanwhile the two generals, the Canadian Romeo Dallaire and the Ghanaian Henry Anyidoho, both struggled in vain to prick the UN's conscience to deploy reinforcements and broker a truce at the same time. Dallaire was a spiky little artillery officer who, as commanding officer, absorbed so much tension as the months went by that by the end he had "tumor" or "heart attack" written on his face. But Anyidoho was a man of laughing, Rabelaisian bigness. He never appeared ruffled.

"De military man most be yoosed to hazards," he'd say. "But do I miss home? I'm dreaming of foo foo, my brother."

The world was ignoring events in Rwanda in May and June 1994 despite all the promises to act.

"Da big man say everything under control," a Ghanaian soldier said to me. "De small man say no, something should be done."

The Security Council was literally starving UNAMIR. They were down to two weeks' rations by mid-June. Three pints of clean water free of corpse scum, per man, per day. The correspondents had the same problem and Dallaire kindly agreed to allow us to fill our jerricans with UNAMIR's thickly chlorinated water. After the morning briefing each day I reported at the quartermaster's office and went away with a sack of rations. Each food pack featured exactly the same menu: tinned cassoulet, tinned potatoes in brine, tinned cheese, and a stick of nougat. I yearned for invitations to eat with the Ghanaian contingent soldiers, who pounded yams to make into their national dish, foo foo. We scrounged for guavas among the trees that lined Kigali's roadsides to get a supply of vitamin C and I consumed so many of those fruits that I couldn't eat them again after Rwanda.

Since the airport had been closed, injured or sick men had to be evacuated a day's journey by road to Uganda. "How am I? I'm alive," people used to tell each other by way of greeting at the UNAMIR headquarters. A Russian officer had an AK-47 bullet that had hit his car and just missed him hanging on a string around his neck. Before going out on patrol each morning he kissed the bullet as if it were an icon and tucked it back into his striped blue and white vest. The car park outside UNAMIR was full of vehicles and armored personnel carriers spattered with shrapnel marks and cannibalized for spare parts. Officers slept where they worked and I interviewed a Canadian major in his room as two Ecuadorians watched a porn video. Turned up loud above the video sound track was the local Radio Milles Collines, with a Hutu voice. Mortar-bomb impacts sent us downstairs for cover; a few minutes passed, then we drifted back to the room and the Ecuadorians rewound to where they'd left off while the voice ranted on the radio.

*   *   *

We found a place to kip at the Hotel Meridien, already occupied by UNAMIR officers and hundreds of Tutsi civilians. The utilities were all on the blink and the swimming pool had been drained by the Bangladeshi contingent for drinking water before they evacuated. It was far too dangerous to loiter outside, because the tennis courts and gardens took regular mortar-bomb hits. Among all this, I was astonished to discover that the concierge Marie Therese soldiered on with room-service food and managed to rustle up fine claret from the cellar.

UNAMIR threw a party at the Meridien one night. It started with a small ceremony, at which Dallaire pinned service medals on some of his officers. He said they deserved them a hundred times over. I guess it was the general's attempt to boost morale, since the Security Council had no intention of reinforcing them. A Senegalese put on reggae music. There were balloons for the kids, scrounged by the Russian officer with the bullet necklace. The genteel Marie Therese circulated with a tray of drinks. People furtively tapped their feet to the music. Then a Ghanaian began jiggling up and down to Bob Marley's "Small Axe." Soon we were all skanking, as the late afternoon sun shone golden down on us all, kids, Tutsis, UNAMIR officers, hacks, and the concierge Marie Therese. Nobody cried and everybody danced.

The hotel was at the top of a hill facing Hutu lines. UNAMIR had already occupied all the rooms on the safe side, facing away from the battle. The only rooms available for us were the ones facing downhill, toward the battle. One had to move about the room on hands and knees and we'd come back at night to find bullet holes, broken glass, and plaster strewn everywhere. An antiaircraft round passed through the wall above my head as I sat writing on my computer one day and a mortar bomb hit the hotel on the floor above us. We slept in our flak jackets in the bathroom because it had an extra inner wall, or in the corridor, which was already crowded. On some nights we climbed the stairs up to the penthouse restaurant to watch the light show of tracer fire and explosions across Kigali. We sat there eavesdropping on the radio traffic with its snatches of orders and panic. During one evening of battle we tuned in to the radio to hear a disembodied voice reciting the French poet Arthur Rimbaud.

Hutu snipers began using our satellite phone dishes positioned on the balconies for target practice. We felt like fish in a barrel. When the snipers hit an Argentine AP photographer on his balcony through both his legs we took him to the Médecins Sans Frontières doctors, then packed up our stuff and moved out of the Meridien. I had met up again with Lieutenant Frank and he told us we could stay at a seminary called the Christus Center, which was within walking distance of the front but protected from the line of fire by the imposing Amahoro football stadium.

The Christus was set in a garden of bananas and bird-of-paradise lilies. The buildings, laid out in two barrack-style H-blocks, stank of bat shit. A dozen or so Tutsi boys had been executed in one room, where the walls and floors and ceilings were caked with dried blood and fragments of flesh, hair, and bone. Their remains had been removed by Frank and his men and buried at the bottom of the garden. I commandeered several rooms for Reuters, reserving the best for Lizzie and me. We even had the luxury of an old mattress on the floor. Various other correspondents quickly turned up and soon we had created a grim copy of the al-Sahafi in Mogadishu. Correspondents used the chapel as a bar. We cooked on an open fire, crapped among the nearby banana trees, and washed out of buckets of brown water. At night Lizzie and I hugged each other close under the sleeping bag as missiles flew far overhead toward distant positions. After some weeks I decided to tidy our room and, raising the mattress to sweep out the dust, I saw that beneath it on the gray concrete floor was the form of a man perfectly outlined in dried blood. I tried to keep it a secret from Lizzie, scrubbing the floor with some disinfectant I had scrounged and replacing the mattress. But from then on I had a macabre impression that the blood man was sleeping between us.

UNAMIR laid on a bus to ferry the reporters around town, the kind of vehicles used by institutions to transport loonies or old-age pensioners on their day trips. It trundled along those terrifying streets so slowly it was horrible. Between the Meridien and the UNAMIR base in Kigali was a road that ran along the contour of a hill where rebel positions were dug in. Cars driving along it were in full view of government guns on the next hill. In the crazy logic of this war people seemed to know exactly when you were likely to get shot or when you were safe. At an RPF checkpoint on the way back to the hotel the soldiers used to display a big soft toy gorilla wearing a tuxedo and a bow tie. When the RPF put the gorilla in the fork of a guava tree at the checkpoint, it meant the road farther down was quiet. When the gorilla was not there it signaled that a fight was in progress. I imagined the real gorillas up there in the Virunga volcanic range, chewing on wild celery and making love in the mist, not daring to ever venture down into the plains where the humans would turn them into umbrella stands and open-handed ashtrays.

We needed a vehicle with a lot more speed than the UNAMIR charabanc. There was a car park full of abandoned vehicles at the Meridien and the only reason they hadn't been looted was that UNAMIR's Ghanaians were guarding the compound. By now I had friends among the Ghanaians and they turned a blind eye while I selected a vehicle to hot-wire. I checked out a glitzy BMW and a roomy Volvo but decided to settle on a gleaming white Mercedes diesel 4x4. Once I got it going, I smeared it with mud and used some of Carlos's black duct tape to write out the words PRESS and TV and REUTERS on the flanks and bonnet. Gas was a problem in Kigali and I became handy at busting off fuel caps and siphoning the contents from other abandoned vehicles.

Bald Sam had also commandeered his own vehicle. We planned to drive our two cars back home to Kenya when the war was over. But one day, the Mercedes ran out of diesel miles from anywhere. We were in a wood of planted gum trees and I remember the eucalyptus aroma, a cluster of burned-out huts nearby, and the roadside littered with broken Primus beer bottles, boots, and ammunition boxes. In the fields beyond the wood, ripe crops rotted on the stalk and coffee berries hung crimson on their bushes. There are people in Africa wherever one goes, even in the remotest of deserts or jungles. Africans live on the land and they are everywhere, even if spread thinly. Stop your car along the road and within minutes a group of children will appear as if they had been hiding behind a bush all the time. If there was anybody alive behind the trees in this landscape, they were keeping their distance. I felt nervous as we sat by the broken-down vehicle watching a column of safari ants. Hutu militias were known to still be roaming around out there among the villages, along with packs of fat dogs gone feral. Frank had told me that the Hutu militias, the *interahamwe*, were too disorganized to represent any guerrilla threat but they were a thorn in the RPF's side. While the war was still on RPF soldiers killed them outright wherever they were encountered. I had seen a group of twenty Hutu men near Gahini, in the east, their arms and legs tied up with banana-leaf strands— not so much corpses as colonies of squirming maggots mimicking the human form. But whenever we drove around I was fearful of an ambush and pictured a tree across the road and a gang of jeering militias.

A guerrilla vehicle finally appeared and it broke my heart to have to abandon the Mercedes right there. The good news was that the next day I simply hot-wired myself another vehicle back at the Meridien car park.

* * *

Below the Meridien was no-man's-land. I crossed the line only in a Red Cross convoy or a UNAMIR armored personnel carrier. At the bottom of the valley was the first Hutu militia checkpoint of *inter-ahamwe*. Once on the Hutu side of the line, the atmosphere was heavy. The sky was lower, darker, the air viscous. It was my imagination, of course, but everyone there was full of hate and fear and guilt about the crime that was taking place all around us. There were so many corpses in the roads and houses that the Red Cross feared a wave of epidemics. Kigali's Hutu mayor had deployed the convicts to clean up and every day big tipper trucks rumbled slowly down the roads, followed by men in pink pajamas who went around tidying up. The mayor told the Red Cross he had picked up sixty thousand corpses.

On the other side of the valley in Hutu territory was the church of Sainte Famille, which we visited whenever we could. Inside were camped a thousand Tutsis, sleeping among the pews and under the altar itself beneath a white Jesus. They lived in twenty-four-hour terror of the militias beyond the perimeter and as you walked through the church they plucked at you, pleading in quavering voices. Hutu boys peered over the compound walls hungrily, dragging their fingers across their throats. At the church gate was a checkpoint of Hutu kids with bows and arrows, guns and nailed clubs. This was a playground to them. One kid in beach shorts and shades ran about holding a big Concorde model looted out of the Air France office and he made jet-plane noises in his throat.

The Sainte Famille Tutsis were ruled over by Father Wenceslas, a Hutu priest who wore his dog collar with a camouflage flak jacket and pistol. He would have you believe he was a version of Oskar Schindler. The militias wanted to get inside the church complex to slaughter all the Tutsis. The priest claimed he kept them out, but the Tutsis said he wrote their names down on lists and handed these over to the Hutus outside. During the hours of darkness, groups of young men, those of "combatant age," would mysteriously disappear from the church and fall into the hands of the militias, who then took their prey down to the valley below the church, where they were lined up to be hacked, shot, and pushed into deep trash pits. Some nights the Hutus would hammer holes through the walls, crawl through, and drag away a few youths to play with before butchering them. Late one night we could hear all hell erupting in the valley around Sainte Famille and next day we learned that the guerrillas had rescued six hundred inmates from the church compound, but dozens had died during the operation.

There are times in a war that will always seem like the beat of silence after the last bar of a piece of music that has come to an abrupt close. The past has had its tongue cut out and it seems that, forevermore, there can be no future because of what's happening this instant.

The Red Cross hospital was in a girls' convent school. The first waves of casualties were Tutsis, some with shrapnel or gunshot wounds but mainly suffering machete cuts. I saw victims with five to ten gashes: cleaving the head and face, opening up the limbs so the white fat popped out like cushion stuffing, with bones exposed.

The hospital ran thanks to the chief Red Cross delegate Philippe, a bearded chain-smoker, who however bad the fighting got always dressed well in a tweed jacket and trousers. I saw Philippe negotiating with killers at a roadblock when trying to evacuate Tutsis from the Hutu side of the line, laughing and joking with the militias as if they were old friends. He saved hundreds, possibly thousands of Tutsis. It all got to him. Late at night during battles he was the one who used to read out Rimbaud's poems on the security radio network.

A prodigious amount of physical labor had gone into this genocide. "Can you imagine how much you have to hate somebody if you're going to chop them to bits with a machete?" commented Philippe.

Sixty thousand dead in Kigali. Numbers. Only Westerners seem so meticulous about death tolls. Ask an African peasant, "How many died?" and he replies "thousands." That can't be true in a hamlet of a few dozen, but if you see things at ground level you comprehend that for the man who has lost his family the entire world has died.

The later casualties at the hospital were from proper war, when the Tutsi guerrillas started fighting back. Now the wounded were mainly Hutus with shrapnel and gunshot wounds.

The doctors and nurses—six expatriates and a hundred locals—did not distinguish between tribes. To them these were all just wounded. They could work twenty-four hours a day and still not catch up, so they had to determine who could be saved and who was left until last because they would die anyway. For hours each day the mortar attacks drove the medical staff into the shelter, while the casualties were brought to the gate and left there screaming.

"You have five patients, but time enough to treat only some of them. Which ones do you choose?" John, an American surgeon, asked. John was the only surgeon. Well, John answered himself. Today a mortar had landed on the government hospital up the hill. Thirty dead and a hundred or so casualties were transferred to the Red Cross facility. The gas gangrene case was taken back outside to die. The disemboweled child went to the operating room. The seven-months-pregnant woman with an abdomen wound and in shock got only fluids. A woman with both feet blown to shreds was waiting for a double amputation. A boy had a leg wound heaving with maggots. This was a *good* sign. Bluebottle larvae debride and disinfect injuries by eating away putrid flesh. Thanks to this, there was a chance John could save the leg. He got a dressing.

I asked John why he was here. "Humanity, adrenaline, and

travel. This is an all-expenses-paid trip to a hospital in hell." John told me he had been in Hawaii on the beach watching the tube four days after Rwanda had exploded. He had been offered a post as general surgeon. Rwanda tempted him more. "Bye-bye normal."

John also told me he had come down with malaria, a fever raging at 102 degrees. Then they brought in a flank shrapnel wound. A left retro peritoneal laparotomy. Blood in his urine. All transfusion blood gone. Just fluids to keep up his pressure. Mobilize. Clamp aorta. No other surgeon. John had a choice. Don't operate and the patient could die. But John would be able to rest, recover in three days, and go on to operate on others. Operate now and the patient could die anyway, while the surgeon would become so exhausted he would take an entire week to recover. John slept and the left flank died.

Patients could be brought in weeks after being carried from a village on foot. They came in with gangrene, fetid pus, and live maggots in wounds. Head-wound victims with what they called their personalities all over the stretcher had a nine out of ten mortality rate. Thoracic and abdominal wounds had good survival rates only if the bowel was ruptured, not so if blood-rich organs such as the spleen, liver, and kidneys were ruptured. But there was the danger of infection. Abdominal ops, laparotomies, involved a lot of digging around and could take two to five hours. Amputations, or disarticulations, were smooth and easy: you could saw off a leg in the space of twenty minutes.

There was no spare blood. I gave my O+ and hoped for good karma. Mostly, family and friends provided blood at the bedside, threatening and complaining if the doctors said they must amputate. You had shock, you had wet lung, respiratory distress syndrome. Anesthetics were basic and in short supply, no cocktails. When you whacked a bump of ketamine into a guy he began hallucinating right there on the slab. He swatted imaginary flies, flipped out on his own out-of-body experience, believing he'd arrived in heaven and the doe-eyed virgins were feeding him grapes for eternity. No wonder he was pissed off with the doctors when he woke up to find he was still a Hutu ax murderer except that his legs had been chopped off at the knees and all his mates were scurrying for the border.

Whether the victims were innocents or combatants, children, women, or men, pity them all if they survive to remember those days, to live on in this place. Nobody will be around to heal them as they stumble, stammer, tic, and tremor through life, pursued by the chimeras and driven into the wilderness by states of fugue. They may not have suffered even a scratch on their bodies. It is enough that they possess eyes with which to see, ears to hear, nostrils to smell. A doctor lets a war injury heal slowly from the inside out. He debrides dead tissue and drains poison. Close the wound up too quickly and the filth gets trapped inside. So it is with the mind. Don't ever walk away and pretend or hope that things can be the way they were before this damage.

As John spoke the orderlies brought a woman by with severe head wounds. They put her down in the triage room and John examined her.

"I feel a slight pulse. I don't want to send her over to the morgue while there's still life."

These were words spoken in the heat of battle. I can hardly believe they were truly said, but there they are, in my notebook.

The Rwandese orderlies and nurses were fleeing. The militias turned up one day demanding to dig up a dead comrade from the mass grave out back. When they did so they got angry and claimed he had a million francs on him, which they accused the hospital of stealing. They promised to return. Mortar attack. Bomb shelter. A woman aborted a live fetus at the gate. The militias came back and agreed to settle on a full tank of gas. Enough to flee the city. A Swiss nurse was evacuated with catatonia.

A mortar bomb hit the hospital and I found myself putting away my pencil and paper to help carry stretchers. We picked up a fat guy who had his hand under his chin. He pursed his lips and his eyes were wide open and he looked like a cartoon character. He appeared to have a joke to tell that was so funny he was fit to burst. I said to myself this was no time to laugh. Then the man spat blood and took his hand away and I could see he had a ragged gash in his windpipe.

An orderly in a red tunic washed blood off empty stretchers with a broom and carbolic soap. We were carrying a casualty when a mortar bomb crashed into the tented triage room. We ditched the stretcher and ran down the slope to see shredded canvas, total chaos in the pharmacy next door. A group of kids was playing nearby. Some of them were wounded and screaming while others were huddled and quaking. There were three casualties parked waiting in the triage room and I do not know what state they were in before, but now they had been ripped to meat. Orderlies wearing masks were scraping bits of flesh off the concrete and collecting it all in wheelbarrows.

Every day, John faxed a letter full of gallows humor and trauma-ward anthropology to Lulu's, his favorite coffee shop in New Haven, Connecticut. He said the proprietors posted them on the wall. I tried to imagine his friends reading his letters during their coffee breaks.

"Give me iron brains to cope with this place!" said Philippe. Shivering, he lit another cigarette from the butt of the last.

"How can a man endure such things?" Tears ran down his exhausted, bearded face. We had walked a little way down the dirt road away from the hospital to talk and out of the way here he could cry without anybody seeing, except me. Philippe, I still see you standing there in your tweed jacket and trousers, smart clothes of a Red Cross delegate, before you had slept in them for weeks without a change. And when you left that place, and took your rest, who knew what you did here, Philippe? Who will remember?

Lizzie found a kid in the hospital, about four or five years old, who skipped and bounced between the wards laughing and playing with patients and medical staff. Nobody laughed or smiled in that hospital, except when that boy appeared. A nurse had blown up two surgical gloves like balloons and tied them to the boy's waist, so that they flapped from side to side like fingery wings on a little brown cherub. The child's mother was very sick with fever. His slightly elder brother lay next to their mum with a shrapnel injury. But that kid laughed and laughed. He ran between the stretchers and even through the open door of the operating theater, making *broom-broom* noises with the glove wings flapping. Lizzie fell in love with that child. She couldn't stop talking about him.

"What happens if his mother dies?"

When the Hutus fled Kigali and a million refugees spilled northward, Lizzie pictured the child tied to his mother's back or running alone among a crowd in the melee.

"What kind of life will he have?"

Jonathan and I decided to go on a tour of the country south of Kigali along with our friend from the BBC, Mark Doyle. One day we visited the Kabgai seminary where hundreds of Tutsis had recently been liberated. It was a disease-ridden compound, part ghetto, part concentration camp. The guerrillas had now moved on but we had Lieutenant Frank and his right-hand man Tony to help guide us and we found a farmstead of brick buildings in which to spend the night. We shared our food and tea with an old man who appeared out of nowhere and built a fire. The old man had been hiding down an ant bear hole for weeks. He said he had ventured out at night to suck dew from the grass and scrounge vegetables, but he had gone a bit mad. We hit a bottle of whiskey and Jonathan started going on about how he missed his wife and daughters. Mark had been wearing his flak jacket all day in the heat and I saw he still had it on as he looked into the fire, rocking back and forth in little, jerky motions. He announced his intention to return to London after all this was over to marry his girlfriend.

"It was not an enjoyable evening," Jonathan recalled years later. "The horror around us just made us focus on what was important in our lives."

I slept fitfully and rose early next morning so that we could get on down the road. Jonathan stumbled out of the shed where we had all bedded down, swollen-eyed and red in the face. The fire was cold and the old man from the hole had vanished. No RPF were around. There was distant mortar fire. It was very spooky. We drove down a road empty of traffic, with just the detritus of fleeing people and empty villages where we didn't dare stop. We had been traveling for an hour when Jonathan grabbed at his finger and said he had lost his wedding ring. "We have to go back." I said that was very dangerous, but he was insistent, so back we went. The farmstead was deserted by now. The area had still not been cleared of Hutu forces and I was worried about who might have heard our car engine. Jonathan kept babbling that he was going to get bad luck if he didn't find the ring. He said he was scared that if he lost it he would never see his wife and kids again. Right now, that was all he cared about. We wandered about inside the mud-floored shed but it was nowhere to be found. I walked outside and saw a glint in a tangle of long grass and bent down to pick up the ring. It seemed miraculous to our guerrilla escort, as if a supernatural hand had intervened to save Jonathan. I thought so too, but I didn't let Jonathan know that.

"I know what you'd say if this were a movie and we got into a really tight spot," I said to Jonathan. "You'd hand me your ring and say: 'If anything should happen to me, give this to my wife.'"

"Well, I bloody well wouldn't rely on you," he said. "You'd go and pawn it or something."

The highland sunshine beat down on us. I missed my home in Kenya. I wished we were in a Nairobi bar, cradling a couple of nicely chilled bottles of Tusker beer.

"Amazing thing," I imagined I'd say to Jonathan, pointing at the yellow and black label of the beer bottle with its classic logo of the elephant's head. "Did you know that the man who founded the Tusker brewery was charged and killed by an elephant in 1912—hence the name?"

"Fascinating," Jonathan would say. "Because it happens to be your round."

Farther up the road was a village called Nyamata. Half of the village was destroyed and I thought I had seen it all. But Lieutenant Frank and Tony had been insistent we come to Nyamata. We climbed the dirt track up to the church. The hill was shrouded in a gray mist of drizzle. Among the blue gums we found a little red-brick church. As we stopped and got out of the car a pack of dogs slunk off into the undergrowth. Then a couple of men appeared and Tony went after them with a stick grenade. There was a bang and a few seconds later he reappeared, adjusting his red beret. We approached the church. The sward was littered with rags, shoes, ID cards, and a couple of dozen individuals sprawled about. One didn't have to be much of a forensic scientist to see that these were the ones who either had been dragged out or had attempted to escape.

Words frequently fail me when it comes to Rwanda. It reminds me how when I was a boy, Granny showed me something my great-uncle Noel had written. It was his eyewitness account of being among the first British troops to enter Bergen-Belsen on April 12, 1945. I remember being disappointed that he had not expressively conveyed exactly what he saw that historic day of liberation. In fact, Noel retired to a pub in Wales. Like many of his generation he never spoke of what he saw in the war, though in a room above the bar he kept the boots of SS Kommandant Josef Kramer, the Beast of Belsen himself, for which he charged patrons "6 D. to view." I don't know why he made this ghoulish joke. Perhaps he needed to deflate the horror of what he'd seen. Or it was his way of telling you he was there.

I have no mementoes I'd want to display from that time. There are big gaps in my memory. I am unable to recall so much of the people, events, conversations, entire weeks of experience. Outside the many lapses, the parts I do recall are explosively vivid. I can instantly recognize years later the scenes at individual massacres when the slaughter is commemorated in books and magazines. It seems the images were branded on my retina, like photographic film. To see them again brings back smell, a time of day, a conversation, everything.

I am then reminded of my feeling that I was there like a Peeping Tom, ogling at the confusion of dead in all their humiliation. I have come to know these men and women with a unique intimacy. I won't ever forget those people at Nyamata church. Some of them were less than human. They had lost heads, limbs, and all form. But there was something very alive about the scene. They were not dead and gone. As I watched, I felt as if I were witnessing their murders before my very own eyes. I was seeing and hearing their last moments. A woman lay right in my path. She was on her back with her gingham skirt hitched up around her thighs. Not much flesh left on her skeleton. Her hair was sloughing off. Her face and position were frozen at the moment after her final rape when her attacker had shot her in the heart. There was an arm lying in the grass. It had been ripped off its owner. The skin was dried and shrunken around the bones. The hand was intact, almost perfect. The lines on the palm and the finger pads were perfectly preserved, like those of an Iron Age man found in a European peat bog. I saw all of this and the memory of it remains as if encased in amber. Yet it all happened in a split second, in the time it took me to stop and look down in the grass at that limb, before passing on.

We shouldered open the door of the church. As we entered the black ground buckled and disintegrated with a yell as thousands of flies took to the thick air. My eyes adjusted to the dark and I saw a tangle of rags and limbs and bags of guts, seething over and between pews up to the very altar on which a half-rotten skull was perched instead of a crucifix. They lay the way they had fallen when the grenades and bullets poured in through the windows, all except for what the dogs had dragged around and the games humans had played with body parts, like the altar skull. I have no idea how many were in there. I tried counting heads but gave up. I saw brownish scratch marks on the walls and realized they were the results of where the victims had clawed up the plaster. I later heard a few intended victims survived, mainly children who were protected by falling adults' bodies. Others were wounded and managed to lay still, even with their limbs chopped off. Some hid in pit latrines and in the hills. A Swiss woman who kept an orphanage near Nyamata told me the militias had initially said they would spare the girls, but "after they had killed everybody else, they had nobody left to kill, so they turned on the girls as well."

Back outside, the sun had come out after the rain shower. "Oh, dear," Jonathan was saying into his white hanky. "Oh, dear, oh dear, oh dear."

Years later, Jonathan told me, "there were no tears. I took my handkerchief out because of the overpowering smell. I was retching but did not vomit as I realized I was standing on a severed hand and the dogs were eating the remains of the people who had tried to flee the church but had been cut down outside." We sat down in the sunshine to watch clouds of butterflies, white with orange-tipped wings, flexing on the edges of mud puddles around the corpses.

What had happened was recent and it had taken place in

churches and schools all over Rwanda. The killing was still going on, but the fury of the genocide had occured within a fortnight or three weeks at most in the month of April. People argue over how many died: two hundred thousand, five hundred thousand, a million. I don't know and I personally don't believe it matters.

Foreigners have struggled to understand what happened in Rwanda. Rwanda was one of the great acts of inhumanity of the twentieth century, alongside the extermination of the Jews, or the Armenians, or the slaughter of soldiers in Flanders, or the mass deaths in Stalin's USSR, Mao's China, Cambodia, and a string of obscure African wars and famines that you haven't even heard about. Commentators from the West wring their hands over why "we" were not in Rwanda. They say we journalists ignored the story for months. We were there all the time. What's true is that we didn't understand at the time the full magnitude of what was happening. I was an ant walking over the rough hide of an elephant. I had no idea of the scale of what I was witnessing. And when I did become aware I discovered Rwanda was way beyond my limited talents as a correspondent. Just as my great-uncle Noel had failed to adequately describe in written words what he had observed entering Belsen, the words, pictures, and video we produced during this time failed utterly to express what we witnessed with our own eyes. We did not have the eloquence to make the world see the truth until it was too late. I am unable even now to properly put into words what I saw in Rwanda. I'm not sure that any of us who saw it ever will. More to the point, none of this is over yet for the people of Rwanda themselves.

I wonder what it meant that I enjoyed being a journalist but spent my time witnessing so much killing and suffering. I told myself that observing extremes gave me a heightened sense of morality, but it might have meant the opposite, that to go on like that proved one was some sort of borderline psychopath. I met a dwarfish European man who said he was a "white Hutu" and fighting on the side of the government. He said he was a journalist for Radio Milles Collines, which exhorted the Hutus to murder every Tutsi they could find. Unlike him, black Rwandans had no choice but to join one side or the other in this war. The conflicts I have witnessed tell me most men are no different from the Serbs, Hutus, or Somalis who became killers. Most of us are entirely capable of torching a village, executing the men, raping daughters, and beating up grandmothers. As far as the killing of Jews or Armenians or Aboriginals goes, most people barely needed the incitement of their leaders. They engaged in it with enthusiasm. Hutus, if they did not actively enjoy murdering their Tutsi neighbors, demonstrated an uncommon efficiency without the benefit of supervision. Think of the sheer physical task of killing hundreds of thousands of people within weeks, using mattocks, pangas, spades, hammers, guns, and grenades. The mark of Cain will separate out the Hutus, collectively, for generations. Were there any that were innocent? After what happened, are any of us?

Thaddee was the agency's Rwanda stringer. I had met him on earlier visits to the country and I found him to be a bourgeois, respectable man who was extremely timid in the face of danger. He happened to be a Hutu, although his wife was a Tutsi, and prior to April 1994 he had been involved in the opposition press. He had even spent time in jail for lampooning the president in his articles. In April we had lost touch with Thaddee. One day in June the sat phone rang and it was him. His voice sounded stretched to the point of hysteria. He said that the *interahamwe* militias had ordered him to man a roadblock outside his house to "search for rebels." He told me where it was and with a chill I realized I had looked down on it from the Meridien roof terrace through a nightscope and seen figures strutting about in the greenish light. On the phone Thaddee repeatedly told me that the Tutsis were coming to kill his people.

"It's true!" His voice was shrill, high-pitched. "Please believe me. It's true!"

A human rights group later claimed in a report that Thaddee had participated in the roadblock killings. Moderate Hutus were known to have carried out orders to kill with a "sullen obedience" but I knew people within the RPF who told me that Thaddee was a good man and could not have done such things. Long after the end of the war, by which time there were millions of Hutu refugees in exile, Thaddee wrote me a letter from Ujiji, the remote Lake Tanganyika village where Stanley had first encountered Livingstone. He told me that he had fled Kigali with his family including his Tutsi wife across the frontier into Zaire days before RPF forces cut off the exit route. In exile he had lived by smuggling cigarettes, kerosene, and soap across the lake from Tanzania to the refugee camps inside Zaire. Thaddee pleaded with me to visit his house in Kigali, where he wanted to have his family photo album retrieved. He also told me that the computer he had used to file his reports to Reuters was buried in the garden. He enclosed a map marking the spot where I would find it with an X, like a treasure chart.

When I visited the house, I discovered that a family of Tutsis had moved in. They told me they had no idea who had lived there before them, but they were certain that the owner had been a Hutu killer. They became suspicious and quite angry when I asked for Thaddee's photo album and said that everything had been thrown away. They asked me to leave and refused to let me search for the Reuters computer buried in the garden. I knocked at the house next door and asked the man who answered if he had known Thaddee. He told me a story about how he was Tutsi and during the fighting Thaddee had sheltered him and his family. The man had no idea what Thaddee did when he went out during the daylight hours, but whatever it was that he did he continued to protect his Tutsi neighbors until one night they were able to escape across the battle lines. If Thaddee had been a killer, each morning he would have said good-bye to his Tutsi wife and children and friends, walked to his roadblock, taken hold of a club, and bludgeoned out the brains of other Tutsis the militias had ordered him to murder. Had he refused to kill, I assumed the militias would have murdered him. I cannot bring myself to believe that Thaddee was a killer. But his story has given me a great deal to think about. When faced with a choice of doing evil or being killed defending a principle, I wonder what I would do.

Thaddee has vanished. For several years I tried tracing him in the refugee camps of eastern Zaire, known later as the Congo, through the International Red Cross. I never heard a single word back. He may have perished in the cholera epidemics that hit the refugee camps after he'd fled into exile. Or he may have been killed. In the Tutsi reprisals against the Hutus in 1997—another war, another massacre in the endless Central African cycle—so many civilians were butchered that the roads exiting the camps were laid with a solid ballast of bones, rags, spectacles, teeth, shoes so that it all crunched beneath the tires of visiting UN vehicles. No action taken. Another footnote in history. For all I know, Thaddee is still alive, a half-starved, crazy desperado fighting in the jungles of Kivu in the Congo. But I hope that instead he's living happily in exile with his family, smuggling soap, kerosene, and gold dust across Lake Tanganyika with its clean blue water and its iridescent fishes.

Jonathan told me to take five days off in June. "Go to the beach," he said. I did exactly that, except that I took Lizzie and drove to the western shore of Lake Victoria to where the Kagera River comes out at the end of its journey from the heart of Rwanda. Lizzie and I were almost happy together again on the story, and had we been able to stay within the envelope of violence, fear, and dependency we'd have ridden off into the polluted sunset and lived happily ever after.

Sales of fish had been banned that week due to fears that the carnivorous Nile perch, which grow as big as a man and swim in the lake's turbid waters, were feeding on the twenty thousand bodies that had washed down the Kagera. A lakeshore rumor said that a human hand had been cut out of a fish's belly. Lizzie and I slept in the car on a beach of black sand scattered with snail shells and next morning we put on rubber gloves and masks and joined a team of young Catholic mission volunteers in dugout canoes. Soon we were out punting along the papyrus-lined shore, looking for corpses for Lizzie to photograph. They were bleached white and snared among the reeds. It became quite a game, spotting bodies. The young Catholics would come up alongside and with their billhooks gaff the corpses, which, when punctured, bubbled and sighed in the water. Along the beaches I observed abstract forms. We ran the canoe aground and I walked a little way until I fell to my knees because of what I saw. A beautiful, shapely woman was facedown and half embedded in the sand. The undulations of her ribs connected to the bumps of her spine blended into the mackerel patterns made by wind and water on the dune. I looked along the beach and realized that the abstract forms were dozens of sea-changed humans.

I boarded the boat again. Some way off, I came along a leg standing upended, the foot sole bobbing flat with the surface of the lake. I grabbed it and pulled. To my surprise, it separated from the thigh with a violent sucking noise. I fell backward into the well of the canoe, the leg in my arms. On my face I felt a spattering of bleached skin and flesh. Whenever our canoes were filled up with corpses, we returned to shore, where they were lifted onto the beach, dusted with quicklime, bagged in polythene, and slung onto the back of a construction truck. This was backed to the edge of a big hole, the hydraulic tipper was raised, and the bags slipped down into the pit. Lizzie's shutter release followed all this, exposing hundreds of frames.

A mission boy standing with me surveying the scene turned to me: "How can we live here now?"

I can't put my finger on exactly how death smells. The stench of human putrefaction is different from that of all other animals. It moves us as instinctively as the cry of a newly born baby. It lies at one extreme end of the olfactory register. Blood from the injured and the dying smells coppery. After a cadaver's a day old, you smell it before you see it. From the odor alone, I could tell how long a body had been dead and even, depending on whether brains or bowels had been opened up, where it had been hacked or shot. A body would quickly balloon up in the tropical heat, eyes and tongue swelling, flesh straining against clothes until the skin bursts and fluids spill from lesions. Flies would get in there and within three days the corpse might stink. It became a yellow mass of pupae cascading out of all orifices and the flesh literally undulated beneath the clothes. The tough bits of skin on the palms of their hands and the soles of their feet were the parts of the body that always rotted away last. As living people, these had been peasants who had walked without shoes and worked hard in the fields. A man who has been dead seven days reeks of boiling beans, guava fruit, glue, blown handkerchiefs, cloves, and vinegar. After that he starts to dry out into a skeleton until he's almost inoffensive and your reaction is "I wonder if that's an arm or a leg?"

The dead accompanied me long after Rwanda. It was months before I could order a plate of red meat served up in a restaurant. I smelled putrefaction in my mouth, or in my dirty socks, or as sweat on my body. I imagined what people I met would look like when dead. To this day I am unable to shake the image of that beautiful woman on the beach of Lake Victoria.

I escaped Rwanda's maelstrom for a short respite to discover that my pigeonhole in the Reuters Nairobi Bunker was stuffed with memos. In accounts, my expenses were turned down since I had no receipts. I had bribed Hutu militias at the roadblocks. I had spent my cash on things like those goats I'd bought off the priest on the walk to Kigali. For once, I was not scamming from the company.

The agency was on one of its drives for corporate efficiency. I looked at my memos. One proposed I work to raise the company profile.

"We suggest staff correspondents fix lunch appointments with local businessmen to persuade them to buy the Reuters service."

I had been lectured often that company strategy was to make all global news regions self-contained. The Reuters accountants wanted a region's reporting budgets to reflect roughly its revenue from the local sale of news services. In other words, Europe, which had healthy revenues, controlled a huge budget to cover the Balkans. Eastern Africa was the world's poorest region and therefore a financial black hole in Reuters terms. Except that we had seen a sequence of what should have been huge stories, like Rwanda.

In a repeat of Somalia, covering Rwanda blew bureau budgets. Jonathan went back to fighting for funds for the charter flights, cash advances, vehicles, TV feeds, and extra staff to beef up the reporting teams. We had two sat phones and we were in a collapsed nation. Reuters in South Africa, which had a better cell phone network than that of the United States, had six—and they wouldn't give us any. Rwanda was a nightmare for those managers who looked only to the bottom line. Before the outbreak of the conflict Rwanda was a country of no importance whatsoever, even in African terms: tiny exports of coffee and tea and a small industry offering trips for rich tourists to see the gorillas in the Virunga mountains. It did not even have a huge debt problem. World markets, and therefore the majority of our clients' interests, were totally unaffected by genocide in Central Africa. For this reason Robin, our Nairobi manager, told me that senior staff wanted our Rwanda coverage to be wound down. It was making the company no money. I became dizzy when he said that. At least he was honest and felt bad about it.

After all the bitterness that Rwanda had bred in us, the loss of faith in humans, I needed to feel there was some institution that was on the side of justice. I wish it could have been Britain, the nation I had grown up to admire as the voice of the World Service, the civilizing empire my mother had told me about. But those symbols were dead and gone. In the modern age I wanted it to be Reuters, the global news agency of record, accuracy, and reliability. As in Somalia I was sorely disappointed. To find that Reuters, my only remaining flag to which I could show loyalty, saw Rwanda as *too expensive* to cover filled me with despair. Reporters were made to feel that we had embarked on some profligate spending spree. It was as if we had been on some vacation out there and needed bringing into line with the company ethos.

Robin announced that we were to attend a compulsory "team-building" weekend. Puzzled, we drove up to a posh tourist hotel on the western slopes of Mount Kenya. During the days, we assembled in a conference room. A suit-wearing management consultant trained in the Myers-Briggs technique lectured us with the aid of a blackboard and an overhead projector on which various charts and bullet points were listed.

Our teacher asked us to assess one another in terms of our "probable team role repertoire." Buchizya and I, for example, were deemed to be "resourceful investigators," whereas Jonathan was a "go-go individual." All three of us were said to "lack sustained concentration or interest in routines." Our teacher advised us to "manage such behavior patterns." We were amused. "What would improve your effectiveness?" the teacher asked me. "More pay," Buchizya chipped in. "More holidays," I added.

In our absence, things had fallen apart at the Ski Chalet. We hadn't been taking any notice of the dogs and our bitch Cassandra produced a litter of puppies without us being aware she had even been pregnant. Lizzie carried them around in her arms cooing. We neglected to have them vaccinated and one day I came back from Reuters to find Celestine looking very grave. Lizzie was sitting on the lawn, weeping. In her lap were several tiny fur balls, all of them dead from tick fever.

We were starting to have full-scale shouting matches. I snarled and yelled. Lizzie ran out cackling or in a torrent of tears, gathering up her things to vanish in the red car. She would not return until after dark and come in and go to bed. If Lizzie needed her solitude, I felt starved of intimacy. I hated being apart from her, but after a few days of tormenting each other the relief of a looming assignment was the only thing that heralded a truce in the war between us.

There will be time to sleep when we die. All I wanted to do was sleep. But for now, sleep was a hard thing to do. We lay in bed, listening to the dogs of the Ongata Rongai slum in the valley below. Waves of barking rolled from the nearest shanties to the far distance and back, hour after hour. Lizzie and I lay side by side and the churning of our brains was almost audible. We lay there in the darkness, like two radios with their dials being flipped through all the frequencies on shortwave.

Our quarrels got continually worse. Our chemistry together took on a beastly, murderous, sexual intensity. I drank, yelled, and grimaced gargoylelike. She spat in my face. "You're the worst thing that ever happened to me!" she screamed.

In our calmer moments, I tried talking.

"Perhaps we get on badly because of what we've been seeing. You know, the job could be making us a bit crazy." Lizzie gave me an icy look.

"What are you saying, that we should go and see shrinks? Why don't you go, since you need one and let me tell you, it's not because of Rwanda."

"You don't think you need to go?"

"No, I'm fine. I'm not crazy just because I've seen a pile of corpses, let me tell you."

We made our friends uncomfortable. I noticed that they were staying away from us. Our strongest bond now was the obsessive jealousy betrayal nurtures. Our respect for each other was that of enemies. Our hit-and-run attacks, our pain and hatred, taught us the exact contours of each other far more intimately than love. This made me ache with sadness, doubly so because I knew she felt the same way.

An evening I will always remember, when we sat alone together on the balcony of the Ski Chalet, watching the clouds drag blue curtains of rain across the plains. A breeze carried faint snatches of Sunday life from the town a mile away: an evangelical preacher's apocalyptic sermon delivered through a bullhorn, the beat of drums from his choir. Then the rain came like a crowd's applause, audible for a full minute before it arrived, splashing down in big warm drops that smelled of the steppe. The shingle roof roared until sunset, and darkness fell suddenly. In the aftermath, flying termites hatched from their mounds by the rain fluttered through the open windows of the lighted house. They spiraled into the bath where we sat at opposite ends, our legs entangled. The water was decorated with their filigree wings. Lizzie began crying, softly at first, then with tormented sobs.

Outside, the notes of a picking guitar cascaded from the nightwatchmen's radio. There was that other host of night noises, each one striking a different bittersweet note: the lonely cry of the nightjar, the honk and shriek of hyraxes, and the symphony of crickets.

"I just want to fuck all pussy," Bald Sam told me on the aircraft returning to Kigali. "Fat pussy, old pussy, young pussy. I don't care. I walk along the street and I want to fuck every single fucking pussy I see. Fuckfuckfuck*fuck*!"

There was no pussy to be had in Kigali. Not even for Sam. Piles of broken glass and rubbish still littered the airport and bored soldiers sat on the carousels, going round and around. Standing in the foyer with a bullet hole in its heart was the giant statue of a gorilla. The Tutsis had got it together to post immigration officers in cubicles to check our passports. Peace equals bureaucracy.

We were just in time to catch the flood of celebrities, world leaders, and aid workers. They came in to gawp at the bodies, by now desiccated like mummies, and shake their heads in front of the cameras. The strangest visitor I saw among them was the Reverend Al Sharpton, a large black New Yorker who appeared at Kigali airport in shoulder-length wet-look hair and combat fatigues, accompanied by two bodyguards of similar size and attire.

The genocide and the war were over. At this point the United Nations finally deployed reinforcements for Dallaire and his thin blue line of 450 brave men. A field hospital unit from the British Paratrooper regiment arrived to tend the sick and wounded through the southwest of the country. Their HQ was at the Amahoro football stadium in Kigali. I remember how the squaddies communicated with the Rwandese workers under them in a sort of pidgin Cockney. They got up to all sorts of mischief that for some of us at least introduced a rare tone of humor into life in Rwanda. When a European high official and his wife flew in to view the devastation, a greeting party of Rwandan road sweepers was lined up with their brooms and wheelbarrows to meet them. The squaddies had been coaching them on the greeting ceremony for days. As the high official and his lady moved off, the sweepers pointed at the man's wife and solemnly chanted, "Cor, just look at the arse on that!"

It was impossible for latecomers to comprehend the evil committed here but the British military top brass were still so scared of what their soldiers might see and what it would do to their minds that they sent a psychiatrist to accompany the forces to Rwanda. Bald Sam and I were amazed at that. We laughed about it. A shrink! It seemed extravagant. But the truth is we stuck close to that man for days. We said it was all for a story, but really it was about us. The psychiatrist, whose name was Ian, told us his special area of interest was the minds of war correspondents. I could see Bald Sam squirming with happiness at all the attention and I felt quite flattered myself.

I had heard about a mental asylum on the outskirts of Kigali. Ian agreed to come along with us on a visit. When we got there we found that the inmates had been fending for themselves. The lunatics had indeed taken over the asylum. We learned they were made up of both Hutus and Tutsis. Some were genocide survivors. One was a woman who had been gang-raped by the militias and who then had been dumped off by her husband when she got too mad to handle. We got out of the car to see a man goose-step into the courtyard, giving Nazi salutes. A woman in rags came out to meet us and offered to show us around. She warned us not to stray out off the paths. Land mines had been sown around the hospital compound but apparently the inmates kept wandering off into the jungle only to get their limbs blown off. Our guide took us first to meet a man who sat jingling his manacles and drawing dozens of round faces against the cell walls using his own shit. They were like smiley faces, only they had no mouths, just eyes. The women took us next to a locked hut from which came noises of snuffling, chuckles, and yelps. The hut shuddered because the thing inside was throwing itself against the mud and timber walls. As we passed by an open palm appeared under the hut door and flicked out a fresh turd. We walked until we came to another hut. Our guide said it was her own cell. As she opened the door she curtsied and smiled sweetly. "Here," she said. "I am ready. This is the place where you can kill me."

I walked back to the car. We were all pretty much silent on the way back to the British base. Later, Ian and the paratroopers returned to the asylum, cleared the mines, got the place running, supplied it with drugs. It was the practical, good thing to do. For me, it was one of the stories that never got written. I just couldn't. I never went back but it's an encounter I still feel badly about. I never suffered like that female inmate, but for years I did endure some sort of payback. I have to try every day to prevent the poison that sits in my mind to spread outward and hurt the people I love. Sometimes I can't stop it and I wonder if in some way the corruption will be passed on from me to my children.

When Kigali fell to the Tutsi RPF, a million or more Hutus fled across the frontier into Zaire. Lizzie and I crossed the frontier into Zaire from Burundi farther south, at a cluster of huts in the centre of a papyrus swamp. Zaire had fallen apart years and years before. In the first of several huts at the border post an official stared at our visas, shook his head, and demanded ten dollars. I handed it over. In the next office a man huffed and puffed at our vaccination cards and demanded another ten. In the third hut we found a fellow in a red beret with his feet up on the desk, reading a book entitled *A Concise Dictionary of Misdemeanours.* He demanded a Zairean document we had never even heard about.

"Oh monsieur, monsieur. Do you think we would just let you break the laws of Zaire?"

I handed over yet another ten dollars and thundered that we had been robbed. The man in the red beret looked at me with an amused expression.

"What did you expect? You come to Zaire with your pockets full. You will leave with them empty."

We arrived at the main crossing point for refugees in Goma and realized in that place what the end of the world might look like. The first we saw of the camps was a cloud of brown mist hanging over the land. A multitude of refugees was huddled across a plain. They built shelters of green grass and leaves and bits of blue sheet plastic the UN had handed out. They set about chopping down the trees, eating away like ants at the rain forest carpeting the sides of the volcanoes. The green wood fires cast a pall of acid yellow mist that clung to the earth. Then, unbelievably, the volcano itself started belching gas and smoke. The acrid fog raked at throats and made eyes and nostrils stream. People wore masks or tied rags about their faces. Some of us, the lucky ones, had plastic goggles to protect our eyes. The noonday sun was a sick brown orb. The smoke so darkened the sky that it was impossible to know what time of day it was except by looking at a clock. One sensed night was falling when the poisonous blanket got even thicker and visibility was reduced to a few yards.

It rained and hordes of cracked feet churned the ground into a quagmire. "It's Woodstock without the music," said a nurse I talked to. Only a handful of foreigners were there to help at the start but they quickly crowded in. Every humanitarian disaster is a golden fund-raising opportunity for the charities. One Christian outfit worked all day praying, rather than distributing food, shelter, or IV fluids. "Yea though I walk through the valley of the shadow of death ..." Africa may be the world's poorest place but it is rich in men of God. It's unfortunate that the Africans no longer boil them up in pots and serve them for dinner.

In the smog life loomed in and out of focus. Memory of those weeks are fuzzy, or are recalled as if they had happened to somebody else. Hence, I'm unsure if we ran over a man with our car, or somebody else did, or if it is another fantasy. I recall speeding too fast through a camp with a local driver at the wheel. A dark, tottering figure stumbles into our path. *Bang!* We hit him. In a split second I see rolling eyeballs, an open mouth, then he's sucked under the right front wheel. The car rises up as we lurch over him. We are all wide-eyed with horror. "What the fuck was that?" We don't want to know. Somebody says we should go back, but he does so only weakly. Nobody wants to get torn apart by a crowd of Hutus. So the driver keeps his foot to the floor. The horde in front of us parts like magic.

They did rip living things to pieces. I had seen them do it. Food could not be delivered to the refugees by the aid agencies fast enough. Truckloads of maize reached the camps but the Hutus needed meat. Wildlife abounded in the forest and bush. The host of refugees, the tents and noise and stench, must have confused the animals. One morning I saw a doe antelope that had strayed into the camp between the tents at dawn. A gleeful shout went up as the refugees began pelting her, leaping now, with sticks and stones. It was such an agile creature with reddish, dew-dappled flanks and it jumped gracefully about, but the crowd formed a closing circle, beating and hacking at her until she collapsed. Too many hands struggled for a portion of the meat and she was torn limb from limb.

The quantities of maize eaten had to come out somewhere and so the plain was swiftly caked in fresh shit. The agencies were working to dig pit latrines but when it rained, rivers of ordure flowed down gullies to the ponds and lakes where the refugees scooped out their water with plastic jerricans. I remember going down to a pond and seeing a line of women drawing water from the shallows. A little farther out a corpse floated head down, bloated. The warnings were there. There was nothing they could do when the cholera epidemic hit.

I remember a cholera treatment tent on a black volcanic plain they called Munigi. Relatives brought victims in on their backs, on stretchers, or in wheelbarrows. Nurses scurried about, jabbing drip needles into the arms of the sunken-eyed sick. I saw one pull the tubing out of a man who had expired and stick it directly into another prone figure who was still alive. I saw a man rip the top off a bag of Hartmann's intravenous fluid and simply drink it, only to throw up milky fluids seconds later. He stood up briefly, defecated in his trousers, and collapsed, his eyes rolling back into his skull.

On the six-mile drive to Munigi that morning, I had seen little clusters of bodies, five-strong or so each, by the roadside. On the way back that evening the groups were much bigger. I stopped to count eight hundred in one line. The statistics were numbing. In a single day a million refugees shat ten tons in weight and drank five million liters of water. In every twenty-four hours some forty thousand liters of IV fluids were dripped into the arms of fifty thousand cholera victims and every day three thousand of them expired. How the hell do I put a snappy lead on that, I asked myself.

It was biblical, all right. A huge King James version. Nothing in modern life prepared you for this. You had to think in bigger adjectives: earthquakes, rains of fire and brimstone, deluges, locusts. And all of us who had witnessed the sin of the genocide saw the Hutus' plague as the Old Testament God's retribution.

I heard, for example, that dozens of Hutu soldiers and militias were sick at a military camp near a traffic roundabout in Goma town. The Red Cross had moved in to take care of them. I went down there with Sam and Lizzie and we moved between the men sprawled on the open ground. I did it anyway, but I knew it was not for me to gloat over them. Perhaps had I been a Tutsi it would have been justifiable, like the Jews I have heard exult over the rape of German women by the invading Russians.

The French Foreign Legion had set up camp next to the runway on the edge of Goma, with a field hospital and a storage site for supplies being flown in. The hacks set up their tents near the French military press-briefing areas and the flyaway, a satellite dish for transmitting pictures. I woke up once and poked my head out of our tent. A man was lying dead a few yards away. In the middle distance, the multitudes were still visible before the smog of the morning fires had descended. Off to one side stood an attractive reporter with one of the networks. She was dressed in an office power suit and a perfect blond hairdo. At that moment she was checking her lipstick, ready to do her piece on camera.

Sleeping in the refugee camp, in an igloo tent with Lizzie, we jumped clean out of our bags when a scream went up in the dead of night. The ululating went from one end of the vast camp to the other, an infectious wave of panic. Smoky flames leapt up from thousands of green fires. We were camped with the Red Cross workers behind a fence of barbed wire, with all the food and medical supplies. Either the camp was coming under attack from outsiders or if it wasn't that, then we decided the refugee inmates themselves were about to overwhelm our compound to kill us or loot the relief supplies. We weighed our prospects of making a run for it in one of the aid trucks. A Red Cross staffer got a bullhorn and began yelling for people to calm down. We knew if the Hutus wanted us dead, we would not make it more than a few feet from the barbed- wire perimeter. The panic washed back and forth in waves for an hour, then subsided. Next day we heard all manner of stories. The *interahamwe* had dragged their own civilians off to be executed. The Tutsis had attacked. A lion had strayed into the camp, so the story went, and became so confused by the smell that it tore around in circles, terrified by the stench of humans.

In July, Washington finally deployed a U.S. Army squad to eastern Zaire. This was the result of the debate that had gone on since April about whether or not to intervene to prevent the massacre of Tutsis. They were now coming in to save the perpetrators of the genocide—and when they landed in their aircraft it appeared that everybody around Goma was already dead or dying. And so instead of protecting civilians from slaughter, or intervening to stop a war that was already over, they joined the French legionnaires in digging mass graves. I recall that the Americans in Goma called the bodies they picked up "cigars." This was because the Hutus wrapped up their dead in the same raffia mats they had slept on. Then they stacked them like billets of wood along the tracks for collection. Each day trucks made rounds of the camps to pick up those who had died overnight. They were dying faster than they could be buried, in pits the size of swimming pools. The volcanic ground was so hard the French were using dynamite to blast holes in the earth. But it was slow work. Meanwhile, the soldiers bulldozed the bodies into pyramids and banks. Once I saw a woman's corpse with a baby emerging from between her legs. I thought that was the worst thing I had ever seen and that it couldn't get any worse.

I was standing next to one of the pits one day taking notes. African volunteer orderlies in face masks, with plastic gloves or socks on their hands, tossed the cadavers out of the trucks and into the hole. French Foreign Legionnaires were directing the burial. At first the orderlies lined up the dead neatly. As the layers increased they began dumping them any old how. There was a smacking noise as bodies landed on top of one another, pulling free of their raffia shrouds. A French legionnaire scattered quicklime over the pile of bodies, which would burn up and dissolve them swiftly. The white powder coated the heap and gave the appearance of a carved relief on a marble monument of many Africans, almost serene with their eyes closed and tangled up in a heap of clothes, feet, hands, and heads.

I was gazing at this and waiting for the bulldozer to move in and cover them with dark volcanic earth when the legionnaire cried out for it to halt. His eyes were wide behind his mask and he pointed into the pit.

"I can't believe this," he exclaimed in a strangled voice. "This is beyond my imagination!"

I looked.

And though it is difficult for me now to write this, I have to tell you. I saw movement. An arm, a raised small hand.

The legionnaire and I leaped into the pit together. We clambered among the dead. I sunk among bodies, stepped on gassy, hollow bellies, slipped on limbs, found purchase on a head, reached down, and pulled free the raised hand. It was a little boy. The legionnaire was crying as he cradled him in his arms and then we stumbled back up the side of the mass grave.

By the side of the pit we washed his face with water from the legionnaire's canteen. Naked and wrinkled with dehydration, the boy's eyes rolled open. I tried to make him drink some water, but he was foaming at the mouth and could not hold it down. He was conscious, just, and began to cry softly. Then he spoke.

One of the gravediggers leaned in, straining to hear what he said. Forgive me for this, but I took out my notebook and demanded he translate as I took notes. For what it's worth, this was his story.

I asked what his name was. What I heard, what is still today in my notebook, was the name Dibadirigwa. He said he had lost his mother and had wandered alone for days, becoming hungry and sick. The day before, he had finally found his mother, lying dead. How could he have found his mother out there? Was it just the body of what he believed was his mother? He lay down next to her and slept.

When the truck came soon after that, the gravediggers in their masks assumed him to be dead. He was too weak to cry out as they picked him up and threw him in the back with the rest of the bodies. By the time the truck was filled it was already dusk, so the soldiers parked it and went away. Dibadirigwa lay there all night, I imagine with the weight of the dead pressing down on top of him. The burial teams returned next morning and drove to the pit, where we saw him a few seconds before he got buried alive.

The soldier wrapped him in a plastic bag and laid him down between ammunition boxes in the back of a jeep. On the way to the French military clinic at the airport, the revulsion gave way to a sense of euphoria. The legionnaire floored the accelerator and we whisked past bodies stacked like firewood. We had saved the boy. A little beam of light shone into the darkness. When we arrived, the legionnaire carried the limp boy to the arms of a female French nurse. I pursued her into the tented wards and watched as she put him on a bed and rigged him up to a drip. "He's going to be all right?" She nodded curtly and I left. I went back and told the soldier. We shook hands and as we parted we both had a spring in our steps.

I went away and filed my story. As I predicted, the agency went mad for it. This little Lazarus made human the suffering of faceless hordes. We were redeemed. Next day, a herogram from the

desk said Lazarus had scored big time on the touchstone impacts.
The papers were clamoring for more.

I revisited the tented clinic, with candy in my pocket for
Dibadirigwa. I walked from tent to tent, between the beds. A
group of children was in there, wide eyed, silent. "Do you know a
boy, he was here yesterday, Dibadirigwa, from Kusingi?" I relayed
the question through a French-speaking Hutu. They shook their
heads. I found the French nurse I had seen the day before when we
had handed the boy over. No, no, he passed away in the night.
From the second he was carried in, it was obvious that he was a
terminal case.

"Didn't he say anything?"

"He said nothing. We tried, but nothing ..."

"What was wrong with him—cholera?"

The nurse shrugged.

"In such cases ... No, I think he decided to not live."

I thought we had saved the child Dibadirigwa. In truth, we
had cruelly disturbed him from his purpose. Had we left him to the
bulldozer's teeth, within seconds he would have been buried in the
pit in his mother's arms. We had separated him from her—body
alive, spirit so horrified he could not bear to live—only long enough
for him to deliver his valediction, to appear in morning papers
around the world next day.

At the daily press briefing, a Foreign Legion colonel declared
that the boy—nobody else had heard his name, Dibadirigwa—had
been revived by antibiotics and IV fluids. I didn't bother to argue
with the colonel. The journalists went off to the hospital where
they were shown lots of kids. Any child would have done. They
filed their stories, saying that the boy was recuperating. I sent mine,
saying that he had died. Not a single paper used my copy. I can't say
I blame them.

* * *

I returned to Rwanda, where victory brought no joy to the guerrillas. With the cessation of hostilities, my Tutsi friends had time on their hands to nurture resentment against the outside world for not intervening to prevent the killings. As a foreigner, I felt a new coldness from them that never again lifted. It was odd to pass the landmarks such as the Sainte Famille, which had returned to being a church rather than a prison camp. Out in the countryside, tracts of land lay abandoned by farmers now dead or in exile. Crops rotted in the fields and a curious odor of yeast and decay hung over the countryside.

We found the prisons bursting with Hutus. The wardens allowed us in without an appointment. They simply locked the gates behind us and there we were, face-to-face with men who had manned the roadblocks and hacked up women and children, now dressed in prison-issue pink pajamas. Inside, I observed a poker game in progress and the Catholic sacrament being given outside the toilets. Genocide had had dedicated followers—I came across an inmate of seven and a paraplegic who had been confined to a wheelchair for twenty years.

Tutsi policy was to incarcerate all Hutu males until they might prove their innocence. In one prison, conditions were those of a killing bottle, such as one uses to asphyxiate bugs with formaldehyde. Men stood four to a yard in the open as the sun beat down on their heads and they pissed and shat where they stood.

After doing the prisons, Lizzie left without me. We hardly talked all the time we had stayed at the Hotel Milles Collines, now vacated by the crowds of Tutsi civilians who had sheltered there under UNAMIR protection during the battle for Kigali. But I planned a surprise for when we next saw each other. I had brought with me a picture of the little boy she had fallen for at the Red Cross hospital. She had often talked about him and said she wanted to adopt him, assuming that his mother had died from the injuries we'd seen her suffering from at the Red Cross hospital.

I showed the photo around at the hospitals and orphanages in the city. Philippe at the Red Cross shook his head. "You want to find *this* child, and you do not have his name, but he was at the hospital in June, before the city fell? Come, come," he said. "It is impossible to find this child, even if you knew his name."

Philippe was right. Millions of people had been on the move. The kid was from a tribe that had lost the war. If he had survived the fighting in Kigali, if his family had escaped the city when it fell to the guerrilla forces, if they had made it all the way to the frontier, if cholera or starvation had not killed him yet, then he would now be huddled in the smog on that volcanic plain among the nameless hordes of refugees.

Philippe continued: "Then, I must ask *why* you are looking for this child?" Of course, he was right again. His mother might still be alive. If she was not, then there was still the rest of his family. I had to question what I was up to.

The boy was lost. So I went home again empty-handed. I often wonder what would have happened if I had picked him up and taken him back to the Ski Chalet. Or if Dibadirigwa had survived and we had taken him instead. They certainly needed the help of somebody, anybody. And not just them. What about all the others I had seen over the years?

I used to scoff at those journalists who got personally involved in the crises they covered by thinking they could somehow help out. Often, their good intentions amounted to nothing more than interference. Yet these days, I can't shake off the sense that I could have done more. Down the years, I had met dozens, hundreds, thousands of individuals I could have helped, by dropping the notebook that was my shield. I had countless opportunities but I rarely lifted a finger to genuinely help out a single person. I could have adopted one child from an orphanage, or brought one out of

the line of fire, or paid for a school education, or even saved my
father's friend Brian Bowden from a squalid murder in Mogadishu,
or the wounded Ethiopian soldier who had pleaded for my help, or
Graham, the English mercenary being tortured by the Serbs. The
truth is I did not do any of this. And what do I have to show for
those years? Only the stories.

Flights out of Rwanda always had malfunctions and bad luck
attached to them. Fate had to pose some sort of ordeal to dash one's
hopes of ever making it home in one piece. "Deliver us from evil," I
whispered as the aircraft gained altitude. We flew in clean, blue
skies. I looked down at green hills and brown rivers. If I prayed for
self-preservation, and were to believe in heaven and hell and an
afterlife, how was it that our wings did not hit the thick, ectoplas-
mic turbulence of a million souls rushing about and sucking us
earthward? "There are no devils left in hell," wrote an American
correspondent that summer. "They're all in Rwanda." But I never
once found a shred of evidence that we had witnessed anything
more spiritual than the operations of a vast abattoir. The appari-
tions eluded me until, down through the years, I have come at last
to understand what it is to be haunted.

Peter Davey's groom and horse, Beihan

One Moment, of the Well of Life to Taste

My father was in Aden when the news of his friend's death was radioed through. Seager called him into his office and on the spot he was given vague orders that were never put on paper, to lead a mission to retrieve Peter's body and next, to punish the followers of Awas. He boarded an RAF transport that flew him up to Dhala with two platoons of government guards, a sapper of the Royal Engineers, Lieutenant Beale, and several crates of explosives. In Dhala they loaded up six camels and donkeys, then set off west as Davey had done a few days before. Some of the guards rode on camels with a machine gun across their knees. The tough Bedu guards, armed with old short-muzzle Enfield rifles, jogged on foot. As they entered Ahmedi country, my father put out a line of scouts. They scampered ahead and up the stony hillsides like ibex. They camped for two nights on the way, observing the few local inhabitants, who moved off quietly from the corn and qat fields when they saw the party advancing down the valleys. Eventually they arrived at Sheikh Mohamed Awas's fort at al-Hussein. The settlement was deserted. Government Guards now occupied the building.

After the shoot-out, the body of Awas had been removed across the frontier to Yemen. His slave man-at-arms had been left to rot where he lay for days in the hot sun. The scene of the fight could be determined exactly from where piles of white vulture droppings and feathers were scattered in a circle. The slave's skeleton had been picked until the white ribs showed and bits of it had been dragged off into the bushes by hyenas or jackals.

In his papers, my father had remembered many years later his reaction to the scene: "I felt great sorrow and respect for this brave servant who came down to shoot Peter, knowing full well that he would be killed. How tragic, how foolish and how wasteful the whole business was."

The force was equipped with a radio. They used this to call the Royal Air Force when the fort was completely vacated. At an agreed-upon time, a flight of three Mosquito fighter-bombers swooped overhead. Unlike Haidara's fort on Jihaf, the target here was at the bottom of a steep-sided gorge and therefore much more difficult to strike. The explosives echoed in roars from one side of the valley to the next, but no hits were scored.

The Royal Engineers Lieutenant, Beale, then set to work. He was a perfectionist. The fort was a large stone construction of about three floors in height. The lower ground floor had been used in the traditional manner for stabling and for storage of grain and forage. The upper floors were for cooking, living, and sleeping. Lieutenant Beale laid heavy explosive charges in each corner of the ground floor, set his detonators, and wired them up. He then placed another massive charge in the center of the ground-floor area. The area was cleared and everybody took cover behind rocks.

Shortly after midday on April 21, an enormous detonation heralded the destruction of the fort. Dad was far away watching the spectacular demolition. The first explosion caused the walls to cave in. Then, as the whole fort collapsed inward, there followed a mighty eruption from the center charge. This flung everything into the air—huge chunks of masonry and beams, furniture and charpoys and chests, and all the contents of the fort. Dad had a narrow escape from flying stones, which rained down around him. The wadi was filled for several minutes with a great wall of dust. The colossal noise echoed through the mountains and valleys along the Imam's frontier.

On the following day some of the Ahmedis returned. They were unarmed and came in submission. They said that after hearing the great explosions, which had totally destroyed the fort, they knew they could expect no mercy from the British. My father decided there was nothing more to be done. It was up to the government in Aden to decide on the future.

Dhala remained an accursed place. There was continual political strife. Several more English officials were assassinated in Dhala in the following years. On Christmas day, 1950, a seyyid stabbed Seager in the face and chest. Seager's wife, Heather, who became my sister Bryony's godmother, saved him by throwing rocks at the attacker, who was then shot dead. The political officer Groom was on hand in Dhala and saw Seager loaded onto an aircraft, and as he puffed on his cigarette the smoke escaped through the gash in his cheek. From exile Haidara organized another assassination attempt against my parents' friend Charles Inge, but the killer mistakenly shot a well-liked man named Bob Mounde through an open window as the Englishman sat eating his dinner. The British Army fought battles in the hills with bands of terrorists in the 1960s. Still, in 1952, Dad was climbing Jihaf on the morning that news was brought to him of my eldest brother Richard's birth in England. My father said it was among the happiest moments of his entire life. But he never did go back down into the country of Mohamed Awas.

Before I left the village where Davey and Awas died, the old man showed me where the ruins of the tower were still scattered about the hillside. A new village had sprung up farther along the slope. It was a curious place. If Rumpelstiltskin had relatives, this was where they would have lived. The entire community was housed in one building, a single floor half sunk in the ground. A warren of stables and rooms were connected by passages. It had thick walls of stone and the ceiling beams were made of entire tree trunks. Goats and sheep trotted about on the roof. Beyond the walls were walnut and peach trees and beehives stacked in great earthenware pipes. The old man took me into his house and showed me his firearms collection, which included a heavy machine gun. "For weddings," he sniffed. With a group of young Awas descendants we ran down the steep hill for a naked swim in the cold, clear river and took potshots at shoals of fish with a .45 pistol. Back in the village, we ate an enormous meal. When it was time for the afternoon's qat session, I wondered if I should even tell the people here the truth.

Eventually I did speak out. The landscape was turning a leaden gray as the sun sank behind the mountains. I told the group that it was my father who had destroyed their village. It may have been a foolish thing to reveal. In a society where blood feuds sputter on through generations, the memory of the punitive mission easily could have still rankled with them. A grandson of Awas had been gunned down here just a few months before in a quarrel over land. The family was determined that the Islamic courts should execute the culprits by firing squad. An eye for an eye, a tooth for a tooth. There was a stunned silence. The seconds crept by. My heart beat faster. My vision narrowed to a tunnel. I experienced the strange sensation that my father and Davey were nearby. The decades peeled away for the villagers too. I know it. Then it was gone.

"Oh," said the old man. He roared with laughter. "Do the British have any plans to return to Yemen?"

He invited us to stay the night in the village, but my driver was strongly against the idea after all this talk of bloodshed. He whispered in my ear, "Eat with a friend, but do not sleep with him!"

I was inclined to agree. And so we left.

* * *

My father rarely had felt such despair and it changed him as a man forever. "I had lost a comrade, a friend of many years and many trips. The government lost a fine man. Peter and Awas and his loyal retainer had been killed. The fort was no more. I decided there was nothing more to be done. Nothing of any good came out of all of this ..."

I remembered again asking Dad what had happened to all of his friends. And how he had replied, "I have no friends. They're all dead."

After destroying the fort, my father's party tied Peter's blood-ied body onto the back of a camel and set off for Dhala, where an RAF doctor cleaned the dead Englishman up in preparation for his burial. I suppose my father's orders were to fly the body back to Aden for burial. But Davey's last loyalty was to the Arabia he loved, rather than to the British who had played a part in robbing him of his happiness. All the Arabs I talked to claimed that a note had been found in the top pocket of the blood-soaked shirt on Davey's body. It was a hand-scribbled will and it asked for a Muslim burial. Davey had just one friend at his funeral. The woman he had loved was not present, nor his family, nor the nobles of Beihan, nor the aviators who had drunk whiskey with him at the club in Aden.

Dad ordered the burial to take place in Dhala's Muslim ceme-tery. Davey's body was washed and wrapped in a shroud. An escort of Government Guards then carried this on a Union Jack–covered stretcher. The Arabs at the graveside recited the verses of the Surat Yasin, regarded as the heart of the Holy Koran. "We belong to God and to him we return." My father then paraded the guards. At his command, they shouldered their rifles and fired a salute to honor the dead Englishman. I have a tattered fragment of paper on which Dad had scribbled a note after the funeral. It might have been a let-ter to Peter's mother. "Peter gave his life for an ideal and it was fit-ting that his [*last journey*—crossed out] resting place should have been in such a setting, among the people he worked for and mourned by his comrades."

I had a map, drawn early in the twentieth century, showing where the British military cemetery was supposed to be. I knew the graves belonged mostly to two dozen English and Irish soldiers who had succumbed to fever and bullets in the first border expeditions. This entire country, it seemed, was brimful with graves. There were the martyrs who had died in all the battles against the British and then against one another; there were graves of Chinese road builders from the communist era; the white-domed tombs of the holy saints and the subterranean, treasure-filled graves of the ancients. I had no luck in finding Davey. The town of Dhala had expanded beyond all recognition from the 1940s photographs. Buildings spilled down the hill and sprawled across the uneven, rocky country, almost to the foot of Jihaf mountain. In the market I found a toothless old man who said he would show me where Davey was buried. He led me to a trash-filled plot, surrounded by ramshackle houses and dead plots of junk. There were a few dozen mounds of earth in the neglected cemetery. The old man pointed at one, marked out by an oval of rocks and planted with bitter aloes.

"That," he declared, "is the grave of Davey." I said he may have been called Abdallah—his Muslim name adopted at his conversion in Beihan which means the "slave of god"—not Davey, and that caused some confusion. A crowd was now gathering and as several of us stalked about the cemetery looking for the name an argument broke out between the old man and another, who declared that the correct grave was at a spot circled with rough stones and beneath an acacia tree. One in the crowd said a madman came to that grave every night to rave about Davey. I imagined the absurdly Gothic scene: moonlight, a ragged figure with legs planted on either side of the grave, imploring the earth beneath his feet. I knew I wasn't ever going to be sure where Davey was. It was a hot and dusty day. I gave up. We had lost him. I chose the most likely looking grave, surrounded by flat stones and grown over with stunted euphorbia. I sat there for a long while, thinking of what my father would have said to his friend had he been sitting with me now. The old man and the small crowd of interested onlookers got bored and dispersed, leaving me alone. My father wasn't the kind of person who revisited graves. Here I was instead, paying my respects to a man who had become a story.

At evening people move about their houses with candles. Shadows cast hugely across housefronts. A procession of men with torches winds its way through the village, past the walled cemetery with its white-domed tomb, on its way to a wedding party. I sleep on the flat roof of a mud tower. Ibex horns jut out from the corners of the building, to ward off the evil eye. The window frames are blue with bright yellow shutters. From the roof I can look out down the gorge. Hamlets of brown mud towers like termite colonies rise up on one side of the escarpment with date groves below.

I wake in the middle of the night to dead silence. The stars have vanished. Am I dreaming? I have the sense my body is beached, embedded in warm sand. The ripples of my windpipe, ribs, and spine hardly break the mackerel wave of the sand dunes around me. From here I could keep very quiet and watch the world. Around me are the dead faces of young men. My father is younger than I ever saw him. He is with Davey. The pilgrimage is complete. Life is a barren waste to cross and along the way we'll see dancing mirages that confuse us and a few scattered wells from which to draw our hope. But we throw ourselves into the journey and when it's done, even while having learned that all experience involves the loss of something beloved, what is left in the residue of memory is love.

Plum-sized raindrops are splashing down from the black sky onto my face. I get up and move the bedroll beneath the sheltered part of the roof terrace. I sit, smoking and listening to the downpour. A blue flash illuminates the village. Thunder. Lightning. I hear children's wails of fear, but there's another sound, of men whooping for joy at the rain, calling out to their neighbors, laughing. By the time I wake again the muezzin is calling and the cocks are crowing. Weaverbirds chatter in the date palms. The braying of donkeys echoes along the narrow gorge in the dawn. The smell of freshly baked bread rises from the floors below.

Carlos Mavroleon, Mogadishu, December 1992

HEROGRAMS

Lizzie and I arrived in the polluted heat of a London summer. We stood frozen at street corners as a blur of pedestrians burst out of subways and spilled like ants down pavements. The crowded bars, the expensive shops, the fashionable clothes—to me it all seemed a population rushing about to no avail. In an art gallery I saw a tank of formaldehyde in which was suspended a shark. In another was half a pig. I thought of the soap gorilla at Kigali airport. Waiting for the Underground train, I stared at a huge poster of a woman in her underwear staring down at her own breasts. HELLO BOYS, she said. At the movies we witnessed sickening violence, except that this time we held tubs of popcorn between our legs and the gunfire and screams were broadcast in digital Dolby. We had escaped a place where evil stared right at you from the sockets of a child's skull on a battlefield, only to arrive in London, where office workers led lines of such tedium and plenty that they had to entertain themselves with all the fucking and killing on the big screen. So, here then was the prosperous, democratic, and civilized Western world. A place of washing machines, reality TV, Armani, frequent-flier miles, mortgages. And this is what the Africans are supposed to hope for, if they're lucky.

Lizzie and I checked into the Park Lane Hilton. We bathed in hot water, had dinner at the Ivy, and fell into bed between linen sheets. I was woken with a shock at dawn by a loud explosion that seemed to come from the south, over Buckingham Palace. We responded the way we always did to incoming fire: we sprang out of bed and crawled naked into the bathroom on our hands and knees.

This was definitely an IRA attack. Not long before, terrorists had bombed the Baltic Exchange in the City. We crouched on the tiled floor and Lizzie shook her head. "This is absurd," I agreed. We had survived Rwanda, flown halfway across the world to civilization, only to witness a bomb outrage on our very first morning.

It struck me that few Reuters journalists lived in Park Lane, which meant it was unlikely that anybody else from the agency had heard the bomb yet. It could be a scoop, I thought: my biggest ever. I decided it was urgent that I call the news desk to at least check as to whether they had heard about the event. I crawled back to the bedside table, pulled the phone onto the floor, and punched out the agency's number. Switchboard answered and put me through to the world desk. I rehearsed in my mind what the snap should be. This definitely deserved a six-belled bulletin.

BOMB EXPLODES IN LONDON'S WEST END

I was still groggy from sleep, not thinking straight. Something was not right. A familiar deskman's voice came on the line and I introduced myself.

"Morning. This is Aidan Hartley. No, I'm out of Kigali. In London ... Yes, I'm fine! You won't believe this but I've got a story to file. A bulletin ..."

My voice was beginning to crack. I felt tired. The nagging sense that something was not right struck me again. I paused. I stared out toward the window. An early morning shower had started. A flash of bluish white electricity lit up the sky through the frame of the balcony window.

"Hello?" said the voice. Suddenly it was raining harder.

"Hello?"

I didn't say another word, but gently replaced the handset. I got to my feet and walked over to the balcony. I stood looking out over Hyde Park at the muggy summer rain.

"Aidan?"

"Thunder," I said over my shoulder.

Lizzie always saved her camera film for work. She used to say, "Do you want some editor on *Newsweek* looking at our happy snaps?" We still mucked around enough in bored moments to gather a photographic diary of our time together. We stand arm in arm with gunmen, in front of a parked Cobra helicopter in Mogadishu, at Kigali's Red Cross hospital with the kid Lizzie loved, at the Rwandan frontier next to a pyramid of pangas, grenades, and semiautomatics. We look happy, unwashed, squinting into the sun. Among all these pictures are a few oddities, taken when we were relaxing away from the wars. I can count the holidays: Mardi Gras in New Orleans, 1992. We're both wearing cowboy boots, lying on a bed above a courtyard that had magnolias in flower. Montauk, Long Island, the same year, windblown by the ocean. The Kenya coast, three times: September 1991, April 1994, and April 1995, when we slept on a desert island and swam in the sea at night with the phosphorescence streaming off our bodies. Italy, August 1995: a balcony over Lake Como, with water-skiers at sunset; then a drive through Chianti vineyards, sunflowers, and lavender. We drank Montepulciano at dinner and Lizzie wore her pearls. Our spirits lifted on a marble terrace, where a duet sang *La Bohème*. I wondered aloud, "And what will we do now?" *Ho tante cose che ti volio dire ... O una sola, ma grande come il mare.* "Live in a house with a white picket fence," she said sarcastically. I shot a last sequence of pictures on our last safari. Lizzie swims under the blue water of a pool. Her hair sleek. She trails bubbles and then vanishes beneath a skin of reflected sunlight.

In 1996 Lizzie moved to Israel while I stayed behind in Africa. It was a fresh, new story for her, but distance and time worked to unravel what had been held together by Rwanda and Somalia. When I visited Israel I heard she was on the Lebanon frontier and I went to find her in the town of Metulla. As I drove north, I was overtaken by fever. By the time I met up with her I could barely stand, and while she returned up the hill to take photographs I took to my hotel bed with a halo of fire fizzing around my brain. Malaria had come back to haunt me like a bad dream, an episode either dormant in my spleen since childhood or left over from a parasite encountered in Central Africa. I went into a delirium and later woke to the boom of guns and helicopters. There was a loud bang outside. I crawled out of bed and onto the balcony in time to see a plume of dust rising from the street in front of the hotel. Hezbollah guerrillas were firing rockets at us. Up the hill, the Israelis opened up with Operation Grapes of Wrath, an artillery barrage that was demolishing southern Lebanon. Hearing the explosions made me weep like a child for not being strong enough to be outside, standing next to the field guns, or scribbling in my notebook among the correspondents I knew and could hear talking loudly in the bar downstairs. I consoled myself that I would be, just as soon as I got better. For a long time I returned to hang about in shitholes and danger zones. Others were getting paid to be there, whereas I wanted only to feed off the atmosphere. I had no peace inside me.

On the day it was time to go we had one of those vacuous conversations typically held at airports, prolonged by a shared, foul-tasting cigarette. I looked at her when it was time for me to go. Her eyes were extraordinarily blue and her face seemed shrouded in mist. We waved one more time from either side of the immigration barrier and I watched her as she turned and was swallowed up by the crowds of travelers.

She returned to her beloved photography. From Central Africa, one letter described looking up at the Hale-Bopp comet glowing in the equatorial sky as a spasm of violence illuminated the night horizon across the River Congo. "How I thought of you as I sat on the roof of the Brazzaville Sofitel, listening to the rifle fire and watching smoke mushroom from the buildings across the river ..." For a long time it was like living with a ghost. I caught myself reading her stars in the paper. I'd wake up and move my leg across the bed to find there was nothing there. At the roulette table I'd stack my chips on the day and month of her birthday. I wrote dozens of letters I never sent. I replayed in dreams everything that had happened between us and lived out an entirely new life. Waking was an interruption to this inner life and I spent void days longing for night and the vivid continuation of what was no longer real. In time the dreams began to fade like old photographs in the sunlight in the slow, final parting.

It was as if a spell had held us briefly together in Africa and when it lifted we were overnight scattered to the world's four corners: to the Balkans, to Afghanistan, to Silicon Valley and Shepherd's Bush.

Jonathan did not stay long at Reuters. After Africa, his next posting was to Brussels, of all places. He was given a corner in the open plan office with orders to report for work in a suit and tie. A new tribe of young correspondents ran about with mobile phones, dictating urgent paragraphs on European Union directives or company balance sheets, racing back from press scrums to file their stories. "It's *streetfighting* out there!" they exclaimed. Jonathan boasted in his letters about the comforts of his new life. Fast trains to Paris and *pain au chocolat* in the cafés. He said he was happy to be out of Africa, but he confessed that he hung out in Congolese music bars when he wanted to laugh. We met up a few times in London and raced our drinks against England's early closing hours. Jonathan was marking time, waiting to be laid off in one of the company cost-cutting pogroms, the corporate bullet to the back of the skull. I'm happy to say he denied them the satisfaction and one day walked out to a better life.

With Jonathan gone, the Bunker was taken over by strangers while I couldn't forget the ghosts of our recent past. I also no longer enjoyed having a boss who, because we were friends and had endured so much together, would turn a blind eye to my failures as a company man, or even indeed as a correspondent. My only option to survive at Reuters was to put in for a posting on the desk at headquarters in Gray's Inn Road. Foreign correspondents described the desk in hushed tones of horror, because no matter how many herograms you'd won in the field, in the end they always called you back in and slapped you on the graveyard shift, or subbing copy from Norway, or writing about soft commodities. I guess it was the company's way of cutting you back down to size. The desk was an office of glass and steel tubing, like an airport or a train station. After Rwanda I'd been up to the third floor, where dozens of reporters were squirreling away under artificial lights. Close to the lifts, I'd found a door marked SMOKING ROOM. I entered and lit up. In the room there were several figures, hanging their heads as they pulled on their fags. At first I assumed they were the floor cleaners and ill-paid skivvies. But in the stale murk I gradually began to recognize the familiar faces of the veterans and great legends of the past three decades of news. On the shelf, in the smoking room. Back outside among the workstations and watercoolers, the new generation of reporters sat in front of curtains of green text, went up and down in lifts, attended their morning prayers, budget meetings, and team building courses. It looked more like a bank than the Baron Reuter's great news agency.

Home in Kenya I handed in my resignation, and the day I left my Nairobi colleagues passed around the hat to buy me a gold watch as a going-away present. Buchizya had been entrusted with buying the gift and on closer inspection his choice turned out to be a "gold" watch, a Chinese-made counterfeit purchased off a pavement hawker. It stopped ticking inside a week and was exactly the kind of present I appreciated. My colleagues jotted messages into a farewell card. "Stay safe, write eloquently and behave yourself!" As I made for the exit the secretary Maggie called after me, "May the Lord Jesus Christ be with you always . . ."

"Amen," added the other secretary, Rosemary.

The dogs and the cat went when the Ski Chalet was sold. "I've heard all about what went on here," said one woman who looked around the place. "I bet you could get stoned just by licking the walls." I said good-bye to Celestine and he returned to his small *shamba* farm. From London I wrote to him and imagined him reading my letters, sitting outside his peasant's mud hut, with its tin roof glinting in the sunshine, surrounded by chickens and children. His replies were in his usual striking prose. "Dear Sir: Get much greetings from me. How is the atmospheric pressure in your quarter? My jubilation is that this letter avails to you in good environmental condition. How are you pushing on with your daily activities? I hope you are very busy and committed towards development. I am just sitting here with my backbone on the shamba. Please to say hallow to anybody who can remember my aura or shadow."

Whenever I see a news headline to this day I half feel I should board the next flight into the heart of it. I'd love to get all charged up again and I could write the story with my eyes closed. I'm sure the sense that I'm missing out while others get in on a great story will never completely pass. I can turn on the radio years later and hear voices I knew back then and wonder how they can go on doing it. Are they brave professionals or numbed-out news junkies? The sight of people committing acts of unspeakable brutality against others fills a hole in some of us. The activity is made respectable by being paid a salary to do it, but there is a cost.

I knew of a foreign correspondent from Sarajevo who won fame for his sympathetic coverage of the Balkans. Reading his stories, you could see he reserved his greatest energies for highlighting the plight of civilians, rather than being attracted to the guns and violence. But while vacationing between assignments in London or New York, he carried with him an audiotape on which were two macabre recorded sequences. The first was a Serb artillery bombardment of Sarajevo, recorded from his window at the Holiday Inn. The second captured the sounds of Iraqi troops overwhelming a Kurdish trench near where the correspondent had crouched. The attackers were bayoneting men who pleaded for mercy amid blood-curdling screams. Would the correspondent ever have got over the wars? I don't know. He died on a lonely road in Sierra Leone when his car drove into an ambush.

And so several years later I am thirty-five and getting drunk with JC, a veteran correspondent of the Middle East. JC drains his glass and flings open the lid of a big trunk stuffed with mementoes, trophies, and files. He rummages about and pulls out a single document. "Look," he says, jabbing his finger at the page, a pay slip from his Spanish newspaper. It reads:

> 27 muertas . . . . 7,000 pesetas
> 38 muertas . . . . 7,000 pesetas

However many dead there were, we still got paid the same. It wasn't about the money, but on the other hand we had sold part of our souls. Forgotten incidents of history become our unforgettable days. Our faraway readers threw out yesterday's papers and a decade later I look at my scrapbooks and understand that all the staccato newsbreaks, the hard news leads, my newsprint words yellowing with age are simply the tear sheets of my own memory.

"Do you think we all paid a price for dipping in and out of other people's misery at whim?" Jonathan said to me in a London bar. "It seems like that to me."

"We'll never see anything like it again," said Eric over his vodka lime and soda one night in another bar, on the beach in Kenya after it was all over. "Where we've just come from was the Old Testament—massacres, plagues, and famines. The only thing we missed were tribes of giants, the archangels singing in the heavens, and Beelzebub himself—though fuck me I've met a few of those in my time."

A long time later I asked Eric in a letter if he missed it. He replied and said: "I've never had a time like that since, when what I wanted to be doing with my life and the life I was living were so utterly intertwined. And I'm old enough now to understand that most people never get anything close to that in the course of their lives. Nor have I ever cared so much about what I was doing. To me, honestly, South Africa was about answering the question: Can we all live together? And the fact that it worked out has given me a kind of secular hope for humankind that I would be lost without. So yeah, I miss it. I miss the intense friendships, the madness, the heat, the Red Cross flights into that week's shitfight, the red-eyed motherfuckers at roadblocks, the African sky at night, the desert cities where dogs sleep in the middle of the streets, the fact that nothing ever fucking works ever, knowing which side of the plane to ask for a seat on to get the best view of Kilimanjaro, the crazed welcome-home dinner parties after a month in (pick one) Somalia, Rwanda, Liberia, Sierra Leone, the long dirt roads, the vast horizons, getting up at 4:30 in the morning to do dawn patrols on the East Rand with the BBC, you and I doing our Big Audio Dynamite dance in the living room of the Ski Chalet, the personal velocity of Julian, the herograms, the sleeping night watchmen who suddenly jerk to life when your car pulls up, the flat-topped trees, seeing a kudu in the park on the drive out from town, freezing cold Tuskers, crunching over empty bullet casings, calling friends from sat phones, the occasional breeze off the ocean and the sundown silhouettes of women with woven baskets on top of their heads. I miss it all but more than anything else I miss the people. I honestly think that despite everything we saw, there's a humanity in Africa that the rest of the world has lost touch with. In the end, I may have been born and raised in St. Joseph, Missouri, but I'll always look at Africa as the place where I grew up."

I received a postcard from Julian. He was at the Prado in Madrid and the picture was of Goya's two men slugging away at each other with cudgels. Julian had written on the back in capitals:

TO HELL WITH OTHER MEN'S WARS
IT'S TIME TO FIGHT OUR OWN!

In the 1970s the Soviets had built a military base on the Dahlak Archipelago, off the Red Sea coast of Eritrea. At the end of the Cold War they left, but before they sailed away they dumped all their weapons on the seabed. Diving on the island's reefs in the late 1990s I found myself drifting above the most beautiful of scenes, of tank turrets and rocket-launching tubes garlanded with coral and sponges and shoals of iridescent tropical fishes.

Looking back, the truth is that we often had the best of times. At Reuters if I'd said I didn't want to go into the field they would have put me on the desk and that was a prison sentence. Having lived for the moment, we never considered that we might end up living alone in an apartment with the utility bills piling up. Re-entry taught me a new sort of fear that was slow and dull rather than quick and thrilling. A long time later I went to see Ian, the British army psychiatrist I'd met in Rwanda, and we sat by the fire at his home talking. "What can I do for you?" he said. Nothing, I realized. "Have a Guinness?" And so we talked over our pints in front of his fire and we agreed that the hardest part of reentry to a humdrum life was not recovering from the bad stuff. It was missing the good times, the friendship, intensity, fear, sense of purpose, the sheer exotic escapism of it all.

On November 23, 1996, Mo Amin and Brian Tetley, the old hack who had been so kind to me from the early days, were en route from Addis Ababa home to Nairobi on Ethiopian Airlines flight 961. After takeoff, three men burst into the cockpit and ordered the captain to fly to Australia. One wore a black glove with a package strapped tightly to it with duct tape. The man said it was a bomb. The other two armed themselves with an onboard fire extinguisher and an ax. They refused to listen to the captain's pleas that he did not have enough fuel for the journey. Sure enough, heading east across the Indian Ocean several hours later the Boeing 767 ran out of gas. The hijackers struggled with the captain and his copilot even as they attempted to bring the Boeing in for an emergency landing on the Comoro Islands archipelago. In those final minutes, Mo got up to appeal to his fellow passengers to help him overpower the terrorists. Nobody volunteered to help him. Mo couldn't take them on alone with his one arm, so he shook his head and returned to his seat. The captain ditched off Grande Comore, close enough to the beach for a tourist to video the crash sequence. The Boeing hit the water on its belly. It was such a smooth, well-executed landing that at first it looked as if it might have come to rest like a big boat. But the port wing hit a submerged coral reef, and the aircraft cartwheeled and disintegrated. Fifty-two passengers survived, but Mo and Brian were among the 123 who perished.

Mo was buried the same day the bodies were returned to Nairobi, in line with Muslim tradition. Brian's funeral was in the seedy Nairobi suburb where he had lived. His friends dressed him in his best suit so that mourners could view his corpse. Somebody put a bottle of Tusker beer under each of Brian's arms. At the funeral the coffin was lowered into a grave and covered over with cement and concrete blocks—to discourage grave robbers from exhuming Brian's body for his good suit and, one imagines, those two good bottles of Tusker.

Mohamed "Mo" Shafi, the only Reuters man to survive the mob attack in Mogadishu on July 12, 1993, never took a breather. He was in Rwanda with us. In 1999 he survived a misdirected NATO aerial bomb attack on the Albanian Kosovo frontier. The explosions knocked him over, but he never stopped his TV camera rolling. In February 2001 he covered Israel's elections and was found dead, apparently of a heart attack, in his Jerusalem hotel room. He was forty-nine and left behind his widow and four children.

Two years after my night out with the correspondent JC, I heard that he had escaped to a remote village in Bolivia. One afternoon, after a long, lost weekend, he sat on his balcony and shot himself in the chest. He left no note.

When I used to meet up with Carlos in London, he had replaced his war-zone chic with the image of Latin cool, in mirror shades and Hawaiian shirt, Marlboro Reds in his top pocket. I remember cruising the streets in his car with the top down, salsa cascading from the stereo. He cooked back at his flat and we'd eat food doused with his homemade hot chilli sauce, sitting on the floor as we had in Mogadishu. He had found happiness with a beautiful, dark-eyed girl and he had launched his own company,

Black Lion Films. "Mavroleon" translates into English as "Black Lion." Carlos still went to hot spots, but many were retrospectives on Afghanistan and Somalia. Before he'd had the chance to lay the old wars to rest, fresh layers of conflict had spread. I observed a new calm in him and it was reflected in the films he wanted to make. Over a drink he suggested doing a documentary on artisan skills of the English countryside. "Like what?" I asked. "Stuff like black-smithing, cider making, house thatching . . ." And he was serious.

In the late summer of 1998 I was getting drunk south of the river in London and, being broke, I had to walk home. I found myself passing Carlos's home after midnight. I decided to bang loudly on his door and he answered, bleary-eyed and wrapped in his *maweis*.

"I thought since I was passing . . . Sorry. Better come back another time."

"Could you? Listen, I really want to see you. Can we talk tomorrow? I'm going away soon."

On the phone next day, Carlos announced that he was getting married. First, he was going on assignment to the Sudan. He aimed to be back in two weeks. We agreed to have a big night out to celebrate the good news on his return. Carlos passed via Nairobi to hitch a flight in and out of rebel-held southern Sudan. He flew back to London on August 5, two days before Osama bin Laden's al-Qaeda detonated a truck bomb outside the U.S. embassy in downtown Nairobi. The blast killed 213 people. Many victims were vaporized or buried alive under rubble from the embassy and from a nearby multistory office block that collapsed like a house of cards.

U.S. Navy ships in the Arabian Gulf on August 20 launched salvos of Tomahawk cruise missiles against bin Laden's training camps near Khost in Afghanistan. Simultaneously, U.S. missiles demolished a pharmaceutical factory outside Khartoum. Immediately following the attack, a producer from CBS News' *60 Minutes* contacted Carlos, now back in London, and asked him to enter the

Khost area to film what he could of the attacks' aftermath. Few possessed either Carlos's courage or his knowledge to do a job like this. I feel I know what went through his mind—that this would be his biggest scoop ever, his one last, big story to do before getting married.

Carlos phoned me the day he got back to London. I had popped out for ten minutes. When I got back the message light was blinking on the answering machine. I was in a black dog mood and I didn't call him back for two days. I finally did so the night before we were to have dinner and all I got was his recorded message. The minute I'd called him, I understood later, he was already boarding his flight to Islamabad.

Carlos traveled up to Peshawar and checked into room 304 of Green's Hotel, a haunt for hacks, smackheads, and cross-border gunrunners. Traveling under his Muslim name, Karimullah, and dressed in the Afghan clothes he wore so comfortably, Carlos might easily have passed for a local. But the dangers of being exposed as a Westerner were great. Following the air strikes, bin Laden had placed a $20,000 bounty on the head of any American in the area. Carlos's disguise would obviously have raised suspicions that he was a spy. He carried a sat phone, which men like bin Laden knew would allow the CIA to get an accurate fix on the bearer whenever it was switched on. In the next two days, Carlos tried crossing the border several times. But his video cameras and sat phone raised suspicions. Pakistani security police detained him, roughed him up, and then released him. He took on the disguise of a doctor and managed to enter the hospital at Miram Shah, on the frontier, where he spoke to guerrillas injured in the Tomahawk strikes. There are friends who believe that Carlos received information during these two days that put him in great danger.

Carlos made it back to his Peshawar hotel room. The next morning, he spoke to his fiancée and also to his producer at CBS. He said he was shaken but would take a shower and sleep it off. At

ten o'clock that night, after he had failed to answer a string of fran-
tic incoming calls from CBS, Green's Hotel staff forced the door to
his room. They found Carlos sitting at his room desk, stone cold
dead. The butt of a Malboro Red was still between his lips, burned
right down with the ash falling on his lap. An empty syringe lay
next to his body. I imagine the scene in the room, because it had
always been the same in Mogadishu: piles of camera equipment
and black duct tape, his copy of the Holy Koran, packets of Marlboro Reds spilling everywhere, a Zippo lighter, five thousand dollars in cash, the sat phone, and photos of himself with his old
mujahideen comrades, which Carlos might have intended to use to
make friends with Taliban militias along the road. The police
claimed Carlos had died of a self-administered heroin overdose.
Anybody who knew Carlos said it made no sense at all. Some
believe Carlos was assassinated and that it was made to appear like
a suicide. A proper investigation was never conducted and friends
who traveled to Peshawar to ask questions were warned off.

At Carlos's funeral back in St. Bride's, the church for journalists off Fleet Street, we sang "Mine eyes have seen the glory of the
coming of the Lord." Readers quoted Kipling's *Kim* and Byron's
Childe Harold. Ned Warwick, ABC News bureau chief, stood up to
pay tribute to Carlos and she summed up his qualities as a questing,
free man, an adventurer, and a stringer journalist: "He cared little
for conventional recognition or television network ratings. His life
in the field was a brutal test of endurance, courage, and knowledge,
of hostile clans, treacherous mountain passes, the habits of scorpi-
ons, and the signature of a rocket."

We filed out to the salsa strains of *Ritmo Caliente,* past plaques,
an open book, candles, and memorial trees in the garden paying tribute to Dan, Hos, Anthony, Mo, Brian, and countless other dead correspondents. And I remembered how Carlos had once said, "In the
midst of carnage, you will see the utter evil and the supreme good,
side by side." Carlos spoke for all of us who long for such clarity. We

will rarely find it in so-called normal life. I know that the privilege of witnessing the extremes stretches something inside the heart or the soul or the mind, so that there is a void we cannot ever hope to fill again in ourselves. In all my pained imaginings of how Carlos had come to his final moment, only one thing really matters. Carlos was on the story, looking for the utter evil and the supreme good.

Dad slept or read books, devouring volumes in a single sitting, as if he were trying to cram in as much information while he still could. These days he tottered about as if he were on a ship's deck in a storm. Elbows out, head down. He refused to see a doctor. He became querulous about the smallest things. House bills. The price of vegetables, compared to what they had cost in some distant past era. He ate little and went to bed soon after sundown. The truth had been there for a year or two. Looking back now, his decline appears as steady and all too mortal. But Old Testament prophets are not supposed to die, at least for several centuries. We tried to ignore the truth until very late, clinging to the belief that he was somehow invincible.

On my visits to the beach house in Malindi, we'd sit on the veranda and I'd try to coax out of him all I could. Memories, ideas, jokes. Talking to my old Dad before he died was like attempting to rescue books from a house engulfed in flames. I took his reticence for modesty until the day it dawned on me that he was being coy because his memory had faded. Oblivion was advancing across his mind while he was still alive. Against this tide he struggled to remain the storyteller he had always been. He had a repertoire, rehearsed down to every pause and phrase, of classic stories, top twenty tales, music hall songs, poems, and jokes. He kept those, but otherwise the details of his past life were being wiped out, leaving behind blurred summaries and strong convictions. He fell out of step with life. He began to loathe appearing in family photographs. I see him in the family picture albums, bent-backed and hurrying for the edge of the frame. He bicycled better than he walked these days, and he would ride along the beach to chat with fishermen over their catches and with traders in town, speaking his perfectly correct Swahili. He did his yoga and drank his cup of tea as the sun came up, with the BBC World Service playing on the radio. There was still the redeeming comedy of my parents together, heroically in love after all they had been through, but still bickering. My father was a man who had spent his life so far away from us in remote places, but at last as his strength drained away his expressions of devotion became warmer than they had ever been.

I have found a note by my father among his jumbled papers, written on his eighty-ninth birthday. It says, "I have had a long, happy and healthy life and I am grateful for this. There is much which I would like to do before I leave. Time is short:

> *One moment in annihilation's waste,*
> *One moment, of the well to taste,*
> *The Stars are setting and the caravan*
> *Starts for the dawn of nothing—Oh, make haste!*

One day quite suddenly he was hopelessly old. He hated the thought of becoming helpless and had secretly joined a euthanasia society that briefed him on methods to commit suicide. For all this, the medicine cabinet at home housed nothing more lethal that a few vitamin tablets and bandages stuck together in the tropical humidity. In my mind's eye, I can't edit out the picture of the way he was at the end. How unfair memory can be.

* * *

On the last day I saw him, Dad and I were sitting talking about all the usual things. And he said to me, "We should never have come here."

It was a preposterous thing to say. Had I misunderstood him it would have been as if the past several centuries had been a party to be avoided because we might bump into people we didn't want to see, or because we always created a spectacle of ourselves in public. But I did understand what he meant. We'd had this conversation many times before, when we talked about the coming of the modern world to Africa. Dad believed that the twenieth century had brought nothing but ruination.

"But it's history, Dad," I'd say.

I recalled the stories he told me when I was a boy, when I thought of us sitting in the pool of flickering light cast by a campfire, with the vast spaces of imagination and constellations of stars all above us. After Rwanda, then sitting with my Dad that day, suddenly it was time to look around and notice that, as we had been telling each other stories, Africa's night had become crowded with the yells of alarm, the smell of burning rubbish, and the winking of slum lights. Cultures had been pulverized. The beautiful places had been violated.

My father said it one more time. "We should never have come. But when we did we should have stayed."

"Dad," I said, "We did."

I asked him about his dreams and what had happened that day on Lake Victoria's shore nearly seven decades before, when he had shot those two impala rams on the anthill. I asked him whether he now thought that the villagers had punished him for killing the impala totem. "They were happy that I had done it," he replied.

Dad was gazing out at the ocean. A fisherman in an outrigger canoe set against the silver of the morning water was hoisting his sail as he bobbed out beyond the surf. My father turned to me and he looked like the saddest of all men.

"They told me I had played my part in fate."

I had heard this before. It never made any sense in the past but at last I knew exactly what he was talking about.

At the beginning of my story I told how my father had believed he was bewitched on Lake Victoria. To me, his repetitive nightmare, in which a dark shadow stalked him, is an emblem of the spell placed on him by the ancestors of the Lake Victoria villagers, or perhaps by Africa itself. His sentence was to become obsessed with Africa. To spend the rest of his days toiling there, as the colonial officer "Bwana Cotton," then as the white settler on the vast ranch land Mother thought we'd have for one hundred years only to have it taken away after fewer than twenty, then as a United Nations development worker, and then finally in his eighties as a charity volunteer in the famine zones of Africa. To see houses built, water flow, animal herds grow fat, and crops swell on the deep red earth. To witness the homes fall into ruin, the trees felled, the land engulfed by dust devils, the people go hungry in the name of freedom and die of pestilence and war. And to know it was done by his hand. If for a moment we can believe this, then the dark shadow was my father's own conscience.

The sins of my father were indeed visited upon me, but also were his dearest loves. We are living out the consequences of history, but at the same time each generation must learn the lessons of experience for itself. For me the journey started on the summit of the pyramid at Giza and one part of it ended at the edge of the pit, overlooking the mass grave where the Lazarus boy had spoken to me. I was the son who grew up loving Africa because of his father. I loved it and wanted it to love me back. In witnessing the suffering and beauty of Africa's story, I have finally become a tiny part of its fabric.

*   *   *

"Breathing" was his very last word. Then he stopped. And so my father, Brian Joseph Hartley, having lived enough to cram the journeys of three restless men into his eighty-nine years, died in the port of Mombasa, on the same Indian Ocean coast where as a young man he had first set his feet down in East Africa.

On the dawn of that last day he swam in the sea, as was his routine. He grumbled to Mother about the fish they ate for lunch. Later he dosed himself with antimalaria tablets. A short time later a blood clot burst an artery inside that huge barrel chest of his that I had hugged for as long as I can remember. An ambulance was summoned. On the two-hour journey he began to lose the struggle to live as he slipped through a landscape of mighty trees, coconut palms, flocks of egrets, villages, past the freedom bell near Nyali Creek that used to be struck every time a slave was emancipated, and finally into Mombasa's crowded streets. He was fading by the time the ambulance arrived at the hospital gates. He would have been happy to know that he passed only momentarily through the hands of the medical profession he had feared and loathed. The warrior lay dying and my mother held his feet as they became cold and his armorlike rib cage grew still.

Dad had meticulously planned his own funeral to appear as if it were entirely offhand. First he had wanted to be cremated, in order, he said, to avoid taking up valuable soil. Then he had wanted to be taken out to sea, weighted down with rocks, and tossed overboard. Next he instructed that he was to be buried in the bush dressed in his khaki shorts and shirt without a coffin, so as not to waste good timber.

In the event, his body was dispatched to the Hindu temple next to the Aga Khan hospital for incineration. The ashes were returned in a wooden box. We decided to set him free on Langaseni, the old ranch on the slopes of Kilimanjaro where he and my mother had been happiest. At the frontier between Kenya and Tan-

ly keeps appearing in the bath, to the consternation of
the delight of our kids.

the morning of the day I write this I rose while the night-
till crying, before even the first cock crow. Quietly, I pulled
clothes and boots by the light of the moon. I brewed *chai*,
the leaves and lots of milk and sugar together in the same
eturning to the bedroom to sip the sweet liquid, I sat by the
nd watched my sleeping family. I have always seen in Claire's
the story of our empire, with features that morph between her
stors from England, Ireland, India, China. I am like my fore-
ers, who tried to conquer others, only to be won over them-
ves. Draining the cup, I set off as I love to do each dawn, driving
t under the bowl of the sky onto plains where the livestock *bomas*
re scattered. The herdsmen with their weathered faces and lop-
ears were stamping the morning chill out of stiff legs, bantering,
spitting, and opening up the night enclosures to release bleating
flocks and humped, dewlapped cattle. The animals spread out
across the savannah. As the day went on clouds built into mountain
ranges. As I write this, black towers of water and wind are moving
across the ochre land. The air is scented with grass. And as I look to
the future, I remember what my mother wrote on the eve of her
arrival in Kenya in 1951. "If ONLY we could be certain of peace, I
can see the most *perfect* and *exciting* life ahead."

zania, a border policeman stopped my brother Richard, who carried
the container, and tapped on the box with his swagger stick.

"What is this?"

"My father."

The policeman raised his eyebrows.

"I mean his ashes," Richard smiled.

"You may pass."

The little gathering took place on a knoll planted with
euphorbia trees that rattled like bones in the cold wind. We looked
out across the thorny plain where dust devils tilted against the sun.
With Kilimanjaro to the east and Meru to the west, the ranch was
the most beautiful place in the world. Richard opened the box and
we each scooped up his ashes to scatter. Holding those fire-
blackened shards in my hands I cried. Our father slipped out
between our fingers and curled away into the air. Then he was gone,
too swiftly for us to have properly said good-bye. We opened a
flagon of red African wine, splashed some onto the ground for
Dad, and toasted him with what was left. I will always recall the
look on my mother's face then, the lark singing overhead, the
clouds swirling around the mountains, and the Maasai shepherd in
his red toga who waved at us as we drove away.

POSTSCRIP

> How can I face such slaughter and be cool?
> How can I turn from Africa and live?
> —Derek Walcott, "A Far Cry From Africa"

I met Claire when I was at my lowest ebb. For some time a
met, she lived with the events that haunted me. When I felt I
not go on she waited for me, she took me by the hand and beca
my companion along the road. She is the only woman with whom
have ever really felt at peace. Soon after we were married, we
decided to abandon the city. We moved to the Laikipia plateau,
west of Mount Kenya, where we were welcomed by friends onto
their farm. These past two years we have been reliving the African
idyll I missed for so long, and here we are raising our young children. This place is what my father would call paradise, with wide
open spaces on all sides and blue hills in the distance. Up here in
the East African highlands we have hot days and cool nights. We
live under a roof of woven papyrus in rooms lit by hurricane lamps.
At night there are no electric lights visible anywhere on the horizon
from our veranda, just stars and moonlight. Our water is from a
spring at the bottom of the hill. An elephant with a penchant for
pumpkins occasionally raids the vegetable patch and a bullfrog

ACKNOWLEDGMENTS

Bringing a book into the world is among life's weirder experiences and one not necessarily to be envied. How fortunate I was, then, to be in the care of my agents and publishers. The individuals among their teams I would like to thank are too numerous to name. They include my agent David Godwin, Michael Fishwick at Harper-Collins, Jonathan Ball Publishers in South Africa, Julie Grau at Riverhead and, most especially, Morgan Entrekin at Grove/Atlantic. Out there in the frontline trenches promoting the book have been Jessica Axe, Anika Ebrahim and Deb Seager. I have also been deeply touched by the support of people in my homeland of Kenya. Many men and women spent time relating for me their memories of the Aden Protectorates and in particular I wish to thank Nigel St. John Groom, former Political Officer to Beihan and Dhala, and his wife Lorna. I have made reference to some of the tales, portraits and place descriptions contained in Nigel's fascinating memoir, *Sheba Revealed: A Posting to Bayhan in the Yemen*. To flesh out the Davey-Awas fight I shamelessly lifted details from a separate, noto-rious Dhala shoot-out, described in Nigel's official reports and other contemporary sources. In Britain I am also grateful to the Rhodes House Library, Oxford, and members of the British-Yemeni Society. I was fortunate enough to enjoy the legendary hospitality of the Yemenis, and for their generosity I am indebted notably to my hosts Ahmed Hussein al-Fadhli, Brigadier-General Sharif Haider al-Habili and the brothers Alawi and Abdallah. The late Peter Davey had no say in the way I told his story, but readers may be interested to know they will be able to read his life in his own words, in a forthcoming edition of his extraordinary diaries. In Africa, countless people helped me on the road: colleagues, my guides and protectors in the field, soldiers, humanitarian aid workers, dreamers and ordinary people. Those who I wish to remember by name include Mohamoud Afrah, whose war diary I referred to in my portrayal of Mogadishu, together with American surgeon John Sundin, whose conversation and faxed letters to the New Haven coffee shop enlivened my description of the ICRC trauma hospital in Kigali. I am grateful for the photographs by Sam Ouma, Judy Walgren, Saskia Spender and Jim Hollander. The following extended many forms of kindness over the years that helped me write: Celestine Achole Sikuku, George Bloch, Miles Bredin, Jonathan Clayton, Carter Coleman, the Eldons, Mike Ivey, Jeffrey Lee, Susan Minot, Buchizya Mseteka, Julian Ozanne, Eric Ransdell, Michael Schutzer-Weismann, Tom and Jo Silvester, the late Tonio Trzebinski and his wife Anna, Toby Young, Nick and Hett Day and their children, who gave us a home on Kamogi ranch, my siblings and their partners, Richard and Helen, Bryony and Rick, Kim and Clusi and my mother, Doreen Hartley. Most of all I thank my wife Claire, my dearest companion, supporter and editor, without whom this book would not have been completed. I love her with all my heart. Readers are welcome to email me at *info@thezanzibarchest.com* or to visit *www.thezanzibarchest.com*. This is in memory of Brian Joseph Hartley, Peter Davey, Tonio Trzebinski, Mohamed Amin, Brian Tetley, "Mo" Shafi Mohamed, Hos Maina, Anthony Macharia, Dan Eldon, JC, Hans Kraus, John Mathai, Carlos Mavroleon, Emma McCune, Brian Bowden, Kurt

Schork, Giles Thornton, Ilaria Alpi and the boy Lazarus. To all the writers of letters to SOON, may your prayers be answered, even if you receive no reply in the mail. La lutta continua!

—Laikipia, Kenya, March 2004

Aidan Hartley was born in 1965. He
lives in Kenya with his wife and children.